LONE STAR POLITICS

LONE STAR POLITICS

TRADITION AND TRANSFORMATION IN TEXAS

SECOND EDITION

KEN COLLIER ★ **STEVEN GALATAS** ★ **JULIE HARRELSON-STEPHENS**

Stephen F. Austin State University

CQ PRESS

A Division of SAGE
Washington, D.C.

CQ Press
2300 N Street, NW, Suite 800
Washington, DC 20037

Phone: 202-729-1900; toll-free, 1-866-4CQ-PRESS (1-866-427-7737)

Web: www.cqpress.com

Cover design: Jeffrey Everett/El Jefe Design
Typesetting: C&M Digitals (P) Ltd.

⊗ The paper used in this publication exceeds the requirements of the American National Standard for Information Sciences—Permanence of Paper for Printed Library Materials, ANSI Z39.48-1992.

Printed and bound in the United States of America

15 14 13 12 11   2 3 4 5

Library of Congress Cataloging-in-Publication Data

Collier, Kenneth E.,
  Lone star politics: tradition and transformation in Texas / Ken Collier, Steven Galatas, Julie Harrelson-Stephens. — 2nd ed.
      p. cm.
  Includes bibliographical references and index.
  ISBN 978-1-60426-638-2 (pbk.: alk. paper) 1. Texas—Politics and government. I. Galatas, Steven. II. Harrelson-Stephens, Julie, III. Title.
  JK4816.C65 2012
  320.4764—dc22

                                                                    2010047680

To parents who always gave us love and support:

Joe and Betty Lyn Collier

Mel and Sherry Galatas

Arthur and Kyrene Harrelson

About the Authors

Ken Collier is associate professor at Stephen F. Austin State University, with a PhD from the University of Texas at Austin. He is the author of *Between the Branches: The White House Office of Legislative Affairs* and is currently researching presidential speechwriting and gubernatorial elections. He has published articles in such journals as *Journal of Politics, White House Studies, Presidential Studies Quarterly, Public Choice,* and *Social Science Quarterly.*

Steven Galatas is associate professor at Stephen F. Austin State University, with a PhD from the University of Missouri. He has published articles in *Journal of Politics, Public Choice, Party Politics, Politics and Policy,* and *PS: Political Science and Politics.* His research and teaching concern comparative elections, voting behavior, and campaign finance.

Julie Harrelson-Stephens is associate professor at Stephen F. Austin State University, with a PhD from the University of North Texas. She has coedited, with Rhonda L. Callaway, *Exploring International Human Rights: Essential Readings* and has been published in *Conflict and Terrorism, PS: Political Science and Politics, Human Rights Review,* and *International Interactions.* Her primary research interests include human rights, regime theory, and terrorism.

Brief Contents

Contents

Maps, Boxed Features, Tables, and Figures

Tables

Figures

Preface

As has often been said, there is no State in the Union whose history presents such varied and romantic scenes as does that of Texas. This alone would recommend it to the general reader and the earnest student. But there is in addition to its interest a weighty reason why every school in the State should give Texas History a place in its course of study. No one who learns well the lessons taught can fail to become a better and wiser citizen.[1]

Anna J. Hardwicke Pennybacker
A New History of Texas for Schools (1888)

Mrs. Pennybacker's "new" history of Texas presents a traditional view of Texas history. The copy we used originally belonged to Earl B. Persons, the great-uncle of one of the authors. In the century since young Earl Persons first read this quotation in his schoolbook, Texans have written some new history and revised some old history. Mr. Persons served in World War I before taking part in the rise of the oil business in East Texas, a time when he saw his pastures become more valuable for the oil under them than the cattle that grazed on them. The next generation of Texans saw America through World War II, the Cold War, and the space race directed from NASA in Houston. That generation grew up on *Texas History Movies,* a comic version of Texas history, sponsored by an oil company. Another generation saw the high-tech boom take root in Texas. Texans born today may never own a printed book on Texas's politics and history and thus will be unlikely to leave their name scrawled in a textbook to remind descendants of the Texas they knew. (However, today's students can preserve the Texas they know by buying copies of this text for their children and grandchildren and setting them aside so that future generations can share the fun of Texas circa 2011—please contact CQ Press for inquiries regarding bulk sales.)

The economic, demographic, and political changes in the state brought new ways of life to its citizens. Over the past century, as Texans moved from the countryside into the cities, ranches and farms gave way to cities, suburbs, and exurbs as the natural habitat of Texans. As small towns gave way to the more impersonal big cities, Texans found themselves living closer and closer together, meaning that they would have to cooperate more with neighbors and fellow citizens. The farmer's lonely but simple commute from farmhouse to field has been replaced by long treks to work on crowded superhighways. For Texans of an earlier time commerce meant the weekly trip into town to sell goods, buy supplies, and check the mail at the post office. Social networking meant gathering at the local coffee shop to swap stories over breakfast. Today, many Texans are in constant contact with other Texans, other Americans, and other people from around the world. Many Texans have trouble working when their Internet connection goes down even briefly.

Clearly, we Texans aren't what we used to be. However, our image of ourselves has not changed quite as much as the circumstances of our lives. During the century since Mrs. Pennybacker wrote those words, most Texans have looked again at our history and found a much more nuanced view of our conflicts with the Mexican government during the revolution and with the U.S. government during and after the U.S. Civil War. While scholars have reviewed and revised the stories of Texas, Texans have often clung to the more romantic version of our history.

Our state's government is in the unenviable position of having to keep pace with all these changes while still remaining true to our traditions and legends. Texas government needs to be both lean and modern, capable of managing the affairs of almost 25 million Texans while still retaining a small-town feel and the frontier spirit. Texas leaders must be both engaged and rooted, nimble enough to respond to global competition and regional hurricane devastation while still able to ride a horse and swap stories with fellow Texans, whether at the counter of the local diner or on Facebook.

One of the most remarkable things about teaching Texas politics is that, while so many Texas students only take it because it's required and so many instructors have trepidations about teaching it, the subject is actually pretty enjoyable. Generations of textbooks have stepped into the breach between these reluctant participants, often with mixed results. Textbooks about Texas politics tend to be rather dry, when the study of Texas politics should actually be very interesting, as our state's history is full of legends, criminals, preachers, hucksters, and even comedians. Somehow, when all is said and done, the life is too often taken out of Texas politics, and we think that's a true Texas tragedy.

We hope to breathe a little of that life back into the study of Texas politics. We can't engage in storytelling for storytelling's sake. However, any effort to put together a dry, story-free (i.e., "serious") textbook on Texas politics would lead us to forget the role that the state's legends and myths play in shaping how Texans think and how our politicians behave. You can't tell the story of Texas without revisiting a few tall tales, debunking some persistent myths in the state, and captivating the readers with the true stories that are often more interesting than the legends.

Reading between the Lines of *Lone Star Politics*

Our book was written by Texans but published by CQ Press in Washington, D.C. We designed our text to work well when partnered with CQ Press's other offerings or when used as a text that can stand on its own.

The plan for the book is relatively simple. We open with an introduction to the state and its history in Chapter 1. While much of this story will be familiar to many readers, we feel it bears repeating, to bring focus to the political history of the state and to refresh the memories of Texas students who haven't seen much of their state's history since middle school. Building on the state's history, Chapter 2 examines the birth and rebirth of the state through its constitutions. The chapter emphasizes that while the Texas Constitution continues to evolve, it has not been able to keep pace with a rapidly changing state. Chapter 3 looks at how the Texas Legislature is elected and how it functions. As the heart of Texas democracy, the legislature is a fine example of how changes have been slow to come. Next, Chapter 4 visits the Texas governor's mansion to see if the executive office is ready to keep up with the state. Chapter 5 explores the justice system in Texas. Chapter 6 looks at local government in Texas. Chapter 7 examines how Texans elect their officials, and Chapter 8 looks at how Texans work together through parties and organized interests. Finally, Chapter 9 investigates what the government produces: policy. We'll also use that chapter to conclude the book and revisit a few themes.

Featuring Our Features

This text is designed to draw readers into the key issues of politics in Texas. Several features of the text are designed to bring the reader's attention to an issue, often in a new light.

Texas Legends

John Steinbeck observed after his first visit to Texas, "Like most passionate nations Texas has its own history based on, but not limited by, facts."[2] We have made a discussion of "Texas legends" a recurring feature of this text. When we look at the characters and stories that fill Texas politics, we often find that Texas's legends differ from reality. These legends play a role in shaping Texans' self-image whether or not they can be proven true. One historian, who suggested that the real Davy Crockett surrendered rather than died fighting like Fess Parker's portrayal in Disney's version of the Alamo, was told by one angry reader that the "Fess Parker image has done more for children than your book can."[3] Discussing what has been termed the "Texas creation myth," one writer concluded, "the mythic Alamo of the American collective imagination has become far more important than the Alamo of tedious historical fact."[4] It is odd that Texans have allowed Davy Crockett, Jim Bowie, and other legends of the Alamo to be recast. Many of the men who defended the Alamo were brave, but their lives were not necessarily family fare. For example, Bowie partnered in a slave-smuggling ring with pirate Jean Lafitte before arriving in Texas.[5] William Travis abandoned a young son and a pregnant wife before he came to Texas.

That these men and women lived hard lives and made serious errors is not the point of retelling their stories. Texas is a place where people have come to start over and find a new identity. The celebrated "Baron de Bastrop" was really a Dutchman named Philip Hendrick Nering Bögel who invented the title when he arrived in San Antonio with very little money. When Moses Austin came to Texas in 1820 to win the right to form colonies in Texas only to be sent packing by a Spanish governor who distrusted foreigners, it was the baron who persuaded the governor to forward Austin's proposal to the Spanish government. As one author put it, "He was among the first, but certainly not the last, loser to come to Texas to reinvent himself and emerge in prominence."[6] The flaws in Texas's leaders remain evident today. George W. Bush was honest—if not always specific—about the mistakes in his past. Despite those flaws, Texans twice chose him as their governor before recommending him to a nation that would twice elect him as president.

Even after the legends of our history reinvented themselves, we Texans have reinvented our own history. Our recollection of history is less fixed than we care to admit. After the Texans won the Battle of San Jacinto with the battle cry, "Remember the Alamo," the Alamo itself would lie in neglect for half a century, a forgotten monument that was used to store onions and potatoes before being restored and elevated as "the shrine of Texas Liberty."

Our explorations of Texas legends are not an attempt to resolve the debate between views of "Disneyland Davy" and other versions of Texas history. Texans need not be sidetracked by the debate about whether their state's heroes were perfect. They were not. Neither were the founders of the United States. What we need to understand is how important these images are to the people of Texas. Describing the "passionate nation" that is Texas, John Steinbeck noted that "[r]ich, poor, Panhandle, Gulf, city, county, Texas is the obsession, the proper study and the passionate possession of all Texans."[7]

The aspirations embedded in our myths play a role in how the state approaches change. Because our legends are about who we once were, retelling these stories now reminds us who we are today and keeps us from drifting too far from our values. At the same time these legends can tell us a great deal about who we want to be and where our hopes come from. As Steinbeck wrote, "I have said that Texas is a state of mind, but I think it is more than that. It is a mystique closely approximating a religion."[8]

Winners and Losers

Politics involves the distribution of goods and by its nature produces winners and losers. While Texas's history, culture, and predilections may seem vague and distant to students today, the politics that spring from them have ramifications that are very real for the citizens of the state. This text is intended to encourage students to think critically about Texas politics, identify problems, and look ahead to solutions. In every chapter we will be looking at who gets what from government by looking at winners and losers in Texas politics. This is especially valuable in studying Texas political history because the victories won by a group in one era most often lay the groundwork for the next battles. Texas is in a constant state of change, and citizens need to consider what needs to be changed and how their fellow Texans might be affected by the changes.

Texas versus . . .

We will occasionally pause to compare Texas to other states, often focusing on those states that provide the most dramatic or interesting contrast to Texas. We want to illustrate how Texas is different and why that difference is significant. Because most citizens of a state seldom consider their options, we felt it was important to illustrate the possibilities of state government and to illustrate the consequences of choices that people face. Comparisons were selected to provide examples from potentially familiar settings, like Louisiana or California, to settings that Texans may have little exposure to, like Vermont or North Dakota. It is our hope that students will come to appreciate why Texas is just a little bit different. Our comparison of Texas to other states is a good place to highlight critical thinking. We pose a set of questions to encourage students to look at options and ponder what would best serve the state.

Companion Website and Instructor Resources

Students and instructors also will benefit from a variety of ancillaries. A companion website, available at http://lonestar.cqpress.com, provides chapter summaries, interactive flash cards of key words, practice quizzes, and annotated hyperlinks to a wealth of online resources and readings. Instructors adopting the text can download test bank questions covering each chapter, along with PowerPoint lecture slides at http://college.cqpress.com/instructors-resources/collier.

Politics changes even between editions of our text, and our blog (http://lonestar politics.wordpress.com) is our outlet for assorted musings about Texas politics that didn't get past our editors and reviewers, as well as for corrections, updates, and other current issues in Texas politics.

Acknowledgments

Obviously, we didn't do this by ourselves. We did make all the mistakes. Against all odds, a small band of dedicated people tried their best to detect these mistakes and set us right.

Don Gregory served as our research assistant early in this project. He provided us a wealth of old Texas texts and sent many interesting clippings. His research skills were exceptional, and we expect that he will do quite well in political science. We also enjoyed assistance from Joe Ericson. We believe that Joe served as a political advisor to Stephen F. Austin himself. We also benefited from many small favors from other colleagues. We thank Laurie Dodson of the Texas Municipal League for her assistance with statistics and resources on city government in Texas. She was also helpful in translating the legalese of local government administration into political science terms. Debra Gaston, Nacogdoches County elections administrator, provided invaluable consultation regarding elections processes and procedures in Texas.

Far from Texas, the good people at CQ Press labored to keep us on schedule and under control. Despite the fact that they still haven't found the pictures we wanted of the "Los Conquistadors Coronado Burro Ride" at the Six Flags Over Texas amusement park (or hid them from us if they did), we would like to thank Charisse Kiino, Nancy Matuszak, and Gwenda Larsen for their benevolence, patience, and diligence. We'd also like to thank the first edition reviewers who offered up a balance of criticism and encouragement: Brian Cravens, Blinn College; Richard Daly, St. Edward's University; Paul J. Pope, University of Texas at Brownsville; and Glenn Utter, Lamar University.

Notes

1. Mrs. Anna J. Hardwicke Pennybacker, *A New History of Texas for Schools* (Tyler, Tex., 1888), v.
2. John Steinbeck, *Travels with Charley: In Search of America* (New York: Bantam Books, 1961), 226.
3. James E. Crisp, *Sleuthing the Alamo: Davy Crockett's Last Stand and Other Mysteries of the Texas Revolution* (New York: Oxford University Press, 2004), 142.
4. Ibid., 144.
5. Ibid., 17.
6. James L. Haley, *Passionate Nation: The Epic History of Texas* (New York: Free Press, 2006), 70.
7. Steinbeck, *Travels with Charley,* 226.
8. Ibid., 227.

Texas borders welcome about 634 new Texans every day. The Census Bureau estimates that Texas gains about 241 people from other states and 393 from other countries daily. Add another 1,121 Texans born every year, and the changing face of the state is clear.

CHAPTER 1

Introduction

After watching immigrants stream across the border into Texas year after year government officials on the Texas side began to worry that their state was being transformed into a part-Mexican, part-Anglo society that would prove unmanageable and ungovernable as the growing number of immigrants asserted their political power. Some immigrants entered lawfully, patiently working their way through the government's cumbersome process; others came without regard to the laws, exploiting a border that was too long and too remote to be effectively monitored. Most of the new immigrants proved both hard working and enterprising, solid additions to Texas society and the Texas economy. Many brought along their families for a chance at a better life or planned on bringing family as soon as they made enough money to do so. A few crossed the border to escape legal and financial problems back home and contributed to criminal enterprises or squandered their wages on alcohol and vice while eventually abandoning their families. Established residents worried that they would become foreigners in their own country or doubted that their new neighbors would ever prove anything but a challenge since many newcomers refused to assimilate or adopt the politics and culture of their new home. Many of the new arrivals stubbornly clung to their native tongue; some even began to demand that official business be conducted in it.

The government felt that much of the problem lay on the other side of the border. Some of these immigrants seemed to be entering the state to foment change, and many had strong political ties to political leaders back home. Sam Houston, who had been governor of Tennessee, was a close political and personal friend of U.S. president Andrew Jackson. Davy Crockett, also a product of Jackson's Democratic Party in Tennessee, had served in the U.S. Congress and was one of the leading political figures of the day. It seemed likely that his political ambitions followed him to Texas.

Many of the early Texans who later fought for independence from Mexico came to Texas against the expressed wishes of the Mexican government. Whereas early American colonists along the Eastern seaboard settled among, and then pushed aside, the more loosely organized Native American populations, early Texans violated a border officially recognized by the American government as they brushed aside Mexican law. The immigration issue—then as today—represents a challenge for a government that struggles to keep up with a rapidly expanding, ever-changing state. While immigrants today generate a great deal of tax money for the state through sales and income taxes, they also cost the counties and local governments a great deal in services. Immigrants contribute greatly to the economic success of the state by meeting the demand for inexpensive labor, but sometimes do so at the expense of native-born labor.

Immigration, then and now, shows us that Texas's placement at the crossroads between new and old has been one of the few constants in the politics of the state. Texas has relished its growth, but often disparaged the new citizens who fueled it. Texans have enjoyed the prosperity that growth brings, but only reluctantly accepted the new Texans and the changes they brought.

While change may be inevitable, a society is rooted by the stories citizens share and hand down from generation to generation. We Texans are especially attached to our state's history and its legends of larger-than-life people and events. Stories from Texas history are more than dramatic scenes we retell and recreate for entertainment; these stories define who we are and remind us of our values. Texas's unique relationship with its history is reflected in a favorite theme park, Six Flags over Texas, an amusement park originally constructed around Texas history themes and which at one time featured rides such as "LaSalle's River Boat Adventure" in the French section and "Los Conquistadors Coronado Burro Ride" in the Spanish section. Today, the legends portrayed at Six Flags are decidedly modern: tourists are more likely to pose for pictures with Batman and Bugs Bunny in front of gleaming metal roller coasters than with the costumed deputies who duel horse thieves in front of the county courthouse.

Legends are stories passed down for generations—but stories that are often presented as history. While not always entirely true, legends play an important role in politics. Legends reveal a desire to be culturally connected to our fellow citizens and to a larger entity, and they also tell us a great deal about who we want to be.

So where, between legend and reality, lies the true Texas? Even as it takes care to project a rustic frontier image, Texas today is home to many of the most innovative businesses in the global marketplace. The gap between the state's political heritage and its future aspirations was never more in evidence than when Governor Rick Perry opened his 2006 reelection bid with an ad depicting a herd of longhorn cattle rumbling down a city street lined with modern skyscrapers. In keeping with the legend, elected officials are left to act like cowboys even as they think like twenty-first century engineers, focused on the intricate demands of expansion and balance that mark the contemporary world.

In this chapter we will chart the contours of this gap. We will start by looking at Texas history and geography, casting an eye toward the traditions and transformations that have shaped the state's politics. We will examine some of the legends behind Texas politics and highlight the differences between Texas and another one-time independent U.S. state. We will conclude the chapter by focusing on the state of Texas today—its people, economy, and culture.

As you read the chapter, think about the following questions:

★ What role do legends play in the political culture of Texas?

★ How does Texas's size affect its political institutions?

★ To what extent do changing demographics and economic diversification shape the state of Texas?

★ Why is there a tension between the rapidly changing nature of Texas and Texas's legends?

Texas Geography

The land mass of Texas defines the state's image as much as it has determined the course of its history. With a land area totaling 263,513 square miles, it is the second largest of the U.S. states, behind Alaska's 663,276 square miles. From east to west the state spans 773 miles and from north to south 801 miles. The 785-mile drive from Marshall to El Paso takes a traveler from the Piney Woods of East Texas to the sparse landscape of the West Texas desert. Driving the 900 miles north from Brownsville to Texline takes the traveler from the border of Mexico and the Gulf of Mexico to the borders of Oklahoma and New Mexico. The Texas Gulf Coast consists of shoreline and marshy areas while the Trans-Pecos region includes the arid desert of the Big Bend and Guadalupe Peak, the highest point in Texas at 8,749 feet.

Texas runs the full gamut from urban to rural. The state's most populous county, Harris County, which contains Houston, had 4,070,989 residents in 2009, making it more populous than half of the states in the United States. Texas also has some of the nation's least populated counties, with Loving County's 677 square miles in the Panhandle occupied by only 45 residents. The state has eight counties with populations under 1,000, and about one-third (eighty-nine) of Texas's 254 counties have populations under 10,000.

Texas's size encourages more than bragging rights. V. O. Key, a native Texan and one of the founders of modern political science, pointed out that the geographic size of the state has limited the face-to-face interactions needed to develop closely knit political organizations. While this helped inoculate Texas from the large party machines that corrupted politics in many places in the nineteenth century, it has also inhibited the formation of beneficial groups that would bring together more benevolent forces from across the state.

The state's size makes campaigning expensive for candidates trying to win votes statewide and has left the state's politicians more dependent on those capable of financing a statewide campaign. The sheer size of the state has also rewarded a dramatic style. As Key observed after surveying the electoral history of his home state, "Attention-getting antics substituted for organized politics."[1] In the absence of closely knit state political networks, and given Texans' fondness for independence, the path to power for the political "outsider" may be a little bit easier. The ability to quickly grab the imagination of voters has given Texas politics a colorful cast of characters rivaled by few other places. Texas's political candidates are often larger than life, and while change has been a constant in Texas politics, subtlety is often lacking.

Size has contributed to the state's mentality in other ways. With its seemingly endless frontier, Texas represents limitless potential to many. At the same time, its spaciousness offers an escape that reinforces Texans' sense of independence and freedom. With Texans dispersed across such an extensive landscape, history and legends become even more important as a shared culture. The vast geographic distances and the differences in human geography leave many wondering exactly what it is that binds so tightly all these people from all these places and makes them into such fiercely loyal Texans. The answer, of course, is Texas's unique history. As John Steinbeck wrote, "there is no physical or geographical unity in Texas. Its unity lies in the mind.[2]

While Texas's history unites its citizens, it also represents a long string of transitions that brought with them conflict between old and new. As we will see, the Texas political system has often resisted the needs and wishes of new arrivals because those that came before were reluctant to give up the power they earned or fought for. While this pattern is not unique to Texas, Texas's history offers a vivid tableau of upheaval along the hard road of change.

History: The Birth of Texas Traditions

The first wave of change began about 12,000 years ago when humans who had drifted across the Bering Strait land bridge into North America some 20,000 years ago eventually found their way into Texas. These earliest Texans hunted mammoths before those large animals became extinct. Later, bison served as a primary food source on the grassy plains that covered present-day West Texas. As changes in the climate began to warm the plains, the land could no longer support the large mammals that the hunting tribes depended on, and as a result hunter-gatherer tribes became more prevalent.

As with native people from other parts of the continent, the native American tribes of Texas were diverse. About 1,500 years ago, the Caddo people developed agricultural tools and practices that gave them a more stable food supply, which meant less need to roam and more time to form a society with social classes and establish trading relations with other tribes. By 1500 an estimated 200,000 Caddos inhabited a society that was extensive enough to lead some historians to call the Caddos the "Romans of Texas."[3] Along the Gulf Coast the Karankawa tribe relied on fish and shellfish for much of their diet. Dubbed cannibals by some, the Karankawas ate only their enemies and were in fact so shocked to learn that the Spanish survivors of the Narváez Expedition had cannibalized each other that some Karankawas expressed regret at not having killed the Spanish explorers when they first came ashore.[4] Coahuiltecan tribes roamed the area southwest of the Karankawas, surviving on a diverse diet of whatever they could gather or catch. Because subsistence needs forced them to move about the prairies, these small hunter-gatherer bands lacked the cohesive society that developed among tribes like the Caddos. The Apaches—who inhabited areas of what would become the Texas Panhandle—lived in large, extended families in a peaceful and well-ordered society.

Christopher Columbus's first voyage brought great change to the Texas region as the Spanish empire in America began to take root in the Caribbean, Central America, and the Southwest. As would many others after them, the conquistadores Álvar Núñez Cabeza de Vaca and later Hernando Cortéz visited the region seeking wealth. One of the most significant instruments of change the Spanish brought with them was the horse. Even though the Spanish forces would never be a large enough presence to transform the region, the horses they brought would change Indian society by giving some tribes the means to move their camps more quickly and become more effective hunters and warriors.

The French, led by René-Robert Cavelier and Sieur de La Salle, managed only a brief presence in Texas. La Salle, who, in the view of one historian, had the sort of personality and exhibited the kind of behavior that "led many to question his mental stability,"[5] had an ambitious plan to build a series of posts down the Mississippi River to the Gulf of Mexico, claim all of the land drained by the Mississippi, and name it Louisiana in honor of the French king Louis XIV. La Salle's venture into Texas failed, and La Salle himself was killed in an ambush. However, La Salle's incursions spurred the Spanish to increase their settlement of East Texas to counter any future French arrivals.

Map 1.1 Independent Texas

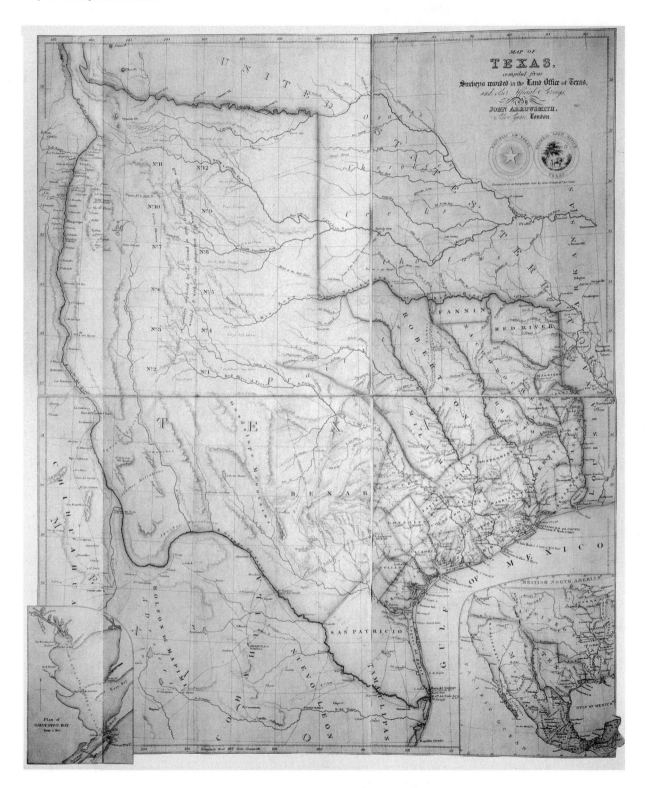

The Alamo, the most famous historic site in Texas, was originally part of the network of missions that the Spanish hoped would establish their presence in Texas.

Although relative newcomers themselves, the Spanish, like the Indian tribes before them, were suspicious of the motives of new arrivals and sought to bar outsiders; they attempted to strengthen their hold on the area by encouraging their own people to establish or expand settlements. Over the course of the eighteenth century the Spanish gradually established themselves in Texas through a system of missions and presidios (forts). The missions were designed to bring the Indians to God while pushing the French out. Native Americans in the area showed little interest in converting to Catholicism, however, and the Spanish had to supplement their religious outposts with presidios. Given the high costs of maintaining these forts, Spanish investments in the area ultimately proved inadequate, and by the 1790s there were fewer than 3,200 Spanish-speaking people in Texas.

Building a border wall to keep immigrants out of Spanish territory was out of the question, but Spanish officials declared in 1795 that local officials should take "the utmost care to prevent the passage to this kingdom of persons from the United States of America."[6] In one of the first recorded verbal assaults on immigrants, one Spanish official colorfully warned that the American immigrants "are not and will not be anything but crows to pick out our eyes."[7]

Despite the efforts of Spanish officials, the tides of change proved too strong to resist, and eventually the Spanish government resorted to giving citizens of the United States land grants to settle in Louisiana (before the territory was acquired by France in 1800). While recruiting Anglo settlers from the United States to serve as a buffer against intrusion by the U.S. government seems self-defeating, the Spanish government had little choice. Many in Spain realized that closing off Texas was futile. Spanish officials hoped that by abandoning Florida and negotiating the Adams-Onís Treaty of 1819, which established clear boundaries between Spanish and U.S. claims, American interest would be diverted away from Texas long enough for Spain to build a stronger presence there.

The Spanish legacy in Texas can be seen on any Texas map, where every major river except the Red River bears a Spanish name. Spanish rule also left a different, but particularly Texan kind of mark: a 1778 Spanish proclamation stated that all unbranded cattle were property of the king, which led to the practice of cattle branding to identify ownership.[8]

The roots of the organized Anglo settlement of Texas in the early nineteenth century can be traced to the last years of Spanish rule in Texas. A Missouri resident, Moses Austin, visited Texas in 1820 in hopes of winning the legal right to form colonies in the area. Unfortunately, the return trip took its toll on Austin after his horses were stolen, and he died soon after returning to Missouri, though not before expressing the hope that his son Stephen would carry on the endeavor. In fact, Stephen F. Austin had little interest in serving as an *empresario* (an entrepreneur who made money colonizing areas), and Texas was initially a somewhat unwanted inheritance. However, Austin, a canny businessman, came to see the potential of the land and ultimately warmed to his task.

Empresario

an entrepreneur who made money colonizing areas of the Mexican territories.

Mexican Independence

The next round of change began on September 16 (still celebrated by many Tejanos—Texans of Mexican origin—as Diez y Seis de Septiembre) when Father Miguel Hidalgo y Costilla launched the Mexican War of Independence against Spain through his revolutionary "Call of Hidalgo" (also known as the "Grito de Dolores"), which demanded that those born in the New World be endowed with the same rights as those born in Europe. Mexican independence would end Spanish control of Texas, but it did not end the desire of local authorities to stop the growing trickle of immigrants from the United States. The fledgling Mexican government eventually approved Austin's colonization plan in the hope that legal settlers brought by authorized empresarios like Austin would become loyal to the Mexican government rather than their United States roots.

By 1824 Austin had assembled the three hundred families allowed under his initial contract and began to settle in Texas. While these colonists suffered more than their share of hardships, Austin's colonies prospered so much that he received four additional contracts to bring settlers over the next seven years. However, in what would become a familiar problem in Texas, the same opportunities that drew legal settlers to the colonies of Austin and other empresarios also drew illegal immigrants unwilling to deal with the encumbrance of law. Soon Austin and other empresarios found themselves laboring to protect their legal colonies from a flood of illegal squatters.

By the 1830s there were about 10,000 Anglo settlers in Texas. Some came to Texas hoping to make money quickly in land speculation, but most were subsistence farmers looking for a chance to own their own land and control their own destiny. Some were fleeing financial ruin brought on by the Panic of 1819; other settlers came to Texas fleeing justice in American states. Tensions between the Anglos and the Mexican government developed as a result of differences in political culture and the Mexican government's insistence on Spanish as the official language. In addition, many Anglo settlers were Protestants who resented the Mexican government's requirement that they become Catholics. Finally, some wanted to use their land to produce cotton, a cash crop that depended heavily on the labor of the approximately 1,000 slaves they brought with them. This too created conflict as the Mexican government was opposed to slavery. In fact, the risk of losing their slaves kept many wealthy southern plantation owners from moving into Texas.

TEXAS FOREVER!!

The usurper of the South has failed in his efforts to enslave the freemen of Texas.

The wives and daughters of Texas will be saved from the brutality of Mexican soldiers.

Now is the time to emigrate to the Garden of America.

A free passage, and all found, is offered at New Orleans to all applicants. Every settler receives a location of

EIGHT HUNDRED ACRES OF LAND.

On the 23d of February, a force of 1000 Mexicans came in sight of San Antonio, and on the 25th Gen. St. Anna arrived at that place with 2500 more men, and demanded a surrender of the fort held by 150 Texians, and on the refusal, he attempted to storm the fort, twice, with his whole force, but was repelled with the loss of 500 men, and the Americans lost none. Many of his troops, the liberals of Zacatecas, are brought on to Texas in irons and are urged forward with the promise of the women and plunder of Texas.

The Texian forces were marching to relieve St. Antonio, March the 2d. The Government of Texas is supplied with plenty of arms, ammunition, provisions, &c. &c.

An 1836 flyer offers free transportation and land to new settlers in hopes of reinforcing the Anglo presence in Texas.

The Texas Revolution

The tension between the Mexican government and the Anglo settlers eventually turned into that most dramatic political transformation—revolution. Initially, Anglo settlers were divided on the issues of revolution and independence. Stephen F. Austin and many of the established settlers advocated a moderate course, asking for separate statehood within the Mexican nation. Mexico's constitution required that Texas have a population of 80,000 before becoming a state, a number far greater than the 30,000 inhabiting the area at the time. During the early 1830s the Mexican government granted some of the Anglos' other requests: the right to trial by jury and the official use of the English language. Despite these concessions, many Anglos remained unhappy and began to openly defy the Mexican government. When Texans in Gonzalez fired on Mexican troops who came to take away the cannon the town used for its defense, the Texas revolution was underway.

Tejanos were in a difficult position. In the 1820s about 4,000 Tejanos inhabited the region, including many former soldiers who had been stationed in the area and remained after leaving military service. Many had become community leaders and owned large ranches. While Anglo settlers were unhappy about life under the Mexican government, Tejanos were uneasy about the possibility of living under the rule of Anglo settlers, many of whom considered Mexicans and their culture inferior. At the same time, Tejanos shared the concerns of Anglo settlers who did not want a central government in Mexico City controlling their fate and hampering their economic development.

The politics of the independence movement was often chaotic. When Mexican president Antonio López de Santa Anna became less tolerant toward the Texans' aspirations and sent troops to enforce his laws, the Texans began to mobilize politically, calling for a meeting to organize their response. They termed the meeting a "Consultation" of the people of Texas to avoid drawing the ire of Mexican officials with the label "convention," which implied the authority to rewrite the constitution. The Consultation assembled on November 1, 1835, and on November 13 passed the Organic Law creating a government with a governor, lieutenant governor, and a General Council with representatives for each geographic district. Henry Smith, the leader of the more radical group favoring immediate independence, was elected governor by a 30–22 vote, beating out Stephen F. Austin who clung to a more moderate course. Perhaps Texans should have worried more about their choice. Smith had been married to—and quickly widowed by—two sisters in succession, only to marry again a third sister, the twin of his second wife. Smith's political relationships died even more quickly than his romantic relationships. Smith resisted compromise and suspended the General Council. Meanwhile, the council impeached him after fewer than four months in office. The effect of all this was a government paralyzed.

The revolution was further hamstrung when the council created a regular army under the command of Sam Houston without formally bringing the volunteers already in the field under Houston's command. The volunteers were notorious for their autonomy and lack of discipline, as Austin would find out on November 23 when he ordered them to attack Mexican troops in Béxar only to have his order refused.

Voters on February 1, 1836, elected representatives to serve as delegates to a new convention that began deliberations on March 1. Shunning most of the more cautious men who had served in the earlier Consultation and in the General Council, Texans chose younger men, many of whom were newcomers—nearly half of the fifty-nine delegates had lived in Texas less than two years. They met in the town of Washington (on the Brazos River) in part because local business owners provided a building without charge. There the delegates adopted without debate a Declaration of Independence, drafted by George C. Childress, who had been in Texas for less than eight months. The convention continued meeting until March 17, when it completed the Constitution of the Republic of Texas. The constitution protected slavery and permitted a freed slave to live in Texas only with the permission of the Texas Legislature. A government ad interim, composed of the members of the constitutional convention, was empowered to run the affairs of the state. One of the first orders of business was the election of David G. Burnet as Texas's first president. For vice president the convention selected Lorenzo de Zavala who had served as Mexican minister to Paris under Santa Anna but left his post when Santa Anna claimed dictatorial powers in 1835.

While united by their struggle against the Mexican government, the revolutionary leaders of Texas often fought among themselves even after independence was won. After Houston's ankle was shattered in the Battle of San Jacinto on April 21, 1836, President Burnet denied the victorious general permission to leave for New Orleans to seek medical treatment. Burnet eventually relented when the captain of the boat Houston was set to embark on refused to take anyone at all if he was not allowed to take Houston.

The Republic of Texas

On September 5, 1836, Sam Houston was elected president of the Republic of Texas by a landslide, receiving 5,119 votes, compared to 743 for Henry Smith and only 586 for Stephen F. Austin. The Republic of Texas Constitution also won approval from voters, as did a referendum on pursuing annexation to the United States. With over 3,000 citizens voting to seek annexation and fewer than 100 objecting, Texas's interest in joining the United States was clear from its first day of independence.

The government was temporarily located in Columbia but soon moved to a new town located on Buffalo Bayou that backers, much to the new president's delight, suggested be named Houston. The new capital city, like much of the republic, was improvised; the legislature met in an unfinished capitol building with tree branches forming the roof.

While the period of Texas independence was relatively brief, it was neither simple nor quiet. The population of Texas doubled. Just after the revolution in 1836 Texas had about 30,000 Anglos, 5,000 black slaves, 3,470 Tejanos, and 14,500 Indians. By 1847 its "white" population (including 12–14,000 persons of Mexican descent) had soared to 102,961 while its black population had climbed to 39,048 (38,753 slaves and 295 freed blacks).

Change was not limited to number of citizens. While the Republic's second president, Mirabeau B. Lamar, helped develop the Texas education system, his administration proved disastrous for the Indian tribes living in Texas. Houston had worked to build friendships with Texas's tribes, but Lamar sought to eradicate them. During the three years of the Lamar administration, the Republic of Texas's debt skyrocketed from $2 to $7 million and the value of its currency plummeted. Lamar opposed annexation by the United States at a time when the United States was expressing doubts of its own. Sam Houston returned to the presidency only after a bruising political battle. Once back in office, Houston helped make peace with the Indians and brought fiscal discipline back to government, spending one-tenth of what Lamar had spent.

The path to statehood would not be as simple as Houston hoped. In the United States northern interests in the U.S. Congress, led by John Quincy Adams, balked at

Sam Houston

By the time he became a Texan and led Texas to independence, Sam Houston had gone through two wives and lots of alcohol and was, in the words of Texas historian James L. Haley, "considered in respectable circles as unsavory as he was colorful."[i] However, no one better reflects the reality that the greatness of Texas's legends can be found in less-than-perfect people, as Houston guided Texas through some of its most dramatic transitions.

In his youth Houston generally preferred sneaking away to live among the Indians to working in the family business. Houston distinguished himself during the War of 1812, serving bravely and winning the admiration of General Andrew Jackson. Houston followed Jackson, his new mentor, into politics and was sometimes mentioned as a successor to President Jackson. However, his first marriage abruptly ended in 1827 in the middle of his term as governor of Tennessee and just two months after his wedding. His marriage over and his political career in ruins, Houston went to live again among the Cherokees. During this time he took a Cherokee wife, without entering into a formal Christian marriage. Over time Houston's state of mind deteriorated and his Indian hosts eventually stripped him of his original Indian name ("The Raven") and began to call him Oo-tse-tee Ar-dee-tah-skee ("The Big Drunk").[ii] After abandoning his second wife and returning to public life in America, Houston narrowly avoided jail after assaulting a member of Congress who had insulted his integrity. Brought before Congress to face charges, Houston delivered an impassioned defense on his own behalf, allegedly because his lawyer, Francis Scott Key, was too hungover to speak.

During the Texas Revolution gossips frequently attributed Houston's disappearances to drinking binges rather than military missions. Some questioned his bravery and military leadership during the war. Many Texans wanted Houston to turn and fight the Mexican Army sooner, despite Houston's protest that his troops were undertrained and outnumbered. While most Texans sided with Houston after his victory at San Jacinto, criticisms of his conduct of the war would reappear in political campaigns for the rest of his career.

After leading Texas through the Revolution, Houston continued to play a major role in the state's changes while serving as Texas's first president during its years as an independent nation. Houston struggled in the years after the Texas Revolution to protect the Tejanos who had served alongside him during the war. Similarly, his years among the Cherokees and his continued fondness for them left him at odds with many Anglos who preferred to see Native Americans driven off or killed.

After playing a central role in winning Texas's entry into the United States, Houston's final political act would be the struggle to keep Texas from seceding and joining the Confederacy. Houston disliked slavery and defied state law by freeing his own slaves. He had been one of few southern senators to speak out against slavery, a sentiment that led the Texas Legislature to vote against his return to the Senate. His final departure from politics came when he refused to support the secession of Texas in the American Civil War and, as a result, was forced by the legislature to resign his governorship. If Texans had followed Houston's leadership, the lives of many Texas soldiers would have been saved and the state spared post–war Reconstruction.

Houston finally settled down after marrying his third wife and finding redemption, but he never denied his faults. When asked if his sins had been washed away at his river baptism, Houston joked, "I hope so. But if they were all washed away, the Lord help the fish down below."[iii]

However numerous his sins, Houston's principles make him a much more heroic historical figure than many of his more sober peers. From the moment Houston arrived in Texas he became a central figure in the transformation of the state and for thirty years he guided Texas through its most turbulent times. While Houston might not be able to be elected today, he did more to shape modern Texas than any other person.

i.   James L. Haley, *Passionate Nation: The Epic History of Texas* (New York: Free Press, 2006) 107.
ii. James E. Crisp, *Sleuthing the Alamo: Davy Crockett's Last Stand and Other Mysteries of the Texas Revolution* (New York: Oxford University Press, 2004) 29.
iii. Haley, *Passionate Nation*, 277.

bringing another slave state into the nation. Houston managed to stir U.S. interest by making overtures to European powers—a course of action designed to pique the United States' jealousy and make it wary of foreign intervention along its borders. As threats from Mexico continued into the 1840s, Texas turned to England and France for help in obtaining the release of Texas soldiers imprisoned in Mexican jails. Houston also positioned Texas for future bargaining by claiming for the Republic disputed land reaching west and north as far as Wyoming, including portions of the Santa Fe Trail used for trade between the United States and Mexico. The Texas Congress went even further and passed (over Houston's veto) a bill that claimed all the land south of the forty-second parallel and west of Texas to the Pacific, as well as portions of Mexico—a claim that would have made Texas larger than the United States at the time.

Texas Statehood

The issue of annexation of Texas eventually became central to the 1844 U.S. presidential election when James K. Polk, the candidate backed by Andrew Jackson, campaigned for the acquisition of Texas. Texas's expansive claim to territory was resolved when Henry Clay crafted a compromise whereby Texas accepted its present borders in return for a payment of $10 million. While the joint resolution inviting Texas to join the United States passed the U.S. House easily, it barely squeaked through the Senate, 27 to 25. John Quincy Adams and Texas's opponents made one final, last-ditch effort to stop Texas statehood by asserting that the admission of Texas through a joint resolution was unconstitutional because that method of admission was not spelled out in the U.S. Constitution.

Texas called a convention for July 4, 1845, to approve annexation and draft a constitution to accommodate Texas's new role as a U.S. state. The only vote in the Texas Legislature against entering the United States came from Richard Bache, who allegedly voted against annexation because he had come to Texas to escape his ex-wife and did not care to live in the same country with her again.[9] Texas was able to retain ownership of its public lands, a term of annexation that other new states did not enjoy. The U.S. Congress accepted the state's new constitution in December, and President Polk signed the bill on December 29, 1845. Texas formally entered statehood on February 19, 1846.

A telling part of the residual folklore of Texas's admission is the notion that Texas retains the right to secede—and if it so chooses, to reenter the United States as five separate states. The origins of this folklore come from a compromise designed to overcome objections in the U.S. Congress to the original admission of Texas. The joint resolution that admitted Texas to the Union provided that Texas could be divided into as many as five states. New states north or west of the Missouri Compromise lines would be free; in states south of the compromise lines, a popular vote would determine the legality of slavery. However, the power to create new states ultimately rests with the U.S. Congress, and the right to divide was not reserved to Texas.

J. Pinckney Henderson earned the honor of serving as Texas's first governor after winning election by a large margin. Texas sent Sam Houston and Thomas Jefferson Rusk to serve as the state's first two U.S. senators. Texas's only Jewish member of Congress for 130 years was among its first: David Kaufman of Nacogdoches, a Philadelphia-born Jew who had worked as a lawyer in Mississippi before arriving in

Texas, distinguishing himself as an Indian fighter, and then serving two terms as the Speaker of the Republic of Texas's legislature. Kaufman was only the second Jewish member of the U.S. House, taking office the year after Lewis C. Levin became the nation's first Jewish representative in 1845. Passed over in the selection of Texas's first congressional delegation was Anson Jones, who had been sworn in as president of Texas on December 9, 1844. Jones was embittered by this perceived slight and set about putting together his own volume of the history of the Republic, published posthumously a year after Jones shot himself on the steps of the old capitol in Houston.

Americans who had resisted the admission of Texas for fear of provoking war with Mexico soon saw those fears realized when fighting broke out in 1846. Many historians believe that U.S. president James K. Polk orchestrated the Mexican-American War by ordering Gen. Zachary Taylor into territory near the mouth of the Rio Grande that Mexican officials had claimed was part of Mexico. Mexico responded by declaring a defensive war on April 23, with the United States responding with its own declaration of war on May 13. The Mexican-American War ended after troops under the command of U.S. general Winfield Scott moved into Mexico City. The **Treaty of Guadalupe Hidalgo** was signed on February 2, 1848, recognizing the Rio Grande as the official boundary between Texas and Mexico. While the treaty offered assurances that the rights of erstwhile Mexican citizens who suddenly found themselves citizens of the United States would be protected, this promise proved fragile.

The rapid population growth following Texas's annexation further transformed the state. However, not every group grew at an equal rate. Despite the general population surge, the Tejano population declined, and by the 1847 census the 8,000 Germans in Texas were the largest ethnic minority in a state with a total population of around 142,000, including 40,000 slaves and only 295 free people of color. Even though the Tejanos had fought for independence, many were forced to move to Mexico as the clash of Mexican and Anglo cultures intensified, marking one of just a few times in its history that Texas saw people moving away.

Texas in the Confederacy

The rise of cotton farming in Texas increased the importance of slavery to the Texas economy as production of cotton grew from 40,000 bales in 1848 to 420,000 bales in 1860.[10] By 1860, Texans held 182,566 slaves, compared to a total population of 604,215.[11] While much of Texas was becoming dependent on slave labor, Sam Houston battled slavery, and in 1855 became one of the few southern members of Congress to publicly oppose it. Once again, Houston's personal popularity would be undone by an unpopular stand on the burning issue of the day. In 1857, two years before his term expired, the Texas Legislature voted to not return Houston to the Senate for another term, leaving Houston to serve the remainder of his term as a lame duck. Houston responded to the insult by running for governor in 1857. Over the course of this campaign, he traveled over 1,500 miles, visited forty-two cities, and gave endless speeches, many lasting as long as four hours. Despite his efforts, Houston lost the election to Hardin R. Runnels by a vote of 32,552 to 28,678. Houston's loss came in part from his association with the anti-immigrant Know Nothing Party, which proved unpopular among voters of Mexican and German ancestry who might otherwise have sympathized with Houston's anti-slavery stance.

Treaty of Guadalupe Hidalgo signed on February 2, 1848, this agreement between the United States and Mexico ended the Mexican-American War and recognized the Rio Grande as the boundary between Texas, now part of the United States, and Mexico.

After serving out the remainder of his Senate term, Houston left the U.S. Senate in 1859 to run once again for governor, hoping that when the South seceded from the Union he could lead Texas back to independence. This time, Houston was successful, defeating Runnels 33,375 to 27,500. Nonetheless, over the objections of Governor Houston, a Secessionist Convention was subsequently convened, and on February 1, 1861, it voted overwhelmingly in favor of secession. A few weeks later, voters statewide approved a secession ordinance by a three-to-one margin. The Secession Convention approved a requirement that all state officers swear an oath of loyalty to the Confederacy. After Houston refused to take the oath, the governor's office was declared vacant.

The Confederate regime in Texas was a disaster for many. Not only were free blacks victimized, but Germans were targeted for harassment because of their opposition to slavery. Tejanos saw their land seized, and many Tejanos chose to align themselves with the Union. Some enlisted, becoming the heart of the Union's Second Cavalry, while others fought as pro-Union guerrillas. Many pro-Union Anglos were forced to flee the state. William Marsh Rice, whose wealth would one day endow Rice University, had to leave Houston and move his businesses to Matamoros in Mexico.

Reconstruction in Texas

Northern rule arrived with the end of the Civil War on June 19, 1865, when Union forces, under Gen. Gordon Granger, arrived in Galveston bringing with them a proclamation ending slavery in Texas. That date, known as "Juneteenth" in Texas, was the day on which the slaves in Texas were actually freed, despite President Abraham Lincoln's having signed the Emancipation Proclamation in January 1863. While many transformations in Texas history involved the arrival of new citizens from outside the state, the end of slavery meant that former slaves were now new citizens in their old state. Joining with a small number of Anglo Republicans, African Americans helped elect Republicans to statewide offices and constitutional conventions.

Freedom proved a mixed blessing for the "freedmen." While legally they were free, in practical terms freedmen endured horrendous intimidation and exploitation. State law would not recognize any marriage involving African American Texans until 1869. While the Freedmen's Bureau was created to help former slaves, the bureau's efforts were sometimes limited by administrators who, while supporting the end of slavery, doubted the goal of racial equality. Texas, like other southern states, passed so-called Black Codes that were designed to limit the rights of the former slaves. In Texas, any person with one-eighth or more of Negro blood could not serve on a jury or vote. With local law enforcement often in the hands of Confederate sympathizers, African Americans relied on Union troops for protection. As elsewhere in the former Confederate states, the Ku Klux Klan became a vehicle for terrorizing former slaves and those sympathetic to their cause, as well as "carpetbaggers" (people from the North who came south to assist or cash in on Reconstruction) and "scalawags" (Republicans of local origin).

In January 1866, Texans elected delegates to a convention to draft a new state constitution aimed at winning the state readmission into the United States. However, the Texas Legislature seemed to have missed the news that the South lost the war: the legislature refused to ratify the Thirteenth Amendment (ending slavery) and Fourteenth Amendment (guaranteeing equal rights) and instead drafted a framework of laws limiting the rights of freed slaves. The Constitution of 1866 failed to meet the demands of the Radical Republicans who had won control of the U.S. Congress in the 1866 election. While much has been made of the influx of carpetbaggers during this time, in fact the political transition to Republican control of Texas government during Reconstruction resulted less from an influx of outsiders from the northeast and more on the right of freed slaves to vote at the same time that supporters of the Confederacy lost their right to vote or hold office after Congress passed the Second Reconstruction Act. With most white Democrats purged both from office and from voting lists, the next constitutional convention was dominated by Republicans, who accounted for seventy-eight of the ninety delegates. The resulting Constitution of 1869 won for Texas readmission to the United States by including many provisions granting rights to freed slaves: the right to vote, run for office, serve on juries, testify in court against whites, and attend public schools.

The End of Reconstruction and Rise of the "Redeemers"

Texas politics was transformed again when Reconstruction ended and more Confederate sympathizers were allowed to vote. The Democrats (the party of the white Confederate sympathizers) won control of the legislature in the election of 1872. Like the emancipation of the slaves, this transformation of Texas politics did not arise from an influx of new Texans, but rather resulted from the renewal of citizenship of old citizens. Republican E. J. Davis was widely despised by Democrats, who considered him at best a symbol of northern oppression and at worst incredibly corrupt. Once in control of Texas government, the Democrats proclaimed themselves "Redeemers" and removed the last remnants of Republican rule. On August 2, 1875, the Texas Legislature authorized a new constitutional convention and elected three delegates each from the state's thirty senatorial districts. None of the ninety members of the 1875 convention had been members of the convention that drafted the 1869 constitution, and the partisan composition was dramatically different. Seventy-five members were Democrats while only fifteen were Republicans. At least forty were members of the Patrons of Husbandry, or "the Grange," an economic and political organization of farmers. Voters ratified the constitution on February 15, 1876, by a vote of 136,606 to 56,652.

The rise of the Redeemers and the impact of the Grange are especially important transitions in Texas politics because the constitution of this era would remain in force long after the politics and politicians responsible for it had vanished. Texas would continue to change and grow, but the Texas Constitution has not been replaced since, only amended—piecemeal changes resulting in minor alterations to the basic design of 1876. The twenty-five years that followed the Civil War spawned the cowboy imagery that Texans still relish. It was during this brief period that the frontier truly existed, when Texas was in fact home to the quintessential rugged cowboy who tended large ranches and oversaw herds of cattle that has remained rooted in the Texan persona ever since. And even then, the image of Texas as the "Old West" was based on the lives of only a small number of Texans. Although Texans hold the legend of the cowboy in high esteem, the cowboy's life was anything but glamorous. Most were young. About one-third were Hispanic or African American. The ranch owners generally regarded them as common laborers on horseback, and the men who rode the range and drove the cattle were paid less than the trail cooks.[12] By the 1890s the fabled trail drives had come to an end, finished by drought, quarantines, barbed-wire fencing across the open range, and competition from the railroads.

The state government encouraged immigration in the last half of the nineteenth century to help settle and populate the western part of the state and drive off Indian tribes. Some state officials saw the immigration of white settlers and farmers as a means of counteracting the increase in former slaves, many of whom had become sharecroppers. Germans flooded into Texas, their numbers surging from 41,000 in 1870 to 125,262 in 1890; at this time Texans of Mexican ancestry numbered only 105,193. While Texas west of Austin may have resembled the Wild West, most Texans resided in the eastern portion of the state, which resembled the "New South" that was emerging elsewhere out of the former Confederacy and was characterized by railroad networks and urbanized cities like Dallas.

Era of Reform

As Texas transitioned from the farming and ranching of the nineteenth century to the industrial and oil economy of the twentieth century, the state began to struggle with the limits of the Constitution of 1876. In 1890, Attorney General James Stephen Hogg decided that his office lacked the resources to adequately enforce regulations on the state's railroads. Hogg's call for the creation of a railroad commission would become a centerpiece of his campaign for governor. The railroads labeled Hogg "communistic," but his economic and political reforms proved popular, and his election represented the first stirrings of the reform movement in Texas. While the creation of the Texas Railroad Commission was heralded as a means to achieve fair competition, in practice it was often used to restrict out-of-state railroads and protect Texas-based businesses from international competitors.

Although glamorized in movies and television shows, cowboys, or *vaqueros*, led a hard life and were often shunned by civilized society.

Frustrated by the lack of responsiveness from the Democrats to their needs, farmers organized the People's Party, more commonly known as the Populist Party. While the populists were short-lived, their call for radical reforms, including public ownership of the railroads, and their willingness to reach out to black voters rattled the political order. After the populists were absorbed into the Democratic Party, the progressives took up the role of reform party. In contrast to the populists' narrow base in agricultural communities, the progressives emerged in the 1890s as a broader reform movement attacking both the railroads that bedeviled the farmers and the big industries that challenged urban labor.

While progressive candidates for governor won elections, their legislative victories were limited. Thomas Campbell won the governorship in the election of 1906 only to see much of his progressive agenda hijacked or sidetracked by the legislature. Most crucially, Campbell was unable to win approval of statewide referenda and recall. Legislation requiring that insurance companies invest 75 percent of their premiums in Texas did change the way insurance companies operated, but mainly benefited Texas businesses and drove foreign insurers from the state.

The progressive movement in Texas became consumed by the alcohol prohibition issue, in part because Texas politics lacked the large corporations and big city political machines that energized the efforts of progressives in the north. Much of the prohibitionists' efforts took place at the local level; they were especially successful at winning local option elections that outlawed drinking. In 1891, the Texas Legislature put a prohibitionist constitutional amendment before the state's voters. The campaign was intense, and voters turned out at more than twice the rate they had in the previous gubernatorial election to narrowly reject the amendment by a 237,393 to 231,096 vote.

While the emergence of a new Texas economy early in the twentieth century and the reforms of the progressive movement captured the attention of many voters, others remained fixated on the old issues of race and the Civil War. In a struggle that foreshadows today's battle over the history that is taught in Texas's classrooms, Governor Oscar Branch Colquitt struggled in his 1912 reelection bid because he had criticized the state textbook board for rejecting a history book because it contained a photograph of Abraham Lincoln. Meanwhile, voters flocked to see Colquitt's opponent, William Ramsay, who played upon southern sentiments in his speeches and had bands play "Dixie" during campaign events. Prohibition was a hotly contested issue on its own and reflected old racial hatreds as alcohol was portrayed as a vice of the Germans and Mexicans.

No one better personifies the failures of Texas progressives to produce reform in Texas than James E. "Pa" Ferguson. While the rest of the Texas political system obsessed over prohibition, "Farmer Jim" shunned the issue and instead won office with promises of capping how much rent tenant farmers could be charged by their landlords. Ferguson's tenant farmer law would ultimately be ruled unconstitutional, but he remained a hero to the state's small farmers. Ferguson could be charming, but his politics were often petty. For example, he used appointments to the board of Prairie View Normal and Industrial College to remove principal Edward Blackshear, who had had the temerity to support a political rival. Ferguson took his personal political fight to the University of Texas as well, where he demanded the removal of William J. Battle, the president of the university. When asked his reason for wanting Battle's removal, Ferguson proclaimed, "I don't have to give any reason. I am Governor of the State of Texas."[13] Later, Ferguson vetoed appropriations for the university. When Ferguson was elected to a second term in 1916, his battle with the university and its allies ultimately brought him down. On July 23, 1917, the Speaker of the Texas House called for a special session to consider impeachment, and in August the Texas House voted on twenty-one articles of impeachment, including charges dealing with Ferguson's personal finances, especially bank loans. The Senate found him guilty on ten charges, primarily those dealing with his finances. While impeachment removed Ferguson from the governor's office and disqualified him from holding other public office, Texas was not so easily rid of his influence.

Ferguson's departure made passage of statewide prohibition easier. The presence of military training camps in Texas led prohibitionists to argue that patriotism required that the state protect young recruits from liquor. Initially, the Texas Legislature simply made it illegal to sell alcohol within ten miles of a military base. The next year, in May 1919, Texas voters approved an amendment to the Texas

Constitution that brought prohibition to Texas a year before it went into effect nationwide.

As with other states, prohibition in Texas proved unworkable as many Texans refused to give up alcohol. The legislature contributed to the failure of the initiative by providing very little funding for the enforcement necessary to make prohibition a success. Organized crime thrived on the revenue that illegal alcohol distribution and sales brought and allegedly worked with prohibitionists to keep alcohol illegal. During prohibition over 20 percent of all arrests in the state were related to prohibition.[14] Galveston became a major center for liquor smuggling as foreign ships anchored along "Rum Row," a line just beyond U.S. territorial waters where boats dropped anchor to distribute alcohol just out of the reach of American law.

While voters were approving prohibition, they also rejected an amendment that would have embraced another item on the progressives' list of reforms: the right of women to vote in all elections. Some of the resistance was based solely on gender discrimination, but some southern voters believed that granting equal rights to women would open the door to "Negro rule" and socialism.

The economic changes that came with the new century resulted from a flood of oil—not of new citizens. While oil's presence in Texas had been noted since Spanish explorers used natural tar seeps to patch their boats, its impact on Texas would not be realized until the early twentieth century. A few wells were drilled in Texas in the 1890s, but the state lacked the refinery capacity to make use of the oil. After the first refinery was built in Texas, interest in oil exploration increased, but the state remained a minor producer. That changed in 1901 when the Spindletop oil rig near Beaumont hit oil and gas, eventually producing 100,000 barrels of oil a day. Investors began streaming into the state in search of oil; by 1928 Texas was leading the nation in oil production, providing 20 percent of the world's oil. And by 1929 oil had replaced "King Cotton" as the largest part of the Texas economy.

Just as oil investors transformed much of the Texas countryside and economy, oil revenues had a huge impact on Texas government, contributing almost $6 million to state accounts by 1929 and reducing the need for other state taxes. Texas's other major business was lumber, which grew dramatically early in the twentieth century, eventually topping 2.25 billion board feet in 1907 before overcutting slowed production. Highway construction boomed in Texas, and by the end of the 1920s Texas had almost 19,000 miles of highway. Fruit trees were introduced into South Texas, providing a new segment of the economy and planting the seeds for future immigration as seasonal, migratory labor was needed to harvest these fruits. By the 1920s Texas seemed well on its way to establishing a strong and diverse economy—a trend that would be undone by the Great Depression.

The Great Depression and the New Deal in Texas

By the late 1920s Texans were beginning to show a little independence from the Democratic Party. The state went for a Republican presidential candidate for the first time in 1928 when Texans shunned Democrat Al Smith, a Catholic New Yorker who drank. However, many Texans regretted their vote for Republican Herbert Hoover as Texas was hit hard by the depression that many blamed on him. As many as one-third of farmers in some areas were driven from their farms by the depression, and the Texas oil boom did little to spare the state. Overproduction of oil caused prices to fall to as low as three cents a barrel. When

Bob Bullock

When Texas governor George W. Bush delivered the eulogy for Bob Bullock in June 1999, he honored him as "the largest Texan of our time." While the state's historical museum in Austin now bears his name, Bullock's path to legendary status was neither steady nor straight. Bullock began his political career aligned with segregationists, transformed himself into a liberal Democrat, and then metamorphosed into one of Republican George W. Bush's most important political allies. Bullock was very much like Sam Houston, a Texan who transcended personal failing to rise to greatness and become a state icon. As Bullock quipped when Hill Junior College put his name on a building: "I'm so happy that they named a gym after me instead of a prison."[i]

Bullock grew up in Hillsboro, Texas, where it seemed to many that he was more likely to end up inside the walls of a state penal institution than atop its political institutions. Some in Hillsboro attribute to a young Bob Bullock a prank right out of *American Graffiti*. One night someone wrapped a chain around the rear axel of a police cruiser, tied it to a telephone pole, and then called the police to tell the officer on duty that evening about a big fight at a local cafe. When the officer leapt into his car it lurched as far as the end of the chain before yanking the rear end of the car clear off.

Bullock battled his way through Texas government as legislator, lobbyist, staffer for Governor Preston Smith, and secretary of state. Even as he worked his way up in Texas politics, he chain smoked and drank a fifth of whiskey daily. In 1974, Bullock won statewide election to the position of comptroller of public accounts, where he modernized the office's accounting practice by replacing paper and pencil account ledgers and mechanical adding machines with computers. Bullock won an expanded budget for his office by promising legislators that, with a few more million dollars provided for auditors and enforcers, he would find a few hundred million more in revenue that the legislature could appropriate. Bullock used these resources to stage dramatic, highly visible seizure raids at some businesses. The raids encouraged other delinquent businesses to settle their accounts. Bullock never shied from a battle, once forcing the Texas Council of Campfire Girls to pay $13,284 for sales taxes on their fundraising candy sales. He also used the comptroller's ability to generate tax revenue estimates that effectively serve as a cap on legislative spending as a tool for influencing state policy.

As much as Bullock mastered political office, he was unable to master his appetites. Bullock occasionally showed up at work drunk and traveled around the state on business accompanied by a companion selected from the secretarial pool. Once, after being caught using a state airplane for personal use, Bullock proclaimed: "Yeah, I'm a crook, but I'm the best comptroller the state ever had."[ii] While he could be blunt in his politics, he wasn't interested in having too much truth reported. When pressed too insistently by reporters at a press conference, Bullock warned: "I keep files on reporters, too. I could name your girlfriends and where they live and what flowers you buy them . . . if I wanted to tell that to your wives."[iii] When the paper began reporting on his use of public funds for a new truck, Bullock mailed boxes of cow manure to the *Dallas Morning News,* a move his spokesman later defended by saying, "He did it on his own time, on his own money."[iv]

By the time he was elected lieutenant governor in 1990 Bullock had put most of his troubled past behind him, telling one person, "there is nothing left for me to do but what's good for Texas." When George W. Bush became governor he immediately realized that Bullock's years of experience, fundraising skills, and legislative connections made him an indispensable partner, especially for a governor new to state government. Working closely with Bullock, Bush built the record of bipartisan legislative success that would help propel him to the White House. The endorsement of Bullock, a long-time Democrat, gave Bush an important boost. Known for closing with "God bless Texas," Bullock found a way to move beyond the personal controversy that often swirled around him and help Texas move ahead.

i.   Dave McNeely and Jim Henderson, *Bob Bullock: God Bless Texas* (Austin: University of Texas Press, 2008), 16.
ii. Ibid., 7
iii. Ibid., 114.
iv. Ibid., 141.

the Railroad Commission refused to act to reduce overproduction, Governor Ross S. Sterling declared martial law and used National Guardsmen to shut down the East Texas oil fields. The desperation of the times brought about the repeal of national prohibition, with "wets" arguing that repeal would aid recovery.

Burdened with a depressed economy and the overproduction of oil and cotton, Governor Sterling ran for reelection against "Pa" Ferguson's legacy, his wife, Miriam "Ma" Ferguson, who trounced Sterling at the ballot box. While the Fergusons finally departed the governor's office for good in 1935, it wasn't long before another character, Wilbert Lee "Pappy" O'Daniel, ushered in a new brand of populist politics. O'Daniel, a former sales manager for a flour mill, became known statewide as the host of a radio show that featured the music of the Light Crust Doughboys mixed with inspirational stories. Purportedly encouraged by listeners' letters urging him to run—although some suggested that wealthy business interests and a public relations expert had done the urging—O'Daniel declared his candidacy, proclaiming the Ten Commandments as his platform and the Golden Rule as his motto. He won the Democratic nomination without a runoff and, facing no real opposition, won the general election with 97 percent of the vote.

Although a colorful personality on the campaign trail, O'Daniel accomplished little of importance once in office, where he lacked the skill to work with legislators and tended to appoint less-than-qualified people to office. After winning reelection to the governorship in 1940, O'Daniel shifted his sights to Washington, D.C., when the death of Sen. Morris Sheppard created a vacancy in 1941. O'Daniel won the special election to replace Sheppard, narrowly edging out a young ex-congressman named Lyndon Johnson in a disputed election.

Transitions to the Twenty-First Century

Texas spent the rest of the twentieth century in transition, shedding some old habits. Even with the landmark *Brown v. Board of Education* Supreme Court decision in 1954, Texas managed to resist desegregation, despite the Court's mandate of "all deliberate speed." Many Texas schools remained segregated well into the early 1970s when federal courts ordered them to desegregate. In 1954 Texas women belatedly won the right to serve on juries, but further progress toward equality was slow. In the 1960s only six women served in the Texas Legislature, and the state failed to ratify the national Equal Rights Amendment (ERA). However, in 1972 voters approved an equal rights amendment to the state constitution and the legislature voted to ratify the ERA (although it would fail to get the required three-quarters of states nationally). In 1975, Liz Cockrell was elected mayor of San Antonio, making her the first woman mayor of a major Texas city.

By the 1960s the partisan legacy of the Civil War was finally beginning to wear off. In 1961, John Tower was elected to the U.S. Senate, becoming the first Republican to win statewide office since Reconstruction. With the Republican Party showing signs of viability, many conservative Democrats shifted their allegiance to the Republican Party in state elections. This followed years of dividing their loyalty by voting for Republicans in national elections while supporting Democrats for state and local offices, a practice labeled **presidential republicanism.** The career of Texas governor John Connally is a case in point. Connally, although friendly with Lyndon Johnson and elected governor as a Democrat, served in the cabinet of Republican president Richard Nixon before eventually seeking the presidency himself as a Republican candidate. Texas did not seat its first Republican governor

Presidential republicanism
the practice in the South of voting for Republicans in presidential elections but voting for conservative Democrats in other races, a practice that continued until animosity over Reconstruction faded and the Republicans demonstrated their electability in the South.

until 1978, when William P. Clements won an upset victory. While Clements' narrow victory was the only statewide race the Republicans won that year, it proved a significant first step as Texas Republicans thereafter began to score more and more successes. Once conservatives saw that they could win elections under the Republican banner, they began to shift their party affiliation. By the 2000 elections, Republicans dominated, winning every statewide office on the ballot.

Texas Today

For generations, waves of people have come to Texas to make new lives for themselves; in the process they have brought with them new ideas and new customs. Texas has always been the meeting ground for different ambitions and cultures. These cultures have clashed, blended, and evolved into a complicated modern state that can be a challenge to govern.

Political culture is the shared values and beliefs about the nature of the political world that give us a common language that we can use to discuss and debate ideas.[15] The **individualistic political culture** that many observers attribute to Texans holds that individuals are best left largely free of the intervention of community forces like government which should attempt only those things demanded by the people it is created to serve.[16] The individualistic subculture is most dominant in western parts of the state, where frontier living fostered independence and a general distrust of government. In contrast, the **traditionalistic political culture** sees government as having a limited role concerned with the preservation of the existing social order. The traditionalistic culture can be seen in areas like East Texas that were more heavily influenced by the traditions of the Old South. Finally, the **moralistic political culture** sees the exercise of community forces as sometimes necessary to advance the public good. In this view government can be a positive force and citizens have a duty to participate. While this view can be found in many places in New England and other parts of the United States, it is rare in Texas.

The size and diversity of Texas makes any discussion of political culture difficult. The idea of a political culture is further clouded by the growth of the state's urban areas, the influx of citizens from other states, and the rise of electronic communication. Traditional analyses of political culture in Texas have suggested that traditionalistic culture dominates in East Texas and weakens moving west across the state, with individualistic culture more prominent in the Panhandle. However, Mexican immigrants bring their own brand of traditionalistic culture, while immigrants from other states have often brought moralistic values into the state. Today, national media and the Internet bring every point of view into Texas homes.

In reality, Texas does not have a single culture. The state is richly diverse, and the mixing of cultures that have been brought to Texas has produced entirely new cultures unique to Texas. In no place is this unique mixture more evident than in Laredo's annual George Washington Birthday celebration, a month-long festival created in 1896 that takes an American-style celebration and unites it with the city's diverse roots. Today, Mexican food and colonial gowns both star in the celebration of the city's bicultural roots, and Laredoans and their guests move easily from jalapeño-eating contests to formal colonial pageants. In this sense Laredo perfectly embraces the tradition of change that defines Texas.

While no state relishes its identity more than Texas, it's increasingly unclear what it means to be a Texan. Much was made of Texans' independent streak after Governor Perry tossed around language about secession. However, a 2009 Rasmussen Poll taken

Political culture
the shared values and beliefs of citizens about the nature of the political world that give the public a common language as a foundation to discuss and debate ideas.

Individualistic political culture
the idea that individuals are best left largely free of the intervention of community forces like government and that government should attempt only those things demanded by the people it is created to serve.

Traditionalistic political culture
the idea, most prevalent in the parts of Texas most like the Old South, that government has a limited role concerned with the preservation of the existing social order.

Moralistic political culture
rare in Texas, the view that the exercise of community pressure is sometimes necessary to advance the public good; it also holds that government can be a positive force and citizens have a duty to participate.

after Perry's comments revealed that 75 percent of Texans wanted to remain part of the United States while only 18 percent would support secession.[17] Clearly, Texans love being Americans just as much as they love being Texans.

A Tradition of Change

Texas continues its tradition of change. For hundreds of years people left their old lives to build new ones in Texas, leaving behind them signs declaring "Gone to Texas." While these generations of new Texans have brought different languages and culture, all consistently brought one thing—change. Change brought by new arrivals has defined Texas since the 1500s when newly arrived Spanish explorers turned the Caddo word for friend (*techas*) into *Tejas,* a term describing the Caddo tribe.[18] In the centuries since, waves of people have come to Texas seeking opportunity and bringing change.

The changes have not always been welcome by established Texans. When explorer Francisco Vasquez de Coronado's expedition arrived and proudly proclaimed to the Zuñi Indians who lived in Texas that the tribe now enjoyed protection as subjects of the Spanish king, the Zuñis answered with a volley of arrows.[19] The arrows bounced off the Spanish armor, and today immigrants arriving from across the nation and around the world generally receive a better reception. Still, new arrivals have often been seen by many Texans as competitors rather than partners in the state's future.

New arrivals remain a constant in Texas. The state's population increased about one hundredfold since joining the United States, growing at an average of just over 40 percent each decade (see Table 1.1). The Census Bureau estimated that there were 24,782,302 Texans in 2009, and that there will be over 33 million people living in Texas by 2030. How today's Texans make room for the nine million new Texans expected over the next twenty years will be an important part of Texas politics.

Change is especially difficult for a political system that must meet the needs of a large, diverse, and ever-changing population. Political systems tend to represent the status quo—and established groups are inherently threatened by changes to the government's base of power. Because politics is, in the words of a classic definition, about who gets what, newcomers compete against established residents, leaving the government to resolve the conflict and determine who wins and who loses. Politics becomes a battle between the old and the new, and this battle is often repeated in Texas. The Texas revolution, which came about when Mexican officials refused to meet the needs of Anglo settlers, is probably the most dramatic—and ultimately literal—example of politics as battle.

A current snapshot of Texas reveals increasing diversity as the state grows. In 2005, Texas became a "majority-minority" state, joining Hawaii, New Mexico, and California as states in which the nation's majority (Anglos) make up less than half

Table 1.1 Population and Percentage of Growth in Texas since 1850

CENSUS	POPULATION	PERCENTAGE OF GROWTH
1850	212,592	
1860	604,215	184.2%
1870	818,579	35.5%
1880	1,591,749	94.5%
1890	2,235,527	40.4%
1900	3,048,710	36.4%
1910	3,896,542	27.8%
1920	4,663,228	19.7%
1930	5,824,715	24.9%
1940	6,414,824	10.1%
1950	7,711,194	20.2%
1960	9,579,677	24.2%
1970	11,196,730	16.9%
1980	14,229,191	27.1%
1990	16,986,510	19.4%
2000	20,851,820	22.8%
2009	24,782,302	18.8%

Source: U.S. Census Bureau.

of a state's population. In Texas today, Anglos account for 47 percent of the state's population. While about 73 percent of Texas residents describe themselves as "white," this category includes both Anglos and Hispanics (see Table 1.2). Almost 16 percent of Texans (compared to 12.5 percent of Americans) are foreign born, and just over one in three Texans speaks a language other than English at home (compared to one in five Americans).[20]

The state's rural nature has been transformed, and today about 80 percent of Texans live in 1,210 cities or suburbs. In fact, Texas has three of the nation's ten largest cities—Houston (#4), San Antonio (#7), and Dallas (#8)—and four of the ten fastest growing counties in the United States. Another measure of the "new normal" of Texas is that today married Texans make up only about half of the population. In Texas in 2008, 49.4 percent of women and 53.3 percent of men were married.[21]

Texans often quip they are "the buckle in the Bible Belt," reflecting on the fact that Texas is home to over 5 million evangelical Protestants. While the state's 4.5 million Baptists are a large presence, the state is also home to almost 4.4 million Catholics. In fact, Catholics outnumber Southern Baptists in every major urban area except Dallas–Fort Worth.[22] As Table 1.3 reflects, the state is home to a range of religious traditions.

The state's economy is as diverse as its people. While the state still has more farms (229,000 farms encompassing about 129,000,000 acres) and ranches than any other state, more Texans work in the information industry than agriculture. While Texas as a ranching and farming behemoth remains the preferred image, in fact residents today are engaged in providing virtually every kind of product and service (see Table 1.4). Educational services and health care are the biggest industries, while agriculture, despite the image, is the smallest.

The Texas economy is massive and growing. In 2009 the state's economy was estimated to have produced over $1.2 trillion in gross state product. If Texas were a nation, its economy would be the eleventh largest in the world, just behind Canada and ahead of Russia. (See Table 1.5.)

Even as Texas grapples with challenges within its borders arising from its diverse and growing population and its expansive economy, it also has to deal with competition from overseas. While Texans have always relished their independence, the state today must work to ensure its place in a growing global economy. Even farmers must look overseas as they attempt to cultivate foreign markets for their products while warding off foreign competitors.

Table 1.2 Race and Ethnicity in Texas, 2008

RACE/ETHNICITY	PERCENTAGE OF POPULATION
Hispanic or Latino (of any race)	36.5%
White	47.4%
Black or African American	11.9%
Asian	3.5%
American Indian and Alaska Native	0.8%
Two or more races	1.3%

Source: U.S. Census Bureau, "State and County Quick Facts: Texas," http://quickfacts.census.gov/qfd/index.html.

Table 1.3 Religious Traditions in Texas, 2008

RELIGION	PERCENTAGE OF POPULATION
Evangelical Protestant tradition	34%
Mainline Protestant	15%
Historically Black Protestant tradition	8%
Catholic	24%
Mormon	1%
Jehovah's Witness	1%
Buddhist	1%
Hindu	1%
Unaffiliated	12%

Source: Pew Forum on Religion and Public Life, "U.S. Religious Landscape Survey," February 2008, 98, http://religions.pew forum.org/pdf/report-religious-landscape-study-full.pdf.

Table 1.4 Texas Civilian-Employed Population, Age 16 Years and Older

EMPLOYMENT	NUMBER EMPLOYED	PERCENTAGE OF EMPLOYED
Agriculture, forestry, fishing and hunting, and mining	319,490	2.9%
Construction	1,016,566	9.2%
Manufacturing	1,103,798	10.0%
Wholesale trade	385,078	3.5%
Retail trade	1,269,674	11.5%
Transportation and warehousing; utilities	635,147	5.8%
Information	251,876	2.3%
Finance and insurance; real estate and rental and leasing	768,623	7.0%
Professional, scientific, and management services; administrative and waste management services	1,149,316	10.4%
Educational services; health care and social assistance	2,193,660	19.9%
Arts, entertainment, and recreation; accommodation and food services	900,219	8.2%
Other services, except public administration	569,986	5.2%
Public administration	464,197	4.2%
Total	**11,027,630**	**100.10%**

Source: U.S. Census Bureau, "Selected Economic Characteristics: 2006–2008, American Community Survey," http://factfinder.census.gov/.

Table 1.5 Gross Domestic Product, 2009

RANK	NATION	MILLIONS OF DOLLARS
1	United States*	14,258,700
2	Japan	5,071,800
3	China	4,909,200
4	Germany	3,343,900
5	France	2,672,100
6	United Kingdom	2,186,100
7	Italy	2,132,300
8	Brazil	1,562,500
9	Spain	1,460,300
10	Canada	1,339,300
11	**Texas****	**1,233,558**
12	Russia	1,229,700
13	India	1,221,200
14	Australia	973,600
15	Mexico	864,900

Source: Texas Comptrollers of Public Accounts, March 15, 2010.

* United States, including Texas.

** If an independent nation.

While the wealthy Texas oil baron or cattle rancher is a familiar image in movies and television, Texans fall below the national average on many measures of wealth. Compared to the national average, Texans have a lower per capita income ($24,709 versus $27,466 in 2009), a higher poverty rate (16.3 percent versus 13.2 percent of all Americans), and a lower rate of home ownership (63.8 percent versus 66.2 percent). The income disparity depicted in Figure 1.1 illustrates that while Texas may be a land of great wealth, it is also a land of great need. One study found that Texas ranked first or second in income inequality, depending on whether you measure inequality between the highest income group and the bottom income group or between the highest and middle income groups.[23]

Texas's years of transformation are not over, as the state continues to change rapidly. In the 1990s, the Texas population grew by 22.8 percent, and between 2001 and 2009 it grew another 15.8 percent. Texas is now second in U.S. state population, with 24,782,302 residents in 2009, though it is still well behind California's 36,961,664 residents.

More change is coming. Texas, California, and Florida are expected to account for almost half of the nation's growth from 1995 to 2025.[24] For Texas this growth will likely come from a balance of internal immigration (about 1.8 million people moving from other states), international immigration (about 1 million people

Figure 1.1 Income Distribution in Texas, 2008

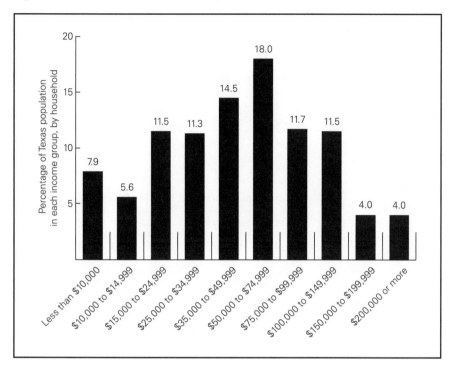

Source: U.S. Census Bureau, "American Community Survey," August 2008, http://factfinder.census.gov.

coming to Texas from other nations), and natural growth (the addition of about 5.7 million people as Texans have babies and live longer).

Thus, the state with a constitution that was authored by isolated farmers who formed the Grange as a way of connecting with other farmers is today a booming high-tech center with citizens connected to each other and to the wider world by the Internet. Visitors arriving in the Texas capital will not find cowboys astride horses on the open plains; instead, they will encounter computer engineers and game programmers stuck in traffic.

Winners and Losers

Certainly one of the most significant forces of change that shaped Texas past, present, and future is immigration. Texas is a state that continues to be largely defined by its ever-changing and constant immigrant population. In understanding Texas's past and trying to prepare Texas for the future, no immigrant population has been more integral to the state than the Hispanic population. As the historical overview in this chapter makes clear, Tejanos in early Texas were central to its development. Unfortunately, as Anglos came to dominate the state, historical revisionists overlooked early cooperation between Anglos and Tejanos, emphasizing and often exaggerating the tensions between the two groups. Just as many Tejanos were driven out of Texas after the revolution against Mexico, their contributions to the war on both sides of the conflict were driven from the pages of Texas history.

Texas versus Vermont

A comparison of Texas and Vermont illustrates the diversity of states within the United States. Vermont, a Northeastern state, got its start when Ethan Allen and the Green Mountain Boys rebelled against attempts by New York and New Hampshire to exert control over the region after the American Revolution. On January 15, 1777, the independent Republic of New Connecticut was declared; later, the name was changed to the Republic of Vermont. Vermont sent ambassadors to France, the Netherlands, and the United States. In 1791, Vermont entered the United States as the fourteenth state to balance the admission of slave-holding Kentucky as the fifteenth state.

While both Texas and Vermont share a history of independence before joining the United States, the similarity ends there. Geographically, Vermont is quite small, at 9,250 square miles. Vermont's size is smaller than the combined area of the largest two Texas counties (10,957 square miles is the combined area of Brewster and Pecos counties in West Texas). Vermont's landscape is dominated by the Green Mountains, abundant forests, and plentiful rivers and streams. As the second largest state by area, Texas covers a vast territory that varies tremendously in land formations, water resources, and natural resources.

The demographics of the two states are also strikingly different. Settled by English settlers and some French colonists from nearby Quebec, Vermont remains among the most homogeneous states in the United States. In 2005, Vermont held the distinction of being one of the "whitest" states in the United States; Texas, in contrast, was among the most racially and ethnically diverse states.

Texas versus Vermont: Ethnic Makeup

POPULATION GROUP	TEXAS	VERMONT
White	47.4%	95.2%
Hispanic/Latino	36.5%	1.4%
African American	11.9%	0.9%
Asian American	3.5%	1.1%
Other	0.9%	0.4%

Sources: Population Division, U.S. Census Bureau, "Quick Facts: Texas" and "Quick Facts: Vermont," 2008, http://quickfacts.census .gov/qfd/index.html.

At some point the Mexican flag failed to appear in the Alamo's "Hall of Honor" that commemorated the country of birth of the Alamo's defenders, allowing Texans to forget that nine of the eleven defenders of the Alamo born in the Mexican territory of Texas had Hispanic origins. Juan Nepomuceno Seguín, who neither wrote nor spoke English, was a close friend of Stephen F. Austin and helped drive Mexican forces from San Antonio before slipping out of the Alamo to seek reinforcements. Later, Seguín joined Sam Houston's army at the decisive battle of San Jacinto. As one historian put it, " 'Remember the Alamo' became a formula for forgetfulness."[25] A rapidly anglicizing Texas replaced the legend of heroic Tejanos with a legend emphasizing dictatorial Mexican rulers seeking the expulsion of the Anglos.

The Tejano population of Texas declined from the time of the revolution until a repressive regime in Mexico, coupled with decades of revolution within that country, created a new wave of immigrants. This tripled the Mexican population in Texas from 1900 to 1920. While these immigrants played important roles in cotton production, they were often not welcomed and took their place somewhere between Anglos and African Americans, unaccepted in either community. Techniques such as "white primaries," which were used to exclude African Americans from voting, were eventually also employed against Tejanos. As the state continued to change, and immigrants continued to move into Texas, Hispanics were marginalized in the political process as well as in the history books.

Vermont also consistently ranks as one of the smallest states in population. In 1850, the first census in which Texas participated, Vermont had a slightly larger population than Texas. Immigration over the following decade saw Texas surpass Vermont in population by the 1860 census, when Texas already had over 600,000 residents. It would take Vermont 140 years to reach that level of population. By the time it did, in 2000, Texas recorded over 22 million residents.

Large cities are found throughout Texas; three of the nation's ten largest cities are located in Texas. Vermont's largest city, Burlington (38,358), is so small that it would rank seventieth in city size in Texas. Even the images of the two states generate contrasts. Texas is the land of open plains, oil wells, cattle, gun-slinging cowboys, and big-time football. Vermont is the land of maple syrup, ice cream, fall foliage, and quaint towns.

Obviously, to govern a diverse population spread over a vast geographic area with extensive mineral wealth, Texas requires a fundamentally different approach than Vermont. In many instances, Texas politics is vastly different in practice than Vermont's political system. However, these differences may not be exactly what we expect.

Thinking Critically

In several places, this textbook presents discussions, tables, and figures to offer comparisons between Texas and other states. At this point, think about the heritage and demographics of your community or hometown.

- Is your community more like a typical Texas or Vermont community?
- What have your experiences in politics been like?
- How would they compare to those in a state like Vermont?

One of the enduring legends of early Texas history is how Anglo order and hard work saved the state from Mexican chaos. According to this view it was immigrants from the United States who, in the words of one public school textbook from the 1880s, "changed Texas from a wilderness into a civilized state: Mexico had nothing but fear and hatred."[26] Like other legacies, this historical "truth" ignores some aspects of history and exaggerates others. So far, Hispanics have been the losers in the formation of historical legend.

By 1930 the Tejano population of Texas had begun to rise with the rest of the population, reaching almost 684,000. Reflecting the return of Tejanos to Texas politics, the League of United Latin American Citizens (LULAC) was formed in Corpus Christi in 1929. LULAC quickly became a major factor in Texas politics. In 1956, Henry B. González became the first Tejano in over half a century to hold a seat in the Texas Senate. During the 1957 legislative session González set the record for a filibuster in the Texas Senate as he fought laws backing segregation in Texas public schools. In 1961, González broke ground again by winning a seat in the U.S. House of Representatives. By that time half a dozen Tejanos were serving in the Texas Legislature and a Tejano was serving as mayor of El Paso. Tejanos won their first statewide office when Dan Morales was elected attorney general in 1992. Hispanics are both the largest and fastest growing group in the state and today hold a variety of offices. In 2009, Eva Guzman became the first Hispanic woman to serve on the Texas Supreme Court when Governor Rick Perry appointed her to fill a vacancy on the court. Hispanics are increasingly successful in organizing and exerting political pressure in Texas. As the Hispanic population continues to increase and organize its interests within the state, Hispanics are in a position to be the winners in a future Texas.

Today Texas is again dealing with an immigrant population whose numbers are increasing so rapidly that they form a majority in some parts of the state. The struggle to deal with this change is part of what defines Texas as a state today. As we will see throughout this text, legends tend to be static and are often at odds with the changing nature of the state. The myth that Texas's story is a primarily Anglo story ignores others' contributions to the state. What's more, the myth of Anglo primacy remains the dominant legend in Texas's history books. Throughout the rest of this book, we will continue to explore this tension between legend and change.

Conclusion: The Lone Star in Transition

In the new millennium, Texas faces fresh challenges as it continues to change. The rising political clout of Republicans, Hispanics, and women at the close of the twentieth century has been only partially reflected in changes to the Texas political system. At the same time, Texas now faces many political issues that have been long deferred by the state's leaders. The funding of public schools, in dispute for over a decade, was only partially resolved by a special session of the legislature in 2006. Texas continues to grapple with air quality, an issue that it hadn't even begun to address until 1965. Toll roads and mass transit have become major issues as the state tries to manage its growing cities and the heavy truck traffic generated by new trade agreements with Mexico.

In 2004, Republicans redistricted the state of Texas to correct what they saw as the underrepresentation of their party in the Texas delegation to the U.S. House. Hispanic leaders continue to struggle to elect officials in proportion to their share of the population. Despite a few highly visible women, representing the state in the U.S. Senate or as Texas comptroller, women remain dramatically underrepresented in state offices, composing only 20 percent of the Texas Legislature in 2009. The struggle of Republicans, women, and Tejanos exemplifies the reality that changes in the state's politics often lag well behind other changes—demographic, social, and economic.

Texans' struggle to define themselves was revived in March 2010 as they witnessed another round of fighting for control of the Alamo. This struggle, played out in Austin rather than San Antonio, was over who among the defenders of the Alamo 174 years earlier would be featured in the Texas public school curriculum. The Texas State Board of Education, the fifteen-member elected board that approves curriculum for the state's public schools, was revising what students must learn about history. The board had previously approved a draft standard for fourth grade classes that included discussion of the Tejanos who died defending the Alamo, but that wording was removed in the March meeting. While the majority on the board approved language that they felt was very inclusive and avoided "number counting and quotas" by focusing on "leaders" at the Alamo, Mary Helen Berlanga asked: "What did James Bowie and Davy Crockett do that the Tejanos did not do?"[27]

Finding a place in the Alamo is an important part of finding a place in Texas politics. The sacrifice of the Alamo's defenders defines the state as much as any single event. While Texans share a fondness for the state's history, what they choose to see in that history can be very different.

Like all democracies, Texas government takes its flavor from the people it represents. While sharing a common history, Texans often take different lessons from it. As this chapter demonstrates, the meaning of "Texan" has changed over the state's history, and today the meaning of the word conjures a different image in each corner of the state. Despite the changes in those who call themselves Texans, and the changes in the places where they live, the basic structure of Texas government has remained largely unchanged.

While Texans relish their colorful history, the state today must work to ensure its place in a competitive, global, high-tech economy. A constitution written in 1876 by isolated Texas farmers who had little interest in government, growth, diversity, big business, or the modern world leaves a government that must struggle to meet the needs of a state that is rapidly growing and increasingly diverse with an economy driven by large multinational corporations on the cutting edge of the information age.

Change does not make the state's history less important. The rapid transformations occurring in the state today make understanding Texas's history even more important as Texans grapple with difficult issues like immigration. Following the legacy of a Declaration of Independence written by men who had lived in Texas only a few years, Texans must both acknowledge the potential contributions of new arrivals and protect what previous generations have created. In the following chapters we will look at how Texas politics and government have adapted to the waves of change over the course of its history and assess how well it is prepared for the changes ahead.

Key Terms

empresario
individualistic political culture
moralistic political culture
political culture
presidential republicanism
traditionalistic political culture
Treaty of Guadalupe Hidalgo

Explore this subject further at http://lonestar.cqpress.com, where you'll find chapter summaries, practice quizzes, key word flash cards, and additional suggested resources.

One of the many Tea Party rallies held in Texas, this one in front of the Alamo was attended by thousands of Texans. The growth of the Tea Party movement reflects the frustration many Texans feel toward the national government.

CHAPTER 2

Texas Constitution

The mood in Texas has changed significantly over the past few years. With the huge federal bailouts of the financial and automobile industries, the national stimulus package, and the battle over national healthcare reform, many Texans question the growth of the national government and the loss of sovereignty at the state level. Texans have long been individualistic, espousing a "pull yourself up by your bootstraps" approach to life and holding individuals responsible for their own welfare. Texans also tend to be fiscally conservative and distrust government, making the recent moves by the national government widely unpopular.

Beginning with the sub-prime mortgage crisis in 2008 and the subsequent recession, the national government has spent a significant amount of money attempting to prevent an economic depression. The 2008 bailout of the financial system was followed by an economic stimulus package in early 2009. President Barack Obama next made good on his campaign promise and engaged in a yearlong battle for healthcare reform. The federal budget, already strained by George W. Bush's domestic and foreign spending, ballooned even further. This expansion of both spending and power at the national level was out of step with Texas's view of the ideal government: we want our government fiscally lean and unobtrusive.

The reaction in Texas to the growth of national government was immediate and significant. The most visible manifestation of frustration is the Tea Party movement, which held rallies across the state. Although the movement is diverse, generally Tea Party activists object to what they perceive as out of control government spending and the looming healthcare reform. Tea Party-goers support limitations on government spending and the establishment of a balanced budget; more generally, they favor keeping the federal government out of state affairs. While the Tea Party movement may represent a vocal minority, the general distrust of government among Texans remains widespread.

Governor Rick Perry immediately picked up on the anti-Washington mood in the state and became the poster boy for the fight against big government in Texas. When Perry attended a Tea Party rally in Austin in 2009, he went so far as to hint that secession from the Union was not off the table. Later that year the Texas House of Representatives passed a resolution affirming the state's sovereignty. Governor Perry has traveled the state with a message that Washington is becoming too intrusive, a message that helped him handily defeat Kay Bailey Hutchison in the 2010 gubernatorial primary. In 2010, Texas Attorney General Greg Abbott joined other states in a lawsuit charging that the national healthcare policy infringed on Texans' individual liberties.

These concerns have to do with a fundamental constitutional arrangement: how much power should the national government have compared to the states? Tea Party participants believe that the national government has become overlarge and over involved and that state governments should more actively protect their power vis-à-vis the national government. The message that Washington is too big and too intrusive has always been a popular one in Texas, whose citizens worry about national tyranny and have often preferred more local policy control. In fact, Article 1, Section 1 of the current Texas Constitution embodies this very idea, stating "Texas is a free and independent State, subject only to the Constitution of the United States, and the maintenance of our free institutions and the perpetuity of the Union depend upon the preservation of the right of local self-government, unimpaired to all the States." In this chapter we will explore the constitutional arrangement of federalism and the development of the Texas Constitution more generally. We will first outline the federalist structure of the national government and how Texas fits into that structure. We will then survey how the Texas Constitution has evolved over time, reflecting our rich history and culture. Finally, we discuss the problems of the current constitution and examine the prospects for constitutional reform.

> **As you read the chapter, think about the following questions:**
> ★ What is the purpose of a constitution?
> ★ How does federalism affect the choices made by state government?
> ★ To what extent have Texas's previous constitutions contributed to the state's current constitution?
> ★ What are the problems with the current Texas Constitution?

Constitutional Government

Constitution
a written document that outlines the powers of government and the limitations on those powers.

A **constitution** is a written document that outlines the powers of government and limitations on those powers to protect the rights of citizens. Ideally, a constitution should be a brief, flexible document that confers broad grants of power to the government. Written constitutions have become the norm in modern times and confer legitimacy on countries. The government, in turn, works within the boundaries of the constitution as it goes about day-to-day operations. The legislature, for example, passes laws that do not violate the basic principles outlined in the constitution. The more fundamental the constitution's provisions, the less likely it will need to be updated over time. The U.S. Constitution, for instance, has lasted over 200 years, with Congress passing and repealing more specific laws to reflect the changing times. Ideally a constitution should protect citizens' rights while being flexible enough to remain relevant even as society changes.

Our country's founders believed that a constitutional or written government was necessary to prevent tyranny. James Madison wrote in *Federalist* No. 51 that "If men were angels, no government would be necessary. If angels were to govern men, neither external nor internal controls on government would be necessary. In framing a government which is to be administered by men over men, the great difficulty lies in this: you must first enable the government to control the governed; and in the next place oblige it to control itself." The founders, concerned with tyranny often displayed by the monarchs at the expense of the people, set out to create a new form of government. The U.S. Constitution checked potential tyrants in several ways: by creating different levels of government (federalism), separating power among different branches of government (separation of powers), and empowering the people to check the government (popular sovereignty).

The idea of **popular sovereignty,** or creating a government where the power to govern is derived from the will of the people, is a critical aspect in limiting tyranny. This idea stands in sharp contrast to the prevailing norm two hundred years ago when the U.S. Constitution was written. Monarchs ruled with little concept of popular representation in government, instead claiming a divine right to rule derived from the will of God. With the memories of a rebellion against a monarch fresh in their minds, the founders included popular sovereignty in the preamble to the U.S. Constitution, with the words "We the people." Similarly, the Texas Constitution begins "Humbly invoking the blessing of Almighty God, the people of the State of Texas do ordain and establish this Constitution." In Texas, popular sovereignty is manifest in the popular election of almost all state officials, including members of the legislative, executive, and judicial branches. Texas voters must also approve amendments to the state's constitution, further extending popular rule to the country's fundamental law.

Popular sovereignty
a government where the power to govern is derived from the will of the people.

As an additional protection for individuals against tyranny, a constitution may place limits on governmental action to curb potential abuses. In the U.S. Constitution, most of these limits are contained within the Bill of Rights.

The United States invented modern constitutional government, and the U.S. Constitution is a model of brevity and flexible language. It remains relatively short, has been amended only twenty-seven times, and outlines the fundamental functions and limits of government while leaving the legislature to pass more specific legislation.

Of course, such an ideal constitution is rarely achieved. The Texas Constitution by contrast is extremely long and specific, creates a relatively weak government, and undergoes constant amendment as the government tries to keep up with a rapidly growing and changing state. The current Texas Constitution, Texas's sixth since its independence from Mexico, reflects Texas's historical experience under Mexico and Spain, its reaction to the Civil War and Reconstruction, and the still prevailing preference for limited government. The current constitution also represents the federal nature of the United States government.

The Federal System of the United States

Federalism—the sharing of powers between two levels of government—is a uniquely American creation. The North American colonies had relatively little influence in decisions made by the central government back in London. The founders were frustrated over lack of representation in the British government, and they believed that governmental tyranny could be checked by separating the powers of government. In an attempt to limit the potential for tyranny, the framers divided powers among the branches of government, as well as between the levels of government. The federalist concept specifies a division of powers between the central or national government and the state governments or lower levels.

Confederal system

a type of government where the lower units of government retain decision-making authority.

Unitary system

a type of government where power is vested in a central governmental authority.

Federalism

a form of government based on the sharing of powers between the national and state governments.

In creating a federal system, the framers compromised between two alternative ideal systems: unitary and confederal. A **confederal system** is a governmental arrangement where the lower units of government retain decision-making authority. The United States experienced a confederacy twice: first under the Articles of Confederation and later in the short-lived Confederacy created by southern states during the Civil War. In both cases, the states retained decision-making authority, leaving a relatively weaker national government. A modern day example of a confederacy is the United Nations, where member countries can participate in various treaties, choose to opt out of treaties, or withdraw from the organization at any time.

A **unitary system,** by contrast, vests power in a central government; lower units of government only have power that is granted to them by the central government. For instance, the North American colonies had only the powers granted to them by the British government. Today, about 75 percent of governments remain unitary, making this the most prevalent type of government in the world. An example of a unitary government close to home is the relationship between Texas and its lower governmental units, cities and counties. Cities and counties in Texas are granted only limited law-making authority by the state constitution and the state legislature.

The founders, having experienced both a unitary and confederal government, created an alternative form of government known as federalism. **Federalism** is a system of government where power is shared between the national and state governments and represents a compromise between a unitary and confederal system. The U.S. Constitution creates a federal system by vesting certain powers in the national government while reserving other powers for the states. Theoretically, dividing power among levels of government prevents the national government from imposing "one-size-fits-all" standards that may not make sense for a particular state or region. On the one hand, federalism allows states to experiment with new policies and permits flexibility as states pass laws that represent their distinct political culture. On the other hand, federalism imposes significant costs on the United States, since different levels of government fight over policy areas, often at the taxpayer's expense. The founders believed that the prevention of tyranny was more important than the inefficiency that different levels of government create.

Vertical Federalism

Vertical federalism

the distribution of power between the national and state governments.

Supremacy clause

the section in the U.S. Constitution that guarantees that the national government is the supreme law of the land, and national laws and the national constitution supersede state laws and state constitutions.

Reserved powers

the specification in the Tenth Amendment that all powers not delegated to the national government belong to the states.

Although the founders generally believed that dividing powers among levels of government would be beneficial, the exact division of power within our federal system is unclear. **Vertical federalism,** or the distribution of power between the national government and the state governments, has been highly contested for much of our history. The difficulty in describing the federal nature of the U.S. government is best exemplified by juxtaposing the supremacy clause and the reserved powers clause of the U.S. Constitution. The **supremacy clause** guarantees that the national government is the supreme law of the land. Thus, the U.S. Constitution and national laws supersede state laws and state constitutions. States can make laws within their territory so long as those laws do not conflict with national laws or the U.S. Constitution. The Tenth Amendment, however, reserves for the states all powers not delegated to the national government. This provision creates a class of powers called **reserved powers,** although the Supreme Court has interpreted these powers narrowly in recent times. These two constitutional clauses generated opposing views of the division of powers between the national government and the state governments. The reserved powers clause seems to indicate a federal system in which states have most of the power, whereas the supremacy clause points to a government of primarily national power.

The U.S. Constitution gives the national government exclusive authority over coining money, establishing a navy, declaring war, and regulating interstate commerce. These **delegated powers** expressly granted to the national government are listed in Article I, Section 8 of the U.S. Constitution. The U.S. Constitution also outlines explicit roles for the states, including the conduct of elections, the selection of electors to the Electoral College, the establishment of voter qualifications, and the approval of constitutional amendments. Moreover, Article I, Section 10 of the U.S. Constitution explicitly prohibits states from entering into treaties, coining money, or granting letters of marque or titles of nobility, among other things. Other powers, such as the power to tax and spend, to establish courts, or to charter banks are **concurrent powers** shared by the national and state governments. (See Figure 2.1.)

Delegated powers

the powers listed in Article I, Section 8 of the U.S. Constitution that are expressly granted to the national government.

Concurrent powers

powers such as taxing and spending and the ability to establish courts and charter banks that are shared by the national and state governments.

Figure 2.1 Distribution of Powers between the National Government and the States in the U.S. Constitution

DELEGATED POWERS (to the national government)	Admit new states to the Union
	Coin money
	Conduct foreign affairs
	Declare war
	Establish courts inferior to the Supreme Court
	Make laws that are necessary for carrying out the powers vested by the Constitution
	Raise and maintain armies and navies
	Regulate interstate and foreign commerce

CONCURRENT POWERS (shared by the national government and the states)	Borrow and spend money for the general welfare
	Charter and regulate banks; charter corporations
	Collect taxes
	Establish courts
	Establish highways
	Pass and enforce laws
	Take private property for public purposes, with just compensation

RESERVED POWERS (to the states)	Conduct elections and determine voter qualifications
	Establish local governments
	Maintain militia (National Guard)
	Provide for public health, safety, and morals
	Ratify amendments to the federal constitution
	Regulate intrastate commerce

DENIED POWERS (to the states)	Abridging the privileges or immunities of citizens or denying due process and equal protection of the laws (14th Amendment)
	Coining money
	Entering into treaties
	Keeping troops or navies
	Levying import or export taxes on goods
	Making war

Source: Adapted from Christine Barbour and Gerald C. Wright, *Keeping the Republic,* 4th brief ed. (Washington, D.C.: CQ Press, 2011), 84.

Horizontal Federalism

Horizontal federalism refers to the relationship between states. Certain provisions within the U.S. Constitution regulate the relations among states. The founders specified certain state obligations to other states, in part to create a sense of national unity among the states. For instance, states are required to grant the same **privileges and immunities** to citizens of other states as they grant to their own citizens. This provision means that states may not fundamentally treat citizens of other states differently than their citizens. The privileges and immunities clause makes travel between states easier and prevents discrimination against citizens of other states. However, exceptions to the privileges and immunities clause have been recognized in two cases.[1] First, states may deny the right to vote to nonresidents. Thus, the laws of one state cannot be unduly influenced by citizens from neighboring states. In addition, states may distinguish between residents and nonresidents in the distribution of certain state-subsidized benefits that may differ from state to state, such as in-state tuition rates or welfare payments. This exception has been deemed reasonable since "individuals could benefit from subsidies without being subject to the taxes that pay the subsidies."[2] States are further required to recognize acts, records, and judicial decisions of other states according to the **full faith and credit clause.** This means that court judgments or legal contracts entered into in one state will be honored by other states. Thus, debt or child support payments cannot be avoided by moving to another state. Finally, the U.S. Constitution requires that states deliver someone suspected or convicted of a crime in another state back to that state so they can face trial and sentencing. This process, known as **extradition,** was designed to keep criminals from escaping justice by moving from state to state.

The Evolving Idea of Federalism

Creating a new type of government generated a considerable amount of uncertainty. It is clear that the founders sought to produce a system of government where powers are shared between two levels of government. It is considerably less clear exactly what that distribution of power would look like. From its inception, the idea of federalism has generated a good deal of controversy, culminating, in part, in a civil war less than a century after the republic was founded. Very few policy areas have escaped this tension. Today the United States continues to grapple with exactly which powers belong to the national government and which should be reserved for the states. Sentimental attachment to the idea of federalism is often usurped by a preference for efficiency and uniformity. The result is that over time the power of the states has eroded significantly. Most notably, states have historically enjoyed policy control over issues such as police power, marriage, education, and election laws. Yet in the last half a century, the national government has begun to encroach on policy areas traditionally reserved for the states.

Perhaps the most effective tool the national government uses to gain control of state policy areas is money. With the creation of a national income tax in 1913, the national government enjoyed a significant increase in tax revenues. Since that time, Congress has used its financial advantage to control issues that were traditionally considered state policy areas. Use of financial incentives to encourage policies at the state level is referred to as **fiscal federalism.** The national government has awarded two types of grants to state and local governments. The **categorical grant** is money given to states and local governments that must be spent for specific activities. When the national government specifies how the money is to be spent, it can then set national policy goals in traditionally state-controlled policy areas. In response to this, Republican administrations favored the **block grant** in an attempt to return policy control back to the states. Theoretically, a block grant is given to state and local governments for a broader purpose and imposes fewer restrictions on the states regarding how the grant money is to be spent. In the 1970s, President Richard Nixon reorganized existing categorical grants into block grants to continue the flow of money from the national government to the states while allowing the states to exert more discretion on how the money was spent. While block grants are a popular means of reviving state power, they have been politically difficult to achieve. Members of Congress prefer to allocate money attached to specific policies, making it easier for them to take credit for the resulting goods provided to their home states.

One example of the national government's use of grants to intrude on state policy issues occurred in the 1980s when Congress wanted to establish a national drinking age. Congress, faced with increasing pressure from the organization Mothers Against Drunk Driving, and absent clear constitutional authority to establish a national drinking age, passed legislation that would take away 10 percent of a state's federal highway funds if the state did not raise its drinking age to twenty-one within two years. South Dakota sued the national government, arguing that the policy amounted to coercion and was a blatant intrusion on states' rights. In *South Dakota v. Dole,* the Supreme Court ruled that the national government could reasonably attach conditions to national grants. In a dissenting opinion, Justice Sandra Day O'Connor concurred with South Dakota that the law violated the spirit of federalism, arguing that "[t]he immense size and power of the Government of the United States ought not obscure its fundamental character."[3] This case illustrates how the national government has used its substantial tax base to considerably increase its policy authority beyond its delegated powers.

One controversial way that the national government has infringed on state policy areas is its reliance on unfunded mandates. An **unfunded mandate** occurs when the national government passes legislation that imposes requirements on state and local governments, which bear the cost of meeting those requirements. Some examples include requirements that all states, including Texas, ensure equal access to public facilities for disabled persons, guarantee civil rights, provide public assistance for single parents, and enforce clean air standards.[4] In each of these cases, the states and local governments must pay for a significant portion of these regulations, imposed on them by the national government.

The debate over the appropriate division of power between the national government and state governments has accelerated in recent years. The expansion of the national government, first with the wars in Afghanistan and Iraq and later with the bailouts of American financial and automobile industries, has renewed America's interest in the proper role and size of the national government. The subsequent stimulus package, followed by a divisive debate on healthcare reform, once again put the issue of federalism at the forefront of the political debate in America. Other issues, such as gay marriage, education policy, and responses to natural disasters such as Hurricane Katrina, serve to highlight the differing views of Americans concerning the responsibilities of government.

One of the most contentious debates over federalism currently is the states' customary authority over marriage. Traditionally, states have enjoyed almost complete control over rules governing marriage, including defining licensing requirements, establishing an age of consent, providing for common law marriages, and determining general guidelines for divorce. Recently, this control has been challenged by

Block grant
national funds given to state and local governments for a broad purpose; comes with fewer restrictions on how the money is to be spent.

Unfunded mandate
legislation passed by the national government imposing requirements on state and local governments, which bear the costs of meeting those requirements.

the issue of same-sex marriage. In 2000, Vermont became the first state in the country to approve civil unions. Three years later, Massachusetts became the first state to allow same-sex marriage. Under the full faith and credit clause of the U.S. Constitution, states have honored marriages performed in other states so long as they do not violate the state's own marriage guidelines. The Massachusetts law caused a national uproar as opponents of same-sex marriage feared that the full faith and credit clause would result in the legalization of gay marriages across the United States. The national government responded by passing the 1996 Defense of Marriage Act, which allows states to adopt legislation excluding same-sex marriages in their territory. With this act, the national government is explicitly attempting to relieve the states of their obligation to grant full faith and credit to public acts in other states. At the state level, many states began to pass state laws explicitly denying the validity of same-sex marriages within their state. Texas did so in 2005, when voters overwhelmingly approved a constitutional amendment defining marriage as a union between a man and a woman. However, the national government may still assume control of this issue in the future. The U.S. Supreme Court could conceivably rule that the Defense of Marriage Act is an unconstitutional breach of a state's full faith and credit obligation. There have also been several attempts by the U.S. Congress (most recently in 2006) to amend the Constitution to ban same-sex marriage. So far, though, these attempts have failed to pass in either chamber.

While the battle over same-sex marriage has been contentious, the battle over the passage of a national healthcare policy has taken the conflict over federalism to a whole new level. A national healthcare system has been a goal of the Democratic Party since President Harry Truman proposed a national health insurance plan in 1945. Indeed, healthcare reform was the hallmark of Massachusetts senator Ted Kennedy's nearly five decades in Congress. Hillary Clinton made national healthcare central to her presidential campaign after championing a similar proposal as first lady. When Barack Obama was elected president in 2008, he promised to make healthcare reform a priority. While national healthcare has been popular among Democrats for some time, it has been equally unpopular among Republicans. When, on March 23, 2010, President Obama signed the healthcare bill into law, the Republican opposition to the bill was still growing. Texans, who tend to distrust government in general, by and large don't want anything approaching universal healthcare. A University of Texas/*Texas Tribune* poll conducted that same month showed that 60 percent of Texans opposed the new bill, while only 28 percent supported it. Only a few hours after the bill passed, Governor Rick Perry released a statement suggesting that "Texas leaders will continue to do everything in our power to fight this federal excess and find ways to protect our families, taxpayers and medical providers from this gross federal overreach."[5] From the beginning of the battle over the current legislation, Perry had described the bill as an encroachment on state's rights and "the largest unfunded mandate in American history."[6] In that spirit, Perry championed a bill reaffirming Texas's commitment to the Tenth Amendment. The so-called Tenthers contend that policies like national healthcare reform, Social Security, and Medicare are an unconstitutional violation of the Tenth Amendment. According to a statement posted on his website, Texas attorney general Greg Abbott has joined other states in a suit against the federal government "To protect all Texans' constitutional rights, preserve the constitutional framework intended by our nation's founders, and defend our state from further infringement by the federal government."[7] Texans' distrust of government, the Tea Party movement, and to a lesser extent the secessionist movement will all likely continue to play a role in Texas politics. As we can see, after two hundred years, federalism in the United States continues to evolve. States have also continued to become more involved in the day-to-day lives of their citizens. Nevertheless, state constitutions vary greatly in their length and specificity, the amount of power they confer to each branch of government, and the structure of their state judiciary, among other things.

Texas Constitutions

Texas's constitutions, including the current document, reflect its experience as a province of Spain and later Mexico. During the time that Texas was part of the Spanish empire, its population was relatively sparse and there was no written constitution. Nevertheless, centuries of Spanish rule left an indelible mark on Texas law. In contrast to English common law, property rights for women were well defined under Spanish law, including the right to hold property, the right to half of all property accumulated during a marriage, and the right to manage their own financial affairs.[8] In addition, Spanish law traditionally protected a debtor's home and farming equipment from seizure for repayment of debt, and this protection has persisted throughout Texas's constitutions under the homestead provisions.

Under Mexican rule, Texas, as part of the state of Coahuila y Tejas, experienced its first federal constitution. Texans were always somewhat frustrated with their

Map 2.1 The United States, 1837

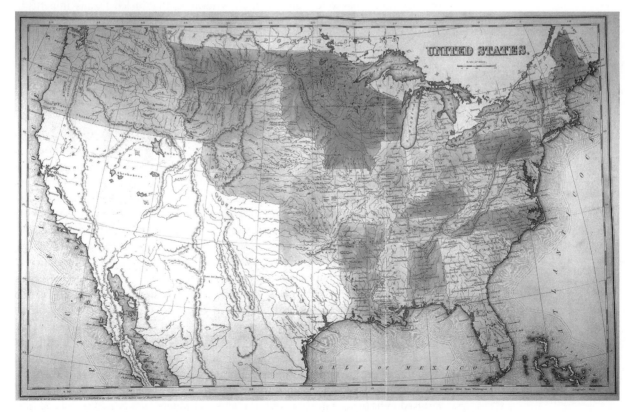

The northern part of Mexico in 1837 extended across most of what is today the American southwest, as well as most of California.

limited voice within the Mexican government. Most Texans felt underrepresented in the state of Coahuila y Tejas where Texans held only two of the state's twelve legislative seats. Anglo-Texans also resented certain aspects of Mexican rule, in particular the establishment of Catholicism as a state religion. Officially Texans were required to join the Catholic Church. Texans also were unhappy with the constitutional provisions prohibiting slavery, although they largely ignored these provisions. In general, Texans favored local control of government and distrusted centralized government, a preference that endures today. However, it was Mexican president Antonio López de Santa Anna's abolition of the Mexican constitution and assumption of dictatorial powers that undoubtedly made independence from Mexico inevitable. On April 21, 1836, Texans defeated Santa Anna at the Battle of San Jacinto, and both sides signed the Treaty of Velasco, granting Texas its independence.

Immigration Rights

When Texans declared independence from Mexico, they brought up a lengthy list of complaints, including unfairness in the judiciary, a lack of adequate political representation, and the imposition of a state religion. White Texans were frustrated with Mexican laws that seemed to ignore their needs. Texas was given only two seats in the legislature, and the Mexican judicial system often seemed to disregard the concerns of the new settlers. But much of the Texans' frustration with Mexico was that Mexico simply didn't represent the cultural preferences of its white settlers. Immigration issues were high among the grievances that fueled Texans' impetus to separate from Mexico.

The Mexican Texans' concern with immigration might seem strange to modern-day Texans. Ironically, much the way the modern economy of Texas depends on its immigrant population, Mexican Texas depended on immigration for the security of the sparsely populated state and initially encouraged immigration from both America and Europe. Under Spain and the early years of the Mexican Republic, immigration laws were quite liberal. However, Mexican authorities became increasingly concerned with the growing influence of Anglos in Texas. Eventually, Mexico sought to halt American immigration with the Law of April 6, 1830, although a significant number of Americans continued to enter Texas illegally.[9]

Anglo immigrants to Texas under Mexico faced a variety of difficulties arising from their inability to speak or write Spanish. Indeed, among the complaints of the Anglos about the judicial system was their inability to understand the laws or Spanish law books. Stephen F. Austin, in an attempt to avoid revolution, wrote to the Mexican government that "[w]ith only two measures Texas would be satisfied, judges who understand English . . . and trial by jury."[10] The basic difficulties of English-speaking immigrants living under a Spanish-speaking government were a primary concern of Anglos in Texas. One of the demands Texans made at the Consultation of 1832 was that the Mexican government create bilingual primary schools, with instruction in both English and Spanish. In 1834, Santa Anna, responding to the unrest in Texas, passed several reforms, including making English the official language of the state of Coahuila y Tejas.[11] Unfortunately, Santa Anna soon abolished the constitution and assumed dictatorial powers in Mexico. Once independent, Texans would not forget their experiences under Mexico, and they resolved to have their new constitution and subsequent laws passed translated into Spanish.

Anglo Texans' experiences as an immigrant minority were manifested in the Constitution of 1836, which established extraordinarily liberal immigration policies. It declared that "All persons, (Africans, the descendants of Africans, and Indians excepted,) who were residing in Texas on the day of the Declaration of Independence, shall be considered citizens of the Republic."[12] Furthermore, the constitution provided that a future immigrant, "after a residence of six months, make oath before some competent authority that he intends to reside permanently in the same, and shall swear to support this Constitution, and that he will bear true allegiance to the Republic of Texas, shall be entitled to all the privileges of citizenship."[13]

Before Texas declared its independence from Mexico, Anglo Texans complained that they were inadequately represented in Mexico. Thus, the framers of the new Texas constitution sought to grant immigrants the right to vote, regardless of citizenship. The current Texas Constitution was drafted to allow "male persons of foreign birth" to vote in the state, so long as they had "resided in this State one year next preceding an election, and the last six months within the district or county in which he offers to vote" and "shall have declared his intention to become a citizen of the United States."[14] Originally, the constitution was designed to ensure that future immigrants could easily and reasonably attain both citizenship and the right to participate in the government. This provision remained in force until 1921, when Texans, by a slim majority (52 percent in favor; 48 percent opposed), approved a constitutional amendment allowing only citizens to vote.

Hispanics in Texas today fight for many of the same rights that Anglos demanded under Mexican rule more than a century ago. Immigrants in Texas today make similar demands for easing citizenship requirements and for language rights. Anglo Texans today, apparently sufficiently distanced from their own experience as an immigrant population, have, in many cases, forgotten the difficulties they faced as the immigrant minority. But historically, the immigration issue was critical in the independence movement of Texas.

The Republic of Texas—The Constitution of 1836

No episode contributes to the mythical history of Texas more than its brief period as an independent country. Delegates from across the state met at Washington-on-the-Brazos to write a constitution for the future Republic of Texas. Of the fifty-nine delegates, almost half had been in Texas less than two years, and most of them had emigrated from southern states. The constitutional convention occurred in the midst of the revolution, and delegates hurriedly wrote the new constitution, well aware that the revolution was in danger of arriving at their doorstep at any moment.[15] The resulting document was largely influenced by the U.S. Constitution in that it was relatively brief and flexible, provided for three branches of government, and established a system of checks and balances. The president was elected to a three-year term, prohibited from serving consecutive terms, and appointed commander-in-chief of the Texas military. A bicameral legislature was established, with one-year terms in the House and three-year terms in the Senate. The short legislative terms and the nonconsecutive presidential term reflected Texans' distrust of government in general, an attitude that continues to dominate state politics today. At the end of the constitution was a Declaration of Rights, which enumerated individual rights similar to those found in the national Bill of Rights, such as freedom of speech, press, and religion. While White and Hispanic males were given a broad range of freedoms, free persons of African descent were prohibited from residing in the state without the consent of the Texas legislature.

There were, however, some notable differences between the U.S. Constitution and the Republic of Texas Constitution. For instance, Texas's constitution was distinctly unitary rather than federal in nature, since the Republic of Texas did not create lower units of government with any independent power. Reacting to the establishment of Catholicism as the state religion under Mexico, the Republic's constitution prohibited priests from holding office. Perhaps the most important feature of the new constitution was its legalization of slavery, a provision that had irreversible consequences for both Texas and the United States. Immigrants moving to Texas were permitted to bring their slaves with them, and Texas slave owners were prohibited from freeing their slaves without the consent of the legislature. However, the constitution stopped short of allowing the slave trade in Texas. As a part of Mexico, the slave population in Texas was relatively small. Once Texas left Mexico, and with annexation into the United States seen as inevitable by many, the slave population exploded in Texas, from an estimated 5,000 slaves (12 percent of the population) in 1836 to 58,161 (27 percent of the population) by the 1850 census, and 182,566 (30 percent) of the population by 1860.[16]

Texas voters overwhelmingly supported the new constitution as well as annexation by the United States. However, annexation was not immediate. There were two significant obstacles to Texas joining the United States. The first was the precarious nature of Texas's claim of independence. Upon his return to Mexico, Santa Anna renounced the Treaty of Velasco and reiterated Mexico's claims to Texas. Any attempt by the United States to annex Texas could potentially provoke a war with Mexico. Second, Texas's constitutional protection of slavery made annexation controversial within the United States. Abolitionists objected to the addition of another slave state; at the same time, existing slave states saw the admission of Texas into the United States as a guarantee of the future of slavery. Initially at least, the annexation of Texas was largely unpopular in the United States, particularly outside of the South. Thus, a first annexation treaty failed to receive Senate ratification. Eventually, though, the idea of **Manifest Destiny**, or the inevitability of the expansion of the United States across the continent, won out. James K. Polk campaigned for the presidency based on expanding the United States through immediate annexation of Texas and expansion into Oregon. In 1845, Texas was finally admitted into the United States. According to the annexation agreement, Texas would retain responsibility for its debt as well as the rights to its public land. In addition, Texas could divide itself into as many as five states as the population continued to expand, and then be admitted to the United States under the provisions of the national constitution.

Some of the greatest legends in Texas are built on this brief period of independence. Today Texans speak fondly of a time when they were masters of their own domain. According to popular imagery, Texas's time as an independent country makes it exceptional among the states. In truth, the Republic of Texas, though unique, was also relatively short-lived, poor, and unproductive. Much of Sam Houston's presidency was spent trying to convince the United States to annex Texas while simultaneously attempting to secure international recognition of Texas's independence by the United States, Great Britain, and France, as well as trying to procure financial aid from these governments.[17] As noted above, Texans overwhelmingly preferred joining the United States. It was the United States that hesitated on bringing Texas into the union. Offshoots of this legend continue to prevail throughout the state. For instance, many Texans believe that Texas is the only state permitted to fly its flag at the same height as the U.S. flag as an indication of its unique status. In truth, all states can fly their flags at a height equal to that of the U.S. flag.

Manifest Destiny
the belief that U.S. expansion across the North American continent was inevitable.

Statehood—The Constitution of 1845

Once Texas was admitted into the United States, a new constitution was necessary. The statehood constitution continued to specify separation of powers and a system of checks and balances while recognizing the federal nature of the United States. The terms for legislators were lengthened to two years for the Texas House and four years for the Texas Senate, although the legislature would now meet biennially, or every other year. The governor's term was shortened to two years, and the governor was prohibited from serving more than four years in any six. The governor's appointment power was expanded to include the attorney general, the Supreme Court judges, and district court judges, in addition to the secretary of state. Texans' experience under both Spain and Mexico was evident in the guarantees of property rights for women and homestead provisions in the new constitution.

The new constitution reflected the experience of Texans in other ways as well. Most Texans were in debt and highly distrustful of creditors, and indeed many individuals, including Stephen F. Austin, came to Texas to try to get out of debt. Thus, the statehood constitution established guarantees against imprisonment for debt. The bill of rights was moved to the beginning of the constitution, an indication of the importance Texans placed on individual freedom and limited government. Most of the Republic's constitutional guarantees, such as freedom of speech and press and protections for the accused, were continued. At the same time, the provisions protecting slavery and prohibiting the Texas legislature from emancipating slaves remained. Voting rights for African Americans and women were not considered in the deliberations, although there was a vigorous debate over enfranchising all free "white" men. Historically, the category of "white" had included both Native Americans and native Mexicans, though some of the delegates expressed concern that the term might now be used to exclude those populations.[18] In the end, the right to vote was conferred on "[e]very free male person who shall have attained the age of twenty-one years . . . (Indians not taxed, Africans and descendants of Africans excepted)."[19] In addition, the constitution mandated that one-tenth of the state's annual revenue be set aside to create a permanent school fund. Overall, the statehood constitution was relatively brief and flexible. Daniel Webster, a U.S. senator at the time, referred to the framers of this constitution as the "ablest political body assembled in Texas," producing the best constitution of the day.[20]

With the election of Abraham Lincoln as U.S. president, however, secessionist movements erupted in many southern states, including Texas. Although the movement to secede was strong in Texas, Governor Sam Houston led a substantial opposition. Indeed, when Texas voted to secede a few months later, several counties in Central Texas and North Texas, as well as Angelina County in East Texas, voted against secession. In the rest of East Texas, where slavery dominated the economy, there was almost universal support for secession (see Map 2.2). There was, however, significant opposition to secession in certain parts of the state. For instance, the Central Texas frontier relied on protection from the U.S. Army, and the ethnic German population there opposed slavery, making secession less popular. Secession was also unpopular in North Texas, where slavery was virtually absent.[21] Nonetheless, on February 23, 1861, Texas voted to secede and joined the Confederate States of America.

Secession and the Confederacy—The Constitution of 1861

Joining the Confederacy meant that a new constitution was needed. However, the 1861 Confederate constitution was primarily a revised version of the 1845 statehood

Map 2.2 Texas Secession Vote, 1861

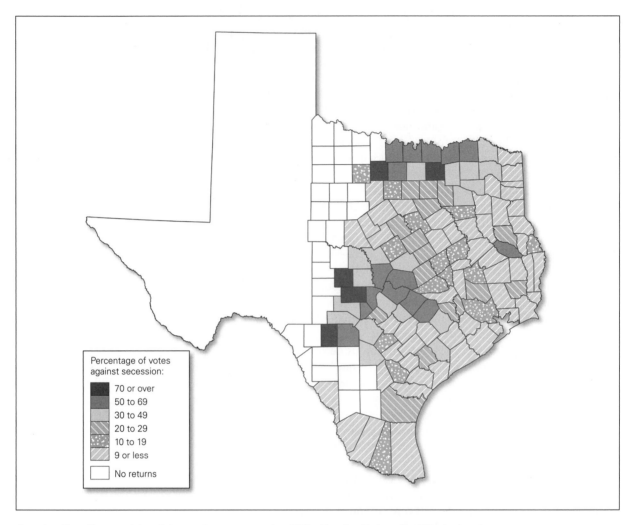

Percentage of votes against secession:

- 70 or over
- 50 to 69
- 30 to 49
- 20 to 29
- 10 to 19
- 9 or less
- No returns

Source: http://www.lib.utexas.edu/maps/atlas_texas/texas_vote_secession_1861.jpg. Reproduced by International Mapping Associates.

constitution, replacing references to the United States with references to the Confederate States of America. One notable difference was that under the Confederate constitution, slavery received even stronger protection. In the statehood constitution, the legislature was prohibited from emancipating slaves without compensating their owners and owners were prohibited from emancipating slaves without permission of the legislature. In the 1861 constitution, both slave owners and the state legislature were prohibited from emancipating slaves under any circumstance. Otherwise the Confederate constitution kept the same general governmental structures as the 1845 statehood constitution.

The First Reconstruction—The Constitution of 1866

With the end of the Civil War, Texas needed a new constitution that recognized the new political reality of the defeated Confederacy and reconstituted Union. Lincoln assigned a provisional governor, A. J. Hamilton, who immediately called for a constitutional convention. Adult white males who swore an oath of allegiance to the United States of America could participate in electing delegates to the convention. Once again, the approach of the drafters at the 1866 constitutional convention was to amend the 1845 statehood constitution rather than write an entirely new constitution. The 1866 constitution specifically renounced secession, repudiated the debts associated with fighting the Civil War on the side of the Confederacy, and acknowledged that slavery was "terminated by this State, by the Government of the United States, by force of arms."[22]

Although slavery was ended, African Americans were not granted voting rights in the 1866 constitution, and other provisions expressly prohibited them from holding office. In addition, the scope of the governorship was altered. Positions that had been previously appointed by the governor, such as the attorney general and state level judges, would now be elected. The governor's term was extended to four years, with the stipulation that the governor serve no more than eight years in any twelve-year time period. In addition, the governor was granted a line-item veto for appropriations bills. Perhaps the most significant contribution of the 1866 constitution was a clause that made it legal for individuals to acquire the mineral rights of their property.[23] In the end, though, this constitution was short-lived as Radical Republicans gained control of the national Congress and passed Reconstruction Acts designed to punish southern states.

The Second Reconstruction—The Constitution of 1869

The Reconstruction Acts passed by Congress divided the South into military districts and assigned military leaders. Texans were required by Congress to write a new constitution in which African Americans would realize full political rights, as well as ratify the Thirteenth and Fourteenth Amendments, in order to end military rule in the state. Moreover, the Radical Republicans who gained control of Congress prevented ex-Confederates, including anyone who had held a political office during the Confederacy, from either participating as delegates at this convention or voting on the resulting constitution. The result was that only six of the ninety delegates that participated in the 1866 constitutional convention attended the 1869 convention.[24] The delegates then, most of whom were unionist Republicans, were viewed with suspicion and resentment by the majority of Texans who had supported the Confederacy. Thus, the 1869 constitution is perhaps best viewed as an anomaly in Texas's constitutional development, as many of its provisions were more radical than the average Texan preferred. For instance, the office of the governor was again given broad appointment powers, including the power to appoint Texas's Supreme Court justices, district court justices, the attorney general, and the secretary of state. The governor's salary was increased and the line-item veto was retained. The 1869 constitution also created a plural executive that consisted of eight offices, including the governor. Perhaps a more radical development for Texans was the 1869 constitution's institution of a broader range of social services and corresponding taxes than Texans had previously experienced. For example, the constitution created a road tax, which would fund bridge building and road improvements in Texas. In addition, this constitution made elementary education compulsory and funded it with one-fourth of the state's annual tax revenues, along with a poll tax and monies from the state's public lands. The constitution guaranteed adult males the right to suffrage, regardless of race, color, or previous condition, and outlawed both slavery and systems of peonage. The delegates also proposed the creation of a new state of West Texas, although this was ultimately defeated.[25]

E. J. Davis

According to Texas legend, Texas needed the "Redeemer" constitution of 1876 to cleanse the state of the despotism endured under Republican governor E. J. Davis. Davis represented the more extreme branch of the Republican Party and narrowly won the gubernatorial election in 1869 with the backing of black voters. This connection to exslaves no doubt helped to alienate former slave owners. In the eyes of many, Davis ballooned the debt, declared martial law in much of the state with his control of the state militia and state police, and sold out the state's farmers to big business, including railroads, at the expense of the mainly agrarian population. And to add insult to injury, when it became clear that Republicans would likely lose the next election, Davis postponed the legislative election and initially refused to leave office after losing the governor's race. This version of events allowed Texans, still stinging from their loss of the recent "War of Northern Aggression," to blame the North for the economic decline of the state, erase from memory the Confederates' military defeat, and give birth to the legend of Democrats as redeemers who saved the state from a corrupt "foreign" invader.

However, if we examine some of the particulars of this story, we get a much more complicated history. Davis sought to create a compulsory education system for all children throughout the state. Any compulsory educational system with its accompanying taxes would have been seen as exorbitant, but it was also the first time that tax dollars would pay for the education of African Americans in the state, and it was the education of African Americans that led to the claims of waste.

It is true that Davis increased the debt of the state, but this is only half of the story. The state of Texas had been financially devastated by the Civil War and would have faced a lack of revenue regardless of who occupied the governor's office. Davis advocated an expansion of social services, which would necessarily translate into higher state taxes. The Republican policies were no doubt more progressive than most Democrats were comfortable with. That does not necessarily translate into wastefulness or dishonesty, though. Moreover, both taxes and state debt were actually higher under the succeeding Democratic administration.[i]

Davis also used the state police and the state militia to deal aggressively with lawless areas in the state. Texas still had large expanses of frontier to protect and there was a good deal of resistance remaining from the Civil War. For instance, Davis declared martial law in Hill County in January 1871, following the arrest of the state police who had attempted to arrest the son of the largest landowner in the county for killing a freedman and his wife.[ii] Similarly, racially motivated attacks and murders in Limestone County along with a mob threatening the

To protest the exclusion of ex-Confederates while including African Americans in the creation of the 1869 constitution, many Democrats boycotted the election to ratify the constitution. Nonetheless, in November 1869 the participating voters approved the new constitution and Republican E. J. Davis was elected governor of Texas. The climate in which the 1869 constitution was written would have lasting effects. After all, the national Congress had mandated many of the provisions of the new constitution, and many Texans had not participated in the election of the convention members, the election to ratify the constitution, or the subsequent election of Governor Davis. Davis would remain the only Republican elected as governor in the state until the 1970s. Because the events surrounding the 1869 constitution occurred during a period of military administration of the state, most Texans doubted the legitimacy of both the new constitution and the new governor from the outset.

E. J. Davis would prove to be one of the most controversial governors in the state's history. The taint of illegitimacy was impossible for Davis—and for the next century, the Republican Party—to overcome. After Reconstruction ended and

state police led Davis to declare martial law there in 1871. So, while it is true that Davis used expanded police powers to maintain order in the state, often the disorder was motivated by whites attempting to dominate the newly freed African American minority and reject the authority of the Republican-dominated state government and police.

Given that many Democrats were disenfranchised during punitive Reconstruction, Davis knew that Republican control of both the governorship and the legislature would be short-lived. Although Davis postponed the legislative and congressional elections, when they finally did take place the Democrats won overwhelmingly. The new Democrat-controlled legislature passed a law calling for the election of state and local offices, including the governor, to be held on December 2, 1873. In that election, Davis was overwhelmingly defeated by Democrat Richard Coke. However, the validity of the election was challenged by Republicans in the *Ex parte Rodriguez* case in the Texas Supreme Court. The 1869 constitution stated that "[a]ll elections for State, district and county officers shall be held at the county seats of the several counties, until otherwise provided by law; and the polls shall be opened for four days, from 8 o'clock, a.m., until 4 o'clock, p.m., of each day."[iii] Democrats argued that the constitution allowed the legislature to change either the allotted time or the place of the election. Republicans argued that the semi-colon after the phrase "provided by law" created two independent clauses and though the legislature could change the location of the polls, it could not change the time allotted for the elections. The Texas Supreme Court sided with the Republicans and earned the moniker "the Semi-colon Court." According to the Texas Supreme Court, Coke's election was thus invalid. Democrats ignored the ruling and inaugurated Coke. Davis, unwilling to resort to force to protect his position, vacated the office.

In many ways vilifying the Davis administration extended the tensions of the Civil War, as Democrats blamed Republican unionists for all of the state's problems. That we still see many textbooks repeat the one-sided view of the Davis administration even today is a testament to the pervasiveness of the anti-Republican and anti-northern myth.

i. Janice C. May, *The Texas State Constitution: A Reference Guide* (Westport, Conn: Greenwood Press, 1996); see also Randolph B. Campbell, *Gone to Texas* (New York: Oxford University Press, 2004).
ii. For more details of this incident, see *Handbook of Texas Online,* www.tsha.utexas .edu/handbook/online/articles/HH/jchka.html, accessed on June 20, 2007.
iii. Texas Constitution (1869), art. 3, sec. 6.

former Confederates were again eligible to vote, Democrats won back control of the state legislature and the governorship, ousting Davis and replacing him with Democrat Richard Coke in the 1873 gubernatorial election. With a Democrat safely in office, Texans immediately set out to write a new constitution. Some sought to prevent such a "tyrant" as Davis from ever again gaining so much power in Texas. Others leapt at the opportunity to replace the constitution that the national government and the Republican Party had imposed on them. Either way, Texans were once again writing a constitution.

The Current System—The Constitution of 1876

The current constitution of Texas emerged from the tangled mess left by the demise of Radical Republican rule and the return to power of the Democrats. The 1876 constitution created three branches of government, with separation of power between the branches of government and a system of checks and balances. Texas's constitution is based on the idea of popular sovereignty, evidenced in the preamble: "Humbly invoking the blessings of Almighty God, the people of the State of Texas do ordain and establish this Constitution." The constitution also embodies the principle of federalism in recognizing that Texas is free, "subject only to the Constitution of the United States."[26]

Several clashes created the context for the current Texas Constitution. First, the Civil War and the subsequent Reconstruction fostered considerable resentment toward northern Republican interests throughout the South. The Reconstruction era in Texas saw a Radical Republican–dominated government exclude the majority of Texans from participating in the creation of a constitution and in the state's political processes in general. Second, a preference for independence and individual freedom along with a deep-seated distrust of government has always characterized the state's political culture. With the exception of the 1869 constitution, Texas has consistently sought to restrict the powers of government. While the current constitution represents the most extreme attempt at restricting Texas government, all of the constitutions, with the exception of the 1869 constitution, sought to create a government that would generally stay out of the lives of average Texans. The constitution drawn up in 1876, in reaction to its comparatively progressive predecessor, went further than any previous constitution in specifying exactly what the government could and could not do. Delegates to the convention that created the current constitution were overwhelmingly Democrats who distrusted government, favored local control, preferred fiscal restraint, and wanted to fix the perceived injustices of the Republican-created 1869 constitution. Third, the delegates who wrote the current constitution were primarily concerned with protecting agrarian interests, as most Texans in 1876 engaged in farming. Indeed, close to half of the delegates were members of the Grange, an organization created to protect the interest of farmers. These farmers sought to limit the power of the railroads, which they relied on to deliver their crops and livestock to market. The Davis administration's policies aided the expansion of the railroads in Texas, which led to exorbitant rail rates that frustrated the farmers in the state. The resulting constitution is one of specific limitations on governmental power rather than a fundamental set of laws.

Table 2.1 Articles of the Current Texas Constitution

PREAMBLE	
Article 1	Bill of Rights
Article 2	The Power of Government
Article 3	Legislative Department
Article 4	Executive Department
Article 5	Judicial Department
Article 6	Suffrage
Article 7	Education
Article 8	Taxation and Revenue
Article 9	Counties
Article 10	Railroads
Article 11	Municipal Corporations
Article 12	Private Corporations
Article 13	Spanish and Mexican Land (repealed August 5, 1969)
Article 14	Public Lands and Land Office
Article 15	Impeachment
Article 16	General Provisions
Article 17	Mode of Amending the Constitutions of this State

Individual Freedom

Texans have always placed a high value on individual freedoms. Since 1845, a Bill of Rights has been the first article in each Texas constitution, demonstrating the importance Texans place on individual freedom (see Table 2.1). The Texas Constitution carries over rights from the previous constitution, such as freedom of speech, press, and assembly, along with the right to bear

Texas versus Connecticut

The constitutions of Texas and Connecticut date from very different eras in the country's history. The Texas Constitution, the state's sixth, was written in 1876 and reflects the agrarian, rural nature of the state at the time. Connecticut's constitution is one of the country's newer state constitutions, having been written and adopted in 1965. It is the state's third, following the Fundamental Orders of Connecticut (1638) and the Connecticut Constitution (1818).

Connecticut's constitution reflects in many ways the world of the 1960s. Its language is less formal and archaic than that of either the Texas Constitution or the U.S. Constitution. An extensive list of civil rights and liberties takes center stage in Connecticut's constitution. We might expect issues surrounding the free exercise of religion and separation of church and state to be reflective of the time and to therefore be more pronounced in the Connecticut Constitution than in the Texas Constitution. After all, Connecticut wrote and adopted its constitution after the U.S. Supreme Court eliminated mandatory prayer and mandatory religious instruction in public schools.

In fact, the Texas and Connecticut constitutions share a number of characteristics regarding religious liberty. For example, both guarantee freedom of worship, prohibit compulsory attendance at religious services, and prohibit any requirement that individuals give money to build places of worship. The constitutions of both states contain a number of prohibitions on their respective state governments. Yet the two documents differ in a number of respects, too. The Connecticut Constitution features specific language that guarantees the right of ministers and religious teachers to pursue their professions. Texas lacks such language in its constitution. In Texas, public lands cannot be given to religious organizations; a similar provision does not appear in the Connecticut Constitution.

The table below lists key provisions of the Texas and Connecticut constitutions in the area of religious liberty.

Thinking Critically

- Which state provides the most guarantees of religious liberty?
- Which state places the strongest limitations on government in the area of religious liberty?
- Which state imposes a greater degree of separation between church and state?
- Are your answers surprising or unexpected? Why or why not?

Religious Liberty: Texas Constitution (1876) and Connecticut Constitution (1965)

ISSUE/TOPIC	TEXAS CONSTITUTION	CONNECTICUT CONSTITUTION
Freedom of worship guaranteed	Yes	Yes
Attendance at services cannot be compelled	Yes	Yes
Contributions to build places of worship cannot be required	Yes	Yes
Preference to any religious society cannot be conferred	Yes	Yes
Equality of denominations guaranteed	Yes	Yes
Equal protection of the law cannot be denied based on religion	No	Yes
Alternative voting permissible where religion forbids act on Election Day	No	Yes
Right of ministers and religious teachers to pursue their profession guaranteed	No	Yes
Religious tests as a prerequisite to holding office are not permitted	Yes	No
Disqualification as a witness in court based on religion is not permitted	Yes	Yes*
State funds cannot be given to religious organizations	Yes	No
Public lands cannot be given to religious organizations	Yes	No

* In equal protection clause.

arms. It also includes protections against unreasonable search and seizure and cruel and unusual punishment and guarantees a trial by jury.

Texans' experiences during the Civil War also influenced the writers of the current constitution. Because President Lincoln had suspended habeas corpus during the war, so that people who were suspected of disloyalty could be arrested and held indefinitely without being charged, the authors of the current constitution specified that the right to habeas corpus shall never be suspended. The authors kept the provisions for freedom of religion while adding a requirement that state officeholders "acknowledge the existence of a Supreme Being." Moreover, the current constitution prohibits public money from being used for the benefit of "any sect, or religious society, theological or religious seminary." Prohibitions against imprisonment for debt and community property and homestead provisions were retained.

The Legislative Branch

The legislative branch is composed of a Texas House of Representatives with 150 members and a Texas Senate with 31 members. The current constitution imposes several explicit limitations on the legislature. Members of the House continue to be elected every two years, while the terms of the senators were shortened to four years. Originally, the constitution spelled out the legislators' salaries, and increasing salaries required a constitutional amendment that had to be approved by the electorate. This restriction persisted until 1991, when the constitution was amended to create the Texas Ethics Commission to set legislative salaries, subject to voter approval. The constitution also restricts the legislature to biennial sessions for only 140 days. While the legislature is limited to a relatively short session, thirty-day special sessions can be called by the governor, who sets the agenda for those sessions.

Much of the Texas Constitution is a list of things that the legislature is specifically prohibited from doing. For instance, the constitution spells out the types of taxes the legislature can and cannot levy. It explicitly prohibits the state from passing a property tax and sets ceilings on the amount of property taxes that local governments can collect. The constitution further forbids the government from imposing a state income tax without approval by a majority of voters. The legislature is additionally prohibited from passing a bill that contains more than one subject and is required to place the subject of the bill in the title. A reading of the current constitution makes clear that the main goal of the framers was to expressly limit the government rather than create a broad governing mandate.

The Executive Branch

One of the most outstanding features of the current Texas Constitution is the creation of a fractured and severely limited executive. According to Article IV, the executive branch is divided between a governor, lieutenant governor, secretary of state, comptroller, land commissioner, and attorney general.[27] Thus, in contrast to the United States executive, the Texas Constitution creates a plural executive. Moreover, most offices that had been appointed by the governor would now be elected, in order to further limit the power of the governor. In fact, the only major appointment left to the governor is the secretary of state. The delegates of the constitutional convention also shortened the term of office for the governor, decreased the governor's salary, and limited the number of terms that a governor could hold office. Later amendments would increase the governor's term to four years and remove the term limits. Clearly, though, one of the main goals of the delegates creating the current constitution was to limit the power of the governor.

The Texas Judiciary

Article V of the Texas Constitution creates a judicial branch with county courts, commissioner's courts, justice of the peace courts, district courts, and appellate courts, as well as "such other courts as may be provided by law." It also specifies the creation of two high courts, a Supreme Court to hear final civil appeals and a Court of Criminal Appeals to hear final criminal appeals.[28] Moreover, the constitution specifies the election of all state judges. The result is a judiciary whose members are constantly raising campaign funds in order to get reelected. This is in sharp contrast to the federal judiciary, which is appointed for the purpose of creating an independent judiciary.

Civil Rights

Two of the most controversial subjects at the 1876 constitutional convention dealt with suffrage and education. One Reconstruction reform that could not be undone was the extension of suffrage to African Americans in Texas, which was now mandated by the U.S. Constitution. There were those at the convention, however, who favored a poll tax in order to vote, ostensibly in an attempt to disenfranchise African Americans in Texas. However, the Grange and other poor farmers objected to the poll tax, which would also disenfranchise poor whites in Texas. In the end, the convention delegates defeated the poll tax. They also refused to grant women's suffrage. Interestingly, the current constitution protects voters from arrest on their way to and from the polls on Election Day.

Perhaps more controversial than voting rights was the educational system that had been mandated in the constitution of 1869. During the Reconstruction period, education was compulsory, regardless of race, and was paid for with tax revenue. At a time when the Texas economy had been devastated by the Civil War, a majority of Texans saw a universal educational system as excessive. Opposition to this system was widespread, as white landowners objected to paying for the education of African American children, and farmers in general favored local control of education, which could be tailored to the needs of particular communities while corresponding to crop cycles.[29] Thus, the 1876 constitution ended compulsory education and required segregated schools. Texas would not reinstate compulsory education until 1915. In 1972, the Texas Constitution was amended to guarantee equality under the law regardless of "sex, race, color, creed or national origin"— the so-called Texas equal rights amendment. A similar amendment failed at the national level. More recently, in 2005, Texas voters overwhelmingly voted to define marriage as "the union of one man and one woman."

Distrust of Government

The most prominent feature of the current Texas Constitution is the general distrust of government. Article I underscores the attitudes of most Texans that "[a]ll political power is inherent in the people, and all free governments are founded on their authority . . . they have at all times the inalienable right to alter, reform or abolish their government in such manner as they may think expedient." We see evidence of Texans' distaste for government throughout the document. For example, the circumstances under which the government can tax and incur debt are spelled out in the constitution. In order to keep the government small, the powers, terms, and salaries of the executive and legislature are severely limited. Instead, the framers of the Texas Constitution created a system where political power is retained by the people. An example of the power entrusted to the Texas voter is the use of the so-called **long ballot,** a system in which almost all positions in the state are elected rather than appointed. This distrust of government continues to pervade Texans' attitudes today and is one of the main reasons why a complete constitutional revision has failed to get support in the state.

Long ballot

a system in which almost all of the positions in a state are elected rather than appointed.

Criticisms of the Texas Constitution

The state's current constitution was written in the era of cowboys and cattle drives. Today's Texas is one of computers and commuters. The population in the 1880s was slightly over 1.5 million people, whereas in 2009 Texas's population was approaching 25 million. While Hispanic and African American populations comprised the two largest minorities in Texas in the 1880s, the Hispanic population has increased significantly since then. The African American population has declined, and other minorities such as Asian immigrants have a greater presence in the state today. Economically, Texas in 1876 was agrarian with small farms and ranches dominating the state. Today, the state's economy is one of the most diverse in the United States and continues to diversify. Texas has a substantial aerospace and defense industry, a significant telecommunications and computer sector, and is an important center of finance, shipping, energy, and other big business. It is not surprising, then, that the current constitution is considered outdated and inadequate for such a large and diverse state.

The desire of the framers to eliminate the last vestiges of Reconstruction, rather than the goal of writing a long-lasting constitution, shaped the current Texas Constitution. One of the most frequently cited criticisms is the amount of specific detail in the document. The Texas Constitution is a long list of specific rules rather than a set of fundamental legal principles for state law. For instance, in 2003 Texans approved twenty-two constitutional amendments, including one permitting cities to donate their surplus fire-fighting equipment to volunteer fire departments. Similarly, of the sixteen constitutional amendments voters passed in November 2007, one was a proposal to create and fund a cancer research institute. While both of these amendments may be commendable, they are the sort of specific policymaking we would ideally see come from a legislature rather than embedded in a constitution.

Writing this sort of specific detail into the state's constitution means that Texas has the second longest constitution in the United States, one that is both disorganized and unwieldy. The problem is compounded because the enactment of statutes often requires the amendment of the state constitution rather than passage in the legislature. This means that the constitution continues to grow; it is now approximately 93,000 words.

In addition, the constitution severely limits the government. The formal power of the executive is limited, leaving Texas's governor one of the institutionally weakest executives in the United States. Moreover, the legislature's session is limited to 140 days every other year. While that may have been desirable in 1876 agrarian Texas, today Texas is the second largest state in the United States with an

Texas versus Massachusetts

The Massachusetts Constitution of 1780, predating the U.S. Constitution by nearly ten years, is the oldest written constitution still in use not only in the United States but also anywhere in the world. The framers of the Massachusetts Constitution included three heroes of the American Revolution: John Adams, Samuel Adams, and James Bowdoin. These larger-than-life heroes established a pattern that many states now follow for state constitutions: a preamble, a declaration of the rights of citizens, a framework for government, and amendments to the constitution. The virtues of the relatively broad language of the Massachusetts Constitution have served the state well, as opposed to the highly specific and technical language of the Texas Constitution. Fewer constitutional amendments (120 total) have been passed in Massachusetts than almost half of the states, certainly fewer than Texas's 467 amendments. Also unlike Texas, Massachusetts still uses the original document, while Texas is on its fifth constitution since statehood (and its sixth if you add the short-lived Constitution of the Republic of Texas).

Thinking Critically

- Why do you think the Massachusetts Constitution is a model for other states?
- What aspects of the Massachusetts Constitution seem unusual to you?
- What aspects seem familiar?
- Do some features in the Texas Constitution seem preferable to you?

A Constitutional Comparison of Massachusetts and Texas

FEATURE	MASSACHUSETTS	TEXAS
Year adopted	1780	1876
Word length	36,700	93,000
Amendments	120	467
Major sections	4	17
Executive offices elected		
Governor	Yes	Yes
Lieutenant Governor	Yes	Yes
Secretary of State	Yes	No
Attorney General	Yes	Yes
Treasurer/Comptroller	Yes	Yes
Other	Yes (1)	Yes (2)
Legislature	General Court	Texas Legislature
Senate		
Size	40	31
Length of term	2 years	4 years
House		
Size	160	150
Length of term	2 years	2 years
Judiciary	Appointed	Elected
Statewide referendum to amend constitution	Yes	Yes
Statewide referendum to make general laws	Yes	No
Initiative petition to amend constitution	Yes	No
Initiative petition to make general laws	Yes	No

increasingly diverse population and economy. Extremely low legislative pay means that average Texans cannot afford to take the job. Instead of creating a citizen legislature, the Texas Legislature is dominated by wealthy individuals and big business. Finally, election of judges in Texas creates a climate of mistrust in the Texas judiciary, with judges constantly having to raise money for reelection. The result is a judiciary that most Texans believe is overly influenced by money.

Amending the Constitution

The current Texas Constitution outlines the process by which it can be amended. Both houses of the Texas Legislature must approve any proposed amendments by a two-thirds vote. Once approved, the amendment must be published twice in major newspapers and posted in each county courthouse thirty days prior to Election Day.

Table 2.2 Comparison of State Constitutions

STATE	NUMBER OF CONSTITUTIONS	DATE OF CURRENT CONSTITUTION	APPROXIMATE WORD LENGTH
Alabama	6	1901	310,328
Alaska	1	1959	15,988
Arizona	1	1912	28,876
Arkansas	5	1874	59,500
California	2	1879	54,645
Colorado	1	1876	45,679
Connecticut	4	1965	16,608
Delaware	4	1879	19,000
Florida	6	1969	38,000
Georgia	10	1983	25,000
Hawaii	1	1959	20,774
Idaho	1	1890	23,239
Illinois	4	1971	13,200
Indiana	2	1851	10,230
Iowa	2	1857	12,500
Kansas	1	1861	12,246
Kentucky	4	1891	23,911
Louisiana	11	1975	54,112
Maine	1	1820	13,500
Maryland	4	1867	46,600
Massachusetts	1	1780	36,700
Michigan	4	1964	27,000
Minnesota	1	1858	11,547
Mississippi	4	1890	24,323
Missouri	4	1945	42,600
Montana	2	1973	13,218
Nebraska	2	1875	20,048
Nevada	1	1864	21,377
New Hampshire	2	1784	9,200
New Jersey	3	1948	22,956
New Mexico	1	1912	27,200
New York	4	1895	51,700
North Carolina	3	1971	11,000
North Dakota	1	1889	20,564
Ohio	2	1851	36,900
Oklahoma	1	1907	79,133
Oregon	1	1859	63,372

Table 2.2, continued

STATE	NUMBER OF CONSTITUTIONS	DATE OF CURRENT CONSTITUTION	APPROXIMATE WORD LENGTH
Pennsylvania	5	1968	27,503
Rhode Island	2	1986	10,908
South Carolina	7	1896	22,300
South Dakota	1	1889	27,703
Tennessee	3	1870	13,300
Texas	**5**	**1876**	**93,000**
Utah	1	1896	11,000
Vermont	3	1793	8,295
Virginia	6	1971	21,319
Washington	1	1889	50,237
West Virginia	2	1872	26,000
Wisconsin	1	1848	14,392
Wyoming	1	1890	31,800

Source: *The Book of the States 2005* (Lexington, Ky: Council of State Governments, 2003), vol. 37, table 1.1, 10.

Finally, the amendment must be approved by a simple majority of voters. The Texas Constitution has been amended 467 times, making it one of the most frequently amended constitutions among the states.[30] Alabama's state constitution has been amended the most, passing 799 amendments, while Rhode Island's constitution has been amended the least, with a mere 8 amendments. (See Table 2.2 for comparison of other facts about the constitutions of the fifty states.)

As Table 2.3 illustrates, the overwhelming majority of proposed constitutional amendments in Texas are approved by electors; 87 percent of all proposed amendments have been adopted since 1985. Almost all constitutional amendments are put on the ballot in odd years, or in special elections. Unfortunately, the voter turnout during special elections is significantly lower than during general elections (see Table 2.4). Since 1985 the average turnout in elections with constitutional amendments is 8.67 percent of the entire voting-age population.[31] Voter turnout remains alarmingly low even when the proposed amendment is relatively popular or controversial. For example, in 2007, when 88 percent of voters approved school tax relief for the elderly and disabled in Texas, less than 7 percent of potential voters actually participated in that election. In 2003, voters approved twenty-two constitutional amendments, including a controversial limit on medical malpractice lawsuits, with a mere 9.3 percent turnout rate. In 2005, 76 percent of voters approved a constitutional amendment defining marriage as a union between a man and a woman. An amendment this controversial was based on a 14 percent voter turnout. Amending the fundamental state law with such low turnout rates raises serious questions about the nature of popular sovereignty in Texas.

Constitutional Revision

Distrust of government has generally translated to suspicion of change in Texas. The current constitution has been criticized since its inception. Demands for

Table 2.3 Texas Constitution of 1876: Amendments Proposed and Adopted, 1879–2009

YEAR PROPOSED	NUMBER PROPOSED	NUMBER ADOPTED	YEAR PROPOSED	NUMBER PROPOSED	NUMBER ADOPTED
1879	1	1	1953	11	11
1881	2	0	1955	9	9
1883	5	5	1957	12	10
1887	6	0	1959	4	4
1889	2	2	1961	14	10
1891	5	5	1963	7	4
1893	2	2	1965	27	20
1895	2	1	1967	20	13
1897	5	1	1969	16	9
1899	1	0	1971	18	12
1901	1	1	1973	9	6
1903	3	3	1975	12	3
1905	3	2	1977	15	11
1907	9	1	1978	1	1
1909	4	4	1979	12	9
1911	5	4	1981	10	8
1913	8	0	1982	3	3
1915	7	0	1983	19	16
1917	3	3	1985	17	17
1919	13	3	1986	1	1
1921	5	1	1987	28	20
1923	2	1	1989	21	19
1925	4	4	1990	1	1
1927	8	4	1991	15	12
1929	7	5	1993	19	14
1931	9	9	1995	14	11
1933	12	4	1997	15	13
1935	13	10	1999	17	13
1937	7	6	2001	20	20
1939	4	3	2003	22	22
1941	5	1	2005	9	7
1943	3	3	2007	17	17
1945	8	7	2009	11	11
1947	9	9			
1949	10	2			
1951	7	3			

Source: Texas Legislative Council, www.tlc.state.tx.us.

constitutional revision have been almost continuous in Texas, with calls for constitutional conventions occurring in 1913, 1917, 1949, 1957, and 1967.[32] As early as 1922 Governor Pat Neff urged the legislature to write a new state constitution, arguing that the 1876 constitution had become a "patchwork"—this after only thirty-nine amendments.[33] However, it wasn't until the early 1970s, in reaction to the Sharpstown Scandal, a banking and stock fraud scandal involving officials at the highest levels of government, that Texas came close to substantial constitutional revision. The legislature created a constitutional revision commission that proposed sweeping changes to the current Texas Constitution. The proposal included providing annual sessions for the legislature, increasing the power of the governor, creating a single high court, and changing the selection process of the judiciary. The proposed document would have contained only 14,000 words and would have reduced the number of articles from seventeen to eleven. The final proposal was considered a well-drafted constitution and contains many of the changes constitutional experts continue to propose today. In the end, though, a joint meeting of both houses of the legislature failed by three votes to get the two-thirds vote necessary to pass. In its next regular session, the legislature revived most of those proposals in the form of eight amendments to the constitution, but Texas voters overwhelmingly rejected each of the amendments.

Another serious attempt at significant constitutional revision came in 1998, spearheaded by Sen. Bill Ratliff and Rep. Rob Junell. The Ratliff-Junell proposal also reduced the document, to about 18,000 words, granted expanded appointment power to the governor, increased the length of legislators' terms while imposing term limits, created a salary commission appointed by the governor to set compensation for legislators (without voter approval), and reorganized the judiciary with a single high court and gubernatorial appointment of judges followed by a retention election. Ratliff and Junell argued that the current constitution is clearly broken and imposes an intolerable cost on the state. Ratliff suggests that "[voters know] that any document you have to try to amend 20 times every other year is broke. It's sort of a Texas tragedy, actually, that we can't seem to come to grips with the fact that we need a new, basic document going into the next century and the next millennium."[34] Moreover, the cost of the frequent elections necessary to amend the constitution is considerable, manifesting itself in the forms of "voter fatigue and the temptation for special-interest groups to push amendments that aren't in the public interest."[35] The Ratliff-Junell proposal unceremoniously died from neglect in the legislature. As with previous attempts at constitutional revision, Texans resisted change and chose to continue to patch up the old constitution. The constitution thus remains mired in legislative detail, and Texans remain unwilling or unable to create a constitution designed for the diversity and complexities of our state.

Absent a constitutional convention, constitutional revision can occur in a variety of other ways. In Texas, constitutional revision has been accomplished primarily through amending the constitution. This incremental change in Texas, while not

Table 2.4 Voter Turnout during Special Elections and Off-Year Elections, 1981–2009

YEAR	VOTER TURNOUT AS A PERCENTAGE OF THE VOTING AGE POPULATION
2009	5.77
2007	6.31
2005	13.8 (Gay marriage amendment)
2003	9.30
2001	5.60
1999	6.69
1997	5.32
1997	8.45 (Special education)
1995	5.55
1993	8.25
1991	16.6 (School tax reform)
1989	9.33
1985	8.24
1983	6.19
1981	8.07

Source: Texas Secretary of State, www.sos.state.tx.us/elections/historical/70-92.shtml.

Initiative

a mechanism that allows voters to gather signatures on a petition in order to place statutes or constitutional amendments on a ballot.

Referendum

a mechanism that allows voters to cast a popular vote on statutes passed by the state legislature; the legislature can place measures on the ballot for voter consideration.

ideal, has been necessary since many Texans resist more sweeping changes, such as wholesale revision through constitutional conventions. Theoretically, change could also be accomplished with the voter-led initiative and referendum. An **initiative** occurs when voters gather signatures on a petition in order to place either statutes or constitutional amendments on a ballot. A **referendum** allows voters to cast a popular vote on statutes passed by the legislature. These two voter-led mechanisms are consistent with Texans' legendary preference for limited government and popular control. So it is particularly surprising that the Texas Constitution does not have provisions for either procedure. While Texans' preference for limited government may be notorious, in this case it is apparently trumped by Texans' equally entrenched resistance to change. In the end, prospects for constitutional change seem limited. Most Texans, even as they acknowledge the problems with the current constitution, still distrust more the potential problems of a new constitution.

Winners and Losers

In Texas, the general distrust of government and resulting resistance to change has created an environment where the fundamental law is unyielding—a difficult situation for one of the nation's most rapidly changing states. The authors of the current Texas Constitution distrusted the Reconstruction government, which they viewed as the government of an occupying army. Their reaction was to create a constitution intended to limit the power of government, curb the potential for abuse by business, and preserve the power of citizens in the state. Ironically, the constitution generated such a high democratic cost to Texas citizens that the goals of the framers were guaranteed to fail. In an effort to safeguard the power of individuals, voters in Texas routinely face a long ballot—and are literally overwhelmed by the number of offices and constitutional amendments put before them at each general election. Instead of ensuring popular control of government, such a burden on citizens ensures voter fatigue and apathy. When citizens don't play their role to keep government in check, professional politicians and narrow special interests fill the gap.

The winners of the current constitutional rules tend to be big business interests. Business in Texas can dominate both the elections of officials and the approval or defeat of constitutional amendments, as overwhelmed voters simply opt out. The voters comprise the losers of the stagnant Texas Constitution. The voters, who continue to distrust government and therefore resist change, must face a political system in which business and political interests often override popular concerns. Moreover, the short biennial legislative sessions stipulated in the constitution create a government that has not kept up with the increasing complexities of the state. The goal of the framers was to create a legislature dominated by citizen legislators. By keeping the legislative sessions fixed and biennial, and the salary small, the framers hoped to preclude the creation of a professional legislature. In fact, in the twenty-first century these constitutional impediments guarantee that the legislature is dominated by people who depend on business corporations or legal firms for their salary, entities that often have interests in state legislation. The constitution has created a legislature that is indebted to big business and special interests rather than one concerned with representing the people.

The election of judges in Texas, when most citizens are already overwhelmed by the number of officials on the ballot, adds to an environment in which citizens' interests may be marginalized in favor of big business interests. Judges must raise significant amounts of money to be elected in the state, even as most citizens are simply not paying attention to judicial elections. Big business and other special interests are willing to fill that gap. In general, the Texas Constitution as it currently stands does not effectively empower the people in the state, and the general distrust of government and change means the people do not favor changing the constitution.

Conclusion: Tradition of Mistrust and Time for a Change?

Texans continues to cling to a constitution written well over one hundred years ago, when Texas was largely dominated by agriculture. The state of Texas has undergone constant and dramatic change since the constitution was written, and there is no sign that change will be slowing down. Gone are the days of the rugged frontier. In today's Texas you are more likely to see a computer chip than a longhorn. Yet even as Texas continues to change, Texans cling to the myth that the constitution continues to serve the citizens of the state. Mistrust of government overrides concerns over an unresponsive governmental structure. Texas continues to face increasingly complex issues, but Texans' tradition of mistrust undermines the ability of the government to respond to the state's transformations. Reliance on its outdated constitution will not serve Texas in the future.

Key Terms

block grant
categorical grant
concurrent powers
confederal system
constitution
delegated powers
extradition
federalism
fiscal federalism
full faith and credit clause
horizontal federalism
initiative
long ballot
Manifest Destiny
popular sovereignty
privileges and immunities
referendum
reserved powers
supremacy clause
unfunded mandate
unitary system
vertical federalism

Explore this subject further at http://lonestar.cqpress.com, where you'll find chapter summaries, practice quizzes, key word flash cards, and additional suggested resources.

Speaker of the House Joe Straus presides over the Texas House of Representatives. The position of Speaker is among the most powerful in Texas government.

CHAPTER 3

Texas Legislature

Amini-revolution occurred when the 81st Texas Legislature opened on January 13, 2009. The Texas House of Representatives began the legislative session with the typical housekeeping activities that start any legislative session: the Pledge of Allegiance was recited to the U.S. flag and to the Texas flag; Archbishop Daniel Nicholas Cardinal DiNardo of the Roman Catholic Church's Diocese of Galveston-Houston offered an opening prayer; new members took the oath of office; and key appointments in the Texas House, like the parliamentarian, chief clerk, and doorkeeper, were announced. As the next order of business, the Texas House began the election of their presiding officer, the Speaker of the House. The members of the Texas House of Representatives replaced incumbent Speaker Tom Craddick (R-Midland) with relative newcomer Joe Straus III (R-San Antonio). In fact, Straus was elected on a unanimous vote.

The election of Straus by unanimous acclamation was not unusual in the history of the Texas House of Representatives. Unanimity is the norm. A relative newcomer to the legislature, Straus arrived via a special election in 2005 to fill a vacant seat. While he had served on several committees, at the time of his election as Speaker, Straus lacked significant leadership experience in the Texas House of Representatives. Craddick, on the other hand, was a longtime member who had served in several leadership positions. However, Craddick's own elections as Speaker, especially in 2005 and 2007, were themselves deviations from the normal process because in both cases several votes were cast against Craddick. In 2007, opposition to his retention of the Speaker's chair reached as high as 20 percent.[1] This figure represented an unprecedented level of opposition in recent Texas politics because most Speakers, as we've already noted, are elected by unanimous consent.

Craddick's removal was an attempt by House members to shift the leadership of the chamber back to "normal" operations—that is, operations as they were conducted prior to Craddick's tenure. Craddick generated tremendous controversy for his autocratic, win-at-all-costs leadership style. For example, during the 80th Legislature, Craddick denied an opponent, Fred Hill (R-Richardson), the right to speak on the floor of the House during a procedural motion.[2] Craddick claimed the ability to recognize members during regular debates or procedural debates was absolute.[3] His opponents went so far as to attempt to seize the Speaker's podium away from Craddick. The House parliamentarian and assistant parliamentarian resigned in protest of Craddick's behavior.[4] In the interim between the end of the 80th Legislature's regular session in May 2007 and the start of the 81st Legislature in January 2009, Republicans from Craddick's own party moved against him. The trigger event occurred when the Democratic Party picked up seats in the Texas House of Representatives during the November 2008 election. The Republicans now held a narrow two-seat margin over the Democrats in the incoming legislature. Sixty-four of the Democratic members of the incoming House of Representatives signed a pledge not to support Craddick as the candidate for Speaker of the House. In addition, a group of Republicans called the Anything But Craddick (ABC) Republicans met to choose a candidate for Speaker other than Craddick. By the weekend before the start of the legislative session in January 2009, the ABC Republicans had selected Joe Straus as their candidate, with his support swelling to as many as 100 of the 150 members of the House of Representatives. Democrats pledged to support Straus included those who had originally agreed to back Craddick. On the afternoon of Sunday, January 4, Craddick's remaining Republican allies convinced him to step down in favor of another member of their faction, John Smithee (R-Amarillo).[5] While Smithee intended to run against Straus for the Speakership, the momentum in favor of Straus proved overwhelming as more and more members of the Texas House of Representatives announced their intention to vote for Straus. In the end, Smithee helped to nominate Joe Straus as Speaker of the House. Straus was elected by unanimous acclamation.[6]

Why does this episode of behind-the-scenes politics matter? What is the significance of the unanimous election of Joe Straus as Speaker of the Texas House of Representatives? What does the lack of unanimous support for Tom Craddick in 2007 tell us about Texas politics? The Speaker of the Texas House of Representatives is one of the most powerful positions in Texas government. The Speaker exercises tremendous power and influence over which bills become laws, which members of the Texas House of Representatives get which committee assignments, and ultimately what the legislature accomplishes during its relatively brief biennial session. If politics is about who gets what, when, and how, the Speaker of the Texas House of Representatives is a key player. Do not count Tom Craddick and his allies out of the game. Republicans dissatisfied with Straus' bipartisanism and emboldened by victories in November 2010 planned to remove Straus and replace him with a party hard-liner prior to the start of the 82nd Legislature in January 2011.[7]

In this chapter, we will examine the Texas Legislature in relation to other state legislatures, including the size of the chambers, the nature of bicameralism, types of state legislatures, and qualifications for office. We will then explore the meaning of representation, examine who is a representative, and consider just how representative the Texas Legislature actually is. A discussion of elections to the Texas Legislature will follow, with a focus on the election system, the issue of redistricting, and the impact of the Voting Rights Act of 1965. Next, we will discuss legislative organization by examining the structure and function of chamber leadership, party organization, and committees in the Texas Legislature. Finally, we will conclude the chapter with an examination of the legislative process, or "how a bill becomes a law" in Texas.

As you read the chapter, think about the following questions:

★ How does Texas's size affect the representative nature of the legislature?

★ To what extent does Texas have a citizen legislature?

★ What limits are placed on the Texas Legislature?

★ Who is included in the leadership structure in the Texas Legislature?

★ What are the obstacles to a bill becoming a law?

The Texas Legislature in Context

The U.S. Congress, as the legislative branch of the U.S. government, serves as a model for most legislative branches of state governments. The Texas Legislature is no exception. (See Table 3.1 for a comparison of some of the characteristics of the U.S. Congress and the Texas Legislature.) The legislative branch in Texas is usually referred to as the Texas Legislature, or simply *the* Legislature. The Texas Legislature is **bicameral,** consisting of two separate chambers or houses. The lower house is called the House of Representatives and the upper house is called the Senate. References to "upper" and "lower" houses developed from the British Parliament where the House of Lords represented the nobility of the "upper" class and the House of Commons represented the ordinary citizens of the "lower" class. These terms carried over into the American, and Texan, experience. States vary slightly in the names of the two chambers. For example, in Virginia the lower house is called the House of Delegates. Most states, however, employ the naming convention that Texas also uses. Forty-nine states possess a bicameral legislature in the state government. Nebraska is the only state with a single-chamber, or unicameral, state legislature.

Bicameral
a legislature that consists of two separate chambers or houses.

The decision to have a dual-chambered state legislature reflects not just a simple desire to mirror the U.S. Congress. James Madison suggested in the *Federalist Papers* that the protection of liberty from passionate majorities rests in part with dividing the power of the legislature.[8] Requiring any new law to pass in two chambers makes it more difficult for a majority to abuse its power. This "divide and subdue" technique of allocating the power of the legislature across two chambers is enhanced when each chamber is chosen by a different means. For example, members of the U.S. House of Representatives are chosen by popular vote based on small geographic districts, while U.S. senators are chosen by statewide popular vote. Another reason, historically, to employ a bicameral legislature is to ensure the adequate representation of different groups. Originally, state governments were directly represented in the U.S. Congress because state legislatures, as opposed to the states' voters, at one time chose the members of the U.S. Senate.

In the past some states mirrored the relationship between the two houses in the U.S. Congress by making counties the basis of representation in the upper house of the state legislature. However, with 254 counties, Texas never really did this. Today

Table 3.1 U.S. Congress and the Texas Legislature: A Comparison

CHARACTERISTIC	U.S. CONGRESS		TEXAS LEGISLATURE	
	U.S. SENATE	U.S. HOUSE	TEXAS SENATE	TEXAS HOUSE
Size of chamber	100	435	31	150
Term in office	6 years	2 years	4 years	2 years
Staggered terms	Yes	No	Yes	No
Minimum age for election	30	25	26	21
Resident of state	Yes	Yes	5 years	2 years
Resident of district	N/A	No	1 year	1 year

Source: Compiled by the authors.

the use of counties as a basis for representation in the upper house of state legislatures is no longer employed in any state. The U.S. Supreme Court rejected counties and local governments as a basis for representation in state legislatures in *Baker v. Carr* (1962), ruling that the Equal Protection Clause of the Fourteenth Amendment asserts the principle of "one person, one vote."[9] The *Baker* decision meant that the population of state legislative districts must be roughly equal and may not differ in population by more than, give or take, 5 percent. Using counties as the basis of representation for state legislatures clearly violated this concept since counties can and do vary tremendously in population size. For example, if counties were used to determine the makeup of the Texas Senate, Harris County, which includes the city of Houston, would have one senator for approximately 4 million people while Loving County in West Texas would have one senator for its forty-five residents. Obviously, people in Loving County would be dramatically overrepresented compared to those living in Harris County. In *Reynolds v. Sims* (1964), the U.S. Supreme Court extended this logic by requiring that both houses of state legislatures represent the population of a state on a one-person, one-vote basis.[10]

Each of the forty-nine states with bicameral state legislatures has an upper house that is smaller than the lower house. The smaller size of the upper house again mirrors the U.S. Congress; the U.S. Senate, with 100 members, is considerably smaller than the 435-member U.S. House of Representatives. However, the size of the membership of a state's legislature is not proportional to the population of the state. Large population states like Texas, Florida, or California do not always have the largest state legislatures. New Hampshire, one of the smallest states, has the largest lower house among the forty-nine bicameral state legislatures, with 400 members.

What may matter more is the relationship between the number of citizens and the size of the legislature. Where there are more legislators relative to the population, each legislator represents fewer people; in some sense the legislator is closer to the people. As shown in Table 3.2, the relationship between the size of the state legislature and the number of representatives is a bit more complex than might be expected. In Texas, with the eleventh largest legislature and the second largest population, each member represents around 137,000 people. When comparing the ratios of representation to population, Texas ranks forty-ninth in the United States. Thus, Texans are less represented in their own state legislature than citizens of almost every other state. Only California has fewer state representatives per person than Texas. Of course, the relative sizes of both houses of legislature change the dynamic a bit. The Texas Senate's 31 members each represent about 800,000 people, but in the Texas House of Representatives the ratio is 165,000 per member.

States vary in the size of their legislature and ratio of legislators to people because each individual state determines the size of its own legislature. Often this number is set in state constitutions and therefore is difficult to change as the state population grows. The Texas Constitution says that the Texas Senate has exactly thirty-one members. In contrast, the Texas Constitution gives a minimum number for the Texas House of Representatives, at ninety-three. The legislature has the power to add additional seats if so desired. As the population of Texas grew, the legislature increased the size of the Texas House of Representatives over time to the current size of 150. Finally, a practical limitation on the ratio of legislators to population is the fact that extremely large legislatures are difficult to organize. If Texas used the same ratio as New Hampshire, where each member of the state legislature represents just over 3,000 people, the Texas Legislature would have to

Table 3.2 Size of State Legislatures

STATE	TOTAL MEMBERS OF THE STATE LEGISLATURE				POPULATION PER LEGISLATOR		POPULATION	
	UPPER HOUSE	LOWER HOUSE	TOTAL MEMBERS	RANK	RATIO	RANK	IN MILLIONS	RANK
New Hampshire	24	400	424	1	3,124	50	1.324	40
Pennsylvania	50	203	253	2	49,821	13	12.604	6
Georgia	56	180	236	3	41,649	20	9.829	9
New York	62	150	212	4	92,177	4	19.829	3
Minnesota	67	134	201	5	26,200	30	5.266	21
Massachusetts	40	160	200	6	32,968	23	6.593	15
Missouri	34	163	197	7	30,394	26	2.951	18
Maryland	47	141	188	8	30,316	27	5.699	19
Connecticut	36	151	187	9	18,814	34	3.518	29
Maine	35	151	186	10	7,088	45	1.318	41
Texas	**31**	**150**	**181**	**11**	**136,919**	**2**	**24.782**	**2**
Vermont	30	150	180	12	3,454	49	0.621	49
Illinois	59	118	177	13	72,940	7	12.910	5
Mississippi	52	122	174	14	16,965	38	2.951	31
North Carolina	50	120	170	15	55,182	11	9.380	10
South Carolina	46	124	170	15	26,831	28	4.561	24
Kansas	40	125	165	17	17,083	36	2.818	33
Florida	40	120	160	18	115,862	3	18.537	4
Indiana	50	100	150	19	42,821	17	6.423	16
Iowa	50	100	150	19	20,052	33	3.007	30
Montana	50	100	150	19	6,500	46	0.974	44
Oklahoma	48	101	149	22	24,745	31	3.687	28
Michigan	38	110	148	23	67,363	9	9.969	8
Washington	49	98	147	24	45,335	15	6.664	13
Louisiana	39	105	144	25	31,195	25	4.492	25
North Dakota	47	94	141	26	4,588	48	0.646	48
Alabama	35	105	140	27	33,634	22	4.708	23
Virginia	40	100	140	27	56,304	10	7.882	12

(continued)

Table 3.2 Size of State Legislatures (continued)

STATE	TOTAL MEMBERS OF THE STATE LEGISLATURE				POPULATION PER LEGISLATOR		POPULATION	
	UPPER HOUSE	LOWER HOUSE	TOTAL MEMBERS	RANK	RATIO	RANK	IN MILLIONS	RANK
Kentucky	38	100	138	29	31,262	24	4.314	26
Arkansas	35	100	135	30	21,403	32	2.889	32
West Virginia	34	100	134	31	13,580	15	1.819	37
Ohio	33	99	122	32	87,444	5	11.542	7
Tennessee	33	99	122	32	47,699	14	6.296	17
Wisconsin	33	99	122	32	42,839	16	5.654	20
California	40	80	120	35	303,014	1	36.961	1
New Jersey	40	80	120	35	72,564	8	8.707	11
Rhode Island	38	75	113	37	9,320	43	1.053	43
New Mexico	42	70	112	38	17,943	35	2.009	36
Idaho	35	70	105	39	14,722	39	1.545	39
South Dakota	35	70	105	39	26,831	28	0.812	46
Utah	29	75	104	41	26,775	29	2.784	34
Colorado	35	65	100	42	50,247	12	5.024	22
Arizona	30	60	90	43	73,247	6	6.595	14
Oregon	30	60	90	43	42,507	18	3.825	27
Wyoming	30	60	90	43	6,047	47	0.544	50
Hawaii	25	51	76	46	17,042	37	1.295	42
Nevada	21	42	63	47	41,954	19	2.643	35
Delaware	21	41	62	48	14,276	40	0.885	45
Alaska	20	40	60	49	11,641	42	0.698	47
Nebraska	49	0	49	50	36,666	21	1.796	38

Sources: Kendra A. Hovey and Harold A. Hovey, *State Fact Finder* (Washington, D.C.: CQ Press, 2007), data compiled from tables on pp. 18, 103, 104; Scott Morgan and Kathleen O'Leary Morgan, eds., *Rankings 2010: A Statistical View of America* (Washington, D.C.: CQ Press, 2010), data compiled from tables on p. 511.

seat over 73,000 members. In general, there is a trade-off between representation and efficiency, as larger legislatures tend to be less efficient.

The Texas Legislature is one of only eight legislatures that does not meet yearly for a regular session, instead convening every two years. State legislatures in Massachusetts, Montana, Nevada, North Dakota, Oregon, South Carolina, and Wisconsin also meet biennially.[11] In 2008, voters in the state of Arkansas amended that state's constitution to shift the Arkansas Legislature from biennial to annual meetings. While the state constitutions of Minnesota and North Carolina stipulate that the legislatures are supposed to meet every other year, these legislatures are permitted to divide the regular session across two years, allowing the legislature in practice to meet annually for regular business.[12]

When in regular session, the Texas Legislature meets for 140 days, making the length of its session the fourteenth longest in the country. Eight states, including large population states like Illinois, Michigan, New York, Ohio, and Pennsylvania, do not limit the length of state legislative sessions.

The length and frequency of legislative sessions directly influences the ability of the legislature to work. Legislatures that meet annually are more likely to manage the state budget, handle new issues, and review actions of the executive branch. The infrequency of legislative sessions in Texas reflects in part the general distrust of government consistent with Texas's political culture and values. A legislature that meets infrequently cannot do as much work—or, theoretically, pass as many laws—perhaps keeping the state government smaller.

The Texas Legislature is not limited to meeting during its regular session every two years. The legislature may hold special sessions limited to thirty days. However, the power to call special sessions in Texas does not rest with the legislature. That power rests with the governor. In addition, the governor determines the topics that the legislature may discuss during special sessions.

When the legislature meets for its biennial session, a tremendous amount of work needs to be accomplished. Certain issues come up every legislative session, such as the state budget. Other issues vary markedly from session to session. In the mid-2000s, the legislature spent a great deal of time unsuccessfully addressing the funding formula for public elementary and secondary schools. The 81st Legislature, which met in 2009, faced several controversial issues. One was the impact of the meltdown in the U.S. banking and financial services sector following the collapse of the U.S. housing market in 2008. The resulting economic recession across the United States affected the Texas economy. The legislature had to address potential shortfalls in the state budget. A related issue involved how to spend money associated with the stimulus package passed by the U.S. Congress and signed into law by President Barack Obama. The stimulus package sought to re-start the U.S. economy by distributing hundreds of billions of dollars above and beyond regular U.S. national government budget outlays. While proponents argued that these expenditures would pump money into the economy and prevent a further collapse of U.S. business, putting the brake on job losses, opponents pointed to the massive increase in the U.S. government's budget deficit and national debt and its consequences for future generations. Governor Rick Perry, in keeping with the sentiments of some Republicans in the Texas Legislature, initially refused to take any stimulus money. Later the governor, with backing from the Texas Legislature, accepted federal dollars in a few key policy areas such as healthcare and education.[13] The legislature also addressed other issues, including expanded healthcare coverage for low income children, reauthorization of a hurricane insurance agency, college financial aid programs, and salaries for correctional officers.

One of the more controversial issues that the 81st Texas Legislature addressed was reauthorization of the Texas Department of Transportation (TxDOT). Like all state government agencies in Texas, TxDOT is periodically required to go through the sunset review process (see Chapter 4). Ultimately, the Texas Legislature had to decide whether to reauthorize the agency. In 2009, the issue of reauthorization of

TxDOT became embroiled in a series of disputes over the use of local option gas taxes for expanding roads, creation of high speed railways, and allegations of abuse of power by toll way authorities.[14] In addition, the overall issue of funding TxDOT projects became a political issue. Until the early 2000s, TxDOT paid for projects when funding was available. When funding was unavailable, roads and highways were not built. In recent years, TxDOT has relied more on establishing toll road authorities and borrowing money.[15] Tolls are supposed to repay the company for building the highway and to pay for any future maintenance to the highways. Yet, in the case of Beltway 8 around Houston, once the company was paid for the building of the road, tolls were used to build new roads in and around Houston. Tolls were never eliminated on some segments of Beltway 8 once the road was paid for. In addition, some new toll roads require travelers to purchase an electronic tag and to set up an account with the toll road authority. On these roads, cash is not accepted. Thus, use of the road is limited only to those who have set up an account.

A dispute between the Texas House and Texas Senate on how to revamp TxDOT ultimately led to adjournment of the House's regular session without a reauthorization of TxDOT or four other state agencies, including the Department of Insurance. The possibility existed that these agencies would be shut down and their activities suspended. In the case of TxDOT, new roads would not be built and existing roads would not be resurfaced. In the end, Governor Perry called the Texas Legislature into a special session in July to reauthorize TxDOT and other state agencies. The session produced two bills and lasted a total of thirty hours.[16]

When the legislature is in regular session or special session, its members possess certain rights and privileges that they do not possess otherwise. For example, the Texas Constitution states that "Senators and Representatives shall, except in cases of treason, felony, or breach of the peace, be privileged from arrest during the session of the legislature, and in going to and returning from the same."[17] Another right is designed to allow members an expansive freedom of speech while engaged in legislative debate: "No member shall be questioned in any other place for words spoken in debate in either House."[18] Essentially, what is said in the legislature supposedly stays in the legislature. Of course, what is said in the legislature may still come back to haunt a member during the next election.

Typologies of State Legislatures

Based upon factors such as length of legislative session, compensation for legislators, and professional resources, state legislatures may be classified as one of three types: citizen, professional, or hybrid. A **citizen legislature** seeks to limit the role of a state legislator to a part-time function so that many or most citizens can perform it. Typically, citizen legislatures meet every other year or for only a few weeks each year. Compensation is minimal for citizen legislators, and in some cases amounts to no more than reimbursement for travel expenses and some meals. The amount of time that a member of a citizen legislature spends in session, committee work, election campaigns, and constituency service is about half of the time they spend on a regular, full-time job. Staffing and other professional resources are minimal. North Dakota and Rhode Island are examples of states that have citizen legislatures. In contrast, a **professional legislature** meets annually, often for as much as nine months of the year. In these states, being a member of the state legislature is a full-time occupation. As a reward for devoting so much time to

Citizen legislature
a legislature that attempts to keep the role of a state legislator to a part-time function so that many or most citizens can perform it; normally, a citizen legislator is provided minimal compensation, offered few staffing resources, and has short or infrequent legislative sessions.

Professional legislature
a legislature that meets annually, often for nine months of the year or more; a professional legislator is provided a professional-level salary and generous allowances to hire and keep support and research staffs.

state government, members of the legislature are well compensated, averaging $68,599 among the eleven states classified as professional.[19] Generous allowances are also provided so that members of the legislature can hire and maintain extensive staffs that typically include secretarial support and researchers. These legislatures average 8.9 staff members per legislator. California and New York are examples of states that have professional legislatures. Given the size and scope of state government, especially in high population states, the development of professional state legislatures is not surprising.

In between these two extremes are hybrid legislatures. In states like Louisiana or Missouri, the legislature typically meets annually for a couple of months. Members of the legislature receive some compensation. Average compensation for states with this type of legislature is $35,326.[20] In addition, members of the legislature receive some funds to hire a small personal staff, on average three staff members per legislator.

The base pay for members of the Texas Legislature is only $7,200. Members also receive $139 per day while the legislature is in session for personal expenses, meaning that they earn a total of $26,660 in years with a regular session. This salary is especially restrictive for representatives from outside Austin, who must pay for a place to live in the capital during the session. To help compensate for the relatively low pay, members of the Texas Legislature enjoy one of the most generous retirement plans among the fifty state legislatures. To qualify a legislator must serve eight years in the legislature. At age 60, they can start receiving the retirement benefit on leaving the legislature. Legislators may start receiving retirement benefits at age 50 if they have served at least twelve years in the legislature. The pension formula is based on 2.3 percent of the base compensation to state district judges times the length of service in the legislature.[21] In 2005, the salary of the district judge was $125,000. This would make the minimum benefit $23,000 per year after eight years of service in the legislature. In addition, members of the legislature may contribute up to 8 percent of their salary per year while they serve in the legislature toward their pension.

In terms of staffing resources, members of the Texas Senate receive an allowance of $25,000 per month to pay for the costs of maintaining offices in Austin and in their district. These funds are used to purchase office equipment and supplies, pay for office space, and provide salaries and other compensation for office workers. Members of the Texas House of Representatives receive $8,500 per month for staff support.

Although the framers of the Texas Constitution sought to establish a citizen legislature, the Texas Legislature today is classified as a hybrid legislature. Labeling the Texas Legislature as "hybrid" takes into account the pension and staffing resources, not just base salary and infrequency of meetings. Peverill Squire, a researcher who developed an index of state legislatures based on the criteria of salary and compensation, staffing and similar resources, and time devoted to legislative activities, found that since 1979 the Texas Legislature has consistently ranked in the middle of state legislatures.[22] Texas was ranked neither in the top third of the list in terms of high salaries and extensive amounts of time spent doing legislative business nor in the bottom third where compensation is low and members of the legislature devote little time to doing legislative business. Absent the generous retirement benefits, the Texas Legislature is structurally similar to a citizen legislature. The low level of pay means that most legislators must maintain other forms of income during their legislative careers or before vesting in their retirement. The attempt to have a largely citizen nature to the Texas Legislature is consistent with the mythology of Texas, which demands that government be staffed by average citizens in order to keep legislators honest and serve the people better. In reality, legislators in Texas hold jobs outside the legislature that allow them to take time off when the legislature is in session, often in professions or industries that have a vested interest in state policy. Most Texans simply cannot leave their job for 140 days every other year to serve in the legislature.

Qualifications for Office and Length of Terms

ndividuals elected to the state legislature must meet both formal and informal requirements. Formal requirements are the legal criteria established in the state constitution. To be elected to the Texas House of Representatives, a candidate must be at least 21 years of age and have been a resident of Texas for two years and a resident of the district for at least one year. Election to the Texas Senate requires that a candidate be at least 26 years of age and have been a resident of Texas for five years and a resident of the district for at least one year. Both senators and representatives must be U.S. citizens and qualified to vote in the state of Texas.[23]

However, some informal elements appear to exist as well. For example, members of the state legislature are typically elected with a **party affiliation.** Members of the state legislature identify themselves to voters as either a Democratic candidate, a Republican candidate, or a member of some other political party. Of course, a party label typically means that the candidate competed in a primary election to win the right to campaign as the party's candidate in the general election. Often another extra-constitutional requirement, then, is a successful run in a **party primary.** This requirement is essential for candidates seeking to run with a Democratic Party label or the Republican Party label. Candidates from other parties like the Libertarian Party need only win the nomination at a party convention. (A detailed discussion of primary elections, including the Democratic Party's use of the "Texas Two-Step," appears in Chapters 7 and 8.) To compete in a party primary requires candidates to be well financed. Once a candidate wins his or her party's nomination in the primary, he or she can then campaign in the general election. While independent candidates do occasionally win election to the legislature without a party label or a primary election, this situation is quite rare.

In common with other legislatures, the Texas House of Representatives and the Texas Senate possess the legal right to refuse to seat a winning candidate. Such refusals are extremely rare, however. Several decades ago a representative from Gillespie County was elected as a write-in candidate. The losing candidate appealed to the Texas House of Representatives, requesting that it not seat the winner because he had not competed in the primary, never announced his candidacy, and never paid a filing fee. The House refused to consider the appeal.[24] The power to decide whether or not an election is valid resides with the legislature. As stated in the Texas Constitution: "Each House shall be the judge of the qualifications and election of its own members; but contested elections shall be determined in such manner as prescribed by law."[25]

The term of office for members of the Texas House of Representatives is two years. Texas senators are elected every four years, but the elections are staggered so that one-half of the Texas Senate is chosen every two years. An exception to this rule

---

Party affiliation

a candidate's identifiable membership in a political party, often listed on an election ballot.

Party primary

an electoral contest to win a political party's nomination for the right to appear as its candidate on the ballot in the general election.

involves **redistricting.** After the release of the U.S. Census data and the redistricting process to adjust election districts for the legislature is completed, the entire Texas Senate is elected at the next election. Then, by lottery, one-half of the Texas Senate comes up for reelection after just two years; a return to the usual four-year term follows at the next election. The other half immediately begins serving a four-year term. This process is highly unusual among state legislatures in the United States. Only the legislatures of Illinois and New Jersey have similar arrangements.[26] Typically, terms in office are fixed and are not affected by the redistricting process every decade. Most states have legislatures in which the lower house serves a two-year term and the upper house serves a four-year term.

The timing of elections to the state legislature also varies significantly by state. Some states hold elections simultaneously with elections for the U.S. president and Congress. Other states hold elections to coincide with midterm elections to the U.S. Congress, for example, in 2006 and 2010. A few states, including Louisiana, conduct elections to the state legislature in the year before elections for U.S. president, such as 1999, 2003, and 2007. In Texas, elections for the state legislature occur simultaneously with U.S. presidential elections and with midterm elections to the U.S. Congress.

In the 1980s some states began imposing term limits on their elected representatives. A **term limit** is a legal limitation whereby legislators are limited to a specific number of terms after which they are no longer eligible to serve in the state legislature. Term limits are typically the result of a **citizen initiative,** or petition drive, rather than self-imposed limits that the legislature itself has enacted. Currently, fifteen states have term limits. Arkansas, California, and Michigan have the most restrictive limits on the amount of time someone may serve in the state legislature: six consecutive years for the lower house of the state legislature and eight consecutive years for the upper house. Texas, along with thirty-four other states, does not have term limits. Proponents argue that term limits encourage **turnover** in office by requiring incumbents, those currently in office, to step down after a specified number of terms or years in office. Turnover is viewed as important to prevent "careerism" among politicians who make serving in an elected office their primary occupation and who thereby allegedly lose touch with the needs and concerns of the average voter.

Opponents of term limits often point to their anti-democratic nature. If voters choose to reelect the same person over and over again, that should be their decision to make; voters should not be denied a chosen representative by an arbitrary limit on the number of terms a person may serve. In addition, the experience incumbents acquire through their years of service in the state legislature is often invaluable.

Interestingly, six states abandoned term limits after their adoption. In four of these, the state's supreme court rejected term limits on constitutional grounds. Idaho and Utah eliminated term limits by action of the state legislature. Interestingly, the legislators' actions in these states did not lead to a massive outcry by voters. It also did not lead to an anti-incumbency trend to vote out members of the legislatures who repealed the limits on their own terms in office.

Do term limits actually increase the rate of turnover in office? Evidence from the 2006 elections suggests that they do. Among the fifteen states with the highest rates of turnover in their legislature, twelve have term limits. California and Nebraska had the highest rates of turnover, at 40.8 percent. Both states have term limits. By comparison, Texas ranked twenty-eighth in the United States in turnover. Sixteen percent of seats in the Texas Legislature changed hands in the 2006 election. Of the

Redistricting
the periodic adjustment of the lines of electoral district boundaries.

Term limit
a legal limitation on the number of terms an elected official may serve in office.

Citizen initiative
a citizen-initiated petition that forces consideration or votes on certain legislation and amendments, rather than having these actions come from the legislature.

Turnover
when current officeholders step down from office and are replaced by new officeholders; turnover may result from retirement, defeat in an election, or term limits.

The Texas Capitol in Austin sits among an impressive set of grounds. The capitol building itself is a source of a Texas legend. According to legend, the building was designed to be slightly taller than the U.S. Capitol in Washington, D.C. However, this legend is subject to debate. The Texas capitol is allegedly taller only if the capitol is measured from the highest tip of the statue at the top of the dome to the lowest level at the back of the building, essentially a partially exposed basement level.

fifteen states with the lowest rates of turnover, only Louisiana imposed term limits on its state legislators.[27] Proponents of term limits point to these higher rates of turnover as evidence that term limits are effective in ending political careerism and returning state legislatures to citizen control.

Rates of incumbency in the Texas Legislature over the last decade have been consistently high, at 80 percent or above. The lowest rate, at 75.7 percent, occurred in the 78th Legislature, which met in 2003. The low rate in this period reflected the historic elections of November 2002, when Republicans won control of both houses of the Texas Legislature for the first time in over 100 years. The Texas House hit a low of 75.3 percent of incumbents returned after the 2002 election while the Texas Senate saw 77.4 percent of senators returned. The 2008 elections returned 85.3 percent of incumbents to the Texas House of Representatives and 93.5 percent of senators to the 81st Legislature.[28]

One interesting effect of term limits is an apparent reduction in the number of women serving in state legislatures. In Missouri, Ohio, Arizona, and Florida, each of which observes term limits, the number of women serving in the legislature has gone down. Ironically, the expectation was that term limits would increase the number of women representatives because more open seats would be available. It appears, however, that when female legislators are term-limited out, the candidates recruited to run in the open seats are often men. In fact, states without term limits, such as Maryland and Virginia, have seen an increase in the number of women serving in the legislature.[29]

Theories of Representation

One of the key functions of a legislature is **representation,** or the relationship between the people and their representatives. There are three views on what constitutes an appropriate relationship between a representative and the electorate. According to the **delegate** approach, the people elect a representative to present the views of the district.[30] The legislator as delegate is expected to carry out specific tasks and hold specific positions, regardless of personal beliefs, on issues like public school funding, crime, and abortion. Essentially, the representative becomes the agent of the majority who elected him or her to office, though majorities can shift as the issues change. In contrast, the **trustee** approach begins by assuming that elected officials have access to information that voters do not. As a result, the representative understands issues from the broader perspective of the best interests of the entire district, state, or country. In this case, the people trust their representative to make the best choices for them when voting in the state legislature. Therefore, the representative, who is better educated about the issue, may go against the wishes of the majority. Finally, the **politico** approach asserts that a representative follows the wishes of the voting majority on the most important issues while on other issues he or she has more leeway.[31] In the latter case, the representative's personal beliefs may conflict with those of the majority and the representative then must choose between conscience and constituency.

In the United States, representation is connected to the single-member district plurality (SMDP) election system that is used to elect both houses of the state legislature. This election system implies a certain type of representation: geographic. Texans, and indeed most Americans, assume that a representative serves a specific geographic area. The Texas Senate consists of thirty-one members elected from thirty-one geographic areas of Texas (see Map 3.1). So, state senator Kirk Watson of Austin is expected to reflect the views of the people from Austin and parts of Travis County from which he was elected. For the 150 members of the Texas House of Representatives, the size of the district that each member represents is even smaller (see Map 3.2). For example, Rep. Linda Harper-Brown serves most of the city of Irving, just northwest of Dallas.

The advantage of geographic representation is the direct connection it provides between the representative and the voters. The voters living in a specific geographic area, or election district, know exactly who their representative is. On the other hand, this theory assumes that a representative can reflect the view of every person, or at least a majority of the people that elected him or her. Of course this is not always possible in view of the large number of issues confronting today's legislators. The passage of a **bill,** or new law or change to an existing law, typically involves numerous and complex considerations. Further complicating matters is the fact that voters often

Representation
the relationship between an elected official and the electorate.

Delegate
an elected official who acts as an agent of the majority that elected her or him to office and carries out, to the extent possible, the wishes of that majority.

Trustee
an elected official who is entrusted to act in the best interests of the electorate based on his or her knowledge; he or she is understood to be generally better informed than the broader electorate.

Politico
an elected official who is expected to follow the wishes of the electorate on some issues but on others is permitted more decision-making leeway; a hybrid of the trustee and delegate.

Bill
a proposed new law or change to existing law brought before a legislative chamber by a legislative member.

Map 3.1 Current State Senate Districts in Texas

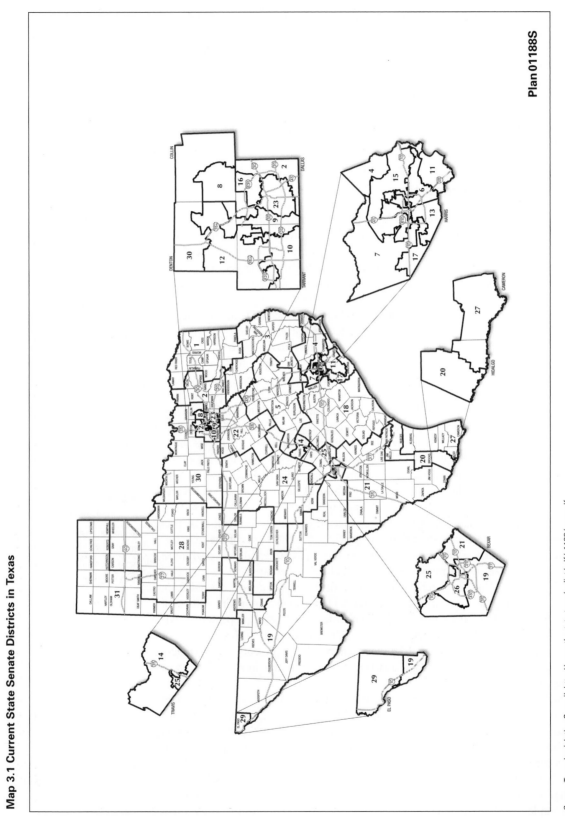

Plan 01188S

Source: Texas Legislative Council, http://www.tlc.state.tx.us/redist/pdf/s1188/map.pdf.

Map 3.2 Current State House Districts in Texas

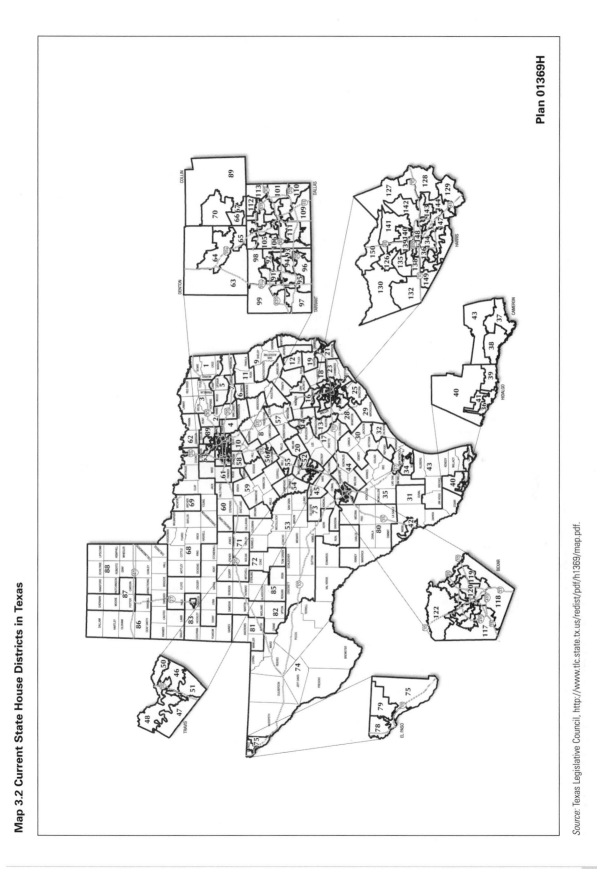

Source: Texas Legislative Council, http://www.tlc.state.tx.us/redist/pdf/h1369/map.pdf.

Plan 01369H

are economically and socially diverse; race, ethnicity, religious background, and other factors shape their understanding of politics, often in opposing ways. A single representative is unlikely to be able to adequately reflect all of these views.

An alternative approach to representation is the microcosm theory. John Adams, the second president of the United States and an early proponent of the theory, believed that a legislature should look like the larger society.[32] The aim is to have the legislature be as close to a perfect representative sample as possible.[33] The microcosm theory proceeds from the view that, while each individual member cannot truly represent the public at large, collectively the legislature represents the whole population. The Texas Legislature, then, should "look like" Texas in, among other things, its gender, racial, and educational makeup. In fact, the current legislature does not mirror the population as a whole (see Table 3.3). In general, Texas legislators are better educated than the public as a whole. The legislature also underrepresents women and racial and ethnic minorities.

Microcosm theory focuses attention on the demographic nature of representation. This demographic focus is an advantage because it raises awareness of whether legislatures truly mirror the larger society. If we assume that a legislator's income, education, race, religion, and gender all shape the decisions that a legislator makes, then microcosm theory offers a starting point to address whether the legislature is truly representative of the population. If the legislature looks like the larger society, citizens may accept its legitimacy and decisions more readily. If the legislature does not seem to mirror the larger society, then legitimacy and decisions may be questioned.

Table 3.3 How "Representative" Is the 2009–2010 Texas Legislature?

	TEXAS SENATE		TEXAS HOUSE OF REPRESENTATIVES		TEXAS POPULATION
	NUMBER	PERCENTAGE	NUMBER	PERCENTAGE	PERCENTAGE
Sex					
Male	25	80.6%	113	75.3%	49.9%
Female	6	19.4%	37	24.7%	50.1%
Race/Ethnicity					
Caucasian/White	23	74.2%	105	70.0%	47.2%
Hispanic	6	19.4%	30	20.0%	36.5%
African American	2	6.5%	13	8.7%	11.2%
Asian American	0	0.0%	2	1.3%	3.4%
Education					
High school or less	2	6.5%	15	10.0%	68.4%
Two-year degree	0	0.00%	4	2.7%	6.3%
Four-year degree	13	41.9%	62	41.3%	17.1%
Graduate study	16	51.6%	69	46.0%	8.3%

Sources: Adapted from Texas Tribune, "Elected Officials Directory" (2010), www.texastribune.org/directory (accessed June 1, 2010); and U.S. Census Bureau, "2008 American Community Survey," http://factfinder.census.gov (accessed June 3, 2010).

Texas Legends

Barbara C. Jordan

Barbara Jordan's career in Texas politics represents both personal and institutional victories. Jordan graduated from Boston University Law School, but her first two efforts at winning a seat in the Texas House of Representatives were foiled by a system that chose the twelve members of the Texas House from Harris County at large through a county-wide vote that diluted the political strength of minorities. Under this system, even though about 20 percent of Houstonians were African American, none of Harris County's representatives were black. However, the *Baker v. Carr* (1962) and *Reynolds v. Sims* (1964) U.S. Supreme Court decisions required that members of the state legislature had to be elected from districts that were roughly equal in population, thus putting an end to the at-large system. Helped by the newly drawn single-member districts mandated by the Court's decisions and by the removal of the poll tax as a barrier to voting, Jordan was elected to the Texas Senate in 1966, where she became the first woman to serve in the Texas Senate and the first African American to serve since 1881.

Initially, Jordan faced insults from some legislators who called her "Mammy" or "the washerwoman" behind her back.[i] However, Jordan's intelligence and political skills won over many of her fellow legislators and the Texas Senate unanimously elected her as president pro tempore in 1972. Later in 1972, Jordan became the first black woman from the South to win election to the U.S. House of Representatives.

While in the U.S. Congress she became an important player in the impeachment of President Richard Nixon, delivering a speech in which she declared, "My faith in the Constitution is whole; it is complete; it is total. And I am not going to sit here and be an idle spectator to the diminution, the subversion, the destruction, of the Constitution." In 1976 she became the first African American woman to deliver the keynote address at the Democratic National Convention, delivering what many observers consider one of the best speeches given at a party convention.

While much of what Barbara Jordan accomplished resulted from her character and intelligence, her political career would not have been possible without the Supreme Court opening the door to more representative legislative bodies through its redistricting decisions that protected the representation of minorities.

i. James L. Haley, *Passionate Nation: The Epic History of Texas* (New York: Free Press, 2006), 545.

Winners and Losers

In creating the Texas Legislature, the framers of the Texas Constitution were thinking about who wins and who loses in politics. In theory, citizen legislatures ensure that citizens do not lose in the contest of politics; their purpose is to protect citizen interests over those of the special interests that so frequently dominate legislatures. Unfortunately, in Texas there are several institutional constraints that preclude the establishment of a true citizen legislature. The low level of compensation forces most legislators to maintain outside sources of income. Those individuals with higher levels of education, higher incomes, and more flexible work schedules may be in a more favorable position to serve in the Texas Legislature. Given the relatively high cost of campaigns, legislators also need to be able to spend time fundraising to seek reelection. The average citizen simply can't afford to take the job. Thus, the effort to maintain a "citizen" legislature may result in a legislature that does not in fact "look like" Texas.

If Texas lacks a true citizen legislature, it is reasonable to ask, just how representative is the Texas Legislature? Evaluating the legislature based on microcosm theory suggests that the legislature is unrepresentative, particularly in terms of gender. Hispanics and African Americans in the state are underrepresented as well, though representation of minorities has improved recently and may continue to do so. In practice, the SMDP system used by Texas tends to favor minority representation. Its use, coupled with federal legislation like the Voting Rights Act of 1965 and Supreme Court decisions, results in an election environment that advances minority representation.

Electing the State Legislature

Single-member district (SMD)
an election system in which the state is divided into many election districts, and each district elects just one person to the state legislature.

Plurality election
a type of election in which the candidate with the most votes wins the election.

Majority election
a type of election in which a candidate must receive 50 percent of the vote plus one additional vote to be declared the winner; simply winning the most votes is not sufficient.

Run-off election
a type of election in SMDM that is held when an election fails to yield a clear majority winner in the initial balloting; the run-off is limited to the top two vote-getters from the initial election, ensuring a majority win.

Instant run-off
a type of election in which second-place votes are considered in instances where no candidate has received a majority of the vote; a winner is determined by adding together the first and second place votes.

Multi-member district (MMD)
an election system in which the state is divided into many election districts, but each district elects more than one person to the state legislature.

Elections to most state legislatures are similar to elections to the U.S. House of Representatives. Typically, states employ some type of **single-member district (SMD)** system—usually the state (or the entire nation in the case of the U.S. House of Representatives) is divided into a number of election districts equal to the membership of the chamber. Thus, for elections to the Texas Senate, the state of Texas is divided into thirty-one districts. Each district elects one and only one person to the chamber. For the Texas House of Representatives, the state is divided into 150 districts. Voters cast a single vote for their most preferred candidate on the ballot. In general elections in Texas, as in most other states, the candidate with the most votes wins the election and the seat in the legislature. This approach is called a **plurality election.** Other states use a single-member district majority (SMDM) system, which requires the winning candidate to receive a majority of the vote, or 50 percent of the vote plus one additional vote. In a **majority election,** if no candidate receives a majority on the initial vote, a **run-off election** is held, usually two weeks to one month later. Because only the top two candidates from the initial election are included in the run-off election, a majority outcome is guaranteed. A variation of this approach is called the **instant run-off.** In this type of election, voters indicate, in addition to their first choice, who they prefer as a second choice. If no candidate receives a majority at the initial election, the second place votes are considered and a winner is determined by adding the first and second place votes.

The main advantage to SMDM elections is that the winner is selected by the majority of the voters who show up. Texas uses both systems: it uses the SMDP system for general elections to the state legislature, U.S. House of Representatives, and U.S. Senate and the SMDM system for primary elections to state and local offices and to the U.S. Senate and U.S. House of Representatives.

Single-Member District versus Multi-Member District

Some states use the **multi-member district (MMD)** system to elect their state legislature. In an MMD system, the state is divided into many election districts, but each district elects more than one person to the state legislature. Voters normally cast a single vote for their most preferred candidate on the ballot. After the votes are counted, the candidates with the highest vote totals equal to the number of seats in the district are elected. The advantage of the MMD system is that candidates from more than one political party (or faction of a political party) are able to win a seat from the district.

For the Texas Senate, the requirement to use the SMDP system was part of the original wording of the Constitution of 1876.[34] Election districts for the Texas House of Representatives were a combination of SMDP and MMD: the MMD system was used sometimes when a county contained enough people to qualify for more than one member of the Texas House of Representatives. Instead of creating separate districts within the county, two or more representatives would represent the entire county. The Voting Rights Act of 1965 forced a shift in Texas and other states away from the MMD system to the SMDP or SMDM systems.[35] The MMD system appeared to depress representation among African Americans and Hispanics.[36] In contrast, the SMDP or SMDM systems concentrate minority voters into smaller population election districts. As a result, more minorities are elected to the legislature and candidates are more responsive to minority voters. Since the 1970s, Texas has used the SMDP system for both houses of the Texas Legislature.

Redistricting Games

One of the challenges of the SMD system is the regular need to redraw district lines. This need to shift district lines occurs because population changes over time. Population change occurs at uneven rates within a state. If election district lines for the state legislature remain fixed, then over time some areas will have many more people per representative than other areas. Consider the fact that Nacogdoches County in eastern Texas, home of the oldest city in Texas, had a population of 9,614 residents in 1870, just prior to the creation of the current state constitution. That same census found that Dallas County had 13,314.[37] By 2000, Nacogdoches County, with a population of 59,203,[38] had nowhere near the population of Dallas County at 2,218,899.[39] In 1876, Dallas County and Nacogdoches County were equally represented in the Texas House of Representatives, with one member each. Obviously, if redistricting never occurred, Nacogdoches County would be drastically overrepresented in the state legislature today and Dallas County would be drastically underrepresented. This situation violates the principle of **one person, one vote,** which requires that the vote of any one person carry the equivalent weight of the vote of any other person. Clearly the resident of Nacogdoches in an election would carry greater weight than the resident of Dallas. Redistricting in Texas normally occurs every ten years, after the results of the U.S. Census are provided to the states.

The Texas Legislature is responsible for drawing the lines for its own election districts, as well as those for the state Board of Education and the U.S. House of Representatives from Texas. Counties, cities, and other local governments also redistrict every ten years, but these governments are responsible for their own redistricting. The state legislature must abide by a number of federal rules and guidelines when drawing election districts. First, the landmark Voting Rights Act of 1965 (VRA) and similar laws seek to ensure the fair representation of minorities who have historically faced discrimination. While the VRA initially applied to African Americans, the law has expanded to include Asian Americans, Native Americans, and Hispanics. A key provision of the VRA is that the federal government must approve any change to election laws in states with a history of discrimination. Second, to boost the number of minorities that win election to the state legislature, the federal government encourages the creation of majority-minority districts. A **majority-minority district** is an election district in which the majority of the population comes from a racial or ethnic minority. In Texas, majority-minority districts have been established to benefit African American or Hispanic populations. In *Hunt*

One person, one vote
shorthand term for the requirement of the U.S. Supreme Court that election districts should be roughly equal in population.

Majority-minority district
an election district in which the majority of the population comes from a racial or ethnic minority.

Texas and North Dakota could not be more different. Texas is the second largest state in the country in terms of population. North Dakota, with 636,000 people, ranks just forty-eighth; only Vermont and Wyoming have fewer people. Population growth rates in Texas make the Lone Star State one of the fastest growing states in the United States. North Dakota ranks near the bottom in growth. Texas is a highly urbanized state. North Dakota remains essentially rural.

Another difference between the two is found in election processes. In North Dakota and a few other states, the lower house of the state legislature is chosen through a multi-member district (MMD) system. Each election district chooses two members of the lower house of the North Dakota Legislature. Each voter in North Dakota casts two votes in his or her election district. The top two vote-getters win seats in the North Dakota House of Representatives. The ninety-four members of the North Dakota House of Representatives are selected every four years from forty-seven election districts. Elections are staggered so that odd-numbered districts elect their representatives in a given election year followed two years later by even-numbered districts choosing their representatives. Other states using this system include Idaho, South Dakota, Washington, and West Virginia.

Because each district elects more than one representative, the possibility exists that candidates from both political parties will be elected to office. In recent elections as many as one in three election districts elected one Republican and one Democrat to serve in the North Dakota House of Representatives. In such cases, voters from both political parties have a representative from their district.

The MMD system may encourage greater party competition than the single member district system used in Texas. Parties have a greater incentive to run candidates. Getting elected in North Dakota means coming in either first or second place, not just in first place. Of course, parties also have an incentive to run more than one candidate in each district. In contrast to Texas, as discussed in Chapter 7, North Dakota has relatively few districts in which the two major parties do not compete. For example, in 2008 every district saw both Republican and Democratic candidates competing for office. In 2006, only three districts lacked a candidate from both major parties.

Thinking Critically

- Do you think the MMD system in North Dakota encourages greater party competition?
- What do you think are advantages of the MMD system?
- What do you think are advantages of the single-member district (SMD) system?
- Are there any drawbacks to either system?
- Which system would you prefer?
- Do you think Texas should maintain its SMD system of elections for the Texas House of Representatives? Why or why not?

Split Results in Recent Elections to the North Dakota House of Representatives

RESULT	2008	2006	2004	2002
Two Republicans elected	57%	42%	61%	62%
One Republican, one Democrat elected	17%	33%	22%	17%
Two Democrats elected	26%	26%	17%	21%

Sources: North Dakota Secretary of State, "General Election—November 5, 2002," http://web.apps.state.nd.us/sec/emspubilc/gp/electionresults.htm (accessed May 12, 2010); North Dakota Secretary of State, "General Election 2, 2004," http://web.apps.state.nd.us/sec/emspubilc/gp/electionresults.htm (accessed May 12, 2010); North Dakota Secretary of State, "General Election—November 7, 2006," http://web.apps.state.nd.us/sec/emspublic/gp/electionresultssearch.htm (accessed July 21, 2007); and North Dakota Secretary of State, "General Election—November 4, 2008," http://web.apps.state.nd.us/sec/emspublic/gp/electionresults.htm (accessed May 12, 2010).

v. Cromartie (1999)[40] the U.S. Supreme Court ruled that while race can be one factor in drawing up Texas's district lines, it cannot be the only factor. Drawing district lines for partisan advantage remains acceptable as long as the principle of one person, one vote established by the U.S. Supreme Court in *Baker v. Carr* is followed.

The Texas Constitution imposes its own restrictions on redistricting in the Texas Legislature. First, districts must be contiguous. Second, districts must respect county boundaries as much as possible. Finally, the state must now use the SMDP system. MMD is not permitted.

Historically, state legislatures in many states simply added new seats as the state's population grew and shifted. Growing counties were rewarded with more seats; those with declining populations or no population growth did not lose representation. Texas followed this pattern in the late 1800s and early 1900s. Between 1921 and 1951, the Texas Legislature neither redistricted nor added new seats, despite periods of rapid population growth in some parts of the state and population decline in others. The Texas Constitution specified that the Texas Senate contain thirty-one members, and the Texas House of Representatives originally held ninety-three members. Since a 1999 amendment to the Texas Constitution, the membership of the Texas House of Representatives has been set at one hundred and fifty.[41]

Either the legislature itself or an independent commission can draw election districts for state legislatures. Many states allow the legislature to draw and redraw district lines. Obviously, the ability of members of the state legislature to define their own election districts encourages incumbents to draw district lines to their political advantage, a process referred to as **gerrymandering.** Some states, for example, Iowa, have created a **nonpartisan or bipartisan independent commission** to draw the district lines. These states attempt to remove politics from the process and, perhaps more importantly, to prohibit the members of the state legislature from drawing their own district lines.

In Texas, the state legislature is responsible for redistricting, with one important modification. If the legislature is unable to pass a redistricting plan, the process is handed over to the **Legislative Redistricting Board (LRB).** The LRB, created by a 1948 amendment to the state constitution, is composed of the lieutenant governor, the Speaker of the Texas House of Representatives, the attorney general, the comptroller of accounts, and the commissioner of the General Land Office. The LRB develops a plan for redistricting that is submitted to the state legislature for approval. The LRB also becomes involved in redistricting the state legislature when a state or federal court invalidates a plan approved by the state legislature. However, the LRB redistricts only the state legislature. The task of drawing election districts for the members of the U.S. House of Representatives from Texas remains the exclusive domain of the state legislature.

In 2000, Texas faced the unusual situation of divided control over the state legislature, with Republicans controlling the Texas Senate and Democrats controlling the Texas House of Representatives. This transition occurred with the rise of the Republican Party and the end of the era of Democratic Party dominance. An impasse developed. The two chambers could not reconcile their differences to pass a final redistricting plan. When the legislature was unable to pass a redistricting plan, the LRB developed a proposal, which became the basis of redistricting the Texas Legislature. This plan was authored by Republican attorney general John Cornyn and passed on a 3–2 vote in the LRB with support from Comptroller Carole Keeton Rylander and Land Commissioner David Dewhurst. The plan ensured that Republicans increased their majority in the Texas House of Representatives.[42]

Gerrymandering
the practice of incumbents creating very oddly shaped electoral districts to maximize their political advantage in an upcoming election.

Nonpartisan or bipartisan independent commission
a system of drawing electoral district lines that attempts to remove politics from the process of redistricting.

Legislative Redistricting Board (LRB)
created by a 1948 amendment to the Texas Constitution, this group steps in if the state legislature is unable to pass a redistricting plan or when a state or federal court invalidates a plan submitted by the legislature; the LRB is active only with respect to redistricting of the state legislature.

Redistricting in Texas leaves the process in the hands of the Texas Legislature and the Legislative Redistricting Board (LRB), all elected officials with a vested interest in engineering district lines. For members of the legislature, protecting incumbents of both parties or securing gains for their party in the legislature can be important. For members of the LRB, assisting their party in gaining or retaining control of the legislature also matters. However, the implications for wider issues like partisan control over state delegations to the U.S. House of Representatives are apparent from the recent battles in Texas.

Arizona voters in 2000 approved Proposition 106, which amended the Arizona Constitution to create an independent commission to oversee redistricting for the state legislature and U.S. House of Representatives. The Arizona Independent Redistricting Commission consists of five persons.[i] By law, two members are Democrats, two members are Republicans, and one member is independent. All five must have maintained the same party affiliation, or no affiliation in the case of the independent, for at least the previous three years. In addition, all five members cannot have served as public officials, lobbyists, campaign workers, or political party officials in the three years prior to their appointment. Nominees are compiled by another independent commission charged with making nominations to Arizona appellate courts and are presented to the leadership of the Arizona Legislature for final appointment.

Proposition 106 contains explicit language to specify how the commission carries out the redistricting process.[ii] For example, the initial mapping of electoral districts cannot consider party affiliations of voters or the history of voting in existing districts. The commission must follow the guidelines of the Voting Rights Act of 1965, other legislation passed by Congress, and relevant rulings by the courts. District lines are to be compact and to respect the boundaries of existing communities, counties, and cities. Also, districts are expected to be competitive between Democratic and Republican candidates. This provision is tested only after the initial plan is developed. Thus, highly gerrymandered districts that clearly favor one party or another are not possible in Arizona.

Thinking Critically

- How does the Independent Redistricting Commission system of Arizona attempt to depoliticize the redistricting process?
- Does Arizona's system accomplish this goal? Why or why not?
- Has redistricting affected your hometown? Would you like to see your state adopt such a plan?

i. Arizona Independent Redistricting Commission, "Frequently Asked Questions," www.azredistricting.org/?page=faq, accessed August 1, 2007.
ii. Arizona Independent Redistricting Commission, "Proposition 106," www.azredistricting.org/?page=prop106, accessed August 1, 2007.

However, redistricting for U.S. House of Representatives seats also became a contentious issue. With the Texas Legislature unable to arrive at a consensus, the federal courts stepped in and drew the lines to favor both Democratic and Republican incumbents. Following the 2002 elections, Republicans gained control of the Texas House of Representatives and retained control over the Texas Senate. With Republicans now in charge of both houses of the state legislature and the governorship, Speaker of the U.S. House of Representatives Tom DeLay, R-Sugarland, proposed to Republican leaders in the state legislature a plan to redistrict Texas. DeLay sought to increase the number of Texas seats controlled by Republicans. After intense debate in the state legislature during the regular session, Governor Rick Perry called the Texas Legislature into special session three times in order to complete redistricting. In the middle of this political drama, Democratic members of the Texas House of Representatives fled to Oklahoma and later to New Mexico in attempts to prevent a quorum to conduct business. However, the state legislature did eventually pass a mid-decade redistricting plan. In the 2004 elections, the new district lines yielded Texas Republicans a net gain of six seats in the U.S. House of Representatives.

A mid-decade redistricting of the U.S. House of Representatives seats by the Texas Legislature, without being ordered to do so by a court, was unprecedented in recent history. Almost immediately, the redistricting plan was challenged in federal courts. Attorneys identified three issues for the U.S. Supreme Court to examine. First, did the mid-decade redistricting violate the U.S. Constitution? Second, did the new districts disenfranchise minority voters, violating the Voting Rights Act of 1965? Third, were the district lines drawn in such a partisan manner as to violate earlier U.S. Supreme Court rulings? In 2006, the U.S. Supreme Court issued a decision in *LULAC v. Perry* (2006).[43] The U.S. Supreme Court stated that mid-decade redistricting was permissible and held that the Texas districts were not drawn in an excessively partisan manner so as to completely dilute Democratic voters. Finally, the Supreme Court did find that some of the district lines violated the Voting Rights Act of 1965, primarily by reducing the strength of Hispanic voters in at least one district. These unacceptable district lines were redrawn to solve the problem identified by the courts. Thus, the transition to Republican Party control of the Texas Legislature ushered in a new era of partisan politics. Redistricting battles shifted from the tradition of defending the reelection chances of incumbents of both parties to securing partisan control over the U.S. House of Representatives and the Texas Legislature for the majority party.

Legislative Organization

Legislative organization is the system through which a legislature conducts everyday business. In doing so, the legislature attempts to provide processes to carry out functions such as developing new bills and revising of existing laws and overseeing the activities of the executive branch. A legislature is typically organized around the chamber leadership, party organization, and committee structure. Each aspect of legislative organization shapes the legislative process in powerful ways.

Chamber Leadership

Leadership of each chamber of the Texas Legislature is important. The leadership, which includes the presiding officers and both a Democratic and a Republican **party caucus chair,** possesses important powers to shape and to model the agendas of the chambers. This ability to control the agenda influences the likelihood that a bill becomes a law.

The presiding officer of the Texas Senate is the **lieutenant governor.** The lieutenant governor is directly elected by the voters of the state, so the senators lack control over the choice of their presiding officer. If the lieutenant governor's position is vacant, as when Lt. Gov. Rick Perry became the governor after George W. Bush was elected president of the United States, then the Texas Senate can appoint a new lieutenant governor. The lieutenant governor exercises immense power in the Senate, including the power to assign bills to committee and to appoint, without limitation, members of the standing committees of the Texas Senate and the chairs of the standing committees. However, the lieutenant governor votes in the Texas Senate only to break a tie. The lieutenant governor also serves on the LRB and the

Party caucus chair
a party leader whose main job is to organize party members to vote for legislation on the floor.

Lieutenant governor
the presiding officer of the Texas Senate, elected directly by the voters.

Legislative Budget Board (LBB). The LBB develops a proposed state budget for the legislature to consider. When the lieutenant governor is unable to attend sessions, the **president pro tempore** takes over as the presiding officer. The president pro tempore is elected by the membership of the Senate.

The **Speaker of the House** presides over sessions of the Texas House of Representatives. The Speaker is elected by the membership of the House as the first order of business at the beginning of the legislative session in January following the elections for the entire state legislature in December. Although the election is often by secret ballot, candidates for the position of Speaker campaign for weeks before the vote is taken. Historically, this process involves a system in which members of the Texas House of Representatives sign cards pledging their support to a candidate before the legislature meets. Thus, a candidate for the Speaker position largely knows which members of the Texas House of Representatives are going to vote for her or him before the balloting occurs.[44]

Unlike in the U.S. House of Representatives, the vote for the Texas Speaker is usually bipartisan and lopsided. As mentioned at the opening of this chapter, current Texas Speaker Joe Straus was elected by a unanimous vote. In 1999, James "Pete" Laney was unanimously elected to the position as well. Even controversial figures like Tom Craddick receive significant bipartisan support. On the one hand, the 27 votes against Craddick during the 2007 election of the Speaker suggest a significant opposition to Craddick, given the unanimity of support for prior Speakers. Yet the 121 votes in favor of Craddick represented most of the Texas House of Representatives, including many of its Democratic members. From the end of Reconstruction in the 1870s through the 1980s, the lopsided votes reflected the reality of Texas politics: the Democratic Party controlled the chamber. As a result, the Republicans in the House often found that supporting the eventual Democratic winner created opportunities for Republicans to have bills and amendments that they favored considered by the majority party. A more pragmatic reason exists for members of both parties to support the Speaker. The powers of the Speaker are extensive, and maintaining a favorable relationship with the Speaker is important. As a consequence, the tradition of lopsided votes continues. For now, the transition to Republican control over the Texas House of Representatives has not produced a shift away from bipartisan support for the election of the Speaker because the powers of the Speaker, regardless of party affiliation, remain extensive.

Powers of the Speaker include presiding over debates and controlling debates by deciding whether to recognize a member to speak or introduce a motion, as illustrated in the vignette at the beginning of the chapter. The Speaker's power also extends over interpretation of the standing rules by which the legislature operates, a power that may be used to help some legislators and hurt others. The Speaker serves on the LRB and appoints part of the membership of the LBB. In addition, the Speaker appoints some standing committee members, the chairs of standing committees, and members of conference committees from the Texas House of Representatives. The Speaker may also create select committees and interim committees. Thus, the Speaker has the ability to influence the size and shape of election districts and the items included in the state budget.

The Speaker also assigns bills to the committees. To be in favor with the Speaker helps ensure a member of the House of Representatives favorable consideration of pet bills and favorable committee assignments. However, unlike the lieutenant governor in the Texas Senate, the power to appoint committee members is limited, since one-half of the makeup of some standing committees is determined by seniority. The Speaker appoints a **Speaker pro tempore** to preside when the Speaker is unable to be at the Capitol.

Unlike some other states, Texas provides its legislative leadership no additional compensation. When the lieutenant governor serves as a presiding officer, no additional pay is given. However, leadership positions do receive additional pay in other states. For example, Oklahoma provides $12,364 per year to the majority party and minority party leaders in both houses of the Oklahoma legislature. Utah gives $1,500 to the party whips. North Dakota gives between $5 and $250 per day the legislature is in session, depending on the position. New York provides over twenty different leadership positions with between $9,000 and $34,500, depending on the position. In fact, only Arizona, New Mexico, South Dakota, and Texas offer no additional compensation to members of the legislature who assume leadership positions.[45]

Party Organization

The political parties provide a basis for organizing the legislature. Because political parties bring together people with similar political beliefs, the parties assist in **structuring the vote,** that is, aligning support or opposition to bills. Parties sometimes play an important role in the selection of committees and the organization of the work of committees. Parties can also form a base of support for the election of the Speaker of the House. Outside the legislature, the political party provides a mechanism for raising needed campaign funds and functions as a tool for mobilizing voters on Election Day. The **party caucus** plays an important role in many state legislatures. At its most basic level, the party *is* the party caucus. A party caucus is simply the members of a specific chamber of the legislature who belong to a specific political party. The historic pattern in Texas has been an absence of party caucuses in the legislature. Several reasons account for this lack of party organization. First, the dominance of the Democratic Party in Texas meant that party caucuses were unneeded. Texas, like other single-party states at the time, had patterns of behavior among legislators that reflected divisions within the Democratic Party itself. Another factor that contributed to the absence of party caucuses was the strength of the leadership positions. The powerful Speaker of the Texas House of Representatives and the lieutenant governor in the Texas Senate historically commanded their respective chambers, rewarding supporters and circumventing the need for party organization. In the Texas House of Representatives, the creation of the Democratic Party caucus in 1981 signaled a shift in the party system within the legislature. The growing number of Republicans spurred Democratic members to increase awareness within the party of policy issues, discuss bills, and discipline party members.[46] From 1981 until 1993, many Democratic members did not join the party caucus, and conservative Democrats often worked on bills in a bipartisan manner with Republicans. By 1993, most Democratic members found that working on a common position on bills within their own party helped to get legislation passed and served as a counterbalance to the growing influence and importance of the Republican Party in the chamber. Additionally, differences between the two political parties were becoming more evident, reflecting the growing trend of partisan politics at the national level. The transition to a more competitive two-party legislature led the Texas Democratic Party, at that time still in the majority, to institutionalize in order to meet a growing Republican challenge. The Democratic Party hoped that by increasing the level of party organization in the legislature, the party could deliver policies and bills more effectively and prevent the loss of additional seats to the Republican Party.

Speaker pro tempore
officer that presides over the House of Representatives when the Speaker is unavailable; akin to the president pro tempore in the Texas Senate.

Structuring the vote
the way in which political parties align support or opposition to bills.

Party caucus
the organization of the members of a specific legislative chamber who belong to a political party.

Although more cohesive in voting than the Democrats, Republicans did not formally create a party caucus until 1989. Republicans resisted forming party caucuses in the legislature in part because they feared focusing on party differences would lead to a loss of influence over legislation. While Democratic control over both chambers of the Texas Legislature existed for many decades, Republicans nevertheless received influential positions on committees, were appointed chairs of committees, and acquired positions of leadership in the chamber. Intensified partisanship was assumed to put Republican access to these positions in jeopardy. However, both houses of the Texas Legislature continued to operate in a bipartisan manner. While battles over taxation and spending in the late 1980s led to the formation of the Republican Caucus in 1987, Republican fears of loss of influence were unfounded during the waning years of Democratic control over the legislature. Ironically, Republican control over the legislature, especially the Texas House of Representatives, beginning in 2003 launched a series of debates and fights within the Republican Party over just how much influence should be granted to the now minority Democratic members and to what extent Republicans should shut out the Democratic Party.

Today, both parties maintain party caucuses in the Texas House of Representatives to provide communication among members of the caucus, to discuss bills before the Texas House of Representatives, and to raise money for campaigns.[47] The Republican Caucus in the Texas House of Representatives also maintains a policy committee that reviews bills under consideration and makes recommendations to the caucus on whether to support the bill, how to amend the bill, or how to defeat the bill.[48] Each party caucus also elects a party caucus chair. The party caucus chair is elected by the caucus to oversee the day-to-day operation of the party. The party caucus chairs in the Texas Legislature do not play as active and important a role as their counterparts in the U.S. Congress. The Republican Party Caucus also has floor whips. A **floor whip** is an individual who reminds fellow members of the party's position on a bill and encourages members to vote with the rest of the party caucus. Because the Texas House of Representatives is larger than the Texas Senate, party organization is more developed and more relevant in the Texas House of Representatives. To date, the Texas Senate lacks real party caucuses as formally organized and recognized organizations that work during the legislative session to shape the legislative process. However, the Texas Senate Democratic Caucus and its Republican counterpart exist to raise money to reelect members of the Senate for their respective political parties. These party caucuses play practically no role in organizing the political parties within the Texas Senate.

At least one study of party caucuses in state legislatures suggests that, relative to other states, party cohesion is relatively weak in Texas.[49] However, this study was undertaken before the emergence of a Republican majority in the Texas Legislature. Under Democratic Party dominance, party cohesion mattered less and legislators could afford to be more independent-minded. Indeed, the individualistic nature of Texas political culture calls upon legislators to exert a degree of independence from their party. Additionally, the powers and influences of the Speaker and lieutenant governor in their respective chambers produce their own centralized system of legislative organization.

Special Caucuses

Sometimes members of the state legislature form special caucuses. A **special caucus** is comprised of members of the state legislature who share a common interest. Special caucuses may include members of both chambers of the Texas Legislature

Floor whip

a party member who reminds legislators of the party's position on a bill and encourages members to vote with the rest of the party caucus.

Special caucus

an organization of members of the state legislature who share a common interest or have constituencies with a common interest.

and may have both Democratic and Republican members. These groups meet regularly to discuss topics of mutual interest to them and to their constituents. Three types of special caucuses exist in the Texas Legislature. The oldest special caucuses are **minority and women's caucuses**. These caucuses exist to represent the unique concerns and beliefs of women and ethnic groups across a broad spectrum of policy areas and political issues. This category includes the Texas Legislative Black Caucus (TLBC), Texas Women's Political Caucus, and Mexican American Legislative Caucus. These caucuses bring together members of the Texas Legislature that share a bipartisan desire to discuss issues affecting women, African Americans, and Hispanics. Often these groups assist in developing new bills or building support for bills that the caucus members believe to be important. A second type of special caucus is an **ideological caucus**, designed to promote a broad ideological agenda. In 1985, conservative members of the Texas Legislature created the Texas Conservative Coalition. In 1993, the Legislative Study Group was created to promote liberal policies. The final type of special caucus is the **issue caucus**. An issue caucus exists to promote bipartisan and cross-chamber support for policies and bills that advocate positions in a relatively narrow range of policy areas or political issues that are important to key constituents in some legislators' districts. Examples include the Rural Caucus, which advocates for healthcare, transportation, and education policies favorable to rural Texas. The Sportsmen's Caucus promotes and protects hunting and fishing rights, while the Environmental Caucus supports policies for environmental protection and conservation of natural resources.

The special caucuses may be formally organized and registered with the Texas Ethics Commission or may be simply informal meetings of members of the legislature. Some special caucuses are not registered with the Texas Ethics Commission, but these groups meet regularly and often informally. Interestingly, one study of the Texas Legislative Black Caucus (TLBC) suggests that the caucus enjoys a high degree of **cohesion,** meaning its members—or members of a political party or special caucus generally—vote together on a bill or resolution. During the 1980s and 1990s, when the TLBC membership voted together as a bloc, the caucus was able to influence legislation related to the group's shared interests.[50] This degree of cohesion suggests that some of the special caucuses play a significant role in the legislative process.

The impact of party and special caucuses on the power of the presiding officers is uncertain. Currently, party caucuses and special caucuses offer an alternative, decentralized base of political power and support to the centralized authority of the Texas Speaker and lieutenant governor. The emergence of caucuses in the Texas Legislature has not directly challenged the power of the presiding officers. Over time, however, power could shift from the presiding officers to the political parties.

Ultimately, special caucuses are important in the legislative process because they provide opportunities for members of the legislature to network on common interests. At a meeting, the members informally discuss bills before the legislature. In some cases, authors of bills or other interested individuals address the caucus. The caucus may also provide a springboard for amendments and other changes to legislation.[51]

Committees

A more formal form of organization that exerts direct influence over legislation is the **committee** system. Like the U.S. Congress, the Texas Legislature utilizes a committee system to assist the legislature in accomplishing its work. The presence of

Minority and women's caucuses
special caucuses in the state legislature that represent the unique concerns and beliefs of women and ethnic groups across a broad range of policy issues.

Ideological caucus
a special caucus in the state legislature that promotes an ideological agenda.

Issue caucus
a special caucus in the state legislature that promotes bipartisan and cross-chamber support for policies and bills advocating positions inside a relatively narrow range of policy areas or political issues.

Cohesion
unity within a group; in politics, when members of a political party or special caucus vote together on a bill or resolution.

Committee
a formally organized group of legislators that assists the legislature in accomplishing its work, allowing a division of labor and an in-depth review of an issue or a bill before review by the entire chamber.

committees allows, among other things, a division of labor so that bills may be reviewed in detail before being considered by the entire chamber. Four types of committees exist in the Texas Legislature: standing, conference, select, and interim.

The **standing committee** is the most important type of committee. These committees are considered permanent because they typically exist across sessions and elections. Standing committees are chamber exclusive, that is, each standing committee is associated with a specific chamber of the legislature and is made up of members from only that chamber. Standing committees are functionally divided. Some standing committees are substantive standing committees. For these committees, each committee handles bills in a specific area of policy such as transportation or higher education, although there are some exceptions. For example, every bill in the Texas House of Representatives that involves spending tax revenue must pass through the Appropriations Committee regardless of the subject of the bill. The Texas House Ways and Means Committee handles every bill involving changes in tax law, the rate of taxation, and the types of taxes levied. Another type of standing committee is the procedural standing committee. These committees handle calendars, procedural issues, and rules. In the 2009–2010 legislature, there were eighteen standing committees in the Texas Senate and thirty-six in the Texas House of Representatives (see Table 3.4).

The appointment process for members of the standing committees varies between the Texas House of Representatives and Texas Senate. As mentioned above, the lieutenant governor appoints the members of the standing committees in the Texas Senate. In the Texas House, the process is a bit more complicated. Seats on standing committees are assigned based upon seniority for the first committee assignment, while the second (or third) committee assignment is made at the discretion of the Speaker of the House. In addition, members of procedural standing committees in the Texas House are appointed only on the basis of seniority.

The membership of the committees has undergone tremendous transition over the past few decades. Prior to the 1980s, so few Republicans were in either chamber of the legislature that placing Republicans on every standing committee proved difficult. As Republicans gained strength in the Texas House of Representatives, Republicans who courted favor with a Democratic Speaker often found themselves receiving favorable positions on committees. In the 1980s and 1990s, Republicans often were overrepresented in committees and even chaired a number of standing committees.[52]

This situation stands in sharp contrast to the party-oriented system of the U.S. Congress and many state legislatures where committee seats are divided so that the party makeup of the committee mirrors the overall strength of the party in the chamber, the majority party is guaranteed a majority of seats on every standing committee, and the majority party holds all of the committee chairs. The control of committee membership and chairs ensures the majority a degree of control over the legislative process since every bill passes through at least one standing committee.

Beginning in the 1990s, committee assignments began to shift in the Texas House of Representatives toward a more party-centered model similar to that of the U.S. Congress. However, this transition is incomplete at best. The Speaker of the House retains powers over committee assignments and makes bipartisan appointments to reward supporters. Every member of the Texas House of Representatives sits on two or three committees, and Texas Senate members sit on at least four standing committees. In addition, after the Republicans became the majority party in 2003, the trend of overrepresenting the minority party on certain committees continued.

Table 3.4 Standing Committees in the 81st Texas Legislature

TEXAS HOUSE OF REPRESENTATIVES		TEXAS SENATE
Agriculture and Livestock	Insurance	Administration
Appropriations	Judiciary and Civil Jurisprudence	Agriculture and Rural Affairs
Border and Intergovernmental Affairs	Land and Resource Management	Business and Commerce
Business and Industry	Licensing and Administrative Procedures	Criminal Justice
Calendars	Local and Consent Calendars	Economic Development
Corrections	Natural Resources	Education
County Affairs	Pensions, Investments, and Financial Services	Finance
Criminal Jurisprudence	Public Education	Government Organization
Culture, Recreation, and Tourism	Public Health	Health and Human Services
Defense and Veterans' Affairs	Public Safety	Higher Education
Elections	Redistricting	Intergovernmental Relations
Energy Resources	Rules and Resolutions	International Relations and Trade
Environmental Regulation	State Affairs	Jurisprudence
General Investigation and Ethics	Technology, Economic Development, and Workforce	Natural Resources
Higher Education	Transportation	Nominations
House Administration	Urban Affairs	State Affairs
Human Services	Ways and Means	Transportation and Homeland Security
		Veterans Affairs and Military Installations

Several committees during the 81st Legislature, which met in 2009, contained a majority of Democratic members, despite Republican control over the legislature.

Presiding over each standing committee is a committee chair. Committee chairs are quite powerful. The committee chair sets the agenda for the committee, determining the order in which bills sent to the committee are considered. The chair also establishes the length of debate and the amendment process for each bill. As a result, the committee chair may schedule bills that he or she supports early in the legislative session to ensure that those bills are considered first by the committee. Likewise, the committee chair may move bills that she or he does not support to the end of the committee's calendar, effectively ensuring that the committee runs out of time before the bills are considered. The committee chair also decides other aspects of the agenda, such as the time devoted to hearings and oversight. This power over the agenda and the flow of legislation in and out of the committee gives the chair of a standing committee tremendous control over the legislative process. Although the majority party could monopolize all of the standing committee chairs in the Texas Legislature, the historic trend of allowing the minority party to chair some standing committees

Amendment

a formal change to a bill made during the committee process.

Mark-up

process whereby a committee goes line-by-line through a bill to make changes without formal amendments.

Oversight

the process whereby the legislature reviews policies and decisions of the executive branch to make sure that the executive branch is following the intentions of the legislature.

endures. In the 81st Legislature, Democrats chaired six of the Texas Senate standing committees. In the Texas House, Democratic members chaired fifteen committees.

Standing committees perform several important functions for the legislature, including the marking-up and amending of bills. An **amendment** is a formal change to a bill made during the committee process. **Mark-up** is the process by which a committee goes line-by-line through a bill to make changes without formal amendments. Because a committee is not required to report every bill to the whole chamber, committees may kill a bill by having a majority of the members on the committee vote against a bill or by not acting on a bill before the legislative session ends.

Another function of standing committees in Texas is to conduct **oversight** of the executive branch agencies. Oversight occurs when the legislature reviews policies and decisions of the executive branch to make sure that the executive branch is following the intentions of the legislature. Because some laws passed by the legislature provide only general guidelines to the executive branch, the specific agency that carries out the law often has discretion to determine exactly how to implement the law. For example, the state legislature in 2005 passed a law requiring state universities in Texas to set the maximum number of hours required for a bachelor's degree at 120 hours.[53] Most degree programs at Texas public universities required more than 120 hours. To make these changes, systems like the University of Texas and independent state universities like Midwestern State University developed plans to reduce the hours required for degrees to 120 hours. The standing committees responsible for higher education in the state legislature review progress toward the 120-hour degree program every two years during the regular session of the legislature.

In addition, new administrative regulations are subject to review by standing committees. For example, if the Texas Department of Parks and Wildlife decides to impose a user fee of $5.00 on everyone who goes fishing at a state park, it is up to the legislature, if it so chooses, to review this decision the next time the legislature meets in regular session. However, the standing committees lack the power to effect changes in new regulations and can only issue advisory opinions.[54] However, executive agencies take these opinions seriously. Keeping the legislature satisfied avoids having the committee, or the legislature, develop new laws to replace administrative regulations.

Committees have the authority to hold hearings when acting on legislation and overseeing the executive. These are meetings of the committee at which experts, invited guests, organized interests, officials from other branches, officials from other levels of government, and private citizens are allowed to address the committee about issues before it. The work of standing committees in all of these functions is enhanced by the research and report-writing of the committees' professional staffs.

To assist the members of the standing committee in their work, each standing committee, regardless of chamber, retains a permanent staff of up to six people in the Texas House of Representatives and up to fifteen people in the Texas Senate. Committee staff helps with research on bills, organization of committee meetings, and other tasks essential to the smooth operation of the committee.

In addition, individual members of the Texas House of Representatives may use the services of the House Research Organization, while senators can access the Senate Research Center. These offices help research issues, draft legislation, and provide information to members of the legislature. The Legislative Reference Library also provides resources for members of the legislature, committees, and committee staff in researching and writing bills.

Standing committees are allowed to create subcommittees in order to provide greater efficiency and division of labor. In the most recent legislature, the Texas

Senate Veterans Affairs and Military Installations standing committee had one sub-committee. The Texas House of Representatives Appropriations standing committee created seven subcommittees.

A second type of committee is necessary because the Texas Legislature contains two chambers. Bills may be passed in different versions in each chamber simply because the two chambers are different in their membership. As a result, when a bill passes both houses in different versions, a single version must be agreed to by both houses before the bill goes to the governor. A committee called a **conference committee** reconciles the differences in the Texas Senate and Texas House versions of a bill. Conference committees contain ten members, five from the Texas House and five from the Texas Senate. Normally some of the members of the standing committees who considered the original bill serve on the conference committee that reconciles the bill. The committee meets on a limited basis to reconcile the differences on a single bill. After producing a single, reconciled version of the bill, the committee disbands. The bill is then reintroduced to both chambers for consideration.

A third type of committee is the **select committee.** These committees are normally temporary committees created by either the lieutenant governor for Senate select committees or the Speaker of the Texas House of Representatives for House select committees. If the lieutenant governor and Speaker of the House create a select committee containing members of the Texas Senate and Texas House, then the committee is called a joint committee. These committees exist for a special purpose. Once the reason for the creation of the committee is resolved or settled, then the committee normally disbands. During the 81st Legislature, the Speaker created several select committees. For example, the Federal Economic Stabilization Funding Select Committee and the Federal Legislation Select Committee addressed the one-time issues of how to deal with funds from the national government's stimulus package. Since the stimulus package was a one-time event associated with the 2008 financial crisis and recession, these committees will be unnecessary in the future. A transportation funding select committee was organized to handle issues surrounding the sunset review process of the Texas Department of Transportation. Three other select committees were also created.

A final type of committee is the **interim committee.** Interim committees are important because the Texas Legislature does not meet each year. During periods when the legislature is not in session, interim committees may be created to provide oversight of the executive branch and to monitor public policy. Typically, interim committees mirror the division of duties and responsibilities used by the standing committees. Often, the committee studies specific problems or conducts research into specific issues as instructed by the state legislature

Legislative Process

Of course, a primary function of the Texas Legislature is making new laws and updating existing laws. Therefore, the legislative process, or how a bill becomes a law, is an important part of the legislature.

Bills must be **introduced** by a member of the chamber in which the bill is considered. Because a bill must pass both houses of the Texas Legislature, the author of a bill will often seek out members of both chambers to help co-sponsor it. The author is attempting to generate interest and support for the bill upon its introduction into each chamber. Members of the legislature and their staff are important sources of bills. Most bills originate in the Texas Legislative Council, a professionally

Conference committee
an official legislative work group that meets on a limited basis to reconcile the different versions of a bill that has passed in the Texas House and Senate.

Select committee
a temporary legislative work group created by the lieutenant governor or Speaker of the Texas House of Representatives for a special purpose; called a joint committee when the lieutenant governor and Speaker of the Texas House of Representatives create a select committee with members from both chambers.

Interim committee
a legislative work group that is created during periods when the legislature is not in session to provide oversight of the executive branch and monitor public policy.

Introduce [a bill]
to officially bring a bill before a legislative chamber for the first time. Introducing a bill is the first step in the formal legislative process.

staffed arm of the legislature. However, organized interests, who often have considerable resources, access to lawyers, and experience in "legalese" (the language of bills and laws), write bills as well.

Each time the legislature meets for its regular session, thousands of bills are filed and introduced into the legislature. In the 81st Legislature's regular session in 2009, a total of 12,238 bills and resolutions were introduced. Just over 60 percent of the items introduced were bills; the remaining 40 percent were resolutions. Of those, 5,910 bills and resolutions were passed into law by the legislature. Most of these were resolutions; only 24.7 percent, or 1,459 of the total, were bills. Bills passed by the legislature are almost always signed into law by the governor. Of the bills passed by the 81st Legislature, only 39 were vetoed by the governor. Even a special session of the legislature generates a considerable amount of activity. The thirty-hour session that took place in early June 2009 to address the funding of several state agencies generated 24 bills and 153 resolutions. The Texas Legislature passed only 2 of those bills into law, but it adopted 146 of the resolutions.

Bills may be pre-filed before the start of each legislative session. However, any new bill may be introduced up to sixty days after the start of the legislative session. To introduce a bill after the sixtieth day requires the agreement of 80 percent of the members of the chamber present. Any bill dealing with the state budget must be considered by the Texas House of Representatives first. Budget bills must be introduced by the thirtieth day after the legislative session opens. Any bill that impacts the state budget must include the cost involved, a projection of future costs, the source of revenue, and the impact on local governments.[55] Texas also requires statements of the impact of the bill on the equalized public education funding formula and on criminal justice policy. These last two provisions are unique to Texas.

In addition to bills, members of the legislature may introduce resolutions. A **resolution** expresses the opinion of the legislature on an issue or changes the organizational structure of the legislature. Three types of resolutions exist: a simple resolution, a concurrent resolution, and a joint resolution. A **simple resolution** addresses organizational issues such as changing the number of standing committees or altering the powers of committee chairs. These resolutions may be limited to a single house of the legislature. A **concurrent resolution** expresses the opinion of the legislature and requires passage in both houses of the Texas Legislature. For example, the legislature may pass a resolution asking the U.S. Congress to change a policy. A resolution may also cover seemingly trivial matters like commending the University of Texas football team for winning the Cotton Bowl or the Texas A&M Women's Golf team for winning a conference championship. A **joint resolution** is particularly important because this legislative act, when passed by both chambers, proposes amendments to the Texas Constitution. Those amendments are then sent to the voters for approval at the next election.

When a bill or resolution is introduced into a chamber, it is assigned a number by the secretary of the Senate or the chief clerk of the House. The number indicates the chamber in which the legislation originated and the order that it was introduced. For example, HR 10 indicates the tenth resolution introduced into the Texas House, while SB 351 is the 351st bill introduced into the Texas Senate.

After legislation is introduced, it is assigned to a standing committee (see Figure 3.1). In the Texas Senate bills are referred to committee by the president of the Senate, the lieutenant governor. Bills in the Texas House of Representatives are referred to committee by the Speaker of the House. Normally, bills are referred to the standing committee with jurisdiction over the policy area. Yet the Speaker of the

Resolution

a legislative act that expresses the opinion of the legislature on an issue or changes the organizational structure of the legislature.

Simple resolution

a legislative act that addresses organizational issues; may be limited to a single house.

Concurrent resolution

a legislative act that expresses an opinion of the legislature; must pass in both houses.

Joint resolution

a legislative act whose approval by both chambers results in amendment to the Texas Constitution; a resolution must be approved by voters at the next election.

House and the lieutenant governor have the power to send the bill to any standing committee in their respective chambers that they choose. In the Texas House of Representatives, if a sponsor of the bill believes the Speaker has unfairly assigned a bill to a committee to kill the bill, the sponsor may seek a "Jim Hogg Committee." Essentially, the standing committee meets in front of the entire House of Representatives to consider the bill.[56] A handful of standing committees in both chambers of the Texas Legislature contain subcommittees to aid in the legislative process. A subcommittee may conduct the detailed examination of the bill and report the bill to the whole committee before the final committee vote is taken.

After a series of public meetings, debates, mark-up sessions, and amendments, the standing committee takes a final vote on the bill. If the committee reports favorably on the bill, the bill returns to the entire membership of the chamber for consideration. In the Texas House of Representatives, the bill now goes to one of two special standing committees. For bills with statewide implications, the bill goes to the calendar committee. The calendar committee places each bill that it receives on the chamber's schedule, determining when a bill will be considered and specifying

Figure 3.1 How a Bill Becomes a Law in Texas

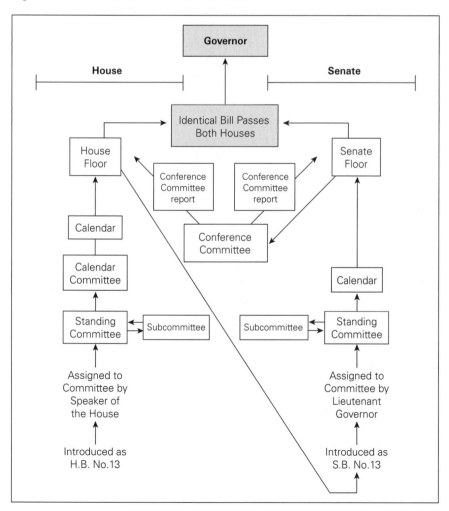

how long a bill will be debated. The calendar committee assigns the bill to one of several different calendars. In the House, at least seven different calendars exist (see Table 3.5). These calendars are arranged in order of importance from most important to least important. Bills on more important calendars are considered first, with bills on less important calendars handled if time remains during the legislative session. If a bill affects only a specific county, city, or other local government, it is sent to the Local and Consent Calendars Committee. This standing committee determines when local and consent bills are considered by the whole Texas House and how long a bill is to be debated. The Rules and Resolutions Standing Committee performs a similar function for memorials and other resolutions. Regardless of whether a bill is assigned to one of the seven calendars by the calendar committee or the local and consent calendar committee, any bill or resolution may be shifted by the whole House of Representatives to a more important (or faster) calendar by a two-thirds vote of the House.

The calendar committee is one of the key differences between the Texas Senate and the Texas House of Representatives. In the Texas Senate, there is no special calendar committee and only one calendar exists with bills listed in the order they were formally introduced. However, the Texas Senate almost never considers bills in this order. Instead, the Texas Senate has developed a trick that allows senators to change the order of consideration. The first bill introduced each session is known as a **blocking bill**, or stopper—a bill that is introduced not to be passed but merely to hold a place at the top of the Texas Senate calendar. This bill prevents bills below it on the calendar from being considered. Like the Texas House of Representatives, the Texas Senate may adjust the calendar by a two-thirds vote of the chamber. Thus, a bill originally scheduled for debate later in the session may be bumped to the top of the calendar, ahead of the blocking bill. Senators use this technique to allow some bills to leap over other bills and to jump ahead of the blocking bill. In this way the Texas Senate chooses which bills to consider first, second, third, and so forth.

Given that there are thirty-one members in the Texas Senate, the two-thirds requirement means that any eleven members can effectively prevent any bill from being moved to the floor for debate. This situation gives the minority party the potential to threaten any bill because the minority party usually holds at least

Blocking bill

a bill regularly introduced in the Texas Senate to serve as a placeholder at the top of the Senate calendar; sometimes called a "stopper."

Table 3.5 Calendars in the Texas House of Representatives (Most Important to Least Important)

CALENDAR	PURPOSE
Emergency	Emergency bills; also used for taxation and appropriation bills
Major State	Important bills with statewide impact
Constitutional Amendments	Amendments to the Texas Constitution
General State	Bills with statewide impact deemed less important than those designated "Major State"
Local, Consent, and Resolution	Bills involving activities of specific counties, cities, and other governments; non-controversial resolutions
Resolution	Votes in which the House offers an opinion on some topic but passes no bill on the topic
Congratulatory and Memorial	House resolution expressing gratitude, thanks, or recognition of some person or event but no bills passed on the matter

Source: Compiled by the authors from data available at www.house.state.tx.us/help/calendar.htm.

eleven seats in the Texas Senate. As such, the majority party must regularly consider the opinion of the minority party in order to get legislation passed in the Texas Senate.

When a bill or resolution comes up for debate before the whole chamber, the entire membership engages in a **floor debate.** The sponsors of the bill will arrange for members to speak on behalf of the bill and opponents meanwhile recruit members to speak against the bill. The trick in both cases is gaining recognition from the presiding officer of the chamber for the purposes of addressing the chamber. Amendments to the bill are made at this time. Sometimes a **killer amendment** is introduced. Killer amendments add language to the bill, often on unrelated or controversial topics, aimed at making the bill unacceptable to a majority of the legislature who will then be more likely to vote against the bill.

After the floor debate, members of the chamber vote on the various amendments and then vote on the final version of the bill. This is the "second reading" of the bill (the "first reading" occurred when the bill was introduced to the chamber). In the Texas Senate, the time of debate is unlimited, so any member may speak indefinitely on the bill. Sometimes, a member of the Senate engages in a **filibuster,** an effort to kill a bill by engaging in prolonged debate and refusing to yield the floor to another member. This stalling serves to prevent a vote on the bill from being taken. A filibuster is ended by a majority vote of the Texas Senate. Because debate time is limited in the Texas House, a filibuster cannot occur in that chamber. Although the filibuster does not occur in the Texas House of Representatives, at times members of the house have engaged in lengthy debate over bills that are not controversial. This action is employed especially late in the legislative session and is used to prevent the Texas House of Representatives from beginning debate on a more controversial issue or bill. This technique of delaying action on a bill to prevent the consideration of another bill is called **chubbing.** The representative engaged in chubbing may or may not be in favor of the current bill but is trying to block consideration of the next bill on the Texas House calendar. Again, the filibuster in the Texas Senate and chubbing in the Texas House of Representatives are important tools employed by the minority party in its effort to influence the legislative process and prevent the majority party from railroading bills through the legislature.

Another tool employed by the minority party to influence voting is the **quorum**. To conduct business, Texas Senate rules require that two-thirds of the membership be present to take a vote. Because there are only thirty-one senators, two-thirds of the membership is equal to twenty members. Therefore, any eleven senators may prevent any business from being conducted if they absent themselves from the chamber. Again, this need for a quorum prods members of the senate to consider the opinion of the minority party. Prior to the 1990s, the two-thirds rule allowed the handful of Republicans in the Texas Senate to join with a small number of Democrats to block legislation. Between 1993 and 2002, Republicans had enough seats to use the two-thirds rule in their favor to compel the majority Democratic Party to alter legislation; Democrats, for their part, were often frustrated by this need to accommodate Republican concerns. When Democrats became the minority party in the Texas Senate following the 2002 election, they too quickly discovered the advantages of the two-thirds rule.

After the chamber vote, a "third reading" takes place just prior to the final vote on the bill. While numerous votes are cast, there are broadly speaking two types of votes that occur in the Texas Legislature. Votes on bills and amendments to bills may be a voice vote, in which members call out "aye" or "nay." In the Texas House, votes are

Floor debate
period during which a bill is brought up before the entire chamber for debate.

Killer amendment
language added to a bill on an unrelated or controversial topic in order to make the bill unacceptable to the majority of the legislature who will then vote against the bill.

Filibuster
an effort to kill a bill by engaging in unlimited debate and refusing to yield the floor to another member, ultimately preventing a vote on the bill.

Chubbing
the act of delaying action on the current bill before the Texas House of Representatives to prevent action on an upcoming bill.

Quorum
the minimum number of members in a legislative body who need to be present for it to conduct business; in the Texas Senate, a quorum is eleven members. In the Texas House of Representatives a quorum is one hundred members.

The Killer Bees

No story better reflects the eccentric politics created by the rules of the Texas Legislature than the story of the Killer Bees. The Bees emerged in May 1970 during a battle over whether Texas should have a separate presidential primary in 1980. One side favored a separate primary so that conservative Democrats could cast a vote in a Republican presidential primary for Ronald Reagan or former Texas governor John Connally on March 11 and then return to the Democratic Party in May to outvote the liberals in the primary for other offices. The other side wanted a single primary that would force conservative Democrats to choose a party. Lt. Gov. Bill Hobby nicknamed some of the liberal legislators who resisted his agenda "Killer Bees" because he said he never knew where they would strike next. Opponents of the separate primary were worked into a frenzy when Hobby slipped the primary into an innocuous election bill that had already passed the Texas House and was coming before the Senate. This would have allowed him to get around the two-thirds vote required to pass most bills. With ten days left in the legislative session the Bees had grown to twelve members but knew that they lacked the majority required to block passage under the new rule. However, they also realized that the Senate would lack a quorum and couldn't pass any more bills if all twelve refused to attend.

The Killer Bees took flight and disappeared. Law enforcement was sent to round them up while the rest of the Senate found themselves unable to leave the Senate building as Hobby kept them in the Capitol. For five days the Bees evaded authorities, although nine of them were hiding in an apartment just over two miles from the Capitol. The Texas Rangers nearly caught Sen. Gene Jones after he left the Austin hideout because of claustrophobia. When lawmen arrived at Jones's new hideout, they mistakenly arrested Jones's brother when he answered the door while Senator Jones jumped the back fence.

While Texans might not have usually sided with the liberal-leaning Bees, there was little sympathy for the political interests behind the separate primary bill, and Texans and the nation found themselves caught up in the spectacle of the small band of Bees eluding a statewide manhunt and foiling the powerful forces aligned against them. Eventually, Hobby relented, inviting the Bees back to the Senate after abandoning his maneuvers on behalf of the bill. While the saga of the Killer Bees reads like a surreal adventure, it highlights the problem with the Senate's requirement that a bill be passed with two-thirds of the vote, a threshold that is high enough to allow a determined and creative minority to resist change.

Roll call vote

a form of voting for which a permanent record of each member's vote is created; used with more important votes.

Rider

an addition to a bill that deals with an unrelated subject such as changing some aspect of law or public policy or spending money or creating programs in a specific member's district.

Closed rider

a rider that is not made public until after the legislature has voted on the bill, either when the bill goes to conference committee for reconciliation or when the governor prepares to sign the bill into law.

recorded electronically; in the Texas Senate all votes are voice votes. Normally, however, an important vote is a **roll call vote.** In this instance, a permanent record of how each member voted exists. Some votes may be conducted on paper ballots.

At any time during committee action or floor debate, a member may attach a rider to an appropriations bill. A **rider** is an addition to the bill that deals with an unrelated subject, usually changing some aspect of an existing law or public policy. A rider may also call for the spending of money. Riders often spend money or create programs in a specific member's district. Riders are common in many state legislatures and in the U.S. Congress. In Texas, a rider may be a **closed rider,** a rider that is not made public until after the legislature has voted on the bill. Riders are revealed when a bill goes to a conference committee for reconciliation or when the governor gets ready to sign the bill into law.

Sometimes, legislators cannot be present for votes on the floor of the legislature. The casting of "ghost" votes—essentially having another legislator cast a vote for the missing member, is common practice. Although members of the legislature are supposed to be present when they cast votes, sometimes the clerk of the chamber is unaware that a particular member is not present when votes are taken. In these circumstances, legislators arrange for another member to cast votes for them. In April 2007, Rep. Mike Krusee (R-Williamson County) attended a conference in

London even as he cast some thirty votes on the floor of the House in Austin. Reportedly, Rep. Marc Veasey (D-Fort Worth) punched in votes for Krusee.[57]

Once a bill has passed one chamber of the legislature, the bill goes to the other chamber for consideration. Again, bills dealing with taxation and spending must start out in the Texas House of Representatives before going to the Texas Senate. All other bills may start out in either chamber before going on to the other chamber. As noted above, once both chambers have passed a bill in identical form the bill goes to the governor for signing. If the House and Senate have passed different versions of the same bill, then the bill first goes to a conference committee for reconciliation. The conference committee may attach several amendments or may rewrite the bill. The recommendation of the conference committee is sent back to both chambers of the Texas Legislature in the form of a report. Each chamber may accept the changes to the bill, reject the changes to the bill, or send the bill back to the conference committee. If both chambers accept the changes, the bill has passed. If the bill fails to pass either chamber or the conference committee cannot reconcile the differences, the bill dies. If a bill has not been passed by the legislature before the end of the session, the bill dies as bills do not carry over to another legislative session. Twenty-four states, but not Texas, allow some form of carryover.[58]

After a bill is sent to the governor, he or she must sign the bill into law or veto the bill. If the governor does not sign the bill into law, after ten days the bill automatically becomes law. While the governor possesses the power to veto legislation, the power of the governor to veto bills is limited. For all bills but those dealing with spending, the governor must veto or accept the entire bill. The governor may use a **line-item veto,** or a selective veto of some parts of a bill, on spending bills only. An override of the governor's veto is possible only by a two-thirds vote of each house of the state legislature. If the legislature ends its session, the governor has twenty days to veto the bill; otherwise, the bill becomes law. Ninety days after the legislature ends its session, any law enacted becomes effective unless the bill contains an **emergency clause,** which makes a bill effective immediately upon being signed into law.

Line-item veto
the ability of the executive to selectively veto only some parts of a bill; in Texas available only on spending bills.

Emergency clause
language that makes a bill effective immediately upon being signed into law rather than subject to the customary ninety-day waiting period.

Winners and Losers

Historically, legislative organization and process have produced clear winners and losers in the game of Texas politics. The relatively weak position of parties, coupled with the dominance of the Democratic Party, produced a system that concentrated power in the hands of the presiding officer. Thus, the two most powerful positions in Texas have been the Speaker of the House and the lieutenant governor in the Senate. The amount of power in these two offices, often unchecked by an institutionally weak legislature and governor, creates the exact type of concentrated power the framers were trying to avoid. While Speaker Craddick attempted to maximize the authority and power of the Speakership, he did so at his own peril. As the opening vignette about Speaker Straus replacing Speaker Craddick illustrates, those offices, although seemingly untouchable, do face limits. Members may revolt and replace the Speaker. The Speaker of the House courts support from individual legislators and rewards supporters with favorable consideration of legislation and committee assignments. To the extent that the Texas model creates a system in which power is concentrated in the hands of the presiding officers of the state legislature, a vigorous system of checks and balances often seems absent.

Paradoxically, recent attempts to organize the party caucuses and raise the level of partisanship within the Texas Legislature may have detrimental effects. The current bipartisan system that allows the minority party significant influence in the Texas Senate and Texas House of Representatives may in fact erode. Because service in the Texas Legislature in Austin may be a precursor to later service in the U.S. House of Representatives in Washington, D.C., the tradition of bipartisan cooperation in the state legislature has historically translated into a bipartisan congressional delegation from Texas in the U.S. Congress. Recently, one group of scholars has suggested that Texas's domination of leadership positions in the U.S. Congress (for example, the Speakerships of Sam Rayburn and Jim Wright in the U.S. House of Representatives and the Senate leadership of Lyndon Johnson) reflects the ability of the Texas delegation to build coalitions and get along with various factions within both parties.[59] The Texas federal delegation has long had a reputation for putting party concerns aside to cooperate in the best interests of the state. As a result, Texas has gained outsized influence in the U.S. Congress and has often received more than its share of favorable national legislation and program funding.

If partisan politics trumps the need to work together to accomplish the state's business, the recent increase in partisan divisions at the state and national level may undermine legislators' ability to get things done. Concentration of power in the hands of the presiding officers of the Texas Legislature, and the bipartisan support that results, historically created a different set of incentives and outcomes in Austin than in Washington, D.C. The Texas Legislature was, and for the near term continues to be, different from the U.S. Congress.

Conclusion

Even though progress has been made in boosting women and minority representation, the Texas Legislature still does not "look like" Texas. Moreover, the legacy of Democratic Party control lingers as the two-party system emerges within the legislature itself. Presiding officers exert tremendous control over legislation and the legislative process, the parties remain weaker than might be expected, and the small Texas Senate continues to check the House by allowing the minority party significant influence over outcomes. As the two-party system develops further, a shift toward a more party-centered model of legislative process and organization seems likely.

Key Terms

amendment
bicameral
bill
blocking bill
chubbing
citizen initiative
citizen legislature
closed rider
cohesion
committee
concurrent resolution
conference committee
delegate
emergency clause
filibuster

floor debate
floor whip
gerrymandering
ideological caucus
instant run-off
interim committee
introduce [a bill]
issue caucus
joint resolution
killer amendment
Legislative Budget Board (LBB)
Legislative Redistricting Board (LRB)
lieutenant governor
line-item veto
majority election
majority-minority district
mark-up
minority and women's caucuses
multi-member district (MMD)
nonpartisan or bipartisan independent commission
one person, one vote
oversight
party affiliation
party caucus
party caucus chair
party primary
plurality election
politico
president pro tempore
professional legislature
quorum
redistricting
representation
resolution
rider
roll call vote
run-off election
select committee
simple resolution
single-member district (SMD)
Speaker of the House
Speaker pro tempore
special caucus
standing committee
structuring the vote
term limit
trustee
turnover

Explore this subject further at http://lonestar.cqpress.com, where you'll find chapter summaries, practice quizzes, key word flash cards, and additional suggested resources.

Governor Rick Perry has transformed himself into a national political figure and critic of Washington.

CHAPTER 4

Governors and Bureaucracy in Texas

Something very interesting is happening in Texas right now. The Texas Constitution creates one of the weakest governors in the country, but Texas politics has produced one of the most visible, charismatic, and shrewd governors today. Rick Perry may have less institutional power than governors in other states, but he has used his informal power to transform himself into a national political figure. Governor George W. Bush and Governor Ann Richards did much the same when they occupied the governor's mansion. Anyone who watched his 2010 primary rout of popular Kay Bailey Hutchison can attest to the fact that he's not just really lucky—he's downright astute. In fact, one analyst called him "one of the best natural politicians Texas has ever produced."[1]

Governor Perry has gained influence by using his position as a leader of a large state to claim a leading role in national politics. He has positioned himself as David to the national government's Goliath. Since the election of Barack Obama, Perry has increasingly identified himself as the center of the opposition to federal power. A few years ago Perry opponents were angry about his HPV vaccine mandate, his plans to turn many of Texas's roads into toll roads, and his plans to use eminent domain to create a trans-Texas corridor. Now all of those sins seem forgotten. In one of the best comebacks since that of John Travolta in *Pulp Fiction,* Perry has redefined himself as a guy who is willing to stand up to the federal government for the rest of us.

Though wildly popular in Texas, Perry's anti-federal government stance has not been without controversy. Governor Perry initially said Texas should say "no thanks" to the federal government's stimulus money. However, he eventually requested—and received—$16.5 billion, even as he rejected $555 million that would have required changes to Texas's unemployment law. Perry also rejected a portion of the education stimulus ($700 million) while accepting $3.2 billion in education funds. Perry has consistently argued that Texas will accept no stimulus money that would entail long-term policy mandates.

This David and Goliath battle intensified when the federal government singled out Texas in a later stimulus package. U.S. representative Lloyd Doggett argued that Texas essentially decreased its education funding by $3.2 billion and then supplanted it with federal funds, allowing Texas to spend $3.2 billion on other things.[2] Congress responded in 2010 with a requirement that Texas can receive further education funds only if the governor certifies it will not decrease local school money to offset future funds. Texas is the only state required to make such a certification.

Despite Perry's stated opposition to federal stimulus money, a report from the National Conference of State Legislatures shows that Texas, more than other states, relied on stimulus money to address its budget gap, using it to cover 96.7 percent of the gap.[3] While it is Washington's bailout that allowed Texas to avoid the tough economic decisions other states have been forced to make, Texas is still expecting an $18 billion shortfall for the next budget cycle. Meanwhile, Perry's anti-Washington rhetoric is wildly popular in the Lone Star State and is largely credited with helping him beat Kay Bailey Hutchison in the 2010 primary.

In this chapter, we will examine the Texas governorship, including the formal and informal qualifications of the office. We will then review the powers of the Texas governor, assessing the extent to which the governorship of Texas is institutionally weak. Finally, we will discuss the other members of the plural executive and the accountability of the Texas bureaucracy in general.

As you read the chapter, think about the following questions:

★ What are the formal powers of the Texas governor?

★ Is the Texas governor weak?

★ How might we change the Texas executive?

★ How is the bureaucracy held accountable in Texas?

The Office of the Governor

Texans distrust executive authority. This distrust, common to many other states, stems from the American colonists' experience under the British king and the vast powers exercised by colonial governors. The result was that early on in America most states created relatively weak executives and preferred to vest power in the legislative branch. Texas was no exception. Distrust of governors in Texas was reinforced by Texans' experience under Mexican president Antonio Lopéz de Santa Anna. Indeed, throughout its history Texans have distrusted government in general and—as governors are the most visible manifestation of state authority—governors in particular. This preference was amplified by Texas's experience after the Civil War when military rule gave way to Reconstruction rule that featured a relatively strong governor and a perceived "illegitimate" government. The Constitution of 1876 deliberately weakened the position of governor, granting the governor little formal power, shortening the governor's term to two years, allowing the governor to make relatively few appointments, and instituting other elected executives to rival the governor's power.

As the state has grown and become more complex, the governor's formal power has increased to some degree; nevertheless, the office has failed to keep pace with the demands of modern Texas. The legislature, for example, has granted the governor more appointment power as it has created a growing number of minor state agencies and commissions. The governor's salary, which was notably decreased by the 1876 constitution, is now fairly competitive. And the governor's term was eventually increased from two to four years, affording governors and citizens alike a break between elections. In addition, Texas governors have become increasingly astute at employing informal powers. Texas's size and geographical position create relatively unique opportunities for the state's governor. For example, Texas's international border with Mexico has allowed the state's governors to participate in national policymaking, as Bush did with the North American Free Trade Agreement and Perry with immigration policy. The national focus on border issues has helped strengthen the Texas governorship and raise its profile. In addition, the highly visible role Texas played in the aftermaths of Hurricanes Katrina, Rita, and, more recently, Ike has garnered national media attention. The power of the Texas governor has grown both formally and informally even as Texans' preference for limited government remains entrenched.

The governor of Texas tends to be a national political figure simply by virtue of being governor of such a large state. Although the Texas Constitution vests few formal powers in the governor, as we shall see governors who are skilled politicians and successfully utilize informal powers can become pivotal political figures. Often the pinnacle of a politician's career, governorships are highly visible and can serve as a stepping stone to appointments to state and federal posts and election to national office, including the presidency itself. For example, former Governor Preston Smith served as chair of what is now the Higher Education Coordinating Board; similarly, after his term as governor Price Daniel was selected by President Lyndon B. Johnson to head the Office of Emergency Preparedness and was later appointed to the Texas Supreme Court. Daniel, who had already served the state in a variety of elected and appointed offices, has held more high offices than anyone else in Texas history.[4] After serving as governor of the state, John Connally, who famously survived bullet wounds received when John F. Kennedy was assassinated in Dallas, became Secretary of the Treasury during Richard Nixon's administration. Pappy O'Daniel resigned the governorship to become a U.S. senator. Most notable, of course, is George W. Bush, who left the governor's office to assume the presidency of the United States. Other governors, for example, Bill Clements and Ann Richards, chose not to seek further elected office after vacating the governor's mansion.

Qualifications

The Texas Constitution specifies three requirements to be governor in the state. The governor must be at least thirty years of age, have resided at least five years in the state of Texas, and be a U.S. citizen. (Table 4.1 compares these requirements against those for the U.S. presidency and for governors in other states.) In addition, the constitution stipulates that all state officeholders, including the governor, must believe in a supreme being, a term left undefined in the constitution. The governor of the state is further restricted from holding any other job or receiving outside compensation, a restriction notably absent from the state's legislature. Specifically, the Texas Constitution states:

> The Governor elected at the general election in 1974, and thereafter, shall be installed on the first Tuesday after the organization of the Legislature, or as soon thereafter as practicable, and shall hold his office for the term of four years, or until his successor shall be duly installed. He shall be at least thirty years of age, a citizen of the United States, and shall have resided in this State at least five years immediately preceding his election. (Amended Nov. 7, 1972.)[5]
>
> During the time he holds the office of Governor, he shall not hold any other office: civil, military or corporate; nor shall he practice any profession, and receive compensation, reward, fee, or the promise thereof for the same; nor receive any salary, reward or compensation or the promise thereof from any person or corporation, for any service rendered or performed during the time he is Governor, or to be thereafter rendered or performed.[6]

Table 4.1 Terms and Qualifications of Elected Chief Executives

CONSTITUTIONAL PROVISIONS	TEXAS GOVERNOR	U.S. PRESIDENT	OTHER STATES
Age	30 years	35 years	34 states set minimum age at 30
Residence	5 years	14 years	5 years or less in 38 states
Terms	4 years	4 years (limited to 2 terms of office or 10 years)	48 states allow a four-year term, but 36 states limit number of consecutive terms

Source: Keon S. Chi, *The Book of the States: 2005 Edition,* vol. 37 (Lexington, Ky.: Council of State Governments, 2005).

Beyond the constitutional requirements, Texas governors have tended to share common characteristics. Since 1876, most governors in Texas have been white, Protestant, wealthy men. As Table 4.2 shows, the vast majority of modern governors have had some higher education—mostly in law—and most Texas governors have also had some military experience, ranging from service in the U.S. Army or Navy to service in the Texas National Guard or Texas Air Guard. Although the myth of the Texas rancher or Texas oilman is often used to tap into the Texas legend during gubernatorial campaigns, few modern governors actually have such experience. Notable exceptions include Dolph Briscoe, who was a wealthy cattleman and horse trader, and Governors Clements and Bush, who made fortunes in oil.

Modern governors of Texas have also, by and large, had previous political experience. Many of the state's governors have risen from the ranks of other Texas offices including the Texas Legislature, the Railroad Commission, and often the lieutenant governor's office. Others held national offices prior to becoming governor of the Lone Star State. After serving as U.S. senator, Price Daniel famously declared he would "rather be governor of Texas than the president of the United States" and returned to Texas to run for governor. Other notable examples include Bill Clements, who had been deputy U.S. secretary of defense, and John Connally, who ascended to the governorship after serving as the secretary of the Navy in the Kennedy administration.

Texas has occasionally expressed a willingness to elect governors with no political experience. While inexperienced gubernatorial candidates can tap into Texans' distrust of government, it is a larger-than-life personality that helps make up for lack of experience in public service. James "Pa" Ferguson, for example, had no political experience when he was elected governor in 1914. His popularity was based less on political skill and more on his self-styled image as "Farmer Jim," representing tenant farmers and poor workers across the state. He also impressed audiences by quoting Shakespeare, Jefferson, or Hamilton whenever the opportunity presented itself.[7]

Equally colorful—and perhaps equally ineffectual—was Governor Wilbert Lee "Pappy" O'Daniel. O'Daniel worked at a flour mill and hosted a weekly radio show during which he sold flour; featured his band, the Light Crust Doughboys; and expressed his opinions. Despite his lack of experience, his popularity on the radio helped him win the governor's office—twice—and afterward a U.S. congressional seat. O'Daniel was highly popular as a radio personality; he inspired a character in the Coen brothers' movie *O Brother Where Art Thou.* As governor, however, he proved ineffectual.

Inexperience does not always equate with ineffectiveness. In 1994, George W. Bush ran for governor having had no prior experience in office. Bush did have the

Table 4.2 Texas Governors since 1876

GOVERNOR	PARTY	TERM	MILITARY EXPERIENCE	OCCUPATION	VETOES
Richard B. Hubbard	Democrat	1876–1879	Confederate Army	Lawyer	0
Oran M. Roberts	Democrat	1879–1883	Confederate Army	Lawyer/Educator	13
John Ireland	Democrat	1883–1887	Confederate Army	Lawyer	10
Lawrence Sul Ross	Democrat	1887–1891	Confederate Army	Farmer/Soldier	7
James S. Hogg	Democrat	1891–1895	None	Lawyer/Educator	21
Charles A. Culberson	Democrat	1895–1899	None	Lawyer	33
Joseph D. Sayers	Democrat	1899–1903	Confederate Army	Lawyer	41
Samuel Lanham	Democrat	1903–1907	Confederate Army	Lawyer	32
Thomas M. Campbell	Democrat	1907–1911	None	Lawyer/Railroad Exec.	32
Oscar B. Colquitt	Democrat	1911–1915	None	Lawyer/Editor	60
James E. Ferguson	Democrat	1915–1917	None	Banker/Lawyer/Farmer	29
William P. Hobby	Democrat	1917–1921	None	Editor	19
Pat M. Neff	Democrat	1921–1925	None	Lawyer/Educator	58
Miriam A. Ferguson	Democrat	1925–1927	None	Housewife	30
Dan Moody	Democrat	1927–1931	TX National Guard in WWI	Lawyer	101
Ross Sterling	Democrat	1931–1933	None	President of Mobil Oil	7
Miriam A. Ferguson	Democrat	1933–1935	None	Housewife	24
James V. Allred	Democrat	1935–1939	U.S. Navy in WWI	Lawyer	48
W. Lee O'Daniel	Democrat	1939–1941	None	Businessperson/Salesperson	48
Coke Stevenson	Democrat	1941–1947	None	Lawyer/Banker/Rancher	56
Beauford Jester	Democrat	1947–1949	U.S. Army in WWI	Lawyer	19
Allan Shivers	Democrat	1949–1957	U.S. Army in WWII	Lawyer	76
Price Daniel	Democrat	1957–1963	U.S. Army in WWII	Lawyer/Educator/Rancher	42
John Connally	Democrat	1963–1969	U.S. Navy Reserve in WWII	Lawyer/Rancher	103
Preston Smith	Democrat	1969–1973	None	Businessperson	92
Dolph Briscoe	Democrat	1973–1979	U.S. Army in WWII	Rancher/Banker	72
Bill Clements	Republican	1979–1983	None	Oilman	78
Mark White	Democrat	1983–1987	TX National Guard	Lawyer	95
Bill Clements	Republican	1987–1991	None	Oilman	112
Ann Richards	Democrat	1991–1995	None	Teacher/Campaigner	62
George W. Bush	Republican	1995–2000	TX Air National Guard	Oilman/Businessperson	95
Rick Perry	Republican	2000–	U.S. Air Force	Farmer/Rancher	204

Source: Compiled by the authors using data from University of Texas at Austin, Liberal Arts Instructional Technology Services, http://texaspolitics.laits.utexas.edu/html/exec/governors/index.html.

benefit of name recognition from his father's presidency and enjoyed a conservative reputation in an overwhelmingly conservative state. As governor, Bush was known for his ability to forge bipartisan coalitions. He successfully supported several education initiatives and state tax cuts and was a relatively popular governor.

One of the most consistent traits of Texas governors throughout the state's history is their conservative bent—and their Democratic Party affiliation. Nothing is more ingrained in the Texas legend than the Democrats' hold on the state, which, until recently, has been nearly absolute. The state has had only three Republican governors since 1876, beginning with Bill Clements who finally broke the Democrats' winning streak in 1978. The dissolution of the Democratic Party monopoly is one of the most significant changes experienced by the state in recent years. The change is particularly noteworthy because it has brought with it an almost complete reversal in party affiliation. Democratic Party dominance has given way to Republican Party control, and the recent trend of electing Republican governors will likely continue in the near future.

Ironically, relatively few early Texas governors were born in the state. Since statehood, just twenty-one out of forty-six governors, or 46 percent, have been native-born. Indeed, Texas's first native-born governor was the state's twentieth, James Stephen "Jim" Hogg, elected in 1890. Hogg was a Democrat who nonetheless brought progressivism to the state. Texans appreciated him for protecting the interests of ordinary people rather than those of big business. Hogg also earned his place in Texas folklore by famously naming his only daughter "Ima." The myth that he named a second daughter "Ura" persists today, though in fact no such person existed. Modern governors have been much more likely to be born in Texas, although Pappy O'Daniel and George W. Bush are both notable exceptions.

Although nearly all of the state's governors have been white men, Texas has also had two women governors. In 1924, Miriam A. "Ma" Ferguson became the first woman governor of Texas and the second woman governor in the United States after Wyoming's Nellie T. Ross was sworn in just two weeks prior to Ma Ferguson. After her husband had been impeached and prevented from holding office in the state, Ma Ferguson ran as a proxy, with the campaign slogan "two governors for the price of one." Ironically, Pa Ferguson had actively opposed women's suffrage, arguing that a woman's place was in the home. Thus, the women's suffrage movement opposed Ma Ferguson's election, though she would go on to appoint the first female secretary of state in Texas, Emma C. Meharg. Ma Ferguson's administration opposed the Ku Klux Klan (she passed an anti-mask law that the courts subsequently overturned), contested prohibition laws, and called for fiscally conservative economic policy. However, Ma Ferguson's administration is perhaps best known for accusations of widespread corruption. During her administration, more than 2,000 pardons were granted leaving the impression that pardons were for sale under the Fergusons. Ma claimed that most of the pardons were given to liquor law violators who were not really criminals, though in fact hundreds of pardons were granted to violent felons as well.[8] Ma lost her bid for reelection in the next two gubernatorial races, but was elected governor again in 1932, becoming the first governor in Texas to serve two non-consecutive terms.

More recently, Ann Richards was elected governor of Texas in 1990. Richards personifies the iconic Texas image: cowboy boots, straight talk, and a reputation for being tough. Richards had experience on the Travis County Commissioners Court and as the Texas state treasurer. A former teacher, Governor Richards decentralized education policy, encouraged economic growth, and promoted women and minorities during her administration. In contrast to Ma Ferguson, Richardson became

Ann Richards

As governor of Texas, Ann Richards reflected both new and old Texas, embracing the transformation of the state while remaining rooted in its traditions. She challenged the historical male dominance of state offices as Texas's "good ole boys" loosened their generations-old grip on state governance. While changing the way things were done, Richards proved equally fluent in the language and symbols of traditional Texas.

Richards moved up quickly in the ranks of state politics. After teaching junior high school social studies while raising her family, she entered government in 1976, winning a seat on the Travis County commission. Richards fit easily into the small-town image revered in Texas, often proclaiming proudly that her father came from a town called Bugtussle and her mother from one called Hogjaw. In 1982 she won election as state treasurer and became the first woman elected to statewide office in Texas in fifty years by winning more votes than any other candidate that year.

She campaigned for the governor's office in 1990, calling for a "New" Texas that would offer opportunities to more residents. In the end, she won a hard-fought battle, besting West Texas rancher Clayton Williams. While in office Richards worked aggressively to bring more women and minorities into state government. She made clear that women could find a place in Texas politics, advising them in patently Texas style: "Let me tell you, sisters, seeing dried egg on a plate in the morning is a lot dirtier than anything I've had to deal with in politics." She appointed the first black regent to the University of Texas Board of Regents and brought more black, Hispanic, and female officers into the ranks of the legendary Texas Rangers.

Richards proved to be just as colorful as her predecessors. She once quipped, "Let me tell you that I am the only child of a very rough-talking father. So don't be embarrassed about your language. I've either heard it or I can top it." Like many of the men who came before her, Richards also had flaws, including alcoholism that ended in rehab and a strained marriage that ended in divorce.

She demonstrated repeatedly that women could be tough on crime, dramatically increasing the size of the Texas prison system and limiting the number of prisoners granted parole. She also championed education and environmental causes. Richards looked to modernize the way in which departments were administered and led the state on insurance reform and ethics reform.

While her tongue was sharp, her language was folksy. Richards' style won her a national following when she delivered the keynote address at the 1988 Democratic National Convention. Complaining about George H. W. Bush, the Republican Party's presidential candidate, Richards suggested the Democrats would expose his shortcomings, or, "we're going to tell how the cow ate the cabbage."

Richards championed political activism, saying, "Sometimes it's serendipitous. Good things happen accidentally. But they're not going to happen unless well-meaning people give of their time and their lives to do that." One of her legacies is the Ann Richards School for Young Women Leaders, a school focused on giving girls the education and confidence to serve as leaders in their community. She preached feminism, telling the nation, "Ginger Rogers did everything Fred Astaire did. She just did it backwards and in high heels."

Beaten by George W. Bush in her bid for reelection, Richards remained in the spotlight, making frequent media appearances and working as a political consultant. Asked what she would have done if she had known she would serve only one term, Richards remarked, "I would have raised more hell."

Richards died of esophageal cancer on September 13, 2006. Governor Rick Perry's eulogy summed up her already legendary status. "Ann Richards," he said, "was the epitome of Texas politics: a figure larger than life who had a gift for captivating the public with her great wit." Richards embodied change in a state that has held fast to tradition. She embraced the traditions of the state more than many of the good ole boys, all the while challenging the state's limited role for women and minorities.

a symbol of women's progress in the state, famously displaying a t-shirt of the state capitol with the caption "a woman's place is in the dome."

Although Hispanics have increasingly added their voices to the state's dialog and are both the largest and fastest growing minority in Texas, Texas has yet to elect a Hispanic governor. In 2002, wealthy oil tycoon Tony Sanchez made an unsuccessful bid for the governor's office, spending a reported $59 million of his own money.[9] Although Sanchez lost to Rick Perry, many observers saw Sanchez's campaign as a test of whether the Democratic Party could tap Hispanic voters to loosen the grip of the Republican Party on the state.[10]

Terms

The Texas Constitution of 1876 originally established a relatively short term of just two years for the governor. A preference for short terms, usually one or two years, was common in early American state politics, reflecting a distrust of executive power carried over from the colonial era. Early on, most governors in Texas were elected to two terms, serving a total of four years. In 1972, however, the Texas Constitution was amended, increasing the governor's term to four years. Despite the fact that Texas has no term limits, few governors have been elected to two terms since that time. Dolph Briscoe served six years after he was initially elected to a two-year term, which began in 1973 before the amendment took effect, and was reelected to a second term under the new rules. Governors elected after Briscoe won only a single four-year term until George W. Bush. Bush was the first governor to be elected to a second four-year term, although he resigned in 2000 to become president. Lt. Gov. Rick Perry finished out Bush's term and then ran successful bids for reelection in 2002 and 2006. In 2010, Governor Perry, already the longest serving governor in Texas, won a third term. At the end of this term, he will have served as governor for an unprecedented fourteen years.

Obviously, the longer a governor serves the more likely the governor will successfully pass his or her own political agenda. That Texas has four-year terms with no term limits is a potential source of power for its governors. For instance, Perry has been able to appoint every appointive office in the state; not surprisingly, this has afforded him a broad base of loyalty to his administration. He has also worked with legislators long enough to have cultivated strong supporters in the Texas Legislature.

Succession

Succession
a set order, usually spelled out in the constitution, denoting which officeholder takes over when the sitting governor resigns, dies, or is impeached.

If a governor is unable to fulfill his or her term, the Texas Constitution outlines an explicit line of **succession.** If the governor resigns, is impeached and convicted, or dies while in office, the lieutenant governor succeeds to the governorship. After the lieutenant governor, the line of succession goes next to the president pro tempore of the Texas Senate, then to the Speaker of the House followed by the attorney general. Thus, after the 2000 presidential election, when George W. Bush resigned the governorship to assume the presidency, Lt. Gov. Rick Perry assumed the office and the Texas Senate elected Bill Ratliff as the new lieutenant governor. Ratliff became the first lieutenant governor in the history of the state to serve as lieutenant governor without having first won a statewide election.

When the governor is out of the state, the lieutenant governor is acting governor. Thus, when George W. Bush was running for president, Rick Perry gained considerable hands-on experience in the governor's office. By custom, both the governor and the lieutenant governor arrange to be out of the state at least one day during their term, allowing the president pro tempore of the Senate to act as governor for the day.

Compensation

Originally, the 1876 constitution specified the governor's salary, which meant that a pay raise required a constitutional amendment approved by a majority of voters. In 1954, however, the constitution was amended to allow the Texas Legislature to set the governor's salary. Currently, the Texas governor is paid $150,000, which puts the state above the average of $131,115 for all governors.[11] California has the highest paid governor, with a salary of $212,179; Maine's governor receives the lowest salary, at $70,000. Ironically, governors are paid well below the average $1.36 million annual salary of NCAA Division 1A head football coaches, who receive the largest salaries among state employees.[12]

In addition to salary, the governor's office includes several auxiliary means of compensation. The Texas governor is allocated a travel allowance and use of a state limousine, state helicopter, and state airplane. All fifty states provide an automobile for their governor, while only thirty-nine states provide a state airplane and twenty-three states provide a state helicopter.[13] The governor also has a staff (a few of whom earn more than the governor) to help coordinate his office, as well as drivers, pilots, chefs, housekeepers, and stewards. Depending on the governor, the staff can number anywhere from 200 to over 300 people. In addition, Texas maintains a governor's mansion around the corner from the capitol. Most governors receive free housing, although according to the Council of State Governments Arizona, Idaho, Massachusetts, Rhode Island, and Vermont do not provide a governor's residence. In 2007, Perry moved out of the governor's mansion so that it could undergo renovation. The following year the mansion was severely damaged by a fire, most probably caused by arson. Perry was criticized in 2010 when he asked state agencies to cut spending by 10 percent even as he spent $10,000 a month in state funds on a rented residence.[14] For most fiscally conservative Texans, Perry's excessive housing allowance is at odds with their expectations of government. Moreover, it comes at a time when Perry is asking the rest of the state to tighten its belt in light of the current budget crisis.

Impeachment

The Texas Constitution vests the power of **impeachment** in the Texas Legislature. According to the constitution, the legislature can impeach the governor, the lieutenant governor, attorney general, commissioner of the General Land Office, comptroller, as well as the judges of the Supreme Court, Court of Appeals, and District Court. In order to impeach the governor, the Texas House of Representatives must approve the articles of impeachment (similar to a grand jury indictment) by a simple majority. Impeachment by the Texas House merely suggests that there is enough evidence to proceed with a trial. Impeachments are then tried in the Texas Senate. Conviction requires a two-thirds vote of the Senate. While the Texas Constitution outlines a clear procedure for impeaching the governor, it is silent on what constitutes an impeachable offense.

Pa Ferguson remains the only governor in the state's history to be impeached and removed from office. Ferguson, whose education was limited to sixth grade, balked when the University of Texas Board of Regents refused to let him handpick university presidents or fire university professors who had opposed his governorship. When asked why he wanted to fire the professors, Governor Ferguson famously quipped, "I am governor of Texas, I don't have to give any reasons."[15] To indicate his disapproval with the Board, Ferguson vetoed the university's appropriations. Up to this point, only six American governors had been impeached, and five of those

Impeachment
formal procedure to remove an elected official from office for misdeeds; passage of the articles of impeachment by the House merely suggests that there is sufficient evidence for a trial, which is then conducted by the Senate.

were Reconstruction-era governors in the South.[16] Nonetheless, the Texas Legislature voted to impeach and remove the governor for misappropriation of public funds, and he was subsequently barred from holding a state office again. In spite of that, Ferguson continued to exert significant influence on politics in the state. The day before the impeachment verdict was announced, Ferguson resigned as governor. He would later claim that this made the impeachment verdict obsolete. Amazingly, in 1924, despite his conviction, Ferguson would again run for governor of the state, although an appellate court upheld his prohibition from holding state office. Even this was not enough to prevent Ferguson's influence, as he subsequently convinced his wife Miriam to run for governor in his place.

Powers of the Governor

The office of Texas governor is formally weak, and the position's strength often depends on the officeholder's ability to generate support informally for a policy agenda. In general, strong governors are granted significant appointment power, exert considerable control over the state's budget, and exercise substantial power to veto legislation. The Texas governor's limited enumerated powers in the 1876 constitution can be traced to the governorship of E. J. Davis, and in particular to the belief that Davis's Reconstruction government did not represent most Texans' preferences. The lack of formal powers in the constitution also reflects a very real preference among Texans for limited government—a preference that continues to be prevalent today.

Executive Role

According to the Texas Constitution, the governor of the state "shall cause the laws to be faithfully executed and shall conduct, in person, or in such manner as shall be prescribed by law, all intercourse and business of the State with other States and with the United States."[17] This means the governor must work with the state bureaucracy to administer the laws passed by the state legislature. The success of the governor in guiding the bureaucracy is directly tied to his or her **appointment power,** or ability to determine who will occupy key posts. A bureaucracy led by gubernatorial appointees will be much more responsive to the governor's policy goals than one which is elected independently of the governor and has its own policy agenda to pursue. In Texas, the governor's appointment powers have traditionally been limited, although they have increased in recent years. The Texas governor's appointment power is a paradox created by continual revision of the 1876 constitution. On the one hand, the governor is part of a **plural executive,** sharing administrative powers with other officials that are elected independent of the governor's office (see Table 4.3). Their independence means that often members of the plural executive are not interested in working toward the governor's goals. Since they serve based on popular election rather than gubernatorial appointment, members of the plural executive may have their own policy goals and will often work against each other. They can even represent opposing parties, making the executive more fragmented and less unified than one where the governor appoints other executive members.

On the other hand, while the governor has little influence over the most important statewide officials, Texas has gradually given the governor more control over thousands of minor appointees in the executive branch. Gubernatorial appointees usually share the governor's basic political philosophies and tend to be loyal to the governor. Governors can also make appointments based on patronage. **Patronage**

Appointment power
the ability to determine who will occupy key positions within the bureaucracy.

Plural executive
an executive branch in which the functions have been divided among several, mostly elected, officeholders rather than residing in a single person, the governor.

Patronage
when individuals who supported a candidate for public office are rewarded with public jobs and appointments.

Table 4.3 Texas's Plural Executive

GOVERNOR OF TEXAS

- Acts as chief executive of the state; is elected by the voters every four years.
- Makes policy recommendations to state lawmakers.
- Appoints the secretary of state, members of the state bureaucracy. The governor also appoints individuals to fill vacancies in elected offices between elections.
- Exercises constitutional and statutory duties of the governor, including:
    signing or vetoing bills passed by the legislature.
    serving as commander-in-chief of the state's military forces.
    convening special sessions of the legislature.
    delivering a state of the state address.
    proposing a biennial budget.
    executing line-item veto on budget approved by the legislature.
    granting reprieves and commutations of punishment and pardons upon the
        recommendation of the Board of Pardons and Paroles.
    declaring special elections to fill vacancies in certain elected offices.
    coordinating policy and resources during a crisis.

LIEUTENANT GOVERNOR

- Elected by voters statewide every four years, with no term limits.
- Acts as presiding officer of the Senate.
- Acts as governor temporarily when the governor is out of the state, or assumes the governorship if the governor is impeached, resigns, or dies in office.
- Co-chairs the Legislative Budget Board (with the Speaker of the House) and appoints the senatorial members of that board.

ATTORNEY GENERAL

- Elected by voters statewide every four years, with no term limits.
- Serves as legal representation for the state in court.
- Ensures that corporations in Texas comply with state and federal laws.
- Collects unpaid child support and delinquent state taxes.
- Issues advisory opinions to the governor's office, the legislature, or other state agencies.

COMPTROLLER

- Elected for four-year terms as state's accountant, auditor, and tax collector.
- Collects a variety of state taxes and fees.
- Manages and invests state funds.
- Estimates the amount of revenue the state will generate each year.

AGRICULTURE COMMISSIONER

- Elected by voters statewide every four years, with no term limits.
- Heads the Texas Department of Agriculture and implements all agriculture law.
- Inspects the accuracy of market scales and gas pumps, regulates the use of pesticides, and regulates the quality of agriculture products.
- Promotes agriculture throughout the state.

(continued)

Table 4.3 Texas's Plural Executive, continued

LAND COMMISSIONER
• Elected by voters statewide every four years, with no term limits.
• Heads the General Land Office and administers the state's public lands.
• Makes low interest loans available to veterans.
• Oversees major source of revenue for the state.

SECRETARY OF STATE
• Appointed by the governor, with Senate confirmation, to a four-year term.
• Serves as state record keeper.
• Maintains a list of lobbyist and campaign contributions, issues corporate charters, certifies notaries public, and keeps the official state seal.
• Administers elections, including conducting voter registration drives and certifying election results.
• Acts as chief administrator for the Texas Border and Mexican Affairs.
• Designated as the chief international protocol officer who receives international delegations.

Source: Compiled by the authors, using information from www.governor.state.tx.us/about/duties.

is the act of rewarding political supporters with public jobs such as appointments. Governor Perry has been very generous with his use of patronage to reward supporters to his campaign. According to a recent study, approximately one-third of Perry's appointees made campaign donations, contributing on average $3,769; Perry received an additional $3 million from his appointees' employers.[18] Governor Perry has earned a reputation for appointing big donors to University Regents positions. One watchdog group reported that the governor collected $6.1 million from 97 of the 155 non-student Regents appointments he has made during his tenure in office.[19] In addition, two Texas Tech regents have alleged that Perry's office pressured them to resign once they announced that they were supporting Kay Bailey Hutchison in her failed attempt to win the Republican primary in 2010.[20]

The governor's single most significant appointment is that of secretary of state, although the governor appoints other important positions, including the adjutant general, health and human services commissioner, and the state education commissioner. The governor also designates over 2,000 appointments to various boards and commissions in Texas. The governor's appointment of board members

Rick Perry is sworn in as governor of Texas while his wife and children look on. In Texas, the governor is part of a plural executive whose other members may have goals different from the governor's.

typically occurs where the legislature has specifically granted the governor that power. The members of two boards, the Railroad Commission and the State Board of Education, were originally appointed by the governor but are today elected. The governor can also appoint members to fill elected positions that are vacated before their term has expired.

The governor's appointment power is limited by the terms of those serving on the board. Typically, members of Texas boards or commissions serve staggered six-year terms that overlap the governor's term. This means that a governor will not have appointed a majority of any board or commission until the end of his or her first term. However, governors who can successfully obtain a second term will eventually appoint all of the members of the boards and commissions in the state. Thus, the longer the tenure of the governor, the more effective the governor's appointment power will be in achieving the governor's policy goals.

The Texas Constitution mandates that all gubernatorial appointments be approved by a two-thirds vote in the Texas Senate. This is a stricter requirement than that of presidential appointments, which are approved with only a simple-majority vote in the U.S. Senate.[21] Since the Texas Legislature is in session only 140 days biennially, often it is necessary to fill a position while the Senate is not in session. In such cases, the governor can make a provisional appointment, but such **recess appointments** require Senate approval within ten days of the next session. The Senate also maintains a custom called **senatorial courtesy.** Any appointees must have approval of their own state senator in order to obtain the support of the Senate. If the appointee's senator does not support the appointment, then the Senate will not consent to the appointment.

Governor Perry, whose long tenure has given him unprecedented control over the state's appointments, has pursued a practice designed to expand the governor's appointment power even more. During the 2007 legislative session, Perry allowed nearly 400 appointments to expire, replacing a mere 12 percent with new appointments or reappointments.[22] If an appointment expires, typically the old appointee continues to serve, thus circumventing senatorial approval. Perry merely had to wait until the legislative session ended to make his appointments to deprive the Texas Senate of its power of confirmation. One of the most controversial examples centers on Transportation Commissioner Richard R. "Ric" Williamson, whose term expired in February 2007. Williamson had taken the lead on Perry's controversial plan to expand toll roads throughout the state. By not reappointing Williamson when his term expired, Williamson continued as Transportation Commissioner while Perry avoided what would have been an ugly battle to try to get Williamson reconfirmed in the Senate. Any appointments made after the end of the 2007 session would not face Senate confirmation until the legislature reconvened in 2009.

Gubernatorial appointment power contributes to the so-called revolving door phenomenon (see Chapter 8). The revolving door refers to the movement of individuals from government jobs to highly paid lobbying jobs. Texas does not require a waiting period between leaving a government job and taking a lobbying position, unlike the national government and the thirty states that require a break of up to two years between a government position and a lobbying position. Texas does have a law prohibiting heads of state agencies and commissioners from lobbying their former agencies for two years, though they are permitted to lobby other governmental agencies during that time. At least seventeen of Perry's former aides now work as lobbyists.[23]

Finally, with the appointment power comes the **removal power.** A governor's appointees are able to exercise much greater autonomy if the governor lacks the power to remove them from their posts subsequent to their appointment. In Texas

Recess appointment
a gubernatorial appointment made while the Senate is not in session; requires Senate approval within ten days of the next legislative session.

Senatorial courtesy
the informal requirement that a gubernatorial appointee have approval of her or his own state senator in order to obtain support within the Senate.

Removal power
the power of the governor to remove an appointee; in Texas, the governor may remove his or her own appointees with the consent of two-thirds of the Texas Senate.

today, the governor can remove his or her own appointees but is required to obtain two-thirds support of the Senate to do so.

In addition to appointment and removal powers, a governor's ability to influence both the legislature and the bureaucracy is significantly influenced by the gubernatorial **budget power.** In a strong executive model, such as that of the national government, the executive exerts considerable influence on the budget by proposing the budget that the legislature will consider. However, in Texas the governor's budgetary powers are notably weak. In 1949, the Texas Legislature created the Legislative Budget Board to seize budgetary power from the executive branch. Since then, the Legislative Budget Board, co-chaired by the lieutenant governor and the Speaker of the House, has dominated the budgeting process. While the governor may still prepare his or her own budget, recent governors have viewed this as a waste of time since the legislature favors its own budget and typically ignores the governor's version.

The governor does exert some power over the budget through the line-item veto, which allows the governor to strike out particular lines in an appropriations bill without vetoing the entire bill. However, even this power is limited in Texas, where a significant portion of the budget each year is earmarked for specific purposes and therefore cannot be vetoed.

Legislative Role

In addition, the governor plays an important **legislative role** in the state. The governor can directly influence the state's legislative agenda through the **state of the state address.** According to the Texas Constitution, the governor will inform the legislature of the condition of the state at the beginning of each legislative session, as well as at the end of his or her term. Thus, at the beginning of the 81st legislative session in Texas, Governor Perry proposed a variety of new initiatives, including a tax cut for small business owners, legislation allowing public schools to adopt e-texts, and increased accountability requirements for Texas K–12 schools. The state of the state address can act as an important means of gubernatorial influence on the legislative agenda.

Governors in Texas also often issue executive orders. Although the power to issue executive orders is not enumerated, governors have often issued them to advance their agenda. For instance, Governor George W. Bush issued executive orders to create a committee to promote adoption, a task force on illegal gambling, and a citizen's committee on tax relief. Governor Perry has also issued a number of executive orders, though he has often been criticized for using them to increase the power of the governor's seat and to circumvent the legislature.

Perry's most controversial executive order would have required that all sixth-grade girls in Texas public schools receive the human papillomavirus (HPV) vaccine, designed to decrease the rates of cervical cancer. The order also provided an option for parents to opt out of the vaccine. Both liberal and conservative Texans across the state opposed the governor's power grab. Eventually, the legislature passed a bill that prevented the vaccine from being required for school enrollment.

Interestingly, this was not the first time Governor Perry attempted to significantly increase his formal powers through the use of the executive order. In 2005, Perry issued an executive order that shortened from one year to six months the time it took coal-fired electric plants to obtain permits. Perry argued that the state was facing a shortage of energy and needed more plants. In 2007, a state district judge ruled that Perry lacked the authority to shorten the hearing time.[24] In several other

Budget power

the executive's ability to exert influence on the state's budget process.

Legislative role

the executive's role in influencing the state's legislative agenda.

State of the state address

the constitutional requirement that the governor address the state legislature about the condition of the state; the state of the state address occurs at the beginning of each legislative session as well as at the end of the governor's term.

instances, Perry issued executive orders requiring the Texas Education Agency to implement changes in education policy that had failed to pass the legislature.[25]

An important legislative function is the governor's power to call the legislature into **special session,** "on extraordinary occasions." According to the constitution, the governor may convene a special session for thirty days and determine the agenda for the session. This process stands in contrast to thirty-six states that allow the members of the legislature or the legislature and its presiding officers to call a special session. Thirty-nine states allow the legislature to determine the topic of the session, including some states that require the governor to call the legislature into session. Thirty-three states place no limit on the length of special sessions.

In Texas, governors have used these sessions to force the legislature to address the governor's legislative proposals. In 2003, for example, Governor Perry called three special sessions after the Texas Legislature had failed to redistrict the state during the regular session. More recently, Perry called the legislature into a special session to address issues left unresolved by the 81st Legislature, including the authorizations of five Texas agencies, including the Texas Department of Transportation, that were under sunset review. Obviously, this tool can be an effective source of power for a governor, although one that may come at a price. The cost of a special session runs well over $1 million per thirty-day session, and governors who use this tool too often risk angering voters.

One of the most important legislative tools of the governor is the **veto power.** The governor in Texas possesses a variety of tools that ensure his or her influence on legislation. Legislation passed by the legislature can be signed or vetoed by the governor within ten days. If the governor does neither, the legislation will automatically become law. If the governor chooses to veto legislation, the Texas Legislature needs a two-thirds vote in both houses in order to override the veto. Vetoes rarely achieve the two-thirds support necessary to be overridden. The last time the legislature successfully overrode a governor's veto in Texas was in 1979. In Texas, the governor's veto power is buttressed by the short legislative session where most bills are passed at the end of the 140 days. Passing bills late in the legislative session increases the likelihood that the legislature will no longer be in session when the veto occurs. After the legislative session is adjourned, the governor gets an additional twenty days to act on all bills still under consideration. A **post-adjournment veto,** or a veto that occurs after the legislature has adjourned, is absolute as there is no way for the legislature to overturn it. Recent governors have been increasingly willing to use the veto; Governor Perry has vetoed more legislation than any previous governor and has made regular use of the post-adjournment veto.

The veto is one of the most important sources of legislative influence for the Texas governor. In order to avoid a veto, the governor's position on any proposed legislation theoretically should be taken into account during the writing of the bill. This makes the true impact of the veto power difficult to assess. It is important to note, however, that a governor who vetoes a considerable amount of legislation runs the risk of being perceived weak; a large number of vetoes indicates that a governor did not exert sufficient influence on proposed legislation earlier in the legislative process.[26] A governor who successfully used the threat of a veto to gain legislative compromise without actually having to veto legislation is doubtless more powerful than a governor who has to actually resort to the veto.

Governor Perry has earned a reputation for frequent use of the veto power. Since taking office, Perry has vetoed an average of fifty bills a session, considerably more than the average of thirty-one bills for Governors Bush and Richards.

Special session
the ability to require the legislature to meet outside its regular session; in Texas the governor can invoke this power "on extraordinary occasions" for a thirty-day period to consider an agenda the governor has predetermined.

Veto power
the formal power of the executive to reject bills that have been passed by the legislature; in Texas, a veto can be overridden only by a two-thirds vote in both houses.

Post-adjournment veto
a veto that occurs after the legislature has adjourned, leaving the legislature unable to overturn it.

Moreover, on Father's Day in 2001, in what has been dubbed the Father's Day Massacre, Perry vetoed a record eighty-three bills, more than any other governor in Texas history. Because these were post-adjournment vetoes, the legislature could not overturn them.

The Texas governor has also been granted line-item veto authority on appropriations bills. The **line-item veto** allows the governor to veto a specific line or lines out of an appropriations bill without vetoing the entire bill. The Texas governor is one of thirty governors in the country given this power over appropriations bills.[27]

Judicial Roles

Framers of the Texas Constitution of 1876 sought to limit the power of the governor by making all state and county-level judges elective rather than appointed posts. In spite of this, the governor of Texas often makes a significant number of judicial appointments to fill vacancies in between elections, subject to senatorial approval. These judicial appointments can be a significant source of gubernatorial influence over the judiciary, since the vast majority of incumbent judges in Texas win reelection.

In addition, the Constitution of 1876 originally granted the governor the authority to "grant reprieves, commutations of punishment and pardons."[28] This power was curbed after Ma and Pa Ferguson were accused of abusing this power by selling pardons. In 1936, a constitutional amendment created the Board of Pardons and Paroles authorized to recommend **pardons** in the state. Today, the governor can grant clemency or mercy only with the recommendation of a majority of the Board of Pardons and Paroles. The governor exercises some influence over the Board, as members are appointed by the governor with senatorial approval. While the governor is not bound to follow the Board's recommendations and grant clemency, he or she can grant no clemency absent the Board's recommendation. The governor can also independently grant a one-time, thirty-day stay of execution in death penalty cases.

Other Roles

The Texas governor fulfills many formal and informal roles. The governor performs a variety of what might otherwise be viewed as **ceremonial duties**. Because the governor is the state's most visible officeholder, the carrying out of ceremonial roles can in fact become important sources of power for the politically savvy governor. Since the September 11, 2001, attacks, the governor's role as **crisis manager** has also become increasingly important.[29] How governors handle crises in the post–War on Terror and post–Katrina era increasingly corresponds with their degree of constituent support. For instance, most Texans had a positive view of Governor Perry's handling of Hurricane Katrina. Perry's policies were generous to evacuees (offering temporary housing and opening Texas's public schools to evacuees) and also fiercely protective of Texas (obtaining reimbursement from the federal government for the costs). Indeed, in a poll taken in the months following Hurricanes Katrina and Rita, Perry's approval rating increased by ten percentage points, and Texans polled indicated that "[t]hey felt like [Perry] was compassionate for those who were displaced and that he fought to make sure Texas did not get stuck for the cost."[30] Though these highly visible roles can be critical sources of power, particularly for a charismatic governor, traditional sources of power for the governor continue to revolve around his or her executive and legislative roles.

Line-item veto
the ability of the executive to selectively veto only some parts of an appropriations bill.

Pardon
an executive grant of release from a sentence or punishment in a criminal case.

Ceremonial duty
an appearance made by the governor as the most visible state officeholder that can function as a source of power; includes appearances at events and performance of ceremonial functions.

Crisis manager
the responsibility to act as a policymaker, coordinator of resources, and point person in the wake of natural and man-made disasters.

Military Roles

Finally, the governor of Texas is commander-in-chief of the Texas National Guard and the Texas State Guard. The governor appoints the Adjutant General to command these units. The Texas National Guard remains under the governor's control unless it is being used for national service. Many in the Texas National Guard have served in Iraq and Afghanistan recently under the direction of the president. If the Texas National Guard is unavailable, the Texas State Guard can be called into action for state emergencies, as it was during Hurricanes Katrina and Rita.

In 2006, the U.S. Congress restricted a governor's power over National Guard troops during natural disasters. During the chaos following Hurricane Katrina, President George W. Bush sought federal control over guardsmen in Louisiana, but Louisiana Governor Kathleen Blanco refused to hand over power.[31] Prior to 2006, governors had sole control of the National Guard during a crisis within their state, though the president could take command of the guard for national service and domestically in times of insurrection. After Katrina, Congress expanded the president's domestic power and now allows the president to take control of troops during "natural disaster, epidemic, or other serious public health emergency, terrorist attack or incident" if the president determines that state authorities "are incapable of maintaining public order."[32] Not surprisingly, all fifty state governors objected to this expansion of federal power.

Texas Governor: Weak?

Most analyses suggest that the Texas governorship is an institutionally weak position. Scholar Thad Beyle has created an index of institutional power that takes into account the extent to which a state's executive is plural; the governor's ability to serve additional terms; the degree of appointment power, control of budget, and veto power wielded by the governor; as well as whether or not the governor's party controls the legislature. Based on these criteria, the governorship in Texas is indeed weak compared to other states' executives. The Texas governor's institutional power score is 3.2 on a five-point scale; thirty-four of the fifty states have governors with more institutional powers than Texas[33] (see Map 4.1). On the other hand, because Texas is such a large, visible state, the governor has the potential to significantly expand his or her power through informal sources. In Texas it is often the case that "personality transcends policy."[34] Thus, in spite of the lack of vigorous institutional powers, the Texas governor has often managed through visibility, charisma, and personal power to become a presence in national politics.

Informal Powers

As we have already pointed out, the ability of the Texas governor to accomplish a legislative agenda will depend in large part on her or his **informal power.** Four important attributes of informal, or personal, power include a governor's electoral mandate, political ambition ladder, personal future as governor, and performance ratings.[35]

The greater the electoral victory of a governor, the more the governor can claim that his or her agenda has a **popular mandate.** The legislature is less willing to challenge a popular governor. Thus, when more than two-thirds of the voters voted for George W. Bush as governor in 1998, the legislature was inclined to work with his policy proposals. During his first term, Bush earned a reputation as a bipartisan

Informal power
an attribute of personal power based on factors such as electoral mandate, political ambition ladder, personal future as governor, and performance ratings rather than on constitutionally enumerated powers.

Popular mandate
the claim that a newly elected official's legislative agenda is the will of the people based on a high margin of victory in a general election.

Map 4.1 Governers' Institutional Powers

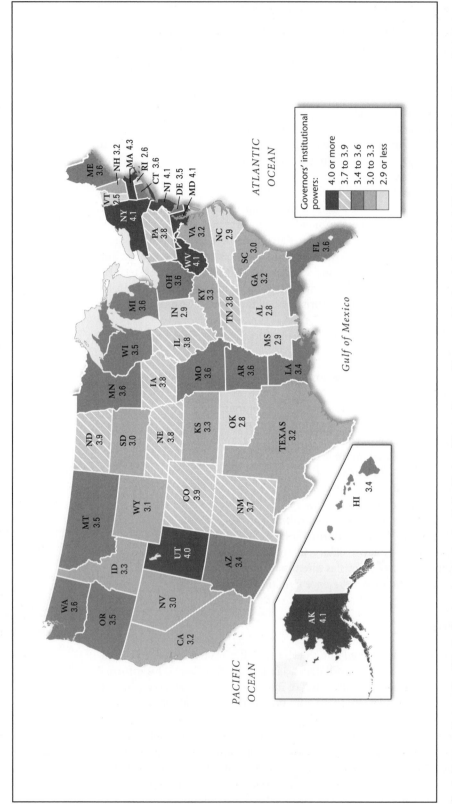

Source: Map created by International Mapping Associates based on data found in Thad Beyle and Margaret Ferguson, "Governors and the Executive Branch," in Politics in the American States: A Comparative Analysis, 9th ed., ed. Virginia Gray and Russell L. Hanson (Washington, D.C.: CQ Press, 2008), Table 7-5.

Texas versus Louisiana

Strong, interesting personalities have often dominated the governor's office in Texas. Sam Houston, Ma and Pa Ferguson, Pappy O'Daniel, and Ann Richards all have left their mark on Texas politics. A neighbor to the east, Louisiana, is not without its own brand of larger-than-life politics. Louisiana's first governor, William C. C. Claiborne (1812–1816), was known for his attempts to arrest the notorious pirate Jean Lafitte, a popular figure who attained "Robin Hood" status in the state. Claiborne went so far as to offer his own money as a bounty for Lafitte's capture, an act which allegedly prompted Lafitte to place a bounty on the governor's head. The twentieth century saw its share of larger-than-life figures who dominated the Louisiana state capitol building in Baton Rouge. Jimmy Davis ran for governor in the 1940s and again in the 1960s. He was known for taking out his guitar at campaign stops and singing the song "You Are My Sunshine," which Davis is credited with having written. Edwin Edwards, who served several terms in the 1970s through the early 1990s, was noted for piling up various indictments in federal court on racketeering charges, some related to his frequent visits to Las Vegas and other world-famous gambling locations. Probably the best known Louisiana politician is Huey Long, the Populist governor and "Share the Wealth" advocate who was assassinated in the state capitol building in 1935.

Lesser known both inside and outside Louisiana is Oscar K. Allen, also known as "O. K. Allen." Allen was a schoolteacher from rural Winn Parish who served in several local elected offices and the Louisiana Senate. In the Senate, Huey Long picked Allen to be the Democratic Party floor leader. Long also appointed Allen chair of the State Highway Commission. In these capacities, Allen served in both the executive and legislative branches of government simultaneously. When Long was elected to the U.S. Senate, he handpicked Allen as his successor.

The subsequent election of Allen as governor surprised no one in Louisiana. More startling was Allen's own willingness to acknowledge Long as the source of his power. Long openly directed Allen's agenda as governor, making almost daily telephone calls to instruct Allen on what to do.[i] Even the special session of the legislature in 1935 that Long was observing when he was assassinated was formally called by Governor Allen per Long's instructions.

Why does Louisiana produce personality-driven politics in the same way as Texas? While the outcome may be the same, the sources are actually different. Texas's geography and weak party system contribute to its personality-driven style of governance. Noted scholar V. O. Key suggested that Louisiana's brand of governance is based upon the tight control of elites over the political system, which serves to produce populist backlash.[ii] Key suggested that Louisiana voters have long been faced with a choice of "outsiders," who use charismatic appeals to the masses to court their votes and then amass political power, versus "insiders," who offer a reform agenda to undo the agenda of the populists.

Thinking Critically

- Why are Texas governors often larger-than-life figures?
- Are Louisiana's governors similar? Why or why not?
- How does this type of candidate affect how you vote?
- Do you feel more connected to interesting personalities? Or are you more interested in campaign issues?

i. Office of the Secretary of the State, "Louisiana Governors: 1877–Present: Oscar K. Allen," www.sos.louisiana.gov/tabid/399/Default.aspx (accessed November 12, 2007).
ii. V. O. Key, *Southern Politics in State and Nation* (New York: Knopf, 1949), 156–182.

player and worked closely with the Speaker and the lieutenant governor to pass legislation on welfare and education reform. In contrast, governors who win by small margins have less political capital when dealing with the legislature and other administrators in the state than governors who can claim an overwhelming mandate. Governor Perry won a second term as governor with support from only 39 percent of voters. Since then, his relationship with the Texas Legislature has become increasingly divisive, and the governor has sought to veto or circumvent the legislature rather than work with it.

Political ambition ladder

the manner in which a political figure has come up through the ranks, working through various levels of state governmental offices and positions on the way to the top position; climbing several levels on the ladder can increase a politician's contacts, allies, and political savvy.

Another indicator of the governor's informal power is the governor's position on the **political ambition ladder.** A governor who has worked his or her way up to the state executive position via other state or local offices will have more allies and political savvy than an individual whose first state office is the governorship and who is learning on the job.[36] Thus, Allan Shivers, a popular Democratic governor, was elected to the Texas Senate and later elected lieutenant governor prior to becoming governor. Shivers was a successful governor, creating the Legislative Council and the Legislative Budget Board, as well as improving education and roads in the state. He is perhaps best known for supporting Texas's claims to Texas tideland by backing Republican presidential candidate Dwight D. Eisenhower who helped Texas maintain control of its off-shore natural resources.

A third indicator of personal power is the governor's personal future as governor. Governors who have the ability to run again or who are at the beginning of their terms have more ability to influence other branches and offices than those governors who are approaching the end of their gubernatorial career.[37] Absent term limits, governors in Texas have the potential to hold office for a significant period of time, amassing political allies and making all important appointments in the state.

A final aspect of the governor's personal power is based on his or her performance ratings. Governors whose public approves of their performance will have greater political capital—and thus a greater ability to influence others in the political process.[38] Since his reelection, Governor Perry's approval ratings have remained low (averaging 40 percent), indicating a limited power base.

Indeed, Beyle's 2007 rating gives the Texas governor a score of 3.8 on a five-point scale, a score that falls just below the mean of 3.9. Only fifteen state governors currently have lower personal power ratings than the Texas governor. Measures of informal power will vary over time and between governors, but it is a good indicator of the importance of informal powers to the governor of Texas.

Personal power in Texas has always been somewhat different than in other states. As noted in Chapter 1, V. O. Key argues that the size of Texas means personal politics frequently gives way to legendary personalities. Texas governors in particular have often been elected for their larger-than-life personalities rather than their ability to lead.

The Texas Bureaucracy

The power of the governor in Texas is limited by the creation of a plural executive. A plural executive results when the power of the executive branch is fragmented among a number of independent offices rather than vested exclusively with the governor.

Texas has six independently elected executive officials. The Texas Constitution states:

> The Executive Department of the State shall consist of a Governor, who shall be the Chief Executive Officer of the State, a Lieutenant Governor, Secretary of State, Comptroller of Public Accounts, Commissioner of the General Land Office, and Attorney General.[39]

Thus, in addition to the governor, the positions of lieutenant governor, attorney general, comptroller of public accounts, public land commissioner, and agriculture commissioner are elected to four-year terms. Because each of these individuals is elected independently of the others, they often disagree on priorities in the state, can be from different parties, and once elected possess their own independent electoral mandate for their policy agendas. A seventh major executive office, the secretary of state, is the only position in Texas's plural executive that is appointed by the governor. Although many other states elect other members of their executive, Texas is one of only eight states without a formal executive cabinet.[40]

Lieutenant Governor

The office of the lieutenant governor is often considered the most powerful position in Texas. The lieutenant governor is elected by voters statewide every four years, with no term limits. If the position becomes vacant, the Texas Senate elects from their membership a person to serve as the lieutenant governor until the next election. The lieutenant governor is the presiding officer of the Senate where he or she exerts great influence on both the debate and the bills that reach the floor. Although this position is mainly legislative in nature (as discussed in Chapter 3), it is also constitutionally granted some executive authority. The primary executive function of the lieutenant governor is to assume the governorship temporarily when the governor is out of the state, or permanently if the governor is impeached, resigns, or dies in office. In terms of executive powers, the lieutenant governor exerts considerable influence on the state's budget. The lieutenant governor co-chairs the Legislative Budget Board (with the Speaker of the House) and appoints the senatorial members of that board.

The current lieutenant governor, Republican David Dewhurst, was elected in 2002 to a four-year term. Previously, Dewhurst had served as land commissioner. As lieutenant governor, Dewhurst pushed through Jessica's Law, which provides for tough penalties for sexual predators. Dewhurst also championed a significant property tax increase and worked to help pass "B on time" legislation, which provides Texas college students zero-interest forgivable loans if they maintain a B average and graduate on time. Dewhurst has become an increasingly controversial leader. Dewhurst's fellow senators have complained about his leadership style, and in 2007 *Texas Monthly* magazine broke with tradition when it included holders of leadership positions (including the governor, the Speaker, and Dewhurst) in its list of top ten worst legislators.

Attorney General

The constitution requires the attorney general to "represent the State in all suits and pleas in the Supreme Court of the State in which the State may be a party."[41] This means that the main function of the attorney general is to serve as legal representation for the state in court. Texas's first constitution provided for the appointment of the attorney general, but subsequent constitutions, including the current one, stipulated that the attorney general be elected. Today the attorney general in Texas is elected in off-year elections to a four-year term, with no term limits. Like Texas, most states elect their attorney general, with only twelve states continuing to appoint the office.

The attorney general's office is involved in a wide range of issues, including pursuing deadbeat dads for unpaid child support, protecting the elderly population of Texas from false consumer and insurance schemes, collecting delinquent state taxes (as it did from Enron in 2005), and recovering fraudulent Medicare and Medicaid payments, to name just a few. The attorney general is also charged with ensuring that corporations in Texas comply with state and federal laws. Thus, in 1894 the attorney general sued John D. Rockefeller's Standard Oil Company and its subsidiary, Waters-Pierce, for antitrust violations. The attorney general successfully made his case, and these companies were barred from doing business in Texas.[42]

One of the most important functions of the attorney general is to issue advisory opinions to the governor's office, the legislature, or other state agencies. For example, in 2007 Governor Perry issued an executive order requiring that all girls receive the HPV immunization before the sixth grade. State senator Jane Nelson disagreed with the governor's mandate and met with Attorney General Greg Abbott, who issued an opinion that the governor's HPV order was merely a suggestion and not legally binding. Once issued, the opinions of the attorney general are rarely challenged and typically carry the weight of law.

The current attorney general, Greg Abbott, was elected in 2002. Prior to becoming attorney general, Abbott had been a judge on the Texas Supreme Court. Once in office, Abbott stressed family and traditional values. As attorney general, he established a Cyber Crimes Unit used to arrest Internet predators, as well as a Fugitive Unit with the aim of arresting sex offenders who violate their parole. In 2005, he also successfully defended the display of the Ten Commandments at the state capitol building before the U.S. Supreme Court. Abbott, who has not been shy about his desire for higher office, recently gained national attention when in 2010 he joined attorneys general from thirteen other states in a lawsuit opposing the national healthcare bill. He also authored an *amicus curiae* brief, signed by twenty-eight other attorneys general, that urged the Seventh Circuit Court to strike down a lower court order declaring the National Day of Prayer unconstitutional.

Comptroller

Elected to four-year terms, the Texas comptroller is the state's accountant, auditor, and tax collector. The comptroller is responsible for collecting a variety of taxes, including the state's sales tax (the largest source of state revenue), fuel tax, franchise tax, alcohol tax, cigarette tax, and hotel tax, to name a few. The comptroller also collects certain fees for the state, including higher education fees, vehicle registration fees, and professional fees. In addition, a 1995 constitutional amendment abolished the office of the treasurer and moved responsibility for managing and investing state funds to the comptroller's office.

Perhaps the most significant aspect of the comptroller's job involves estimating the amount of revenue the state will generate each year. The legislature is prohibited from exceeding the comptroller's estimations, unless four-fifths of both houses approve appropriations that exceed the estimates. Thus, the comptroller exercises a great deal of influence on the state's budget.

This influence can put the comptroller in an unpopular position in the state. Legislators and the governor, often motivated to spend as much money as they can get away with, prefer generous estimates. The comptroller holds the job based in part on making accurate estimates and therefore not creating debt for the state. This can be a particularly difficult job given the biennial time frame of legislative sessions, since the state's budget is based on two-year projections. This tension was behind the 2003 battle between Comptroller Carole Keeton-Strayhorn and the Texas Legislature. Strayhorn, the state's first female comptroller, rankled the governor and the state legislature when she informed them that they faced a $9 billion budget shortfall. The feud between Strayhorn and the legislature culminated in legislation that transferred the comptroller's authority over two programs to the Legislative Budget Board.[43] Strayhorn's insult-trading public brawl with Governor Perry culminated with her run against Perry for governor in the 2006 election.

In 2006, Susan Combs, who had previously been the agriculture commissioner, was elected comptroller. As comptroller, Combs has sought to make finances in the state more transparent by creating a website where citizens can track how money is spent in the state. Her office also transferred hearings on tax disputes to another office in an effort to create a means of settling tax disputes independent of the comptroller's office.

Agriculture Commissioner

The agriculture commissioner is head of the Texas Department of Agriculture, which implements all agriculture laws in the state. The agriculture commissioner inspects the accuracy of market scales and gas pumps, regulates the use of pesticides, and regulates the quality of agricultural products. The office is also charged with promoting agriculture throughout the state. The commissioner oversees school nutrition and in 2003 created the Square Meals program designed to educate children about healthy eating habits. The state also began to limit access to sodas and candy in Texas schools.

The office of agriculture commissioner can be an important rung on the Texas political ambition ladder. After serving three terms as a state legislator, Rick Perry was successfully elected commissioner of agriculture. Perry served two terms before running for lieutenant governor, a position he held until Governor Bush resigned to move to the White House. When Perry vacated the office, Susan Combs became the first woman in the state to hold the position of agriculture commissioner. Combs held the position for two terms before successfully running for comptroller. The current agriculture commissioner, Todd Staples, served as a state representative and state senator prior to his election as agriculture commissioner in 2006.

Land Commissioner

The Texas General Land Office is the oldest agency in the state, dating back to shortly after Texas declared its independence. The head of the General Land Office is the land commissioner, whose primary job is to administer the state's public lands. The land commissioner manages just over 20 million acres of land; she or he is charged with supervising mineral leases and ensuring environmental protection of public lands such as the state's beaches. The general land office also makes low-interest loans available to veterans in the state as part of the Veterans Land Board (which is also chaired by the land commissioner). Since Texas boasts such abundant public lands, the land commissioner's office is a major revenue source for the state. Much of the revenue generated from public lands in Texas is allocated to the Permanent School Fund.

The General Land Office recently began harvesting another natural resource—wind. The vast plains of West Texas produce a lot of wind, and Texas has built large banks of wind turbines in the area. In 2006, Texas surpassed California to become the nation's leader in wind production.[44] In 2007, current Land Commissioner Jerry Patterson added off-shore wind leases to Texas's already profitable off-shore oil industry. Texas has begun leasing wind rights in the Gulf Coast, generating millions of dollars for the state over the life of the leases. Reflecting the Land Office's traditional role as income generator for the state, Patterson boasted that "[t]he future of offshore wind power in the [United States] is right here in Texas, and the Land Office is open for business."[45] Patterson, who has served as land commissioner since 2002, is the sort of larger-than-life character that political scientist V. O. Key suggested would emerge in Texas politics. He flies a 1944 World War II–era plane, chews tobacco, and reportedly carries a gun in his boots. Nonetheless, Patterson remains a controversial land commissioner who has been accused of selling off Texas's public lands and was roundly criticized for his attempt to sell the Christmas Mountains in West Texas.

Secretary of State

The Texas Constitution mandates the office of secretary of state, which is appointed by the governor with Senate confirmation to a four-year term. The traditional function of the secretary of state is that of state record keeper. The office is responsible for keeping records concerning banking and other business activities. The secretary maintains a list of lobbyist and campaign contributions, issues corporate charters, certifies notaries public, and keeps the official state seal. The *Texas Register,* a list of all rules and regulations for the state's bureaucracy, is also published in the secretary of state's office.

An increasingly important function is the secretary of state's role in state elections. The office administers elections, including conducting voter registration drives and certifying election results. The importance of this function was evident in the 2000 election when the Florida secretary of state certified Florida's electoral results for George W. Bush. The Texas secretary of state also oversees Project V.O.T.E. (Voters of Tomorrow through Education), which is designed to teach school-aged children about the process and importance of voting.

Through executive orders, recent governors have expanded the job of the secretary of state, adding three roles to the office. First, the secretary of state is now the chief administrator for the Texas Border and Mexican Affairs, charged with overseeing border issues and Mexican-Texas relations. The secretary has also been designated the chief international protocol officer, in which capacity the secretary receives international delegations. In 2010, Governor Perry added a third role, appointing Secretary of State Hope Andrade as the Texas Census Ambassador. In this role, the secretary was charged with promoting participation in the 2010 census.

The secretary of state is one of the oldest and most honored offices in the state. Texas's first secretary of state was Stephen F. Austin, who, along with Sam Houston, is often referred to as the father of Texas. This office was also one of the first to have a woman in a highly visible state position after Ma Ferguson appointed Emma C. Meharg as the first female secretary of state. In 2008, Governor Perry appointed Andrade, who became the first Latina to serve as secretary of state.

Boards and Commissions

The Texas bureaucracy is a complex system of elected and appointed officials working in conjunction with a wide range of boards and agencies. There are close to 300 boards and commissions in the state—some specified in the constitution, although most have been created by the legislature. Depending on the political mood and particular needs when a board or commission was created, the membership, size, and autonomy of these entities vary greatly. Some boards are elected, providing them a good deal of autonomy; others are appointed, and therefore obligated to the governor or the legislative leadership that appointed its members. Three of the most important state agencies are the Texas Railroad Commission, the State Board of Education, and the Public Utility Commission.

Texas Railroad Commission

The Texas Railroad Commission was created by Governor Hogg to regulate the railroads, decrease corruption, and protect the state's large agrarian population from crooked railroad practices. The Texas Railroad Commission was the first

Texas Railroad Commission

One of the legends of Texas government is the Texas Railroad Commission. While the commission is the oldest regulatory agency in Texas and one of the few elected regulatory agencies in the nation, today the commission fails to live up to its name. In November 1890 Texas voters approved an amendment to the Texas Constitution that empowered the legislature to create an agency to regulate railroads. While the state had initially encouraged the railroads, by the 1890s many Texans, especially farmers, had grown to resent the railroads. The "Texas Traffic Association," an organization made up of the major railroads, set the rates, and with poor roads and unnavigable rivers, Texas farmers had no real alternatives for shipping goods. In 1891 the legislature followed up by establishing the Texas Railroad Commission. Initially, commissioners were appointed by the governor. However, in 1894 voters approved an amendment making the commissioners officials who were elected to six-year terms. Since that time the Texas Railroad Commission has had the unique designation of a regulatory agency headed by elected officials.

Attorney General James Stephen Hogg had made the call for creation of a railroad commission the centerpiece of his campaign for governor. The railroads labeled Hogg "communistic," but his reforms proved popular and his election represented the first stirrings of a populist reform movement in Texas. The creation of the Texas Railroad Commission was proclaimed a way of producing fair competition, but in its actual workings, the commission was used more to restrict out-of-state railroads and protect Texas-based businesses from international competitors.

In the 1920s the Railroad Commission was given responsibility for regulating motor carriers, in addition to railroads. However, responsibility for motor carriers ended in 1994 when trucking was deregulated and responsibility for trucking safety moved to the Texas Department of Transportation (TxDOT).

Today the Railroad Commission oversees oil and natural gas exploration and production, natural gas and hazardous liquids pipeline operations, natural gas utilities, LP gas service, and coal and uranium mining, with about three-quarters of the commission's efforts focused on regulating oil and natural gas exploration and production.

In 2005 the commission's responsibility for rail safety was transferred to the TxDOT, the last step in removing the railroads from the responsibility of the Railroad Commission. While the commission retains the distinction of the state's oldest regulatory agency, nothing remains of its original mission and the Texas Railroad Commission no longer regulates railroads.

regulatory agency in the state and one of the most important commissions in the state's history. The commission is comprised of three members, each independently elected in a statewide contest. The members serve overlapping six-year terms, with one member reelected every two years. By custom, the chair rotates every two years and is the member who is in the last two years of his or her term. Originally created to regulate railroads, the commission's mandate has expanded over time to include regulation of the oil and gas industry, protection of the environment, and promotion of alternative energy sources. There have long been charges that oil and gas interest groups exert too much influence over the commissioners, and the commission struggles with a reputation for emphasizing protection of the oil and gas industry at the expense of environmental protection.

State Board of Education

The State Board of Education is another example of an elected board. It is composed of fifteen members, each elected from single-member districts. The state board's main jobs include approving state curriculum and textbooks, determining passing scores for state educational testing, and managing the Permanent School Fund.

The commissioner of education is appointed by the governor, with Senate approval, from a list of candidates supplied by the board. The commissioner administers the Texas Education Agency, which develops curriculum standards, administers state testing requirements, and accredits and rates schools in the state. In May 2010, the Texas State Board of Education made national news when it adopted new social studies curriculum standards. The new standards questioned the basis for the separation of church and state, stressed the Christian background of the founding fathers, and emphasized states' rights as a cause of the Civil War. Because Texas is such a large textbook market, and publishers accordingly tailor their textbooks to its standards, the board's actions have stirred controversy as Texas's new standards will likely translate into textbook changes across the nation.

Public Utility Commission

The Public Utility Commission (PUC) is an example of an appointed regulatory commission in Texas. The commission is made up of three members, each appointed by the governor, with Senate approval, for six-year overlapping terms. Traditionally, the PUC was charged with regulating phone and energy companies in the state. The commission, acting on its mission to protect consumers from unfair rates and practices, set rates that phone companies and energy companies could charge. The role of the commission has changed over time. In 2002, for example, Texas legislators voted to deregulate energy. Since then, energy prices have fluctuated. The commission continues to be charged with protecting consumers. For instance, in 2001, the Texas Legislature authorized the PUC to create a Texas no-call list.

Bureaucratic Accountability

As we have seen, the bureaucracy of Texas is a complex and diverse array of agency heads, board members, and commissioners who may be elected or appointed to their post. Executive control of the bureaucracy is tenuous at best. As a result, several tools have evolved in Texas that aid the executive in exerting control over the bureaucracy.

Texas utilizes so-called **sunshine laws,** or laws designed to make government transparent and accessible to the people. One such law, the Texas Public Information Act, grants citizens access to government records in the state. Similarly, the Texas Open Meetings Act generally requires governmental bodies to notify the public of the time, date, and nature of scheduled meetings and to open those meetings to the public. City council members from smaller cities have challenged the constitutionality of this requirement in federal court, since for a small council it may mean that two people cannot discuss city business in private. Attorney General Greg Abbot has adamantly defended the Open Meetings Act. Sunshine laws received a significant boost in November 2007 when Texas voters overwhelmingly passed an amendment that requires both houses of the Texas Legislature to record a final vote on bills and make that vote available on the Internet.

In addition, the state enacted a **sunset review process** (see Figure 4.1) to assess all of the statutory boards and commissions in the state. The Sunset Advisory

Sunshine laws
laws designed to make government transparent and accessible.

Sunset review process
a formal assessment of the effectiveness of all statutory boards, commissions, and state agencies.

Figure 4.1 Sunset Review Process

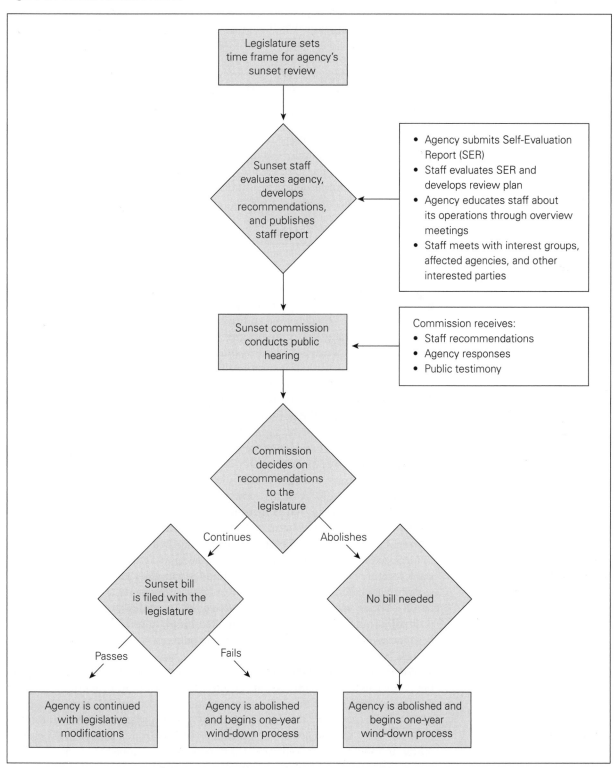

Source: Sunset Advisory Commission, *Guide to the Texas Sunset Process* (December 2009).

Commission was created by the Texas Legislature in 1977 to review the effectiveness of agencies. The commission is made up of twelve members; five members are from the Texas House, appointed by the Speaker of the House, and five members are from the Texas Senate, appointed by the lieutenant governor. The other two members are public members, one appointed by the Speaker and one by the lieutenant governor.

The sunset review process requires most governmental commissions or agencies to be reviewed every twelve years. The commission reviews a self-evaluation report submitted by the agency under review, as well as developing its own reports and holding a public hearing. The commission can then recommend that an agency be continued, reorganized, or merged with another agency. If the commission takes no action, the sun automatically sets on that agency. According to the Sunset Advisory Commission's estimates, since its inception fifty-eight agencies have been abolished and twelve have been consolidated. Estimates from the period 1982–2009 suggest that the commission has saved the state $784 million in that twenty-seven-year span.[46]

Winners and Losers

The creation of an executive who is both vigorous enough to lead the state and act as a check on the legislature but not so powerful as to promote tyrannical tendencies is difficult. The political culture in Texas continues to support the idea that executive power should be relatively limited. However, the potential cost of a weakened executive branch is the lack of a check on the legislative branch—and Texas, with its institutionally weak governor, maintains few checks on its legislative branch. By not making the governor responsible for the budget, Texans lose direct accountability. By denying the governor significant appointment power, Texans stymie the governor's ability to coordinate policy and ensure that laws are executed. In general, Texas's fragmented executive branch leaves a government often working at cross purposes, while the state's citizens pick up the tab. The cost is not only taxes for inefficiency in government, but also a loss of accountability, as few Texans truly know who is in control of any particular process.

A governor who lacks formal power, however, will generally attempt to gain power by other means. When there is a vacuum created by a lack of executive authority and a part-time legislature, a crafty politician can successfully step in. As Governor Perry's influence began to wane he launched an all-out strategy designed to increase the governor's power. Perry's refusal to make most appointments while the legislature is in session denies the Texas Senate their check on gubernatorial appointments. Perry's use of executive orders also indicates a desire to pass preferred policies while circumventing the legislative process. His extensive use of post-adjournment vetoes, often without attempting to inform the legislature that he opposes a bill until he actually vetoes it, subverts the traditional negotiation process between the legislature and the executive.

When the formal structure lags too far behind the needs of the state, enterprising politicians will step in, allowing constraints on power to be left to day-to-day partisan politics rather than to a clear system of checks and balances. The ambiguities of the current system leave politicians scrambling to grab power and make deals. In Texas, the people have continued to resist an overall change in the formal powers granted to the governor even as the state has continued to change and face increasingly complex problems. Texans remain content to allow their political institutions to evolve rather than address a wholesale change in institutional design.

Conclusion

The current structure of the Texas executive was created over 100 years ago in a Texas that was far less complex than the Texas of today. It derives from a political preference for a weak executive that is a legacy of both colonial Americans' dislike of centralized power and an unpopular Reconstruction government in the wake of the Civil War. Historically, Texas voters have favored personality over skill, and governors have typically adopted some version of the legendary "Texan with cowboy boots and straight talk" image in developing their governing persona. This image continues to resonate in the state today. Although the governor's powers remain institutionally weak, strong personalities and the clever use of informal powers have produced governors who can often foil the legislature.

Rather than creating an institutional structure in which an energetic legislature and an energetic executive each possesses enough power to check the other, the Texas system creates an institutional arrangement designed to keep the executive weak. Within that system, especially in recent years, the governor has sought to increase the power of the office informally and, more importantly, undermine the unequal and entrenched institutional distribution of power.

Key Terms

appointment power
budget power
ceremonial duty
crisis manager
impeachment
informal power
legislative role
line-item veto
pardon
patronage
plural executive
political ambition ladder
popular mandate
post-adjournment veto
recess appointment
removal power
senatorial courtesy
special session
state of the state address
succession
sunset review process
sunshine laws
veto power

Explore this subject further at http://lonestar.cqpress.com, where you'll find chapter summaries, practice quizzes, key word flash cards, and additional suggested resources.

County courthouses, like this one in Bandera, Texas, sit in the center of a town's square and epitomize the state's respect for tradition.

CHAPTER 5

Texas Judicial System

Texans have an odd relationship with the death penalty. In recent years, the general mood has shifted palpably away from support for the death penalty, both in the United States and in the world at large; Texans, however, continue to prefer it as a method of punishment. For Texans, support for the death penalty indicates a politician's resolve to be tough on crime. To outsiders, the state's devotion to capital punishment often appears to supersede any rational arguments against particular cases. The subject, in fact, is a hot button issue for the state's politicians, both Democrats and Republicans.

Public support for the death penalty remains so strong in Texas that politicians have strong incentives both to favor the death penalty and to refrain from questioning its use. It was within this political culture that the state executed Cameron Todd Willingham in 2004. Willingham was convicted of setting his family's house on fire, killing his three daughters. In the thirteen years that Willingham spent on death row, forensic science made considerable advances in the study of fire. Shortly before his execution, experts sent evidence to Governor Rick Perry and the Texas Board of Pardons and Paroles that suggested that the arson evidence used to convict Willingham had since been discredited by forensic science. Both the governor and the Board of Pardons and Paroles declined to issue a stay of execution, however, and Willingham's execution was carried out.

Nationally, people began to question whether Texas had executed an innocent man. The Texas Legislature created the Texas Forensic Science Commission in 2005, in part in reaction to the Willingham case. The first case the commission took up was Willingham's; it hired an independent and nationally recognized fire expert to review the case. That expert called the Willingham investigation "slipshod and based on wives' tales about how fire behaves."[1] Three days before the commission was set to hear this report, Perry replaced three of its members, including the commission's chairman, Samuel Bassett. Perry was widely criticized for his actions and accused of attempting to influence the commission's work. Bassett later contended that he had been pressured by the governor's office.[2] Death penalty opponents point to the Willingham case as an instance in which Texas would have to admit that it executed an innocent man. They have accused Governor Perry of attempting to stall the report in an election year. The governor, for his part, maintains that replacing the commissioners was business as usual. Either way, the case highlights Texans' ambivalence when it comes to errors in the state's death penalty system, a strong desire to maintain the death penalty, and a fear that any acknowledgment of error would give political power to death penalty opponents.

The political culture in Texas that views adherence to the death penalty as proof of toughness on crime is the same political culture that patently distrusts government. Imposition of the death penalty is not an act that is typically associated with a populace that distrusts its government; however, in demanding that the state execute its own citizens Texans are in fact exhibiting a particularly high degree of trust in the actions of their government. How do we account for this inconsistency? In order to explore the nature of justice in Texas, we will start by outlining the structure of the Texas judiciary. The structure of the judiciary is central to a consideration of justice in Texas, as the system reflects ad hoc changes rather than a cohesive system of justice. Next we will examine the role of judges in the state and explore questions concerning the method used to elect judges, as well as other methods of judicial selection. Finally, we will explore issues of justice, including the controversial issue of capital punishment.

As you read the chapter, think about the following questions:

★ What contributes to the lack of a cohesive court structure in the state?

★ Should Texas retain its current system of selecting judges?

★ How might Texas decrease its incarceration rate?

★ Why are Texans so committed to the death penalty?

Texas Courts

The Texas court system is part of the larger American judicial system. The American court system is based on **judicial federalism**, where judicial authority is shared between levels of government. The U.S. Constitution created a national system of courts that included trial courts, appellate courts, and a Supreme Court to hear questions of national or constitutional law. At the same time, the states create the court system for their respective state and local levels of government. Questions of local or state law, as well as questions regarding the state's constitution, are heard at the appropriate local- or state-level court. As we shall see, in Texas determining which court will hear which case is far from straightforward. The state's constitution says this about the state's court system:

> The judicial power of this State shall be vested in one Supreme Court, in one Court of Criminal Appeals, in Courts of Appeals, in District Courts, in County Courts, in Commissioners Courts, in Courts of Justices of the Peace, and in such other courts as may be provided by law.
>
> The Legislature may establish such other courts as it may deem necessary and prescribe the jurisdiction and organization thereof, and may conform the jurisdiction of the district and other inferior courts thereto.[3]

The court system in Texas, which is outlined in Figure 5.1, is a highly complex, confusing, and muddled judicial system. Courts in Texas are divided by their jurisdiction, their origin, and their geographical coverage. A court's **jurisdiction** refers to the court's sphere of authority. One issue of authority concerns whether a case is at the original or appellate stage. Courts with **original jurisdiction** hear the initial cases. Typically, courts of original jurisdiction hear evidence and establish the

Judicial federalism
a system in which judicial authority is shared between levels of government.

Jurisdiction
the court's sphere of authority.

Original jurisdiction
the authority to hear the initial case; the evidence and the case record are established in this court.

Figure 5.1 Court Structure of Texas as of November 1, 2010

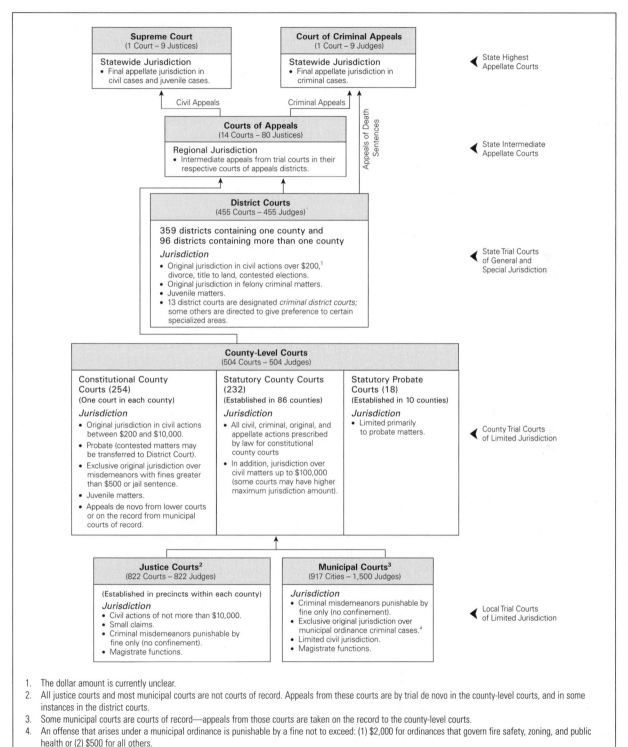

1. The dollar amount is currently unclear.
2. All justice courts and most municipal courts are not courts of record. Appeals from these courts are by trial de novo in the county-level courts, and in some instances in the district courts.
3. Some municipal courts are courts of record—appeals from those courts are taken on the record to the county-level courts.
4. An offense that arises under a municipal ordinance is punishable by a fine not to exceed: (1) $2,000 for ordinances that govern fire safety, zoning, and public health or (2) $500 for all others.

Source: http://www.courts.state.tx.us/oca/pdf/Court_Structure_Chart.pdf.

Appellate jurisdiction

the authority to hear an appeal from a lower court that has already rendered a decision; an appellate court reviews the court record from the original trial and does not hear new evidence.

Exclusive jurisdiction

a particular level of court with the sole right to hear a specific type of case.

Criminal case

a case in which an individual is charged by the state with violating the laws and the state brings the suit.

Civil case

a case in which an aggrieved party sues for damages claiming that he or she has been wronged by another individual.

Concurrent jurisdiction

a system where different levels of courts have overlapping jurisdiction, resulting in a confusing and ill-defined system.

record of the case. Courts with **appellate jurisdiction** hear appeals of cases where a decision has previously been rendered by a lower court. Rather than hearing new evidence, appellate courts are restricted to reviewing the court record from the original trial and determining whether specific points of law or procedure were applied correctly. In addition, courts are sometimes given **exclusive jurisdiction,** meaning a particular level of court has the sole right to hear a specific type of case.

A second issue of jurisdiction distinguishes whether a case is a criminal case or a civil case. In a **criminal case,** an individual is charged by the state with violating the law, and the state brings the suit. In a **civil case,** an aggrieved party sues for damages based on claims that he or she has been wronged by another individual. In Texas, the lower-level courts (the municipal courts, justice of the peace courts, and county courts) are limited to the least serious criminal and civil cases. By contrast, the most serious criminal charges, called felonies, and civil suits over a certain dollar amount are heard in district- or state-level courts.

A third issue of jurisdiction concerns geographical coverage. Jurisdiction in the Texas lower courts is based on the geographical municipality, precinct, or county where the court is located. There are 455 district courts in the state, 96 of which overlap with more than one county. The geographic jurisdiction of district courts therefore often overlaps with county courts. Conversely, in larger counties such as Harris and Dallas County there may be more than one district court. The state is also divided into fourteen appellate districts. The two highest courts, the State Supreme Court and the State Court of Criminal Appeals, serve the entire state of Texas. These distinctions often become confused because, depending on the population of a city or county, courts have evolved to serve different functions and often have overlapping jurisdiction.

Courts in Texas are further distinguished by their origin. The Texas Constitution specifically provides for justice of the peace courts, county courts, district courts, and appellate courts, including the two highest courts. The legislature is left to determine the exact number of courts. In addition, the legislature can create other levels of courts. As such the legislature creates all municipal courts, statutory county courts, and probate courts.

The end result is a judicial system that is confusing, costly, and inefficient. Jurisdiction is often unclear as district courts overlap in many counties in Texas. The state court system is even more confusing since courts often have overlapping original jurisdiction, called **concurrent jurisdiction.** The distinction between original and appellate jurisdiction is also blurred in Texas, where lower-level courts often do not keep official records, meaning that the appellate court has to treat the case as if it were new. Further, the Texas Legislature can create courts to serve specific functions and often does so on an ad-hoc basis. The result is a judicial system with an ill-defined and confusing structure.

Local Trial Courts

t the local level there are two types of trial courts, each with limited jurisdiction: the municipal courts and justice of the peace courts.

Municipal Courts

Municipal courts are courts created by the state legislature for cities in Texas. There are currently 917 municipalities in the state, with larger cities often having more than one municipal court. Municipal courts have original and exclusive jurisdiction over violations of municipal ordinances—those that typically deal with zoning requirements, fire safety, litter laws, or dog regulations. Municipal courts can impose fines of up to $2,000 for violations of municipal ordinances. In addition, municipal courts have jurisdiction over class C misdemeanors (criminal matters punishable by a fine of $500 or less, with no possible jail time). Because justice of the peace courts also have jurisdiction over class C misdemeanors, this is an example of concurrent jurisdiction. Typically, if an officer of the city issues the citation, then the case is heard in municipal court; citations issued by county officers (such as sheriffs) are heard in the justice of the peace court. By custom, the municipal courts also perform **magistrate functions.** As magistrates, municipal courts can issue search and arrest warrants, conduct preliminary hearings, and set bail for more serious crimes. The magistrate functions allow municipal courts to help decrease the workload of higher-level courts. Today, the vast majority of the cases heard in municipal courts, approximately 83 percent, deal with traffic or parking violations.[4]

Appeals from municipal courts are typically heard in county-level courts. If the municipal court is a court of record, then the county-level court exercises appellate jurisdiction. However, most municipal courts are not courts of record, meaning no official transcript is recorded in cases that are brought before the court. Absent an official record, appeals from municipal courts are heard *de novo,* or with a new trial, in county-level courts.

Municipal judges are typically appointed by city councils to two-year terms. The city council also determines the salary for municipal judges, which varies substantially throughout the state. When the state legislature passes statutes creating municipal courts of record, they require that the judges presiding over those courts be licensed attorneys in the state of Texas. Since most municipal courts are not courts of record, however, most municipal judges are not required to be attorneys. Even in the absence of the licensed attorney requirement, 52 percent of all municipal judges are licensed attorneys.[5]

Magistrate functions
the authority to conduct the preliminary procedures in criminal cases, issuing search and arrest warrants, conducting preliminary hearings, and setting bail for more serious crimes.

De novo
to hear an appeal with a new trial, most commonly taken in the absence of an official case record.

Justice of the Peace Courts

Justice of the peace courts, or JP courts, are precinct-level courts. The number of judicial precincts in a county depends on the size of a county's population. Currently, there are 822 JP courts. The constitution provides that each county have between one and eight justice of the peace courts:

> Justice of the peace courts shall have original jurisdiction in criminal matters of misdemeanor cases punishable by fine only, exclusive jurisdiction in civil matters where the amount in controversy is two hundred dollars or less, and such other jurisdiction as may be provided by law. Justices of the peace shall be ex officio notaries public.[6]

Like municipal courts, JP courts are courts of original jurisdiction only. Civil jurisdiction of JP courts extends to cases that involve $10,000 or less. This jurisdiction is concurrent with county and district courts in cases involving amounts of $200 to $500. The JP has nearly exclusive jurisdiction in civil cases involving less than $200. The criminal jurisdiction extends to misdemeanor cases with fines up to $500 and no jail time, concurrent with municipal courts. Approximately 87 percent of all JP cases are criminal cases, and 68 percent of these are traffic cases.[7]

The presiding officials of JP courts perform marriages, act as notaries public, and serve as magistrates for higher courts. JPs also serve as small claims courts. One of the more interesting responsibilities of the JP is to act as coroner in counties without medical examiners. The job of the coroner is to determine cause of death, even though JPs do not generally have any medical training. JP courts are not courts of record, so any appeals are heard *de novo* in the county courts.

JPs, like other state judges, are elected in partisan elections to four-year terms. Lack of educational requirements is one of the most consistent criticisms of JP courts. There are no formal qualifications for JP judges. In 2009, the *Annual Statistical Report for the Texas Judiciary* reported that 93 percent of JP judges graduated from high school, 33 percent graduated from college, and a mere 9 percent graduated from law school.[8] Salaries vary significantly by county and are set by the county commissioners court.

County-Level Trial Courts

At the county level there are three types of trial courts: constitutional county courts, county courts at law, and statutory probate courts.

Constitutional County Courts

The constitution mandates a county-level court in each of the 254 counties in the state; these courts are sometimes referred to as constitutional county courts.

> There shall be established in each county in this State a County Court, which shall be a court of record; and there shall be elected in each county, by the qualified voters, a County Judge, who shall be well informed in the law of the State; shall be a conservator of the peace, and shall hold his office for four years, and until his successor shall be elected and qualified.[9]

Constitutional county courts exercise exclusive and original jurisdiction over misdemeanors where fines can exceed $500 and jail time can be imposed (class A and class B misdemeanors). Original civil jurisdiction extends to cases involving amounts from $200 to $10,000, and is concurrent with JP courts. These courts can also exercise probate jurisdiction, including cases involving guardianship, uncontested wills, and determination of mental competency. Constitutional county courts also possess appellate jurisdiction over cases from either the JP and municipal courts. Appeals from these courts are by and large *de novo,* which increases the workload of the state court system. Since the workload of JP and municipal courts is for the most part traffic-related and county-level courts tend to be overworked, lawyers often use a strategy of appealing traffic offenses in an attempt to get these cases dismissed. Often traffic appeals are not a priority in an overworked county-level court. Constitutional county courts are required to be courts of record.

The constitution requires county judges to be "well informed of the law," which has been interpreted to mean that they do not have to have law degrees. In 2009, the office of court administration reported that 63 percent of county judges had graduated from college and 14 percent had graduated from law school.[10] In larger counties, the county judge often works exclusively on administrative duties and acts as a judge in name only. County judges are elected in partisan elections to four-year terms. Their salaries vary by county and are set by the county commissioners.

Judge Roy Bean

Roy Bean, a legend of the Texas judiciary, reflects the lax nature of frontier justice in Texas and the state's fondness for amateur justice. Born in Kentucky in 1825, Bean had no formal education that prepared him for service as a judge. However, Pecos County needed a judge, one that would allow the Texas Rangers to clean up the area without having to make a 400-mile round trip to the nearest courthouse and jail. Thus, for lack of a better choice, Roy Bean became a Texas judge on August 2, 1882.

Prior to serving as a judge, Bean's legal experience had been on the other side of the bench and cell door. After fleeing legal trouble in several states, Bean settled briefly in San Diego, California, where his brother was mayor. In 1852 he was arrested and charged with assault with intent to murder for participating in a duel over a woman. He eventually escaped from jail, allegedly using a knife smuggled inside some tamales to dig himself out. After relocating to San Gabriel, California, Bean became involved in another duel in 1854, killing a romantic rival. This time, he didn't appear before a court; instead, he narrowly escaped lynching by his victim's friends.

Bean supplemented his judicial earnings by running a bar called "Jersey Lilly," named for Lillie Langtry, a British actress with whom Bean was obsessed. (Contrary to rumor, Langtry, Texas, was not named after her. The city, originally named Eagle Nest, was renamed in honor of George Langtry, an area railroad engineer.)

While occasionally voted out of office, Bean mostly held onto the position of judge until his retirement in 1902. Despite his lack of training and his possession of only one law book, Bean's justice was creative. Because he lacked a jail, he favored setting fines over jail time when sentencing. Horse thieves were generally released after payment of a fine if the horses were returned. When a man died after falling off a bridge, Bean discovered that the man had been carrying forty dollars and a concealed pistol. He fined the man forty dollars for carrying a concealed weapon and used the money to pay for his funeral expenses.

Bean's legal and bartending careers complimented each other nicely; Bean required that jurors buy drinks at his saloon during every judicial recess. His most famous venture came in 1896 when he organized a world championship boxing title match. Since boxing matches were illegal in Texas, Judge Bean arranged for Bob Fitzsimmons and Peter Maher to box on an island in the Rio Grande. While the fight lasted less than two minutes, word of the match and its promoter spread throughout the United States.

Portraying himself as the "Law West of the Pecos," Judge Roy Bean epitomized Texas justice in its infancy. He died in 1903, but his legacy continues to shape the town of Langtry. In 1939 the State of Texas purchased Bean's "Jersey Lilly," making it the centerpiece of Langtry's Old West tourism, with over one million visitors to date.

In addition to judicial responsibilities, the county judge exercises administrative duties over the county government.

County Courts at Law and Statutory Probate Courts

Statutory courts, also called county courts at law, are so called because they are created by legislative statute rather than by the constitution. In counties with larger populations, statutory county courts help with the caseload. There are 232 statutory county courts, concentrated in larger counties. Jurisdiction of these courts varies greatly, according to the statute, but is generally consistent with part or all of the constitutional county courts. Thus, statutory courts may be conferred civil, criminal, or probate jurisdiction, or all of these, for the county. Like constitutional county courts, statutory courts are courts of record. The legislature can also create courts that specialize in probate. Statutory judges are elected in partisan elections to four-year terms. They are required to be trained in the law, and nearly all of these judges have law degrees.[11]

District Courts (State-Level Trial Courts)

State-level trial courts in Texas are called district courts. Every county in the state is served by at least one district court, while more populated areas often have several. According to the Texas Constitution, district court jurisdiction is

> exclusive, appellate, and original jurisdiction of all actions, proceedings, and remedies, except in cases where exclusive, appellate, or original jurisdiction may be conferred by this Constitution or other law on some other court, tribunal, or administrative body.[12]

Thus, the jurisdiction of district courts can vary according to the jurisdiction of other courts in a particular area. In some areas of the state, there are family district courts, criminal district courts, or civil district courts. Generally, though, district courts are granted civil jurisdiction in cases involving $200 or more (concurrent with JP and county courts). District courts exercise original jurisdiction over contested probate issues, divorce, land title claims, slander, child custody, and contested elections. Their original criminal jurisdiction includes all felony cases. They also have jurisdiction over misdemeanors when the case involves a government official. In larger areas, these courts often specialize in just one of these areas. Appeals from district courts are heard at the courts of appeals, with the exception of death penalty cases, which go directly to the Texas Court of Criminal Appeals.

A judge in the district courts must be at least twenty-five years of age, a resident of Texas, and a U.S. citizen. In addition, the judge must be a licensed attorney with at least four years experience as either an attorney or a judge. District judges are elected in partisan elections to four-year terms.

Appellate Courts

The Texas judiciary has two levels of appellate courts. Initial appeals are heard at the court of appeals. After the initial appeal, cases can be appealed to one of the state's two highest courts. Texas is one of only two states with two high courts (the other is Oklahoma). The Texas Supreme Court hears final appeals in civil cases and the Texas Court of Criminal Appeals hears final appeals in criminal cases. Appellate judges must be at least thirty-five years of age, residents of the state, and U.S. citizens. An appellate judge is also required to have at least ten years' experience as a lawyer or a judge and be a licensed attorney. Judges are elected in partisan elections for six-year terms.

Courts of Appeals (Intermediate Appellate Courts)

There are fourteen courts of appeals in Texas. Each court has between three and thirteen judges, including one chief justice. With the exception of death penalty cases, all civil and criminal appeals from the county and district courts are initially heard in the courts of appeals. Appellate courts hear no new evidence or new witnesses. Instead, judges make their decisions based on a review of the written record from the trial, as well as written briefs and oral arguments by attorneys arguing legal or procedural points. Typically an appeal is heard by a panel of three judges, although they can be heard *en banc,* or by the entire court. A panel of judges, rather than a single judge, is traditionally used in appeals courts since there are no juries. Including more than one judge provides some limits on the power of individual judges. The case is decided by a majority vote of the judges. The court can affirm, reverse, or modify a lower courts decision, or can remand the case to the trial court for reconsideration. Civil cases heard by the court of appeals can be appealed to the Texas Supreme Court, while criminal cases can be appealed to the Texas Court of Criminal Appeals.

En banc
an appeal that is heard by the entire court of appeals, rather than by a select panel of judges.

Texas's Highest Appellate Courts

Texas has two courts to hear appeals from the courts of appeals: the Supreme Court, for final civil appeals, and the Court of Criminal Appeals, for final criminal appeals including automatic appeals in death penalty cases.

Texas Court of Criminal Appeals

The Texas Court of Criminal Appeals is the state's highest court for criminal appeals. Like other appellate courts, the Texas Court of Criminal Appeals hears no new evidence and is limited to reviewing the trial record and briefs filed by the lawyers in the case. The court consists of nine judges, including a presiding judge. The court can hear appeals in panels of three judges, though most cases involve the entire court. Cases are decided by majority vote. The most important job of the Texas Court of Criminal Appeals is to hear automatic appeals in death penalty cases. The court typically considers death penalty cases *en banc.* In 2009, the court heard twenty-two death penalty cases, affirming each of those convictions. The court is the final court of appeals for questions of state law and the state constitution. However, cases involving questions of federal law or the U.S. Constitution can ultimately be appealed to the U.S. Supreme Court.

Supreme Court

The Texas Supreme Court is the highest court in Texas for civil cases in the state. The Supreme Court consists of eight justices, plus one chief justice, and cases are decided by majority vote. The Supreme Court also makes procedural rules for lower courts, approves law schools in the state, and appoints members of the Board of Legal Examiners. Like the Court of Criminal Appeals, the cases from the Texas Supreme Court can be appealed to the U.S. Supreme Court if they concern issues of federal law or the U.S. Constitution.

Texas Judges

Historically, the Texas judiciary, like other elected positions, was dominated by Democrats. Since the late 1980s, however, Republicans have dominated the judiciary, holding almost all appellate posts. In addition, judges in Texas today come largely from upper middle-class families. Recall that microcosm theory (introduced in Chapter 3) stipulates that true representation occurs only when the makeup of a society's institutions mirrors the makeup of society as a whole. Although women account for about half of the Texas population, the vast majority of judges in the state are men. In terms of lower courts, female judges constitute 34 percent of municipal and JP judges, 13 percent of constitutional county court judges, and 31 percent of statutory court judges. Women do not fare much better at state-level courts, composing 28 percent of district judges and 41 percent of appellate judges. At the state's highest courts, females currently comprise 11 percent of the Texas Supreme Court and 44 percent of the Texas Court of Criminal Appeals.

The racial distribution of the courts is even more troublesome, particularly given the overwhelmingly low representation of both Hispanics and African Americans in the judicial system (see Figure 5.2). Although African Americans comprise about 12 percent of the state's population, African American judges remain relatively rare in lower-level courts in the state, ranging from less than 1 percent of constitutional county court judges to 5 percent of municipal judges. African American representation on state-level courts is uneven, comprising a mere 4 percent of district judges, 3 percent of appellate judges, and 22 percent of Texas Supreme Court judges. Hispanics make up approximately 35 percent of the state population, but their representation in the Texas judiciary remains well below this figure. Hispanic representation on lower-level courts ranges from a paltry 10 percent on constitutional county courts to 22 percent on statutory county courts. Hispanics comprise 17 percent of the judges at the district level and 14 percent at the appellate level, but only 11 percent of the Supreme Court justices. The Texas Court of Criminal Appeals, the court responsible for all death penalty appeals, has no racial minorities at this time.

The issue of minority representation in Texas remains a major concern, and the manner in which judges are selected is a starting point for critics of the system. Some minorities charge that partisan elections and the dominance of the Republican Party in Texas make it difficult for minorities to get elected. According to this perspective, merely removing party labels from the ballot will increase the likelihood that a minority candidate will be elected to the judiciary.

The nature of judicial districts may also prove an important impediment to minority representation in the state. Large counties in particular often treat the

Figure 5.2 Racial Representation of Justices and Judges in Texas, 2009

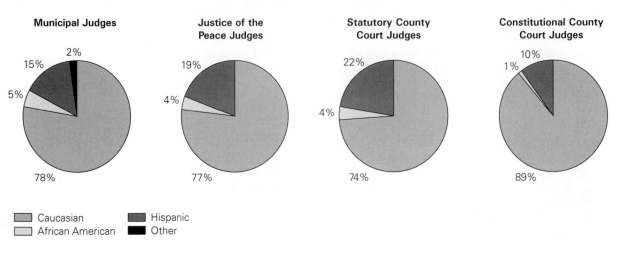

Municipal Judges: 2%, 15%, 5%, 78%

Justice of the Peace Judges: 19%, 4%, 77%

Statutory County Court Judges: 22%, 4%, 74%

Constitutional County Court Judges: 10%, 1%, 89%

Legend: Caucasian, African American, Hispanic, Other

county as one district and then elect quite a few judges from that district as a whole. Minorities contend that using an **at-large election** system to select district and county judges makes it less likely that minorities will win. (See Chapter 3 for more information on at-large elections.)

Some minorities contend that **cumulative voting** would benefit minority candidates. Cumulative voting allows voters to take the total number of positions in a district and divide their votes for those positions among a few candidates or even give all of those votes to a single candidate. For example, in Harris County, which has fifty-nine judges, a voter could vote for fifty-nine candidates, or vote fifty-nine times for one candidate. This system allows voters to concentrate all of their votes in a district on one or two candidates, making it more likely that a minority candidate will be elected. (See Chapter 6 for a discussion of cumulative voting.)

Judicial Selection

One of the more controversial aspects of the Texas judicial system is the selection process for judges. With the exception of municipal judges, judges in Texas are elected in partisan contests. In order to become a judge, candidates have to raise enough money to win the election. Once on the bench, judges need to continue raising money for reelection. Texas is one of just nine states that use partisan elections to select their Supreme Court justices. Another thirteen states elect their judges in nonpartisan elections, a system that decreases the likelihood that votes will be based solely on partisan labels.

The argument for the direct election of judges is rooted in democracy. The people are theoretically retaining political influence, since it is the people who choose the judges. Unfortunately, there are several impediments to the actual popular influence on judicial elections. Foremost, Texans are faced with a long ballot that features almost every major office in the state. In addition to choosing the country's president and the state's national congressional delegation, Texans elect members of the plural executive and other bureaucratic offices, members of the state legislature, and a wide range of judicial offices in the state. The democratic charge for the average Texan is literally overwhelming and the issues in judicial selection are often relatively subtle. The result is that most Texans simply do not pay

At-large election

an election in which a city or county is treated as a single district and candidates are elected from the entire district as a whole.

Cumulative voting

a system that allows voters to take the total number of positions to be selected in a district and concentrate their votes among one or a few candidates.

Figure 5.2, continued

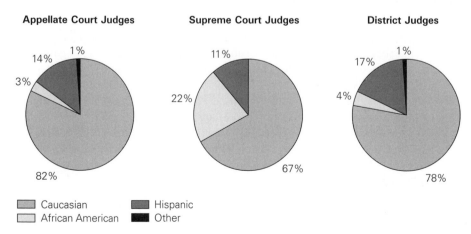

Source: Compiled by the authors from the *Annual Statistical Report for the Texas Judiciary,* 2009.

much attention to judicial campaigns. Rather than voting based on judicial competency, voting in judicial elections often amounts to little more than voting on the basis of partisan labels or image and name recognition.

One of the most important outcomes of requiring Texans to elect so many positions in the state is the tendency for many to vote along party lines or even **straight ticket voting.** Texas is one of sixteen states that allow straight ticket voting in the election of state officers. The problem is that party labels are less meaningful in judicial races compared to other political contests. Party labels in judicial campaigns can have substantively different meanings than party labels in other political campaigns. For instance, Republicans tend to favor big business and defendants in civil trials, whereas Democrats are more likely to side with plaintiffs. A watch group called Court Watch estimates that the 2005–2006 Republican-dominated Supreme Court ruled in favor of big business, insurance companies, medical practitioners, or government agencies 84 percent of the time.[13] Moreover, the Supreme Court has become progressively more anti-consumer in recent years, overturning 81 percent of the cases decided by juries in lower-level courts.[14] Thus, Republican dominance of the state judiciary in recent decades has had a significant impact on the rights of individuals in the state, rights most Texans still vigorously seek to protect.

In addition, **name recognition** provides a common method of voting in Texas, where knowledge of judicial credentials is limited. In one study, Dallas County voters repeatedly recognized the name of only one in eight district judges.[15] Texans often vote on names that they recognize or even names that sound respectable. This tendency has produced some particularly peculiar effects in a state where most judicial candidates are unknown to the voters. One of the most visible examples of the power of a name in judicial campaigns is that of Don Yarbrough. Yarbrough successfully ran for the Texas Supreme Court in 1976, claiming God wanted him to run. Yarbrough ran against a respected judge who was endorsed by the Texas State Bar. Yarbrough was elected in spite of the fact he had a number of suits pending in court (including charges of business fraud) and was facing disbarment proceedings by the Texas State Bar Association. Most observers agree that Yarbrough was elected largely because voters confused him with another man, Don Yarborough, who had mounted several unsuccessful bids for governor. Others may have confused him with progressive Ralph Yarborough, who had served in the U.S. Senate. Eventually, after being indicted for a felony and facing impeachment proceedings, Yarbrough resigned and fled the country.

The long campaign season exacerbates the tendency for judicial candidates to run unopposed. According to retired Supreme Court chief justice Thomas Phillips, the "filing deadline is a year before you take office if you win, and so a lot of lawyers feel like they really don't want to be running against the judge—it's not going to be the best way to attract business for a year. So most of our rural judges, literally a majority, have never been opposed."[16] The tendency for candidates to run unopposed means the perception of popular control on the judiciary remains largely a myth. Moreover, the **incumbency advantage** in Texas is especially robust. In fact, most incumbents run unopposed, since incumbents tend to win reelection. This tendency undermines the effectiveness of popular control on the judiciary.

Judicial Appointment

Although judicial selection in Texas technically occurs with partisan elections, a large number of judges initially reach the bench through appointment. The constitution provides that the governor can appoint judges to fill vacancies on district and

---

Straight ticket voting
the practice of selecting all the candidates for office who are running under a party label simply by checking off a single box marked with the party label.

Name recognition
making a voting choice based on familiarity with or previous recognition of a candidate's name.

Incumbency advantage
the advantage enjoyed by the incumbent candidate, or current officeholder, in elections; the advantage is based on greater visibility, proven record of public service, and often better access to resources.

appellate courts. These gubernatorial appointments must be confirmed by the Texas Senate. In 2009, 39 percent of district or appellate judges originally assumed office by gubernatorial appointment. The fact that the governor ends up making judicial appointments in a system that purports to leave the choice of judges up to the voters is an important aspect of the judicial election system in Texas, since a significant number of the judges chosen by the governor will run unopposed in future elections where voters will be essentially rubberstamping the governor's choice.

Judicial Removal

There are three primary means of removing judges in Texas. The most common means of removal is for the voters to not reelect a judge in the next election. In addition, the constitution grants the Texas Supreme Court the power to remove district judges for incompetence, official misconduct, or negligence. Judges can also be impeached by the Texas House and tried in the Texas Senate, with a two-thirds vote necessary in each house.

Moreover, a 1965 amendment to the constitution established a Commission on Judicial Conduct. The thirteen-member commission investigates allegations of judicial misconduct. According to the Texas Constitution, judicial misconduct includes

> willful or persistent violation of rules promulgated by the Supreme Court of Texas, incompetence in performing the duties of the office, willful violation of the Code of Judicial Conduct, or willful or persistent conduct that is clearly inconsistent with the proper performance of his duties or casts public discredit upon the judiciary or administration of justice.[17]

If the commission finds a judge guilty of misconduct, it can issue a public or private censure or warning, issue an official reprimand, order additional education, or make a recommendation that the judge be removed from office.

Of the 1,110 cases disposed of by the Commission on Judicial Conduct in 2009, 48 percent evidenced no judicial misconduct.[18] Some level of discipline, including public sanction, additional education, or suspension, was ordered in seventy of the cases. In two cases the judges agreed to voluntarily resign to avoid disciplinary action.

Problems with the Texas Judiciary

As we can see, one of the most significant problems of the Texas judiciary is the lack of a coherent court structure. Overlapping and unclear jurisdictions coupled with ad hoc creation of powers in some levels of courts, depending on the population of the area and the other courts serving that area, produces one of the most cumbersome legal systems in the country. In 1991, the Texas Research League, a nonprofit group, concluded that the "Texas court system really is not a system at all. Indeed, Texas' courts are fragmented without a central focus and are going along in their own direction and at their own pace."[19] Two years later a commission established by the Texas Supreme Court concluded that "the Texas trial court system, complex from its inception, has become ever more confusing as ad hoc responses are devised to meet the needs of an urban, industrialized society. No one person understands or can hope to understand all the nuances and intricacies of Texas's thousands of trial courts."[20] The lack of a clear system is exacerbated by problems in the lower courts, which operate without court reporters and thereby create the need to hear appellate cases *de novo*.

In addition, a significant number of judges in the state have no legal training. The lack of trained judges at the city and county level creates real questions about the quality of justice meted out across the state. Texas judges are infamous in the nation for sleeping during hearings, making inappropriate comments, and, in at least one case, using sock puppets to communicate to the court. Moreover, in rural areas where medical examiners are not available the use of JP judges, most of whom have no medical training, to determine cause of death undermines the validity of death certificates. More generally, when judges perform duties absent professional training or expertise it serves to further undermine the credibility of the entire judicial system to the people of Texas. Mistrust of the judicial system is aggravated in a state perceived to sell justice.

Perhaps even more detrimental is the need for judicial candidates to raise campaign funds to compete for judicial positions. The need to raise funds opens the Texas judiciary up to potential influence by campaign donors. Since the average Texan doesn't pay attention to judicial races, special interests, big business, and attorneys are the primary contributors to judicial contests. Inappropriate influence is likely to be greatest in Supreme Court races, where campaign costs can exceed one million dollars. In 2006, Texans for Public Justice reported that a little over half (51 percent) of the contributions to the candidates for the 2006 Texas Supreme Court race were donated by attorneys and law firms. According to its report, "Leading contributors to high-court candidates include some of the court's busiest litigators, including Vinson & Elkins ($95,000) and Fulbright & Jaworski ($50,412)."[21] In addition to attorneys, big business in Texas actively supports judicial candidates. In the 2006 Supreme Court race, the largest donors after law firms were "Texans for Lawsuit Reform PAC ($75,000), HillCo PAC ($40,000), and the Texas Medical Association ($26,037) . . . [who] have a vested interest in the court interpreting tort, labor, and environmental laws in favor of business—even when such rulings come at the expense of consumers, workers, or communities."[22] The need to raise substantial sums of money to compete in a judicial race in the state opens judges up to undue influence, or at the very least the potential for influence. The result is a perception, if not the reality, that the judicial system in Texas protects business at the expense of the individual.

One of the most visible recent cases of influence is that of Supreme Court Justice Nathan Hecht. Hecht incurred extensive legal fees when he appealed a public reprimand from the State Commission on Judicial Conduct. In order to pay his legal debt, he received so-called late-train donations, or donations provided after the election, from several law firms and business groups. Texas Watch, a nonpartisan group, reported that seventeen parties, who had each contributed at least $5,000 to Hecht, subsequently brought cases before the Texas Supreme Court. Hecht's vote on the court sided with his donors 89 percent of the time.[23]

The perception of justice for sale in Texas remains strong throughout the United States. National media often cover the more explicit appearances of injustice in Texas, including most notably a segment produced by the investigative television news program *60 Minutes* in the late 1980s and again in the late 1990s and more recently in a PBS *Frontline* Special Report. Still, there has been little momentum within the state to change the selection process of judges. One notable exception is the 1995 Judicial Campaign Fairness Act. The purpose of the act is to limit contributions of individual donors to no more than $5,000 per election for statewide judicial campaigns. The primary election and general election are treated as separate elections, meaning that an individual can contribute up to $5,000 to a candidate in each election. PAC (the fundraising arms for interest groups) contributions (including contributions from law firms) are limited to up to $30,000 per election for judicial candidates. Additionally, candidates are prevented from receiving more than $300,000 total from PACs. However, a candidate's participation in the limits set by the Judicial Campaign Fairness Act is voluntary. Any candidate who consents to these voluntary limits can advertise their compliance in their campaign material and television ads.

Alternative Systems of Judicial Selection

here are a variety of alternative judicial selection processes used throughout the country. Two of the most widely used systems for selecting judges are lifetime appointment of judges and a merit system.

Appointment

At the national level, undue influence of the federal judiciary is stymied by lifetime appointment of judges. The advantage of appointing judges rather than electing them is that the judiciary can remain independent and free from political pressure. Three states use this model, allowing the governor to appoint state judges. Another two states allow the state legislature to appoint judges to appellate courts, including the states' Supreme Courts.

Merit System

One alternative to electing judges in partisan elections is use of a merit system to select judges. Sometimes referred to as the Missouri Plan, the merit system relies on a panel of experts in an attempt to balance the need for judicial independence with the accountability associated with electing judges. The panel of experts typically includes judges, lawyers, legal scholars, and sometimes ordinary citizens who are charged with reviewing potential candidates and developing a list of potential judicial nominees. The governor then nominates judicial candidates from the list. Once on the bench, the judges will face periodic retention elections. Judges are able to keep their job as long as a majority of voters approve. A retention election allows voters to vote to retain or remove a judge without the competition that would make campaigning necessary.

Although the United States has long embraced the necessity of an independent judiciary, and many Texans support changing the current process in Texas, the businesses and professions that benefit most from the current system continue to forcefully—and effectively—oppose change. The opposition to change the system remains strong, as proposals to abandon partisan elections have "passed the State Senate four times . . . it's never been allowed to have a vote in committee much less on the floor of the House of Representatives, and that's due to the power of political parties."[24] For now, there appears to be sufficient political opposition to thwart the adoption of a merit-based judicial selection system.

Winners and Losers

he Texas judiciary is fraught with impediments to justice for the average Texan. The system is overly complex and unnecessarily confusing, making it difficult for most Texans to understand. In addition, the large number of judges elected in the state creates an excessive democratic cost. As a result, it is not surprising that democratic mechanisms to protect individuals in the state provide very little protection in practice. Ironically, Texans resist change in the judiciary largely because they want to guard their individual rights, such as the right to choose judges. But more often than not that right buckles under the weight of the system's complexity and the regular onslaught of judicial campaigning. Texans—fiercely protective of their independence and their influence on government—in the end relinquish their authority over judicial selection to big donors in judicial campaigns. And it is those big donors—for the most part business and law firms—that reap the benefits and continue to dominate the Texas judiciary. Because these groups remain ever attentive to their own interests, individual Texans lose.

Minorities also lose. Minorities hold few judicial posts in a state that is tough on crime, has one of the largest prison populations in the country, and is rarely sympathetic to appeals. The judicial system in Texas remains dominated by middle- and upper-middle-class white males, even though the state's demographic makeup continues to diversify. The current system of electing judges, particularly in a Republican-dominated state, ensures that minorities will continue to be underrepresented in Texas. The perception that the Texas judicial system is unjust endures for good reason: the prevailing system harms all Texans.

Justice in Texas

Criminal cases deal with individuals charged with violating criminal laws or committing crimes that, although there may be a victim, are technically crimes against the state. The **prosecutor** in a criminal case is the lawyer who represents the government. The **criminal defendant** is the person charged with committing a crime. Criminal law ranges from traffic violations to robbery, sexual assault, or murder. Lower-level criminal violations, such as public intoxication or resisting arrest, are referred to as misdemeanors. Misdemeanors typically involve fines or prison sentences of less than a year. Felonies are more severe criminal offenses, such as sexual assault or murder, and involve harsher punishments. In criminal cases, a twelve-member **grand jury** determines whether there is enough evidence to warrant a trial. If nine of the twelve jurors on the grand jury agree that a trial is warranted, the grand jury issues an **indictment,** a document formally charging an individual with a crime, indicating that there is enough evidence to warrant a trial. The trial jury, or **petit jury,** determines whether or not an individual is guilty. Petit juries are guaranteed in criminal cases and may also be used in civil cases. The accused is presumed innocent and the state must prove that the individual is guilty. In order to determine guilt, the burden of proof in a criminal trial is based on whether the state has submitted sufficient evidence to prove the guilt of the accused **beyond a reasonable doubt.** Texas requires a unanimous verdict in criminal cases. If an individual is found guilty in a criminal case, the punishment can include fines paid to the government, imprisonment, or, in certain cases, the death penalty.

Civil cases, by contrast, involve disputes between individuals. The **plaintiff** in a civil case claims to have been wronged by another party, the **civil defendant.** Civil law cases often involve breach of contract and other contractual disputes, but also include family law issues such as divorce, neglect, custody, or probate questions. Civil cases also include tort cases, claiming personal injury or property damage. Civil cases can be tried by a jury or, if both parties agree, can simply be decided by the judge. The burden of proof for civil cases is based on a much lower standard than for criminal cases. To win the civil case a plaintiff merely has to show through

Prosecutor
a lawyer who represents the government and brings a case in criminal trials.

Criminal defendant
a person charged with committing a crime.

Grand jury
a panel of twelve jurors that reviews evidence, determines whether there is sufficient evidence to bring a trial, and issues an indictment.

Indictment
a document that formally charges a defendant with committing a crime.

Petit jury
a trial jury; jurors attend a trial, listen to evidence, and determine whether a defendant is innocent or guilty.

Beyond a reasonable doubt
the standard burden of proof necessary to find a defendant guilty in a criminal trial; the defendant is presumed innocent.

Plaintiff
the party claiming to have been wronged and bringing the suit.

Civil defendant
the party alleged to have committed the wrong at issue in the suit.

The Texas Rangers

The iconic Texas Rangers vividly illustrate the power of a state's legends both inside and beyond its own borders. The Texas Rangers have become defining symbols of law enforcement, originally galloping through serials like *The Lone Ranger*, featured on the radio and television, and in the movies where they were played by western stars like Roy Rogers, Gene Autry, and Tex Ritter. Long after the early western stars rode off into the sunset, the Texas Rangers continue to capture the imagination of viewers across the country on shows like *Walker, Texas Ranger* and in movies like *Man of the House,* starring Chuck Norris and Tommy Lee Jones.

The Rangers can trace their origins back to Stephen F. Austin, who first referred to the citizens asked to protect his settlements as "rangers" because they had to range over the countryside. The Rangers became official extensions of the temporary government of Texas in 1835, when they were called upon to protect the frontier during the Texas Revolution.

While generally revered, the Rangers' image has suffered from time to time. When Sam Houston wanted to move the state's capital out of Austin, the two Rangers who went to Austin to retrieve the archives met resistance from the local citizens and returned with their horses' manes and tails shaved. In 1918, Governor William P. Hobby allegedly used the Rangers to suppress turnout for James Ferguson in South Texas during that year's Democratic primary. During the 1932 election the Texas Rangers made the mistake of backing Governor Ross Sterling. When Miriam "Ma" Ferguson won office she retaliated by firing the entire force of 48 Rangers and replacing them with 2,300 "special" Rangers, many of them criminals. The legislature responded by authorizing the hiring of just 32 Rangers, leaving the state virtually unprotected as Bonnie Parker and Clyde Barrow (the infamous Bonnie and Clyde) roamed the state robbing banks. The Rangers' image was further tainted when they were accused of being instruments of discrimination and intimidation against Tejanos. Captain Leander McNelly, whose tactics included piling the bodies of dead Mexican rustlers in the Brownsville town square, made the Rangers particularly unpopular among Tejanos in the 1870s.

The Rangers' image today combines independence with law and order—qualities on which all Texans can agree. While the details of the story vary, a common tale depicting the Rangers' uncanny abilities involves citizens of a town who called for a company of Rangers to stop a prize fight. When the local people arrived at the train station to greet the twenty Rangers they had anticipated would be needed to quell the expected riot, they were disappointed to see just one Ranger get off the train: Legendary Ranger Captain Bill McDonald. When the citizens' disappointment over the arrival of only a single Ranger became evident, McDonald responded by saying, "Hell! Ain't I enough? There's only one prize-fight!" Since that time, "One riot, one Ranger" has been a common slogan associated with the Rangers.[i]

Today, the Texas Rangers are a highly professional and modern law enforcement organization that has been part of the Department of Public Safety since 1935. Perhaps less colorful than many of their predecessors—and their television and cinema image—today's Rangers are trained to meet the demands of a high-tech state. The Rangers include 144 commissioned officers, 24 noncommissioned administrative support personnel, a forensic artist, and a fiscal analyst. Rangers assist local law enforcement with criminal investigations, help with the suppression of major disturbances, and conduct special investigations. While twenty-first century Texas Rangers may look little like their predecessors, they still abide by the creed set down by Captain McDonald: "No man in the wrong can stand up against a fellow that's in the right and keeps on a-comin."

i. Quotations from Captain McDonald taken from Texas Department of Public Safety, www.txdps.state.tx.us.

a **preponderance of evidence** that the defendant is likely to have been guilty. Whereas criminal cases may result in jail time, plaintiffs in civil cases may ask the court to redress the grievance, or award monetary damages. **Compensatory damages** are monetary awards designed to compensate the injured party, for instance for medical bills incurred or lost income due to missed work. If the court wants to send a message, it may also award **punitive damages,** which are typically larger monetary awards intended to punish the defendant.

Incarceration in Texas

Everything is bigger in Texas, including the prison system. Several things contribute to the Texas-sized prison system. First, U.S. culture supports high incarceration rates. According to the International Center for Prison Studies, the United States currently has the highest incarceration rate in the world.[25] America imprisons more of its citizens than any other country in the world, both in absolute terms and when population is controlled for. Currently, Texas has the fourth highest incarceration rate in the country. As of 2009, the Texas prison incarceration rate was 649 inmates per 100,000 residents. If Texas were a country, it would rank third in incarceration rates, incarcerating at a higher rate than Iran, China, and Russia.[26] Not only is Texas a world leader in imprisonment, but the number of prisoners is projected to increase significantly in the next decade.[27] Texas political culture continues to demand politicians and policies that are "tough on crime." This means that policies in Texas tend to criminalize more types of behavior and favor tougher sentences than policies of other states. In addition, in the last two decades the Texas population has increased, and stiffer immigration and drug laws have combined with this growth to produce a glut of potential prisoners.

Given its high levels of imprisonment, it is not surprising that Texas jails struggle with overcrowding, and legislators predict this problem will only worsen. Many existing jails are aging, and often maintenance is not a priority. In 2007, the Texas Commission on Jail Standards found that one-third of the jails in Texas failed to meet state standards. Inspections revealed buildings with structural problems and mold, and prisons that were overcrowded and understaffed. In addition, substandard or scarce medical care has often contributed to death or injury of inmates.[28] As Texas's existing prisons have deteriorated and its prison population has increased, Texas, more than any other state, has embraced private prisons.

Privatization of Prisons

One way Texas has tried to deal with its increasing prison population is by embracing the **private prison** option. Texas is firmly on board the privatization craze and currently leads the country in utilizing privately run prisons, housing about 18,000 of its 154,000 prison beds in private facilities.[29] In addition, private prisons based in Texas often have contracts with other states, meaning violent criminals from other states are transferred to Texas. Defenders of privately owned prisons argue the costs for the state are significantly lower than state or locally run facilities. They often point to jobs created by private prisons that are built in rural areas of the state. Opponents point to the poor conditions, underpaid and poorly trained guards, and high-profile scandals involving the largest private prison corporations. Because these prisons are motivated by profit, providing adequate facilities and services often takes a back seat to the bottom line. Moreover, research suggests that the few jobs created by the prison facility are outweighed by negative job growth, as private prisons have

In 1940, Missouri took the radical step of moving from partisan elections for state judges to the Nonpartisan Retention Plan, often called the "Missouri Plan." Under the Missouri Plan, an independent commission nominates three candidates to fill a vacancy on a court. The governor chooses one of the three candidates to serve on the court. After one year on the court, the judge faces a retention election in which voters decide if the judge remains on the court or must step down. After the initial retention election, the judge faces another retention election every four, eight, or twelve years depending on the court. All judges must retire at the age of seventy.

Missouri uses this system for state courts of appeals and the Missouri Supreme Court. Courts in Clay, Jackson, St. Louis, and Platte counties, as well as courts in the city of St. Louis, use the retention election system. Many other local courts in Missouri use partisan elections for selecting judges. Twelve states have adopted the "Missouri Plan," and a few other states, like Florida, use a modified version of the plan. Texas uses partisan elections for staffing all state and local courts.

Proponents of the "Missouri Plan" point toward the use of independent commissions to nominate judges as shifting the focus of judicial selection to finding better-quality judges. The use of a retention election allows the public to have periodic say on whether a judge remains in office, providing a degree of democratic accountability.

Opponents of the system point toward the fact that most judges are retained election after election, in effect, creating a lifetime appointment. No Missouri Supreme Court or appeals court judge has ever lost a retention election and been voted out of office. One study found that over a thirty-year period, only 1.3 percent of judges lost a retention election.[i] Based on these results, critics question the point of the retention elections.

Thinking Critically

- Do you think the "Missouri Plan" offers advantages that the partisan system of electing judges used in Texas lacks?
- Does the low rate of rejecting judges in Missouri undermine the "Missouri Plan"?
- How do you think a plan similar to the "Missouri Plan" would affect the Texas court system and Texas politics?
- Would you favor adopting such a plan?

i. Larry Aspin, William Hall, Jean Bax, and Celeste Montoya, "Thirty Years of Judicial Retention Elections: An Update," *Social Science Journal*, vol. 37, no. 1 (2000): 1–17.

---

actually impeded economic growth overall.[30] In addition, critics contend that inmates moved to private facilities from other states, faced with poor conditions, often are more likely to be clinically depressed and less likely to have access to family or other visitors, making rehabilitation more difficult. The state's choice to allow further construction and use of private prisons means that Texas is increasingly choosing to take on other states' and the national government's prisoners.

Several high-profile scandals have drawn attention to these facilities. For example, in 2007 a GEO Group, Inc., prison company was fired by the Texas Youth Commission (TYC) for squalid conditions after one prisoner (transferred from Idaho) committed suicide.[31] Shortly after the suicide, Idaho corrections officials visited the facility and concluded it "was the worst correctional facility" and was "beyond repair or correction." In spite of chronic questions regarding the conditions in these private jails, a *Dallas Morning News* study found "only a few instances of TYC not renewing contracts because of poor performance" and no cases where the TYC has fined for-profit contractors for problems, though it has the authority to assess such fines.[32]

While Texas maintains its proclivity for being tough on crime, recently legislators have turned their attention to rehabilitation and reducing **recidivism,** or

Recidivism

a former inmate's resumption of criminal activity after his or her release from prison.

a return to crime after release from prison. Rather than focus on building new prisons, the 80th Legislature expanded state rehabilitation facilities, including mental health and substance abuse facilities, as well as increasing the number of halfway houses and drug treatment programs in state prisons. These actions represented a significant shift in policy and were specifically designed to deal with the state's ever-increasing incarceration rates.

Capital Punishment

In 1923, Texas adopted the electric chair (referred to as "Old Sparky") as the state's official method for carrying out capital punishment. Prior to the 1920s, hanging was the preferred method of state execution. In 1972, the Supreme Court ruled that the imposition of capital punishment amounted to "cruel and unusual punishment," since its selective application violated due process. Up to that point, Texas had electrocuted 361 people. Following the Court's ruling, some states, including Texas, began to change their procedures to make them less arbitrary. The most significant change was the adoption of a two-stage process: first, guilt or innocence is decided, then, where a guilty verdict has been pronounced, appropriate punishment is decided separately. By the time Texas implemented its new procedures for imposing the death penalty, lethal injection had become its official means of execution. Between 1982 and 2010, Texas executed 462 individuals with lethal injection. Most executions in the United States occur in the South, accounting for approximately 82 percent of all U.S. executions since 1976. Texas executes far more people than any other state in the United States and has carried out almost 40 percent of all executions in the country since 1976. Internationally, the death penalty has become increasingly unpopular. Currently, 130 countries ban the death penalty, including all western industrialized countries except the United States. Texas not only leads the nation, but also consistently ranks among the top ten countries worldwide in conducting executions (see Table 5.1).

The state may implement the death penalty if a person is found guilty of the murder of a public safety officer, firefighter, correctional employee, child under the age of six or is found guilty of multiple murders. Other actions that may invoke capital punishment include murder during a kidnapping, burglary, robbery, sexual assault, arson, or prison escape; murder for payment; as well as the murder of a prison inmate serving a life sentence for murder, kidnapping, aggravated sexual assault, or robbery.

The U.S. Supreme Court has recently recognized some significant limits on the death penalty. In 2002, the Court ruled that it is unconstitutional for the state to execute defendants who are mentally retarded (see *Atkins v. Virginia*).[33] A few years later, in *Roper v. Simmons*,[34] the Supreme Court ruled that juveniles could no longer be subject to the death penalty. As of July 2010, the Texas Department of Criminal Justice reported that since 1976 46 percent of executed prisoners have been white, 37 percent African American, and 17 percent Hispanic. Critics of the death penalty continue to emphasize that minorities disproportionately receive the death penalty. Texas has also executed three of the eleven women executed in the United States since 1976.

Why does Texas execute significantly more people than other states? Texans have a strong sense of right and wrong and are deeply attached to the idea of the death penalty as a deserved punishment. Whereas other states that use the death penalty may see it as a necessary evil, Texas culture embraces the state's right to execute its

Table 5.1 Countries with the Highest Number of Confirmed Executions in 2009

RANK	COUNTRY
1	China (1,718)*
2	Iran (388)
3	Iraq (120)
4	Saudi Arabia (69)
5	United States (52)
6	Yemen (30)
	Texas (24)

Sources: Death Penalty Information Center, www.deathpenaltyinfo.org/article .php?did=127&scid=30#interexec; Amnesty International, "Death Sentences and Executions 2009," 6, www.amnestyusa.org/ abolish/annual_report/DeathSentences Executions2009.pdf; Texas Execution Information Center, "Execution Reports: 2009," www.txexecutions.org/reports .asp?year=2009.

* Most recent confirmed execution data for China is from 2008.

citizens for the violation of certain laws. Texans' attachment to the death penalty remains as strong as their attachment to guns. Frontier Texans were often left to secure their own towns—indeed preferred it that way, suspicious as they were of governmental interference. Imposition of the death penalty is viewed as a right, one in keeping with Texans' sense that there are no gray areas—right is right, and wrong is wrong. This attitude still prevails throughout most of the state. It can be found among Texans sitting on juries, among Texans sitting on the Texas Court of Criminal Appeals, and among Texans serving on the Texas Board of Pardons and Paroles. As a former Smith County district attorney put it, "the death penalty in Texas is primarily a function of the fact that it is in our law. We have conservative jurors and district attorneys run for election and so it's very important that DAs . . . [who come up for reelections] make decisions on cases that are consistent with the feelings of their constituents."[35]

Support for the death penalty in the state remains strong. Recent polls indicate that while 58 percent of Americans support a moratorium on the death penalty, 70 percent of Texans continue to support the death penalty.[36] As DNA evidence has increasingly revealed that innocent people in the United States have been put to death, national support for the death penalty has waned. More recently, budget crises have motivated some states to abolish the death penalty due to the expense associated with it.

Texans' preference for the death penalty, however, remains so strong that often the actions of Texas courts seem downright odd to the rest of the country. In one now infamous case, a panel of three judges from the Fifth Circuit Court of Appeals upheld a death penalty sentence, even though the defendant's attorney had slept through portions of the trial. The panel ruled that since they could not determine whether the attorney had slept through critical parts of the trial, there was no basis to overturn the conviction. Although the full Fifth Circuit Court later overturned this ruling, the initial ruling is indicative of prevalent attitudes toward justice in Texas.

As opposition to the death penalty grew, Texas again made national news as the country seemed to be going in one direction and Texas in another. In the face of growing DNA evidence that innocent people are on death row, a number of states announced moratoriums on their death penalty, and in September 2007 the Supreme Court announced it would review the death penalty to consider whether lethal injection violates the Eighth Amendment's prohibition against cruel and unusual punishment. Michael Richard was scheduled to be executed in Texas that same day, and his lawyers scrambled to put together a request to stop his execution until the U.S. Supreme Court made its ruling on the constitutionality of lethal injection.

Richard's attorneys were working on their appeal late in the day when their printer malfunctioned. The attorneys called the Texas Court of Criminal Appeals, the highest criminal court in the state, and requested that the court stay open an extra twenty minutes so they could file the

Death Row was located in the Ellis 1 Unit in Huntsville, Texas, from 1965 until 1999. The death penalty symbolizes Texans' strong preference for politicians who are tough on crime.

The death penalty, or capital punishment, is a controversial topic. Attitudes and orientations toward it reflect deeper values associated with the political culture of a society. Within the United States, various states have adopted different constitutional provisions and statutory laws regarding the death penalty. While both Texas and California carry the penalty, they offer differing perspectives on the issue.

Texas permits use of the death penalty, and specific language in the state constitution spells out the process for appeals. The Texas Penal Code permits capital punishment in cases of capital murder, including murder of on-duty public safety officers, intentional murder of another person, hiring another person to commit a murder, and the murder of individuals under age 6, among others. In contrast, California's state constitution prohibits forms of punishment that are "cruel or unusual." In 1972, California became the first state in the country to ban the death penalty when the justices on the California Supreme Court ruled that capital punishment met the cruel or unusual criteria. The state's voters, however, disagreed; later that year the death penalty was restored to the California Constitution by constitutional referendum.

A key difference between the two states is that Texas regularly carries out the death penalty as a punishment while California does not. However, even as Texas has executed more persons than California since 1976, California has actually sentenced more people to death as a punishment for a crime. Several explanations exist for this difference in the rates of execution over time. First, prior to 1976 Texas and California each had executed over 700 individuals. Although both states reinstated the death penalty at approximately the same time, Texas began executing prisoners again in 1983. California did not execute a prisoner until 1992. Simply put, since reinstating the death penalty, Texas has been executing prisoners for a decade longer.[i] The reason for this involves the differing natures of the two states' court systems. In fact, the two states' court systems vary markedly in their orientation to the death penalty. The California court system focuses on minimizing error to ensure that an innocent person is not put to death. In contrast, the Texas court system focuses on a speedy process, and in so doing accepts a higher possible rate of error. As a result, California's appeals process requires both more time and more money be spent on the appeals process.[ii] The states also differ in their funding of a public defenders system. California has a statewide public defenders office that represents some death row inmates; Texas relies on pro bono work or contracts with local or regional lawyers. In addition, California falls under the jurisdiction of the U.S. Ninth Circuit Court of Appeals, whose Democratic-appointed majority is more likely to accept death penalty cases from the states in its jurisdiction, which serves to delay the carrying out of a sentence. The same cannot be said of the U.S. Fifth Circuit Court of Appeals that oversees Texas.[iii] Finally, in California, the death penalty's true purpose may be to serve as a symbol, one charged with acknowledging the seriousness of the offense in order to deter crime or express society's distaste for the act. In this case, the death penalty is not really designed as a punishment since the individual sentenced to death will not actually be put to death quickly.

appeal. Although courts have stayed open in the past to hear last-minute appeals, Sharon Keller, the presiding judge, refused the request. Keller did not consult Judge Cheryl Johnson, who later told the *Austin American-Statesman* that she would have accepted a last-minute filing, nor did Keller consult with the three other judges on the Texas Court of Criminal Appeals who stayed late that night anticipating a last-minute filing based on the U.S. Supreme Court's announcement.[37] Governor Perry, who could have issued a thirty-day reprieve, said that this was a matter for the courts to resolve. Unfortunately, as Judge Keller explained, the Texas Court of Criminal Appeals "close[d] at 5:00." Although Judge Keller has since been reprimanded by the State Commission on Judicial Conduct, the strong preference for carrying out executions remains clear.

	CALIFORNIA	TEXAS
Total inmates on death row, 2009	694	339
Executions in 2009	0	24
Executions before 1976	709	755
Executions since 1976	13	462
Females executed since 1976	0	3

Instead, convicted prisoners are far more likely to live out the rest of their lives in prison. Contrast this with Texas, where the death penalty is most certainly intended to deter crime—the convicted prisoner in Texas sentenced to death will be put to death.

Debate over the death penalty in California resurfaced recently when the state was faced with a serious budget crisis and began looking to cut expenses. A recent study indicates that it costs California an extra $125 million a year to retain the death penalty rather than to put everyone in death row in prison for life; this is in addition to $95 million per year for additional staff.[iv]

On top of this, the state currently needs to build a new "death house" to keep up with its large death row population, the construction of which would cost another $400 million.[v] Finally, the costs of a capital murder trial in California typically run over $1.9 million, three times the cost of a noncapital murder trial.[vi] Cost estimates in Texas place the figure at $1.2 million.[vii] In short, in California today it is the economic costs incurred by retention of the death penalty, including the higher trial costs and the

need to update the system, that is driving debate about the utility of capital punishment.

Thinking Critically

- Why does the "cruel or unusual" provision of the California Constitution change the orientation toward the death penalty and its legality?
- Why would California keep the death penalty in a symbolic sense but not actually use the death penalty?
- Does the cost of execution matter in the decision to impose the death penalty?
- Should Texas reevaluate its use of the death penalty based upon the costs of executing a prisoner?

i. Death Penalty Information Center, 2010, State by State Database, www.deathpenaltyinfo.org/state_by_state (accessed August 16, 2010).
ii. Rone Tempest, "Death Row Often Means a Long Life; California Condemns Many Murderers, but Few are Ever Executed," *Los Angeles Times*, March 6, 2005.
iii. Ibid.
iv. John Van de Kamp, "California Can't Afford the Death Penalty," *Los Angeles Times,* June 10, 2009.
v. Ibid.
vi. Tempest, "Death Row Often Means a Long Life."
vii. Logan Carver, "Death Penalty Cases More Expensive Than Lifetime Imprisonment, but Local CDA Says Costs Never a Consideration," *Lubbock Avalanche-Journal,* December 13, 2009, http//lubbockon line.com (accessed August 16, 2010).

Proponents of the death penalty in Texas and elsewhere argue that it acts as a deterrent on crime. This argument is consistent with Texans' preference for politicians and courts in Texas to be tough on crime. However, opponents of the death penalty point out that states without the death penalty have lower murder rates than states that use the death penalty. One study by the *New York Times* concluded that ten of the twelve states without the death penalty have murder rates that are lower than the national average whereas half the states with the death penalty have murder rates that are higher than the average.[38]

Moreover, opponents point out the added expense of death penalty cases, which involve automatic appeals to the state's high court, among other things. The average time spent on death row is slightly over ten years, although the longest time spent on death row was twenty-four years. In 1992, a *Dallas Morning News* study estimated that taxpayers pay $2.3 million for the average death penalty case in Texas, compared to $750,000 to imprison someone in a single cell at the highest level of security for forty years.[39] This higher cost comes in every case, even those in which the death penalty *may* be imposed. The cost of the death penalty, coupled with the comparatively large number of executions in the state each year, places a significant burden on Texas's taxpayers.

Winners and Losers

In many ways, Texans' preference for a tough approach to crime, demands for justice, and ardent support of the death penalty sets them apart from the rest of the country. However, these political preferences come at a high cost to the average Texan. Money spent on imprisonment rather than rehabilitation means that Texas's high imprisonment rates translate to higher taxes in Texas. Embracing the privatization of prisons also entails significant costs. When these for-profit centers experience high-profile breakouts, it is local and state law officials who conduct statewide searches for the escaped convicts—and it is Texas's taxpayers who pick up the cost. Although private prisons are often cited for poor conditions, Texas has yet to impose fines on these facilities. Texans are also willingly taking on other states' criminal populations, with Texas leading the way in building private prisons intended to house both Texas's prisoners as well as the prisoners of other states. However, recent actions by the Texas Legislature may help the state become a winner as rehabilitation rather than punishment becomes a major focus of the Texas justice system.

Texans win and lose with the death penalty. Although increasingly unpopular nationwide, in Texas the death penalty is revered. On the one hand, Texans, in persisting with their policy preference for executions, "win" in terms of leading the country in number of executions carried out. On the other hand, Texans pay the high costs associated with ensuring that potential death penalty cases follow due process. In appropriating to themselves this cost—one that is significantly higher than the cost of life imprisonment—Texans lose.

Conclusion

Justice in Texas is a complicated affair. The judicial system is complex and confusing. There is a widespread perception among Texans that justice is for sale. Many outside the state view the justice system as medieval and unyielding. Texans' strong affinity for the death penalty and the state's frequent use of it makes Texas unique among the U.S. states. While Texans proclaim a strong desire for justice, in fact the current judicial system rarely satisfies. In order to develop a more responsive judicial system, Texans may need to reevaluate how their preferences are represented in the current system. For instance, the preference of voters to retain control of judicial selection via the ballot entails a high cost. The overwhelming job of selecting nearly all of the judges in the state comes with very little payoff. More generally, Texans' resistance to change means that the Texas judiciary, like other institutions in the state, evolves in a piecemeal manner. The result is a system that in many ways no longer makes sense for the state.

Key Terms

appellate jurisdiction
at-large election
beyond a reasonable doubt
civil case
civil defendant
compensatory damages
concurrent jurisdiction
criminal case
criminal defendant
cumulative voting
de novo
en banc
exclusive jurisdiction
grand jury
incumbency advantage
indictment
judicial federalism
jurisdiction
magistrate functions
name recognition
original jurisdiction
petit jury
plaintiff
preponderance of evidence
private prison
prosecutor
punitive damages
recidivism
straight ticket voting

Explore this subject further at http://lonestar.cqpress.com, where you'll find chapter summaries, practice quizzes, key word flash cards, and additional suggested resources.

Suburban sprawl and urban towers characterize the city of Houston. The aerial view offers a perspective suggesting the unity of the Houston metro area. In reality, Houston, like all other Texas population centers, is governed by a multitude of overlapping local governments.

CHAPTER 6

Local Government in Texas

W ater is the "new oil," according to oil baron T. Boone Pickens.[1] When Fort Stockton Holdings applied for a permit in July 2009 to pump water from the Edwards-Trinity Aquifer in western Texas, the company found itself in a fight that placed several local governments at odds with each other and focused attention on the overlapping concerns and jurisdictions of local governments in the state. Fort Stockton Holdings planned to draw the water from under land in Pecos County owned by Clayton Williams Jr., the former Republican candidate for Texas governor. Williams not only owned the land but also the company planning to draw the water from the aquifer. For Williams, the issue was simple: He owned the land, and he had a right to pump the water.

The city of Fort Stockton in Pecos County had other ideas. Fort Stockton draws its water from the aquifer as well. The permit to pump the water from Williams' land had to be approved by the Middle Pecos Groundwater Conservation District, a local government created by the Texas Legislature to manage water resources in part of western Texas. The situation was complicated by the fact that Williams planned to sell the water to the city of Midland, some 100 miles to the northeast. Fort Stockton challenged the right to pump the water because the planned sale of water to Midland in effect transferred large amounts of water to a city outside the conservation district.[2] Midland needed additional water resources to fuel growth and development in that city. However, the matter was further complicated by the fact that the aquifer serves as the source of springs and creeks that flow eventually into the Rio Grande River—the source of water for Laredo. Environmentalists and elected officials in the Laredo area alleged that the pumping of water would adversely affect their water supply.[3] By May 2010, the Board of Directors of the Middle Pecos Groundwater Conservation District had agreed to hold a hearing on the permit request by Fort Stockton Holdings.

While the Middle Pecos Groundwater Conservation District supervises water rights for parts of Pecos County, the Edwards-Trinity Aquifer extends over a much larger area of Texas, extending in an arc over to San Antonio and up to Austin. Hundreds of cities and counties draw water from the aquifer. The right to draw water from the aquifer is considered by at least ten different conservation districts. A decision to increase the amount of water pumped from the aquifer affects not just a neighboring city or community, but potentially many other cities, counties, and conservation districts in Texas. As the attempt to secure additional water resources by Midland illustrates, even cities and counties outside a region become involved in order to secure their future as well.

While the Texas Water Development Board, an agency of the state government, is supposed to provide leadership on water usage in Texas, cities persist in fighting over access to this important resource. County governments may also become involved to assure residents who live outside of cities that they will have access to water. Additional layers of local government, like water conservation districts and municipal utility districts, also become embroiled in the fight. Meanwhile, land owners become frustrated by the overlapping—and confusing—levels of local government involved.

In this chapter, we will review the basic foundations of the myriad of local governments in Texas, discussing the creation, powers, and organization of county government. Then, we review city government, focusing on the differences between general law and home rule cities. We will also examine the functions of city governments and survey its elections processes. Finally, we will conclude with a review of other forms of local government, including public education and special districts like municipal utility districts.

As you read the chapter, think about the following questions:

★ To what extent does the structure of Texas counties limit large counties such as Harris County or small counties such as Loving County?

★ How do the functions of county government differ from the functions of city government?

★ What are the different types of city government?

★ How are local elections conducted in the state of Texas?

★ How are public schools organized in Texas?

★ Why are special districts, like municipal utility districts, community college districts, and hospital districts, important in Texas?

★ What are the issues with funding local government?

Local Government: The Basics

Local government involves a wide range of entities. Most often, local government refers to cities and counties. In Texas, local government also includes school districts, community college districts, municipal utility districts, water conservation districts, and airport districts, among others. Local government does not just end with water supply concerns. Numerous local governments exist to provide for public schools, junior colleges, hospitals, parks and recreation, economic development, ports, airports, libraries, and fire protection. For example, residents of the Cypress-Fairbanks area of northwest Harris County have at least eight local governments governing their lives, providing necessary services and levying taxes to fund those services. These separate and distinct local governments include the Cypress-Fairbanks Independent School District, Harris County; Harris County Flood Control District; Port of Houston Authority; Harris County Hospital District; Lone Star Community College District; Harris County Education Department; Harris County Emergency Services District 9; and a municipal utility district. One reason for the large number of local governments is that Texas's counties often do not provide the same services that counties in other states provide. In the absence of strong county governments, Texans have found other ways to obtain the services they desire, in part by creating many other types of local governments.

Texas has the third highest number of local governments of any state in the United States (see Table 6.1). Adjusting for the size of population, smaller population states like North and South Dakota possess more governments per person than Texas. In fact, Texas does not even rank in the top half of states ranked according to governments per person, coming in at thirty-third. Thus, although Texas and other high population states like California seem to host a lot of local governments, when population size is taken into account, they do not.

The common characteristic of all of these local governments is that they exist as an arm of the state government. Regardless of the type of local government, all local governments are creatures of the state government, a concept known as **Dillon's Rule.** In an 1868 case before the Iowa Supreme Court, Justice John Forrest Dillon affirmed the principle that local governments have only those powers specifically granted to them by the states.[4] The U.S. Supreme Court later echoed this view. The high court ruled that states may change the powers of their cities, even if the residents living in the city do not approve.[5] By extension, this concept applied to all forms of local government within a state, including county governments and special districts.

In other words, the powers, duties, and very existence of each and every local government are determined by the state government. This legal status exists between local governments and their respective state government in every state of the United States. In Texas, the constitution provides a basic framework to define the types, powers, and responsibilities of local governments in Texas. Statutory laws like the Texas Local Government Code, Texas Education Code, and Texas Utilities Code, and even the Texas Water Code supplement the framework found in the Texas Constitution. For example, the Texas Constitution specifically grants to the Texas Legislature "the power to create counties for the convenience of the people."[6] These constitutional provisions and statutory laws go so far as to specify how local governments elect officials, which administrative offices must exist, and what types of taxes local governments may use to fund their activities.

Because there are fifty states in the United States, essentially fifty different systems of local government have developed. States diverge tremendously in the structure and functions of local governments. As examples, Connecticut and Rhode Island lack county government in the sense that Texas and other states use county government. In both states, counties serve primarily as a method of reporting population for the U.S. Census. Most functions that Texans associate with county government are performed in

Dillon's Rule
the principle that regardless of the type of local government, all local governments are creatures of the state government and have only those powers specifically granted to them by the state.

Table 6.1 Units of Local Government Compared to State Population (2007)

	NUMBER OF LOCAL GOVERNMENTS	
STATE	NUMBER	GOVERNMENTS PER 100,000 PEOPLE
Top Five		
Illinois	6,994	54.2
Pennsylvania	4,871	38.6
Texas	**4,835**	**19.5**
California	4,344	11.7
Kansas	3,931	140.4
50-state average	1,789	28.9
Bottom Five		
Maryland	256	4.5
Nevada	198	0.7
Alaska	177	25.3
Rhode Island	134	13.4
Hawaii	19	1.5
States Bordering Texas		
Oklahoma	1,880	50.8
Arkansas	1,548	53.4
Louisiana	1,346	29.9
New Mexico	863	43.2

Source: U.S. Census Bureau, *Census of Governments,* Table 417, "Number of Local Governments by Type—States: 2007."

Connecticut by township governments and in Rhode Island by cities and towns. Other states, like Georgia, maintain countywide school districts. Arkansas allows school district boundaries to cross county lines. A number of states, like Tennessee and Louisiana, allow cities and counties to merge into a single local government, and in Virginia some cities are independent of or outside of counties.

Because local governments of all types are extensions of a state government, a second relationship necessarily exists: the relationship between local governments and the national government in Washington, D.C. This relationship is more complex. The U.S. Constitution mentions explicitly only state governments and the national government. On a legal and technical level, then, local governments do not exist in the eyes of the U.S. Constitution. In practice, however, the national government recognizes that state governments and state constitutions create local governments and that such governments exist within states. The norm is to hold state governments responsible for the policies and procedures of their local governments. For example, if local school districts are unable or unwilling to comply with a federal law or federal court decision, the U.S. government ultimately requires the state government to solve the problem. A dramatic example involved the failure in the 1970s and 1980s of the Kansas City, Missouri, public school system to integrate its schools following the Supreme Court's ruling in favor of desegregation. The federal courts went so far as to hold the Missouri state government responsible for the problem and to require the use of statewide taxes to pay for integration of Kansas City schools.[7]

A federal system of government, as described in Chapter 2, exists where the powers of government are divided between a national government and state governments, with each level of government having an independent base of power. This arrangement contrasts with a unitary system of government in which all power is centralized and other levels of government are allotted power at the discretion of the central government. The exact division of powers in a federal system may be dual federalism, in which each level has distinct and separate powers, or cooperative federalism, in which the state governments and the national government jointly carry out some tasks.

Two other arrangements within federal systems are fiscal federalism and administrative federalism. Under **fiscal federalism,** the U.S. government sets goals and objectives or develops new programs, then the national government provides financial incentives for the state governments to participate in the program. In response, states begin to develop their own programs or change their own policies to match the goals of what the national government wants. States typically receive money from the national government to cover some of the costs of these programs. For example, if the U.S. Congress and the president believe that providing computers and Internet access to students in elementary, middle, and high schools is essential to learning in the twenty-first century, then they will fund a federal program that provides money to those states that decide to buy new computers and equip new and existing schools with Internet access according to the terms of the federal program. The money provided by the national government is matched with contributions from the state government and then given to schools for implementation. In some cases, the local government may be asked to contribute funds also. There are numerous examples of this type of program spanning a variety of policy areas, including healthcare for the disabled, immunization programs for poor children, road construction, and draining and sewer system improvements, among others.

Fiscal federalism

use of national financial incentives to encourage policies at the state and local level.

Administrative federalism works in a similar manner, however, minus financial input. The national government sets up guidelines for policy, then expects the state governments to pay for the programs on their own without matching funds from the national government. The best current example of administrative federalism is probably "No Child Left Behind" (NCLB). NCLB sets a broad set of objectives for states to follow regarding the performance of elementary and secondary schools. These objectives include lowering high school dropout rates and heading off student truancy. States and school districts are expected to provide methods of assessing whether students are learning essential knowledge and skills. However, the national government does not provide money to states to implement NCLB. States must pay for it themselves.

How do fiscal and administrative federalism connect to local government? In fiscal federalism, the national government provides money in the form of grants, or sums of money given to state or local governments to fund a program or policy. Usually, states allow local governments to apply to the state for a share of the money, often through a competitive process. Thus, local governments must develop the skills and staffs to write the applications, provide evidence of the need for the funds, and develop budgets. In addition, once a local government receives a grant, it must report back in detail to the state government how the money was used. Local governments become the key agents of program implementation. In terms of administrative federalism, local governments again serve as agents of implementation. However, state governments establish how best to achieve the national government's objectives, outlining an approach that is then handed to local governments to carry out. Using NCLB as an illustration, the Texas Education Agency (TEA) developed a set of guidelines to meet the objectives of NCLB, using the Texas Assessment of Knowledge and Skills (TAKS) test. However, the TEA does not give the test to school students. Instead, the TEA gives the tests to each school district, which then administers the TAKS test. If a specific school does not perform well, the local school district is charged with developing a plan to bring up test scores.

County Government: Texas Style

Texas counties vary tremendously in population, natural resources, and land areas. However, all Texas counties are structured the same way, and this structure is grounded in historical development and constitutional provisions. As a result, Texas county government exhibits a one-size-fits-all approach. The lack of variation in government structure makes Texas unusual compared to some states.

History and Function of Counties in Texas

Local government in Texas is rooted in the old municipality system of the Mexican Republic. Under Mexican rule, Texas contained four municipalities, large areas containing a town and surrounding rural areas. Initially, the four municipalities were San Antonio, Bahia (Goliad), Nacogdoches, and Rio Grande Valley. The number of these governments increased as the population and settlements grew. When the Republic of Texas was established, twenty-three counties were created based upon these Mexican municipalities, including Nacogdoches, Bexar, and Brazos. At statehood in 1845, the county system was retained. The Confederate Constitution of 1861 created 122 counties, and the number of counties continued to increase

Administrative federalism
the process whereby the national government sets policy guidelines, then expects state governments to pay for the programs they engender without the aid of federal monies.

under subsequent state constitutions. In 1931, Loving County became the last county to be established. Interestingly, the organization of Loving County marked its second era of existence. The first Loving County had originally been carved in 1893 from Reeves County as part of a get-rich-quick scheme to defraud landowners and the state of Texas by the organizers of the county. The scandal surrounding Loving County, which involved falsified county records, illegitimate elections, and low population, prompted the Texas Legislature to abolish the county in 1897. The arrival of the oil industry to western Texas later spurred its reestablishment.[8]

Texas today has 254 counties, more than any other state. Georgia is the next closest with 159 counties. Hawaii and Delaware have the fewest, with three counties each. In Texas, counties are created by laws passed by the state legislature, subject to a few limitations from the Texas Constitution. For example, new counties may not be smaller than 700 square miles and existing counties from which a new county is created cannot be reduced to less than 700 square miles.[9] Historically, county boundaries were drawn so that its citizens could travel to the county courthouse and return home in a single day.[10] By population, Harris County is the largest county in Texas, with over 3.4 million people. Only two counties in the United States are larger in population: Cook County, Illinois, and Los Angeles County, California. The smallest county in Texas by population is Loving County, with just 45 people. As a result, Loving County holds the distinction of being the smallest county in terms of population in the country as a whole. In terms of geographic area, Brewster County is the largest in Texas at 6,204 square miles, an area larger than the states of Connecticut and Rhode Island combined. Rockwall County, near Dallas, is the smallest at 129 square miles.[11]

County names in Texas reflect a variety of historical and cultural influences. Twelve counties are named for defenders of the Alamo, including Bowie, Fannin, and Taylor Counties. Several reflect geographic features like rivers, streams, and landforms, such as Pecos and Sabine Counties. Some are named for governors and other figures in Texas politics, like Coke County and Lamar County. Panola County is named for the Native American word for "cotton," while Lampasas County comes from the Spanish word for "lilies." Freestone County is named for a variety of peach.

More importantly, county government is essential in Texas because counties carry out many duties for the state government. In this respect, counties are essentially extensions of the state government. The role and function of counties is especially important in rural areas of the state, where cities and towns are few and far between. In the days before well-maintained roads and highways, the state government in Austin was largely inaccessible to many Texans. So, county government was designed to bring state government closer to the people. County government is also essential to the function of both administrative and fiscal federalism because counties are often the front line for the delivery of a variety of policies.

Texas's counties perform at least six key functions for the state government. Counties operate courts for the state, including justice of the peace, county, and district courts. Counties make available public health clinics, conduct immunization programs, enforce state health regulations, and inspect restaurants. They also maintain vital records for the state, including marriage licenses, death certificates, birth certificates, and property deeds. Another function of counties is to collect funds for the state government, for example, in the form of property taxes, license plate fees, and motor vehicle title fees. Counties are also responsible for conducting elections; they maintain election equipment, oversee the registration of voters, and operate polling places. Finally, counties work jointly with state government to carry out other functions. For example, counties help with law enforcement by maintaining sheriff or constable offices and operating county jails. They also build roads and bridges that connect to the state's network of roads and highways.

In a strange twist on Texas politics, the Texas Constitution contains a strong provision against imprisonment for debt. However, the Texas Constitution also allows each county to provide a "Manual Labor Poor House and Farm, for taking care of, managing, employing, and supplying the wants of its indigent and poor inhabitants."[12] Apparently, being in debt is not grounds for state judicial action, but being poor is. This provision of the state constitution is an arcane one that counties have replaced with a variety of national, state, and local programs to provide assistance to the poor. The state permits counties to carry out certain activities that may also be provided by other forms of local government, including cities and special districts. Counties sometimes operate parks, run libraries, own airports, and manage hospitals. Services such as water, sewer, and garbage collection may also be provided through a county government.

Governing Texas Counties

All Texas counties are governed the same way. This means that counties are controlled directly by state laws, the most important being the Texas Local Government Code. Adherence to state law means that all 254 counties in Texas have the same form of government (see Figure 6.1). Every county government is led by a **commissioners court**. The commissioners court is made up of four elected commissioners and the county judge from the county constitutional court. The selection of the commissioners and the county judge is conducted by **partisan election,** that is, an election in which each candidate's name and party affiliation are listed on the ballot. The elections for the four commissioners in every county are by the single-member district plurality (SMDP) system. (See Chapter 3 regarding the state legislature, and again later in this chapter, in reference to city council elections.) The county judge is elected at large by voters across the county. The members of the court, including the county judge, are elected for four-year terms. Commissioners are elected to staggered terms of office.

Each commissioner is responsible for running the county government in his or her own district. One of the primary responsibilities of a commissioner is the maintenance of roads and bridges in the district. Each commissioner determines which roads are paved and repaved, when bridges are repaired, and which company receives the contract to perform road projects in his or her district/precinct. Commissioners do not have to work collectively but may act solely in the interest of his or her precinct. In some counties, the commissioners do agree to pool resources and make these decisions about roads and bridges collectively in the interest of the whole county.

County commissioners may also collectively pass ordinances concerning the sale, possession, and consumption of alcoholic beverages. Yet state law permits residents to override the commissioners court regarding alcoholic beverage control policy. In this instance, it is the county commissioner's election district, or precinct, that determines alcohol control policy. Voters in a commissioner's district may file a petition to hold an election in the precinct to change the alcoholic beverage control policy. The election is limited to just that precinct, and any policy change affects the possession and consumption of alcoholic beverages only in that precinct. For example, at one point in time in Angelina County in East Texas alcohol

Commissioners court
the governing body for Texas counties, consisting of four elected commissioners and the judge from the county constitutional court.

Partisan election
a type of election in which candidates' names and party affiliations appear on the ballot.

Figure 6.1 The Structure of County Government in Texas

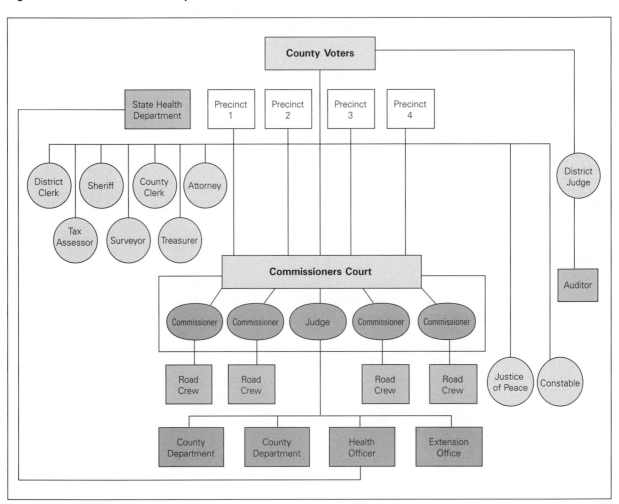

Source: John A. Gilmartin and Joe M. Rothe, *County Government in Texas,* issue 2, V. G. Young Institute of County Government, Texas Agricultural Extension Service, Texas A&M University.

policy varied slightly across the county because voters in one precinct voted to permit individuals to purchase alcohol in public places if the purchaser was an adult over age 21 and had also bought a private club membership. In another precinct, the sale of beverages was permitted only in restaurants and bars to those over age 21 who showed a valid I.D. In still other parts of the county the sale and possession of alcoholic beverages remained illegal because voters had not petitioned for a change in policy.

Students of Texas politics are often confused by the term "commissioners court," which implies a judicial function. This confusion is increased by the presence of the county constitutional court judge on the commissioners court. In fact, the commissioners court serves as a legislative body for the county rather than a judicial body. The commissioners court passes laws that govern the county, determines types and rates of taxes to fund the county government, and passes the annual county budget. The commissioners court also serves as a collective executive for the county.

Law enforcement in Texas is a function of city, county, and state government. While cities like Austin have police departments, county governments use sheriffs, justices of the peace, and constables to enforce the law. At the state level, the Texas Rangers and Texas Highway Patrol serve as law enforcement agencies.

The court administers state and federal funds for local government use, oversees the various county departments and agencies, and holds final responsibility for the conduct of elections in the county. The county constitutional court judge serves as the presiding officer of the commissioners court and appoints temporary replacements when a commissioner resigns. Thus, the commissioners court fuses the power of the legislative and executive branches into a single entity.

The county constitutional court judge, of course, also serves as the justice for the county court. Thus, the role of the county judge crosses all three branches of government. The county constitutional court judge is in charge of the county budget, an executive function; serves on the commissioners court, a legislative function; and hears cases before the county court, a judicial function.

When it comes to Texas county government, the traditional concept of the separation of powers between the U.S. Congress, president, and U.S. Supreme Court entrenched nationally in the U.S. Constitution does not apply. Likewise, although the Texas Constitution (1876) and its predecessors also mirrored the U.S. Constitution's separation of powers at the state level, similar provisions were not included for county government. When the Texas Legislature established county government in Texas, it left no provision for the separation of powers. In a state that prides itself on small and limited government, the structure of county government seems at odds with the prevailing political culture.

To assist the commissioners court, the voters elect a variety of other county officers. Typically, these officers are elected for four-year terms. Voters elect a county **sheriff** to oversee law enforcement in the county. The sheriff appoints deputy sheriffs and operates the county jail. The **county clerk** is responsible for maintaining county records including births, deaths, and marriage licenses. In some counties the county clerk also serves as the county elections officer and

Sheriff
the elected county official who oversees county law enforcement.

County clerk
the elected county official who maintains county records and in some counties oversees elections.

County attorney

the county official who represents the county in legal activities and offers legal advice to the county government.

Tax assessor

the elected county officer who collects county taxes and user fees.

Justice of the peace

an elected county officer who acts as a judicial officer for minor criminal and civil cases.

Constable

an elected county officer who acts as a judicial officer for minor criminal and civil cases.

Auditor

a county officer appointed by the district judge to oversee county finances.

Merit-based civil service system

a system in which people receive government jobs based upon a set of qualifications and formal training; job promotion and pay raises are based upon job performance.

registrar of voters. The **county attorney** serves as the chief prosecuting attorney for misdemeanors in local courts, represents the county in legal activities, and offers legal advice to the county government. The county **tax assessor** collects property taxes and license plate fees, issues title certificates for cars and trucks, and, in many counties, acts as the registrar of voters and chief elections administrator. Since 1978, many counties have created a unified tax assessor district, which provides property tax assessment and collection for the county, cities, and school districts in the county. The county tax assessor's involvement with voter registration is a holdover from the days of the poll tax (see Chapter 7). The **justice of the peace** and **constable** serve as judicial officers for minor criminal and civil cases. Normally, each of the four districts of the county has a justice of the peace and a constable.

Several other officers may be elected or appointed. A district clerk maintains court records for county and district courts. For larger counties, an **auditor** is appointed by the district judge to oversee county finances, a county public health officer directs local public health clinics, and a county agricultural agent assists in rural counties with the needs of the farming community. Some counties have a county elections officer.

These officials are assisted by a host of employees that work for the various departments of the county government. From receptionists and administrative assistants to county land surveyors, counties employ thousands of Texans to perform the day-to-day operations of county government. In all but a handful of Texas counties, these jobs are essentially patronage. In a patronage system, elected officials give out government jobs to whomever the elected official wishes to have the job, often a loyal supporter. A person hired for a government job then serves at the wishes of the elected official and may be fired at will for any reason. Historically, under patronage government jobs were handed out as political favors by the person winning an election. In some cases, the person who got a job in government service lacked any qualifications for the position. Of course, many of the men and women who work for county governments throughout Texas are competent, qualified people. They hold jobs without the protections of a **merit-based civil service system.** In a merit system, people receive government jobs based upon a formalized system of qualifications, usually holding formal training for the position, including college degrees or vocational certification. Often, merit systems require an applicant to take a test or examination to determine if the applicant is qualified. Individuals receive promotions and salary increases based upon a standard scale or series of performance goals. A patronage system may mimic the merit system by writing qualifications for offices or setting minimal standards for getting a job, yet the fact remains that these standards are not mandated by anything other than the decisions of county commissioners.

The Texas Local Government Code allows counties with 200,000 or more people to create a merit-based civil service system. Counties with less than 200,000 retain a patronage system. The creation of a merit system may be initiated by a vote of the county's commissioners court or by the county's voters.[13] In counties with over 500,000 people, a civil service system may be limited to the county's sheriff's department. As a result of the 2000 census, twenty counties in Texas qualified to implement a civil service system; however, only eight created one. Harris County, the most populous county in the state, lacks a civil service system for county employees. All seven of the counties with populations large enough to establish a civil service system for the sheriff's department have done so. Thus, in Harris County, sheriff's department employees operate within a civil service system, but the rest of the county's employees do not.[14]

A civil service system for a county is administered by a **county civil service commission.** The commission is appointed by the commissioners court for terms of two years. The civil service commission develops job definitions, qualification processes, classification of employees, and requirements for promotion. The commission is also charged with additional responsibilities, such as developing disciplinary procedures for employees who violate policies and procedures and a grievance process to handle employee complaints.

County civil service commission
the agency administering the county's civil service system; develops job definitions, qualification processes, employee classifications, and other aspects of the system.

County Finances and Operations

To provide for day-to-day operations, counties in Texas rely on property taxes as their primary source of income. Other sources of revenue are motor vehicle license fees, service fees, and federal aid. Service fees include the costs of obtaining official documents such as marriage licenses and birth certificates, as well as court fees to file a case with the county court.[15] In counties without incorporated cities or transportation districts, the county may also use sales taxes to finance the county government. While county governments face an upper limit on the rate that may be assessed for property tax rates, voters may agree to additional property tax rates to fund roads and bridges in the county or for additional special services that the county may provide, such as flood control. Additional services that citizens desire beyond those financed by the county budget may be funded by creating special districts to fund hospitals, libraries, ports, airports, and so forth. Some counties have created special districts, called municipal utility districts, to provide basic utilities such as water, sewers, and electrical delivery. However, such districts may be created to provide services in only parts of a county. Special districts are discussed later in this chapter.

In some counties, the county government contracts with private businesses to provide the basic services counties normally offer through their budgets and related property taxes. This process involves either **privatization** or **contract outsourcing** of government services. Often services such as trash collection and recycling are targeted for privatization and contract outsourcing. A new outsourcing trend is the building of toll roads. In some counties, a private company is contracted to build and maintain a highway for the county or state. Individuals who use the highway pay a fee to drive on the road. This fee helps to repay the private company for the cost of building it and for routine repairs to the highway. Harris, Dallas, Tarrant, Bexar, Travis, and Smith counties now have toll roads.

In 2009, the city of Kennedale near Arlington in the Dallas–Fort Worth Metroplex decided to save money and to help balance the city's budget by eliminating its recycling program. In response, a local resident decided to create a recycling program herself. Theresa Picard created a business called America Can Recycle; she began offering to pick up recyclables from residents and local businesses for a small fee. All proceeds that the business generates are given to the Kennedale Independent School District. While this approach is not the traditional route to privatization, America Can Recycle does illustrate privatization in action.[16]

Property taxes provide the primary source of funding for county governments in Texas. However, rates of property taxes vary tremendously in the state. In 2008, Sutton County represented the low end of property tax rates in Texas, with rates at $0.18 per $100 of the assessed value of the property, while Jim Hogg County maintained the highest rate at $1.09 per $100. In Jim Hogg County $1.09 per $100 included $0.16 in special taxes to fund roads and bridges and an additional $0.19

Privatization
a process whereby a government entity sells off assets or services to a private company which is then responsible for providing a service; for example, a school district sells its buses to a private company and then allows the company to provide transportation to schools.

Contract outsourcing
a process whereby a government entity contracts with a private company to perform a service that governments traditionally provide, such as a contract to collect trash and garbage.

for other services such as flood control. The average for counties in Texas is $0.50 per $100 of the assessed value of property. Real estate in the state is the only property that is routinely taxed for the purposes of funding local governments. Other states assess personal property taxes as well. Personal property may include recreational vehicles, furniture, electronic appliances, and animals. Some states include the cars and trucks that a family or business owns in their personal property tax assessments as well. In states like Missouri and Kansas, the tax on cars and trucks can be quite substantial. For example, Greene County, Missouri, assesses cars at 33.3 percent of the assessed value of the vehicle per $100 times the local tax rate. So, a person with a $20,000 car in Greene County follows this formula to determine the tax. $20,000 (the value of the car) divided by 100, multiplied by 0.333, then multiplied by 4.26 (the property tax rate). The tax in 2010 on the car, not counting other forms of property, would be approximately $280.[17]

The use of property taxes as the primary source of funding for county government is not without controversy. For counties with high property values, the use of property taxes provides ample revenue to fund county services. The reliance on property taxes stems in part from the inability of many counties to levy sales taxes to fund local government. In addition, property taxes permit the state of Texas to avoid the imposition of income taxes, common in many states. However, property values vary tremendously across the state's counties (see Table 6.2); in many rural areas without significant natural resources or economic development, lower property values might mean an inability to raise adequate revenue. In some instances, property tax rates are substantially higher in these counties to compensate for the relatively lower value of property in the county. Critics of property taxes also point out that the taxes are paid only by individuals who actually own property. If an individual does not own property, he or she does not pay taxes but still has use of public services. In some communities, 30 to 35 percent of residents do not own property, and therefore enjoy services provided by counties, cities, and local governments without contributing directly to the provision of those services, though costs may be passed on to them indirectly through higher rents.

Table 6.2 Property Tax Rates in Texas, 2008

COUNTY	TOTAL TAX RATE PER $100	GENERAL FUND	ROADS AND BRIDGES	OTHER
Five Highest Rates				
Jim Hogg	$1.09	$0.75	$0.16	$0.19
Foard	$0.95	$0.80	$0.15	$0.00
Delta	$0.93	$0.75	$0.00	$0.18
Throckmorton	$0.91	$0.75	$0.13	$0.03
King	$0.88	$0.69	$0.00	$0.19
Five Lowest Rates				
Dallas	$0.23	$0.23	$0.00	$0.00
Borden	$0.22	$0.22	$0.00	$0.00
Freestone	$0.21	$0.21	$0.00	$0.00
Midland	$0.21	$0.21	$0.00	$0.00
Sutton	$0.18	$0.15	$0.00	$0.03

Source: Texas Comptroller, "County Self-Report Data—2008," www.window.state.tx.us/taxinfo/proptax/annual08/2008_county_values.xls (accessed July 26, 2010).

The structure of county government in Texas reflects the continuity and tradition of the state. While the number of counties has increased, and their populations as well, the Texas Constitution and statutory law prevent variation in the structure of the commissioners court and its powers. This lack of variation is true for most other county officials and their duties as well. As a result, Harris County and Loving County essentially share the same system of government, despite the tremendous difference in population and demand for government action. While Harris County's government is larger in terms of total staffing and size of budget, the county basically does what Loving County's government does, in about the same way. County governments cannot adapt to the realities of their situation or the changes that occur over time. In order for counties to significantly adapt and update the uniform, single approach to county government required of all counties in Texas, the state legislature would have to either alter the Texas Local Government Code or propose amendments to the state constitution.

Cities

Although counties perform essential services to Texans as an extension of the state government, cities develop more directly from citizen input. In addition, the Texas Constitution and statutory laws give cities more discretion than counties to adapt to change in such areas as city organization, election system, local laws, and form of government. Given the wide divergence in population size, geographic location, and resource base, the flexibility given to cities better equips them to carry out local government functions in a rapidly changing state.

A city is created in Texas when the population of an area that is not already incorporated as a city reaches at least 200 people. To form a city, the residents must also define its exact boundaries and negotiate with the county regarding the services the new city government will provide versus those the county already provides to the residents. At this point, residents of the area may gather signatures of others living there who support the creation of a city. After gathering the required number of signatures—up to 10 percent of the registered voters of the proposed city—the petition is presented to the county constitutional court judge, who places the issue on the ballot at the next county election. A city may also be created when residents living within an existing city receive permission to leave it and form a new one. Once a city is created, it continues to exist even if the population drops below 200 people. Only a majority vote by the registered voters living in the city can dissolve it.

The Texas Constitution provides for two categories of status for cities: general law and home rule. A city is normally a **general law city.** In other words, the default status of cities is general law. The Texas Local Government Code specifies the exact forms of government, ordinance powers, and other aspects of city government. However, general law cities often find that this arrangement is too rigid to adapt to the demands of population growth, demographic change, and economic development.

Three types of general law cities exist in Texas. These are General Law Type A, General Law Type B, and General Law Type C cities. General Law Type A cities are typically larger cities that contain at least 600 residents. They must have the strong mayor form of city government.[18] Type A cities may choose between SMDP and at-large election systems (discussed later in the chapter) and are required to have a wider range of city officials, either appointed or elected, than the other types. For example, Type A cities must have a tax assessor, a treasurer, a city secretary, and

General law city
the default organization for Texas cities, with the exact forms of government, ordinance powers, and other aspects of city government specified in the Texas Local Government Code.

Buffalo Gap

Founded in the 1850s, Buffalo Gap in Taylor County promoted itself as "The Athens of the West," an indication of its founders' high aspirations.[i] Its name is derived from the importance of buffalo hunting to the town's economy at the time of its founding. Presbyterians opened a college there in 1883, making Buffalo Gap a center of higher education. Sitting along the Old Center Line Trail, which ran from Texarkana to El Paso, the town benefitted from two other major trade routes that also ran through the town at the time, allowing it to flourish as a center of commerce. At its peak in the 1880s, 1,200 people called Buffalo Gap home. It boasted four grocery stores, a jail, a sizable hotel, a drugstore, and other businesses. Enrollment grew at the college, leading to the construction of several buildings and a dormitory on the campus. Buffalo Gap became a natural choice for the county seat when Taylor County was created in 1878. The town was among the more prosperous in the region. Buffalo Gap eventually possessed its own schools, banks, two newspapers, and a blacksmith shop. In short, Buffalo Gap was a thriving community poised for additional growth.

However, economic growth soon left the town behind. In 1883, ranchers north of town heard about the plans of the Texas and Pacific Railroad to build rail lines in the area and met with officials from the railroad, offering portions of their land for its use. They also agreed to help found the town of Abilene to serve as the railroad's headquarters, and the Texas and Pacific Railroad moved into Abilene. Within two years, Abilene surpassed Buffalo Gap in population, and shortly thereafter the county seat relocated there.

While Buffalo Gap was able to attract the Santa Fe Railroad in 1895, Abilene continued to thrive and prosper where Buffalo Gap did not. Unable to halt its decline, Buffalo Gap lost over half of the population it had once claimed. Abilene, meanwhile, grew into a transportation and business hub, profiting from the advent of the oil industry and the establishment of a U.S. Air Force Base after World War II. Buffalo Gap became one of those easily overlooked West Texas towns of legend. Abilene's position was further enhanced by three U.S. highways and an interstate passing through its city limits, even as Buffalo Gap remained a sleepy town several miles off of any major highways, with two Texas Farm to Market Roads intersecting it.

Buffalo Gap's renown flared briefly again in the 1960s when the town's marshal, Floyd Earl, turned the community into a speed trap, stringently enforcing the town's 30 mph speed limit. The marshal, however, did not have the normal provisions of a city police department. There was no police cruiser, and the marshal used his own car, using a flashlight to flag down and stop speeders at night. If a car failed to stop, Earl shot at the car. The marshal also did not have a standard issue police pistol or rifle. Early used his own unlimbered six-gun.[ii]

Today, Buffalo Gap is a quaint community of approximately 452 that seems locked in the past.[iii] Its founders' aspirations—"The Athens of the West"—were not realized; a fire at the college led to its temporary closure in 1895, and it closed for good in 1906. Today, many locals commute to other communities, including Abilene, to work and shop. The Buffalo Gap school system has been consolidated with those of several surrounding towns into the Jim Ned Consolidated Independent School District. Students now travel to the nearby town of Tuscola to attend school. Ironically, the town's major attraction is the Buffalo Gap Historical Village, a recreation of life in the late 1880s. One of its key components is the "Vintage Baseball" living history interpretation, which recreates the changes in the game since the late 1880s. The town's most recent claim to fame is Colt McCoy. McCoy grew up on a Buffalo Gap ranch and graduated from the local high school before becoming the starting quarterback for the University of Texas Longhorns. McCoy now plays for the Cleveland Browns of the National Football League.

i.   Texas State Historical Association, "The Handbook of Texas Online: Buffalo Gap," http://www.tshaonline.org/handbook/online/articles/BB/hlb60.html (accessed July 25, 2010).
ii. "Texas: Trouble in Buffalo Gap," *Time,* September 12, 1960, http://www.time.com/time/magazine/article/0,9171,897522,00.html (accessed July 25, 2010).
iii. U.S. Census Bureau, "Population Estimates, Incorporated Places and Minor Civil Divisions: Table 4. Annual Estimates of the Resident Population for Incorporated Places in Texas: April 1, 2000 to July 1, 2009," www.census.gov (accessed July 25, 2010).

a city attorney. In contrast, General Law Type B cities contain between 201 and 9,999 residents. These cities may choose between the strong mayor and weak mayor forms of government (discussed later in the chapter). Normally, Type B cities with the strong mayor form of government have six members elected to the city council using an at-large system. The city council may create any city offices it deems necessary. State law does not mandate the creation of specific offices.[19] General Law Type C cities have between 201 and 4,999 residents. These cities are required, unless otherwise approved by the state government, to have a weak mayor system of government.[20] The mayor and commission normally serve two-year terms in office.

Almost a century ago, a 1912 amendment to the Texas Constitution began to give cities more flexibility by allowing some to become home rule cities. A **home rule city** is a city that has been granted greater freedom in the organization and function of city government. A general law city with 5,000 or more people is permitted to shift to home rule. The advantages of home rule include the ability to adopt any of the three forms of city government, change the administrative structure by creating or abolishing departments, and alter systems of electing city officials without seeking the permission of the state. Home rule cities are governed by a **city charter,** subject to voter approval.[21] A city charter is a plan of government that details the structure and function of the city government. The city charter also discusses land usage within the city limits, specifies the election system for elected city officials, and details the types of **ordinances,** laws passed by a city government, the city may enact. General law cities of all types lack a city charter and are governed directly by state law and city ordinances. Home rule cities have more freedom to pass ordinances and have some influence over land usage just outside the city boundaries. The land usage power varies from half a mile for cities over 1,500 people to five miles for cities over 25,000. Home rule cities have greater powers of **annexation,** the addition of areas adjacent to it into the city limits. Once a city becomes a home rule city, it retains this status even if the population falls below 5,000.

One survey of cities conducted in 2007 found that the overwhelming majority (71.9 percent) of Texas cities are general law cities. This figure includes many cities with populations of more than 5,000. The residents of these cities have chosen to continue as general law cities despite their large size. Almost all other cities are home rule cities. A very small fraction of Texas cities—less than one-half of 1 percent, or just two cities—are classified as "other." These cities have exemptions from the general law–home rule dichotomy. Josephine in Collin County and Latexo in Houston County make up this category.

Forms of City Government

There are three basic forms of city government in Texas: the weak mayor–council system, the strong mayor–council system, and the council-manager system (see Figures 6.2–6.4). The strong mayor–council system occurs when the voters of the city elect a mayor as the chief executive and a city council to serve as the city's legislature. Together, the mayor and city council make policy for the city, pass ordinances for law-making, and oversee the city's various departments.

The mayor develops the city budget, appoints the heads of the departments of city government, sets the agenda for the council, and serves as chief administrator of the city's departments. The mayor also serves as a representative of the city's citizens at important functions: opening businesses, speaking on behalf of a city's citizens, attending conferences with other mayors, and negotiating on behalf of the city.

Home rule city
a city that has been granted greater freedom in the organization and functioning of city government; can make structural and administrative changes without seeking permission from the state.

City charter
in home rule cities, a plan of government that details the structure and function of the city government; similar to a constitution.

Ordinance
a law enacted by a city government.

Annexation
a process whereby areas adjacent to a city are added to the city, thereby extending the city limits.

Figure 6.2 Mayor-Council Form of City Government with a Weak Mayor

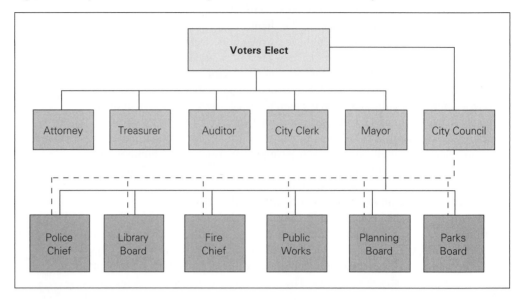

Figure 6.3 Mayor-Council Form of City Government with a Strong Mayor

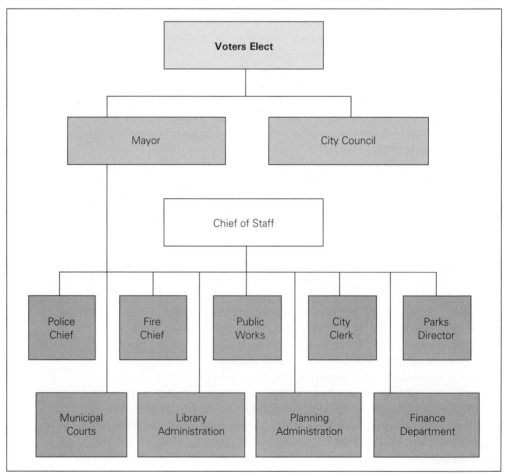

Figure 6.4 Council-Manager Form of City Government

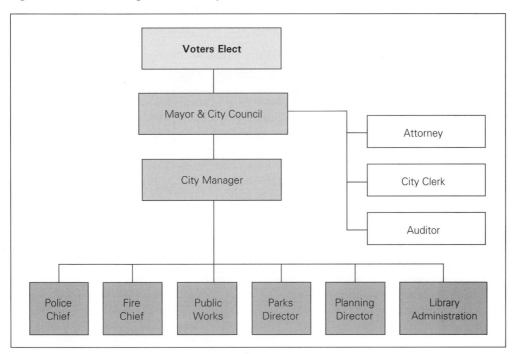

In many cities, the mayor may veto ordinances passed by the city council. The city council is responsible for passing ordinances; in some cities, the council may override a veto by the mayor. In addition, the council approves the city budget. In small cities, the mayor and council members may be part-time positions. In large cities both positions may be well-compensated because serving as mayor or sitting on the council are full-time jobs. In Texas, the strong mayor system is sometimes called the mayor-council, mayor-commission, or mayor-alderman form of government.

The advantage of the strong mayor system is the concentration of power in the hands of the mayor. The mayor provides leadership on issues of the day and sets the priorities of the city. The mayor's control over the city budget and over the city's departments allows for greater harmony and efficiency in policy implementation. In addition, the strong mayor system mirrors the separation of powers between the executive and legislative branches of government found in the national government. However, the concentration of power in the hands of the mayor may lead to personality-driven politics, to the detriment of the city. The power of the mayor also reduces the influence of the city council, which is designed to be the representative branch of city government.

In contrast, the weak mayor–council system features a directly elected mayor whose powers are much more diluted relative to those of the city council. The mayor and city council share power over the creation and adoption of the city budget. Ordinances are jointly determined by the mayor and council. Collectively, the mayor and city council choose the heads of the various city departments and jointly oversee the city bureaucracy. In some systems, voters directly elect the heads of the various city departments, such as the chief of police and city attorney. In Texas, the weak mayor system is often referred to generically as the "council" form of government or the "commission" form of government.

Chicago is the third largest city in the United States, ranking just one place above Houston. Like the Texas Constitution, the Illinois Constitution sets out the specific duties and responsibilities of city governments. Illinois also allows home rule for its cities and counties; but unlike in Texas, in Illinois cities are automatically granted home rule status when their population reaches 25,000 residents.[i]

The City of Chicago and the City of Houston both are home rule cities. Both also possess strong mayor–council systems of government. In Chicago, the city council consists of fifty aldermen elected from single-member districts or wards. The council divides itself into nineteen standing committees to assist in the process of developing and reviewing new ordinances. In this sense, the city council operates in a manner similar to a state legislature. Voters in Chicago directly elect the mayor, treasurer, and city clerk. To organize the city's bureaucracy, over forty city departments and agencies exist. In Houston, voters elect the mayor and city comptroller directly. The Houston City Council is chosen by a combination of single-member districts and at-large seats. Houston's city government consists of over twenty different departments and agencies. Some of Houston's agencies correspond to Chicago's departments. For example, both cities have fire, police, library, and aviation departments. However, there are differences between the two city governments as well. For example, Chicago's city government contains a Board of Ethics, the Chicago Film Office, the Environment Department, and the Cultural Affairs Office. Houston has none of these. Control over some agencies and departments differs too. In Houston, for example, parks and recreation is under city control. In contrast, in Chicago parks are controlled by a related but independent government agency.

City Government in Chicago and Houston

FACTOR	CHICAGO	HOUSTON
Population	2.8 million	2.3 million[a]
Elected executive offices	3	2
Size of city council	50	14
Members of council per person	56,000	160,000
Number of city departments and agencies	40+	20+
City employees (full-time)	40,000	21,700[b]
City expenditures	$7.6 billion	$4.0 billion[c]
Spending per person	$2,714	$1,739

a. U.S. Census Bureau, "Incorporated Places and Minor Civil Divisions: Vintage 2009," http://www.census.gov/popest/cities/cities.html (accessed July 26, 2010).
b. U.S. Census Bureau, "The 2009 Statistical Abstract, Table 455: City Government Employment and Payroll–Largest Cities," www.census.gov/compendia/statab/cats/state_local_govt_finances_employment.html (accessed August 12, 2010).
c. U.S. Census Bureau, "The 2009 Statistical Abstract, Table 446: City Government Expenditures and Debt for Largest Cities: 2006," http://www.census.gov/compendia/statab/2010/tables/10s0446.pdf (accessed August 12, 2010).

Thinking Critically

- How do Houston and Chicago compare in the size of their city councils?
- Are these cities similar in the election systems that they use for their councils?
- How do the cities compare in size of city government in terms of number of departments and city employees?
- How do you think these differences and similarities affect each city's citizens and local politics?

i. Illinois Constitution (1970), art. 7, sec. 6.

By dispersing the powers of city government and balancing the powers of the mayor and council, the weak mayor–council system attempts to avoid the problems of the strong mayor system. Essentially, the mayor becomes just another member of the city council. On the other hand, the weakened position of the mayor means that the city government may be less able to act quickly, since in essence, the city is governed by a committee.

According to a survey by the Texas Municipal League, the strong mayor–council system is more common than the weak mayor–council system in Texas. Only a handful of cities used the latter system, while nearly 40 percent of cities employ strong mayor systems. The most common system, however, is the council-manager system, accounting for 58 percent of cities in Texas.[22]

A council-manager system has the voters in a city elect a city council. The city council in turn then hires a manager to run the day-to-day administrative functions of the city. The manager proposes new ordinances for the city council to consider and develops the city budget. The city manager also hires the heads of the city departments and oversees the city departments. The city manager is essentially CEO (chief executive officer) of the city, similar to a business. Usually, the city manager is hired based on professional qualifications, including prior experience in city government and academic background in public administration. Confusion sometimes arises when a council-manager system includes an elected mayor who serves merely as a spokesperson and representative for the city. In this situation, the mayor is merely a figurehead and holds no significant power beyond that of a member of the city council. In other cities, the role of mayor as spokesperson for the city is performed by a member of the city council. Council-manager systems, sometimes called the commission-manager system, are most common among Texas's home rule cities.

The advantage of the council-manager system is the removal of day-to-day administration of the city from the turmoil of politics. Routine decisions can be made outside partisan politics or personality politics common to the elected offices of the mayor-council system. The resulting management of city government in a council-manager system is assumed to be both more professional and more efficient than in alternative systems. Yet, because city managers are involved in formulating policies for the city and are charged with initiating the city budget, in practice city managers almost inevitably become involved in politics as well.

City Elections

The Texas state government distinguishes between general law and home rule cities with respect to the type of election system that a city uses. Home rule cities are permitted to choose among four different election systems for elections to the city council. These cities may choose at-large, at-large by place, single-member district (SMD), or cumulative voting systems. Some cities also employ a combination of SMD and at-large systems.

The SMD system, discussed extensively in Chapter 3, occurs when the city is divided into several election districts. The number of districts equals the number of seats on the city council. Each district elects one member of the city council, so that if there are seven seats on the city council, then there are seven districts. Voters in each district cast a single vote for their most preferred candidate. In a single-member district plurality system, the candidate with the most votes in the district wins the seat on the city council. Some cities adhere to the single-member district majority system, which requires the winning candidate to win a majority of the votes, or 50 percent of the vote plus one additional vote.

In an at-large system, candidates compete for seats on the city council without reference to specific districts or seats on the council. Instead, voters are allowed to vote for as many candidates as there are seats on the council. For example, if there are seven seats on the city council and eighteen candidates running for office, each voter will vote for up to seven of the eighteen candidates. The candidates with the most votes, up to the total number of seats on the city council, win election to the city council. If there are seven seats on the council, the seven candidates with the most votes of the eighteen are elected to the city council.

A variation of the at-large system is the at-large by place system. In this system, candidates declare that they are running for particular positions or seats on the city council. The candidate for each seat that receives the most votes wins the seat. Thus, if there are seven seats on the city council, a candidate decides for which seat he or she is running. At the election, a voter has seven votes and chooses one candidate running for each of the seven seats. The key difference between the at-large and the at-large by place system is the fact that in the at-large by place system, candidates are grouped into different seats or "places" on the ballot. In contrast to the single-member district system, the seats or places for which candidates compete lack any connection to specific geographic areas or neighborhoods in the city.

The final system is the cumulative voting system. Like an at-large election, all candidates compete for seats on the city council without reference to specific seats, places, or districts. Voters possess a number of votes equal to the number of seats on the council. However, voters may choose to give all of their votes for the same candidate or may spread their votes among several candidates. Thus, if the city council contains seven seats, a voter may give all seven votes to the same candidate or may give three votes to one candidate and four votes to another candidate. The voter may spread the votes among as many or few candidates as the voter desires, so long as the voter casts no more votes than there are seats on the council. The candidates with the most votes, up to the number of seats on the council, win election to the city council. Again, if there are seven seats, the top seven candidates win.

Advocates of the single-member district system suggest that the direct connection between a member of the city council and the voters is an advantage. Each voter knows that a specific member of the council represents the voter's area of the city. If a problem occurs, the voter knows exactly whom to approach. Thus, government should be more responsive to citizens. Another advantage is that SMD city elections appear to increase racial and ethnic diversity among the candidates that are elected to the city council. This prospect for minority representation is an outgrowth of the Voting Rights Act of 1965 (discussed in Chapters 3 and 7). Since the 1970s, many cities in Texas have moved from at-large systems to SMD systems, including El Paso, Fort Worth, and San Antonio. However, district systems suffer from the same issues of partisan gerrymandering that occur with the state legislature and U.S. House of Representatives. In the late 1800s and early 1900s, the SMD system became associated with city-based **machine politics,** in which political organizations headed by a local party boss controlled specific seats on the city council by using city jobs, government contracts, and other giveaways. The party boss ran the city for personal power and gain.

The advantage of the at-large system is the ability of the city council to act on behalf of the entire city and to consider ordinances and policies from the perspective of the whole city, not the particularistic views of an area or neighborhood in the city. Citywide campaigns may also produce better-qualified candidates with broad-based, citywide appeal. At-large systems were also offered in the past as a method of solving the machine politics problem associated with single-member district systems. However, at-large systems were used in Texas to suppress minority votes, especially those of African American and Hispanic voters. Very simply, the Caucasian majority historically voted exclusively for white candidates, effectively

Machine politics

a system of patronage whereby political organizations, led by a local party boss, disperse city jobs, government contracts, and other benefits to maintain control of city governance; power once acquired is typically used for personal gain.

overwhelming minority voters and candidates. In some cities members of the council have consistently come from wealthy areas in town, and less well-off and minority voters have found themselves governed by officials who see or understand little about where minority voters live.

Cumulative voting advocates point to the ability of voters to express intensity of preference among the candidates running for the city council. By giving three or four votes to the same candidate, a voter indicates a greater preference for that candidate than if the voter gives only one or two votes for a candidate. Another advantage is the ability to enhance minority voting by concentrating votes. If minorities concentrate their votes among one or two candidates while whites disperse votes among several candidates, the likelihood of minority candidates winning is increased. Evidence from school board elections in Texas suggests that minority representation is enhanced under cumulative voting.[23] However, because few local governments use this system the question remains whether or not minority representation is actually increased. Also, the concentration or dispersal of votes creates a greater possibility of spoiled ballots, especially in comparison to SMD systems. A spoiled ballot occurs when a voter mismarks a ballot in such a way as to invalidate the ballot, causing the ballot not to be counted. In an SMD system, a voter simply chooses the most preferred candidate and casts only the single vote. In cumulative voting, the voter must be careful not to cast more votes than positions to be elected. If there are six seats on the city council, accidentally casting seven votes would spoil the ballot. The ballot and the votes on the ballot would not be counted. Because a voter may give multiple votes to candidates and may spread the votes across several candidates, the likelihood of spoiled ballots increases relative to the SMD system.

Some cities attempt to keep the best of both worlds by creating a hybrid of the SMD system and at-large system. Houston is an example of a city that pursues a hybrid approach. The fourteen-member city council in Houston consists of nine members elected from single-member districts and five members elected at large. A candidate chooses to either run in the district in which he or she lives or conduct a citywide campaign for an at-large seat. Proponents of this system point to the ability to balance the geographic link between a particular neighborhood or a part of the city and a specific member of the city council found in the SMD system and the broader, citywide orientation of the at-large members that a hybrid system allows. In addition, ethnic and racial minorities continue to benefit by the preservation of the district system in electing minority candidates to the city council.

Election systems in city politics remain an area of change and transition in Texas. City governments, especially those that utilize home rule, are more successful than county- or state-level governments in securing more representative outcomes, for example, the election of minorities to the city council. The shift away from at-large and at-large by place systems to SMDs is indicative of this change. In some cities, experiments with hybrid systems containing both at-large and single-member district seats also demonstrate the adaptability of Texas cities. Whether cities will make additional changes to election systems based upon the recent success of cumulative voting in producing more diverse city councils and school boards remains uncertain.

Issues in City Government

Because city government is typically the level of government closest to the people, cities address a large number of issues that will most directly and immediately affect

The Galveston Hurricane

By the start of the twentieth century, Galveston had become the state's leading port and one of its largest cities. By 1900 about 37,000 people lived in Galveston and the city was often referred to as the "Queen City of the Gulf." The prosperous city enjoyed gas streetlights and theaters, funded by the commerce from one of the nation's leading ports and investment flowing through twenty-three stock companies. Until a few years earlier, it had the largest population in the state, briefly edging out San Antonio. Galveston reflected the optimism of the time. It had been hit by hurricanes in 1867 and 1875, but continued to rebuild and thrive despite dire warnings about future storms.

The storm that hit on September 8, 1900, proved to be more powerful than any before, producing 120-mile-per-hour winds and a 15-foot storm surge on an island whose highest point was only nine feet above sea level. The storm killed about 6,000 people and destroyed 3,600 buildings—more than half the buildings in the city.

After the devastation of the hurricane residents feared that Galveston would suffer the same fate as Indianola, which went from being the second largest port in the state to obscurity after being hit by storms in 1875 and 1886. In response to the crisis, the citizens created a new system of government designed to facilitate the rebuilding. Under the "Galveston Plan" the city was initially governed by five commissioners that were partly elected and partly appointed by the governor, although later the legislature modified the system requiring citywide election of all commissioners. Commissioners were chosen citywide to promote cooperation across parts of the city and minimize the corruption brought by localized "bosses," who might dispense jobs in return for political support. Collectively, the commission wrote the basic policies of the city as did other city councils. However, in addition to these general duties, each commissioner administered a specific portion of the city's functions, like safety or public works.

The city's recovery under the Galveston Plan was considered remarkable. The city constructed a seawall seven miles long and seventeen feet high. Thirty million cubic yards of sand were pumped from the Gulf of Mexico to raise the ground level of the city by seventeen feet and the houses that survived the storm were raised and placed on new higher foundations. These preparations would help the city survive hurricanes in 1909 and 1915.

The Galveston Plan would become one of the most widely adopted reforms of the Progressive era. Houston would adopt the system in 1905, and by 1917, about seventy-five Texas cities and 500 cities nationwide were using the commission form, which was embraced by reformers, including Presidents Theodore Roosevelt and Woodrow Wilson.

Ironically, the Galveston Plan can no longer be found in Galveston or anywhere in Texas. The city, like many others, has adopted the council-manager form. Economically, Galveston lost much of its luster as Houston succeeded in dredging a ship channel that would allow it to create a port that brought railroads and ships together in a safer inland location. While Galveston's charming historic residences and buildings remain a popular tourist destination, it is no longer a major commercial center. In addition, Galveston is once again facing a challenge as recent surveys have indicated that the island is gradually sinking, meaning that the city will once again have to band together to hold off the sea.

Texas residents. Most of the streets within a city's boundaries are maintained by the city government. Cities often provide a variety of services to residents, including libraries, museums, and parks. Cities offer public health and safety services like police protection, fire protection, restaurant inspections, and child-care facility inspections. Many also engage in policies to attract new businesses to the community for the purposes of economic development.

Zoning and planning policies are among the most controversial issues that cities confront. Given the average Texan's attitudes toward land, including a commitment to the idea that individuals retain maximum rights to use their property as they see fit, conflicts between individual property owners and the broader needs of the city are inevitable. This desire to allow individual owners to maintain absolute control over their property is a key reason why the city of Houston, despite being among the largest in the United States, has largely avoided the issue of zoning. In **zoning policy,** the city restricts what property owners may do with their property. Most often, zoning involves designating parts of a city for residential use, commercial use, and industrial use. Among these, residential use restrictions may include designating an area single-family housing only, limiting the number of houses that can be built per acre, or permitting apartments and condominiums only in certain areas. Commercial zoning restrictions may include specifying where large-scale shopping centers and shopping malls may be built, limiting the number of entrances or exits to businesses' parking lots, or restricting the location of establishments that serve alcoholic beverages. Industrial zoning restrictions involve identifying where large factories, industrial plants, and high technology firms may build their facilities. Other issues in zoning policy range from the size of signage that a business may erect to regulations on how residential homes are built.

Zoning and planning often pit those seeking to develop property, build new shopping centers, and construct more houses against established neighborhoods. These battles are usually played out in local politics. Sometimes the state legislature becomes involved in conflicts over zoning and planning. In such cases, one of the sides in the battle tries to go around city government by appealing directly to the state legislature. For example, a bill introduced into the Texas Legislature in 2007 tried to restrict the ability of cities to regulate the size of lots and homes within the boundaries of the city. At issue was the building of so-called McMansions, large homes of over 3,000 square feet. Major property developers attempted to get the state legislature to enact a law to prevent cities from passing ordinances prohibiting the construction of McMansions. The bill ultimately failed because time ran out on the state legislature. Often historic districts require that changes to buildings in the area be approved by a review board so that they conform to the historic look of the area.[24] In some instances, local zoning laws in historic areas prevented developers from buying older homes, tearing down the homes, and building McMansions.

Related to zoning and planning is the issue of annexation. When a city wishes to expand its borders, the expansion occurs for several reasons. The residents of the area that the city plans to expand to may want to be annexed. The residents may see benefits to being within the city limits, including access to services the city provides—perhaps the city has a good police department or excellent fire protection or maybe the city's water system is superior to that of the county.

Economic development may be spurred by annexation, making it a reason for annexation. The city adds new territory in order to entice new businesses to locate in the area. Similarly, cities seek to expand to prevent themselves from becoming

Zoning policy

policy whereby the city restricts what individuals and entities may do with their property, usually by designating certain areas of the city for industrial, commercial, or residential uses.

hemmed in, surrounded by other cities. Once a city is surrounded on all sides by other cities, it is developmentally, and hence perhaps economically, limited. Population growth and economic development can then occur only within the existing city's land capacity. Cities may also annex areas to increase revenue. Newly annexed areas provide new sources of property and sales taxes. Cities especially desire to annex areas that are economically and financially well-off. In addition, the annexation of new areas allows cities to receive more money from the state and national governments. Often funding formulas for grants are tied to a city's size. Politically, larger cities receive more seats in the state legislature as well. State law permits cities to annex up to 10 percent of their land area each year. If a city annexes less than 10 percent, then the difference may be carried over to another year. However, a city may not annex more than 30 percent of its land area in any year.[25]

Beyond annexation, cities are interested in economic development for other reasons. Attracting the right businesses into a community produces the rewards of population growth and economic growth. These results in turn may allow a city to attract even more businesses to the community. New businesses generate new jobs and pay taxes, giving city governments more reason to welcome newcomers. To attract businesses, cities often provide incentives such as rebates on city sales tax and reductions on property tax rates. Cities often build infrastructure for businesses as well: access roads to the business, water lines to the property, and other essentials that the business may require. On the down side, more development means more traffic to channel, more children to educate, more garbage to collect, and more services of every kind.

City budgets are often a source of conflict. Budgets are generated by a variety of sources. Cities levy property taxes just like counties do. They may collect franchise fees, for example, fees paid by cable television, electrical power, and natural gas providers operating within the city limits. Cities also raise revenue from hotel and motel occupancy taxes and from fines from traffic tickets issued by police. They may also raise money by levying sales taxes on purchases made within the city limits. To fund special projects, such as acquiring land for parks, building city courthouses, or establishing a city museum, cities may issue **municipal bonds,** which are certificates of indebtedness. When a city issues municipal bonds, the city is essentially pledging to pay back a loan over time with interest. Regardless of the sources of revenue, the city must prioritize how to spend the revenue it raises. Because revenues are limited, emphasizing the expansion of the city park system or the building of new sidewalks inevitably means less money for other projects such as public health initiatives or erecting new streetlights.

A variety of contrasts between cities and counties exist in Texas. At a basic level, counties are the creation of the state government and exist solely to carry out specific functions the state legislature and constitution designate. Cities in contrast are created by citizens and residents who seek additional services from local government that counties are not able to provide. While the Texas Legislature and Texas Constitution determine ultimately what cities may or may not do, cities are established by citizens.

Another key difference is that cities, unlike counties, are allowed some flexibility in the form of government and election system they employ. This allows them a degree of transition and change to adapt to new circumstances. As Texas continues to experience high population growth rates in the early twenty-first century, the needs of citizens for more, better, and faster services require flexibility. The concentration of the state's population in metropolitan areas, including the development

Municipal bond

a certificate of indebtedness issued by a city that serves as a pledge by the city to pay back the loan over time with interest; used to raise money for services and infrastructure; may also be issued by other forms of local government such as counties, school districts, and special districts.

of massive suburbs and bedroom communities in former pine forests, farms, and ranches, has created—and continues to create—profound challenges to city and county governments. Although flexibility is most evident in home rule cities, General Law Type B cities possess a degree of flexibility as well. Because cities can collect revenue from a wider variety of sources, they can adapt to change more readily than counties. They can also exert influence on the zoning and use of land just outside their boundaries. Counties lack this ability. In fact, a city's influence may infringe on the rights of property owners outside the city limits and on the ability of counties to regulate land use within unincorporated areas of the county near the city's boundaries. Larger cities with home rule status are also freer of state control over their plan of government, the content of city ordinances, and the process of changing these arrangements.

Other Forms of Local Government

n addition to counties and cities, Texas contains a variety of other forms of local government. These include districts to handle the conduct of K–12 public education across the state. Special districts such as community college districts and municipal utility districts also complete the variety of local governments in Texas.

Public Education as Local Government

An important function of state government is the education of its citizens. The state constitution makes specific references to education, including public schools, universities, and community colleges.[26] Texas, like other states, uses several forms of government to provide for the education of its citizens through universities, community colleges, state technical schools, elementary schools, middle schools, and high schools.

Among local governments most familiar to Texans is the local school district. In most instances these are referred to as independent school districts (ISDs). Basic elementary and secondary education is the responsibility of the local board of education. These boards exist at the discretion of the Texas Legislature and operate under the authority of the Texas Constitution. The Texas Education Code, a statutory law passed by the legislature and signed by the governor, provides additional guidelines for K–12 education. Most students enrolled in K–12 education in Texas attend a school that falls under the jurisdiction of one of the more than 1,000 separate independent school districts. However, a handful of public schools continue to operate under the pre-ISD system. Under the Texas Education Code, pre-existing school systems like common schools, county schools, and municipal schools may still operate.[27] County and city governments, and the voters in these counties and cities, determine whether or not a pre-existing school should continue to stand or be converted into an ISD.

The term "independent school district" refers to the fact that the local school district is governed separately from, or independent of, any other form of local government or state government control. Previously, county schools and municipal schools were funded and operated by county or city governments. Under the ISD system, each local school district is governed by a board of trustees that is elected by the voters living within the boundaries of the school district. Boards are elected by at-large, at-large by place, or cumulative voting systems.[28] Members of the board serve four-year terms in office, with staggered elections so that half the board is elected every two years. The board of trustees of an ISD consists of three to seven members. To be a trustee, a candidate must reside within the school district and must be registered to vote. County and municipal school districts may have an elected board of education or may have a board chosen by the county or city government. The boundaries of an ISD may be contained within a county, may include parts of two or more counties, and may include a city or parts of a city.

The ISD system is not unique in the United States, although the term to describe the system is. Under federalism, states are allowed to create school systems however they choose. Two neighboring states illustrate this approach. Arkansas's school districts are similar to those of Texas. School districts are independent of local governments. In Arkansas, school district lines may cross county lines or may be contained within a single county. District lines may also be limited to a single city or include several cities. Some school districts in Arkansas are drawn based on the proximity of a road or highway to a school. In the Ozark and Ouachita Mountains, sometimes the closest school by road may be in another county. Louisiana, by contrast, has county-wide school districts. All public schools in a county are part of the same public school system. Most school systems are parish-wide, with just a handful of exceptions like the city of Monroe or three of the suburbs around Baton Rouge. Even in Louisiana where, with a handful of exceptions, parish-wide (county-wide) school systems exist, local school boards are elected separately from parish and city governments. The parish school boards make decisions independent of the parish government.

In Texas, the board of trustees of an ISD oversees the schools of the district by authorizing construction of schools, selling bonds to finance projects, collecting property taxes to fund operations, and providing guidelines for schools. Guidelines may include directions on the hiring of teachers and administrators, curriculum decisions, discipline policies, and budget decisions.[29] In effect, the board of trustees runs the schools in the district.

Although the ISD system is designed to give citizens local control over their schools, the state of Texas exerts control in specific areas. In particular, the state uses its power over the creation, existence, and support of school districts to enforce statewide policies. These policies include the classes that students must take, the textbooks that students use, and the structure of district budgets.[30] To this end, the Texas Constitution provides for a State Board of Education.[31] The State Board of Education consists of fifteen members elected from single-member districts across the state. The structure, function, and policy implications of the State Board of Education are discussed in Chapter 9.

Special Districts

Special districts are created when the residents within the proposed boundary of the district petition to create it. Examples of special districts are airport authorities, library districts, municipal utility districts, and community college districts. The process is similar to the process of creating a city. In contrast to a city or county, a special district provides a single service or a limited number of services to the residents of the district. To fund these services, special districts are allowed to levy property taxes above and beyond those imposed by cities, counties, and school districts. If the district crosses county lines, then arrangements are made for the tax

Texas versus Tennessee

Because local governments, like cities and counties, are created by state legislatures and state constitutions, the United States has fifty different systems of local government. Some states give a lot of responsibilities and powers to counties, while others do the same with their cities. Some states allow cities to be independent of counties, while other states allow the merger of city and county governments into a single entity. Tennessee is one such state.

In 1963, the Tennessee state government permitted the city of Nashville and surrounding Davidson County to merge. Called the Metropolitan Government, the consolidated government was intended to improve services, especially in areas of Davidson County outside of city limits—essentially rural areas of the county. These unincorporated areas wanted better police protection, fire and ambulance services, parks and recreation, and mass transit. Services to these areas would be uniform across the county. However, residents of rural areas did not necessarily want all of the services that Nashville provided to its residents and the accompanying higher level of taxes, nor did residents in the county want annexation into the city.[i] As a result, the Metropolitan Government created two different levels of service. A general services district (GSD) provides a uniform level of services throughout the county at the same property tax rate regardless of location in Davidson County. As part of the GSD, a common city-county court system and jail replaced separate city and county operations. An urban services district offers additional services to the City of Nashville and other communities that opt into the district. These include street lighting, water, refuse collection, street cleaning, and sanitation.[ii]

The Metropolitan Government is governed by a Metropolitan Council with forty members who are elected by a combination of single-member district plurality and at-large election systems. A Metro mayor serves as the chief executive, and a finance director oversees the budget. Decisions relating to the urban services district are made by a three-person committee whose members are part of the Metropolitan Council.[iii] Davidson County is served by a single, consolidated school district. The school board is directly elected, but the school budget must be approved by the Metro mayor and finance director.

However, the merger of the city of Nashville and Davidson County is only a partial consolidation because seven other cities and towns located in Davidson County that existed prior to the merger remain independent. Communities like Belle Meade and Goodlettsville participate in the general services district. However, the additional services of the urban services district must be provided separately or by a contract with the Metropolitan Government.[iv]

The creation of the Metropolitan Government allowed the city of Nashville and Davidson County to harmonize the level and quality of services provided to citizens in the city and county. Zoning and planning became a function of the consolidated government, forestalling competition between the city and county and producing a common approach to economic development. Economies of scale developed in the provision of services so that many services are provided at a lower cost to taxpayers than if the city and county provided the services separately. In addition, supporters of consolidation maintain that the result has been more local government accountability and a better national image for Nashville.[v]

Thinking Critically

- How many local governments, including school districts, municipal utility districts, cities, and other special purpose districts, are there in your county?
- Do you think the level of services varies tremendously across your county?
- What advantages might there be if the services provided by the various local governments in your county were consolidated as in the case of Metropolitan Nashville–Davidson County in Tennessee?
- Are there disadvantages to city-county consolidations?

i.   Pennsylvania Economy League of Southwestern Pennsylvania, "A Comparative Analysis of City/County Consolidations," February 7, 2007, 78.
ii. Ibid.
iii. Ibid., 79.
iv. Ibid.
v.   Ibid.

assessors in each of the counties to collect the taxes and transfer funds to the district. Thus, special districts often can overcome the problems of coordinating services across multiple cities and counties. This approach is very useful in major metropolitan areas such as the Dallas-Fort Worth Metroplex. Some special districts are authorized by voters to issue municipal bonds, while others charge user fees for the services provided.

The creation of a special district can be complicated, depending on the type of district. Hospital districts are created by first passing an amendment to the Texas Constitution, then by the approval of voters in the proposed district. Community college districts are first authorized by the Texas Legislature. The Texas Commission on Environmental Quality approves the creation of municipal utility districts. Special districts have even been created to build and manage sports stadiums for professional sports teams in Texas.

Normally, special districts are created when a county or city government is unable or unwilling to provide a service itself or when the existing local government prefers to allow a special district to provide the service. Because counties face limits on the amount of property tax they levy, special districts allow counties to overcome this limit by essentially "farming out" new services to a special district. In some instances, residents of a county may choose to join a special district that exists in another county. In this case, the residents take a vote to join the special district or a local government may request that the special district start providing services in the area.

Special districts are governed by a board of usually five members. The board is often elected by voters in the district. In some instances, it is appointed, usually by the mayors, city councils, and commissioners courts operating within the district. The board oversees the regular operation of the special district, hires necessary staff and professionals, and makes policies regarding the provision of services. For example, the Port of Houston Authority is governed by an appointed board of seven members. Some members are appointed by the Harris County Commissioners Court, while other members are appointed by cities within Harris County. The authority oversees the collection of public and private dock facilities along the Houston Ship Channel as well as ship traffic on the channel and in Galveston Bay.

Likewise, the board of trustees of a community college hires the chancellor or president of the college. The board decides, within state guidelines, the degrees that will be offered and the coursework that is required. The board also enters into agreements with four-year universities to determine the transferability of courses, harmonization of degree programs, and ease of transfer to four-year institutions. It establishes pay scales for faculty and staff, qualifications to be on faculty, and rates of tuition and fees for students. In some cases, community colleges have services areas defined by a law passed by the Texas Legislature. Angelina College in East Texas has the exclusive right to operate in twelve East Texas Counties. In contrast, Harris County contains several community college districts, including Houston Community College, Lone Star College, and San Jacinto Community College. Currently, fifty separate college districts exist in Texas. Community colleges educate over 550,000 Texans each year.

The advantage of a special district is the ability to provide services that ordinarily might not be provided. In addition, the services may be provided to promote economic development. In the case of **municipal utility districts (MUDs),** which provide water, sewer, and similar services to individuals and businesses outside city limits, these services may entice new businesses to relocate to the area or developers

Municipal utility district (MUD)
a special district that provides water, sewer, or similar services to individuals and businesses outside city limits.

to construct new homes. Again, in some instances the special district aids in bridging disputes between cities or counties over the provision of services. However, like other local government elections, special election district elections are low turnout events, and thus the decisions made by voters may reflect the wishes of only a few. Also, the proliferation of special districts in an area creates confusion among residents, who may not know who is responsible for what. Special districts also encourage conflict among local governments as multiple districts compete for property tax resources and pursue contradictory goals.

Winners and Losers

As we have seen in previous chapters, choices about the structure of government, the distribution of powers within government and between levels of government, and how government is selected directly impact citizens. In Texas, various levels of local government provide different services and create additional tax burdens on citizens. To the extent that local government in Texas creates flexibility, citizens win. To the extent that each level of local government creates additional, obscure taxes, citizens lose.

Cities are clear winners in the state because they are relatively powerful entities that provide a significant number of government services to citizens. Home rule cities are even bigger winners. They have tremendous freedom to choose their form of government, election system, and organization of city government. However, counties are often losers. Counties, especially high population counties, are strapped with the same form of government that all other counties in Texas possess. Little freedom exists for them to tailor their plan of government and structure to their needs.

The winners in education and special district local governments are often the residents of the districts. In the case of the ISDs, residents benefit by having local school boards that govern smaller areas than might otherwise occur under a countywide system. School boards should be more responsive to voters and parents, especially in smaller enrollment school districts. Schools are also more likely to be community-based. This arrangement reinforces the small-town and rural bias common in Texas political history. Regarding the special districts, residents are winners if they are willing to create the district and are willing to see their property taxes rise to cover the additional services that the special district provides. In addition, residents within a city or in part of a county may elect to create the district to provide selected services to a particular area even if the majority of residents in the entire city or county do not want those services. Thus, the creation of special districts gives Texans the freedom to choose whether to accept certain services and the corresponding taxes and to reject those services (and taxes). However, this buffet-style approach produces significant variation in the services that residents receive and results in divergent rates of property taxes within cities and counties. Residents also find themselves subject to several local governments, a confusing array that offers little coordination of services throughout a county or metropolitan area. Moreover, the heavy use of property taxes to fund all of these services may depress property values in some parts of the state, causing significant variation in taxation levels between rural and wealthy areas of the state; it also places the burden of paying for services largely in the hands of property owners.

On the other hand, the funding of local government through a variety of property taxes and fees often creates a significant and obscure tax burden on citizens throughout the state. Reliance on property taxes, discussed here and in Chapter 9, overburdens citizens who live in larger metropolitan areas where property values are significantly higher than in rural Texas. The property tax is a distinct burden on retirees, whose spending and income often decrease while property taxes remain at the same level. By amendment to the Texas Constitution, retirees are protected from increases in property tax rates. As noted above, the property tax burden is not evenly shared in local government, as individuals who do not own property utilize basic services such as emergency care or education without contributing to their cost. In addition, as local governments wrestle with increased demands on their resources, the current trend toward building and use of toll roads creates yet another tax on citizens. The citizens of Texas pay city sales and property taxes, county property taxes, and special district property taxes and are responsible as well, though indirectly, for paying the interest on municipal bonds. Government in Texas, clearly, is proving unnervingly complex and, arguably, costly. In the end, the citizens of Texas lose.

Conclusion

Local government in Texas is a diverse set of governments. Ultimately, all local governments are dominated by the state government, which determines the powers of local governments and the organizational structure of local governments. Local government in the form of cities, counties, and special districts exists to aid the state of Texas in delivering public policies and public services in areas such as transportation, education, and public health. Citizens also create, with the permission of the state, some forms of local government like cities and special districts to provide specific services that the citizens want. Texas provides little flexibility to its local governments, although cities are afforded more freedom under home rule provisions than other forms of local government. However, residents of cities of sufficient size must choose to adopt home rule status before they can take advantage of it. In the end, Texans are confronted with a set of overlapping jurisdictions providing a variety of public services and overseeing a plethora of public policies with various degrees of effectiveness.

Key Terms

administrative federalism
annexation
auditor
city charter
commissioners court
constable
contract outsourcing
county attorney
county civil service commission
county clerk
Dillon's Rule
fiscal federalism

general law city
home rule city
justice of the peace
machine politics
merit-based civil service system
municipal bond
municipal utility district (MUD)
ordinance
partisan election
privatization
sheriff
tax assessor
zoning policy

Explore this subject further at http://lonestar.cqpress.com, where you'll find chapter summaries, practice quizzes, key word flash cards, and additional suggested resources.

Getting on the ballot is a challenge for minor political parties like the Libertarians and Greens. Ballot access for minor parties often entangles them in the political fights between the two major parties, as Democrats see the Green Party as a threat and Republicans fear losing votes to Libertarians.

CHAPTER 7

Elections: Texas Style

Elections in Texas are dominated by contests that pit Republicans against Democrats. However, other political parties do exist, and in some elections voters are offered a third choice. For example, in 2006 candidates nominated by the Libertarian Party appeared on the Texas ballot. Libertarians contested several statewide races that year and competed in some Texas Senate and Texas House of Representative races. Not only does the presence of third parties on the ballot provide voters with additional choices, but, as significantly, third-party candidates can act as "spoilers," impacting the prospects of major-party candidates. Their presence on the ballot can also divert votes away from one or both of the two major political parties, and in some instances influence the outcome of the election.

Access to the ballot, including whether or not an individual running for office actually gets his or her name on the ballot and which political parties are officially listed there, is often a political football. Getting on the ballot is an essential first step in promoting and maintaining electoral competition. More candidates and more parties on the ballot offer more choices to Texas voters. The 2010 Texas elections for statewide office and for the Texas Legislature illustrate this point.

The Libertarian Party qualified to have its candidates and its party label on the ballot in the 2010 elections thanks to the 2006 general election success of Libertarian William Bryan Strange. Strange took 18 percent of the popular vote in that election for the Texas Court of Criminal Appeals. By securing more than 5 percent of the vote in a statewide race, Strange guaranteed Libertarians a place in every election for the next four years.[1] By 2010, Libertarians were ready to do battle. In the November general election, Libertarians nominated 160 candidates for office, including key statewide races like governor and lieutenant governor, as well as many races for both houses of the Texas Legislature. Some Libertarians believed that 2010 was going to be their best year ever in Texas.[2] Republicans, long in ascendance in state politics, were especially watchful. Electoral competition from Libertarians could potentially affect election results for the Republicans because Libertarians typically endorse small government, low taxes, and fiscal conservatism—all of which Republicans support. Competition for votes from Libertarian candidates would more than likely come at the expense of Republican candidates, splitting the conservative vote. The ultimate winner would be the Democrats, whose chances of winning seats in the Texas Legislature could improve as a result.

Democrats had their own worries. In the summer of 2010, Democrats argued in Texas courts against allowing the Green Party label to appear next to its candidates' names on the November 2010 ballot.[3] They claimed the Green Party received illegal financial contributions from a prominent Arizona Republican, Tim Mooney. Mooney allegedly funded the petition drive to get the Green Party on the ballot in Texas. His efforts were funded in turn by the Missouri-based Take Initiative America. Mooney's financial contributions helped the Green Party collect the 92,000 signatures needed to petition the Texas Secretary of State's office to get the party on the ballot in November 2010,[4] which Democrats alleged was a tactic intended to divert votes from Democratic Party candidates and ease the way for Republicans to win seats. More intrigue occurred with allegations that lobbyist Mike Toomey, former chief of staff to Governor Rick Perry, was also a Republican operative working with the petition drive to get the Green Party on the ballot.[5] When the Green Party lost its district court battle to get on the ballot, the party's lawyers appealed their case all the way to the Texas Supreme Court, which ultimately upheld the lower court's decision denying the Green Party access to the ballot.

In this chapter, we will explore the nature of elections in Texas. We will begin by considering who is eligible to vote in the state. The struggle for the right to vote among African Americans, Hispanics, and women will be explored. Then, we will look at the issue of ballot access. A discussion of the various types of elections, including general and primary elections, follows. Next, we will discuss voter turnout in Texas elections and will review characteristics of electoral competition between political parties, focusing on changes over the past few decades. Finally, we will conclude with a consideration of the campaign finance system.

As you read the chapter, think about the following questions:

★ What obstacles to voting were faced by various groups in Texas?

★ To what extent is low voter turnout impeding democracy?

★ How might Texas make participation in voting more likely today?

★ Why does the type of primary election used to nominate candidates matter?

★ Are Texas elections competitive?

★ How are campaigns for office financed in Texas?

★ What are some consequences of the campaign finance system?

Background to Elections in Texas

The conduct of elections in the United States is largely a function of state governments. Coming out of the Constitutional Convention of 1787, whose attendees wrote the U.S. Constitution, was a compromise that left elections as a responsibility of state governments. As a result, states determine who is qualified to vote in an election, how potential voters register to vote, how candidates and parties get onto a ballot, and what types of voting equipment are used to collect and count votes. However, since the Civil War (1860–1865), states have faced some degree of national oversight, primarily by the U.S. Department of Justice. National supervision of elections became even more prominent during the civil rights era of the 1950s and 1960s.

Voting Registration and Voter Qualifications

Access to the voting booth is a vital issue in a democracy. The rules of who may vote, how they vote, and under what conditions they vote significantly impact the legitimacy of the government and its responsiveness to the people. Thus, voting rights and qualifications are essential to determining who gets what, when, and how. For example, if voting rights are denied to a group of people based upon their race, candidates running for office might ignore the issues and concerns of people of that race. Prior to the civil rights era of the 1950s and 1960s, the state of Texas through a variety of laws and practices attempted to deny African Americans the right to vote. Candidates often ignored issues of concern to African Americans, like the condition of their schools and crime in their neighborhoods. As a result, government policy made upgrading schools in white communities or addressing crime in white areas the priority. African American neighborhoods and schools were neglected and ignored.

Because state governments in the United States are responsible for voter registration, there are fifty different sets of voter registration processes, procedures, and qualifications. For example, North Dakota lacks any formal voter registration process. On Election Day, a voter simply shows a driver's license or state identification card indicating that he or she lives in the state and community in order to vote. Minnesota allows same-day voter registration, meaning if a person is qualified to vote, then that person may register to vote and vote in the election on the same day.

Voter registration in Texas is a bit more complicated. To register to vote, a person must be a citizen of the United States, have attained at least eighteen years of age, and must have resided in Texas for at least thirty days. To vote in a county or other local government election, the thirty-day residency requirement applies, even if a voter is already a resident of Texas. So, a voter who moves from San Antonio to Amarillo must live in Amarillo at least thirty days before voting in an Amarillo city election. If a voter owns property in several locations within Texas, the voter chooses which address serves as his or her primary residence for the purpose of voting.[6]

To register to vote, a voter registration form must be completed. The form is available from county voter registration offices or online from the Texas Secretary of State. The completed form must be submitted in person or by regular mail to the voter registration office in the county in which the voter resides. Electronic submissions are not allowed. Since 1993, residents of Texas may register to vote when applying for a driver's license or when renewing a license. This development occurred when the U.S. Congress passed the National Voter Registration Act, more popularly known as the **Motor Voter Act.** As an election nears, local civic organizations like the League of Women Voters or a university's student government association often hold voter registration drives to get more people registered to vote. Those interested in registering to vote fill out the form and return it by mail, or the civic organization returns all of the cards to the county elections office. Some public libraries and schools make voter registration forms available. Regardless of how a person registers to vote, the form must be submitted to the county voter registration office no later than thirty days before an election.

In addition to age and residency requirements, Texas maintains other qualifications to vote. Individuals determined to be partially or totally mentally incapacitated by a probate court may be denied the right to vote. The determination is usually made by a county or district court. Likewise, convicted felons over the age of eighteen are stripped of the right to vote until they have completed their

Motor Voter Act
the National Voter Registration Act that allows citizens to register to vote when applying for or renewing their driver's license.

sentence, including parole or probation.[7] This limitation reflects the traditionalistic political culture of Texas, which emphasizes the need to punish criminals and the idea that the rights of citizenship are not automatic.

Texas is one of thirteen states to require registration at least thirty days before an election. Only Georgia and Nevada are more restrictive, at thirty-five days. In contrast, several states, including Minnesota, New Hampshire, and Wyoming, allow registration on Election Day or the day before. As mentioned above, North Dakota has no registration process.

Since 1972, Texas has maintained a permanent list of voters. The maintenance of the voter registration list is the responsibility of county governments. In most of Texas's counties, the responsibility is retained by the county tax assessor, a relic of the pre–civil rights era when the tax assessor was responsible for collecting poll taxes as a prerequisite to voting. Having the same office collect the poll tax and maintain voting records made sense. Even though the poll tax has long since been discarded, 62 percent of Texas counties, or 159 counties, continue to assign the responsibility of voter registration to the tax assessor's office. Eighteen counties (7.1 percent) have moved responsibility for voter registration to the county clerk's office. Because the county clerk also keeps other vital records, for example, birth records, having the county clerk serve as the voter registration officer makes sense. Finally, seventy-seven counties (30.3 percent) have a separate county elections office that, in addition to its other duties (discussed below), maintains the voter registration list.[8]

Note that Texas allows its counties to separate the functions of voter registration from the functions of elections administration. Elections administration refers to the conduct of elections such as setting up polling places where people vote, maintaining voting equipment, and similar activities. While some counties use the same office both to register voters and to conduct elections, other counties do not. Seventy-seven counties (30.3 percent) maintain a separate elections office for voter registration and also make those offices responsible for the administration of elections. Only nine counties (3.5 percent) have the tax assessor's office register voters and administer elections. Most counties (168 counties, or 66.1 percent) have their county clerk's office conduct elections and serve as the elections administration office.[9]

Voting Rights in Texas

Under the Republic of Texas Constitution, the right to vote in Texas elections extended only to white and Hispanic males. Women, Native Americans, and African Americans were denied **suffrage,** or the legal right to vote. The Texas Constitution of 1845, adopted when Texas joined the United States, continued to deny access to voting to both of these groups. The Civil War and its aftermath spurred an increased role for the national government in state election processes, primarily in securing to African American males the right to vote. The expansion of the role of the national government in the area of voting rights continued into the twentieth century with the addition of women's suffrage and the passage of voting rights legislation during the civil rights era.

Suffrage
the legal right to vote.

Legal Barriers to Voting in Post-Reconstruction Texas

After the U.S. Civil War, the U.S. Constitution was amended to include the Thirteenth, Fourteenth, and Fifteenth Amendments. The Fifteenth Amendment specifically requires that state governments ensure the right to vote regardless of race or prior status as a slave. Here we see the first steps by the national government to regulate voting rights of all Americans. With the end of military occupation of the southern states and the end of Reconstruction in 1876, states like Texas officially maintained the right of African Americans to vote even as they imposed a series of barriers to effectively bar former slaves from actually exercising that right. For example, Texas, like other southern states, used the **grandfather clause** to prohibit African Americans from voting. Essentially, the grandfather clause reserved the right to vote to those whose grandfathers had the right to vote. Given that most African Americans in Texas at the time were former slaves, as were their fathers and grandfathers, the right to vote for African Americans was greatly restricted. Another technique to discourage African Americans from exercising their right to vote was the **literacy test,** a test of the prospective voter's ability to read and to understand aspects of American government. When registering to vote, the potential voter had to answer a series of questions, to read one or more paragraphs, and to explain the material. The poor state of public education in African American communities throughout the South from the end of Reconstruction into the 1950s ensured that many African Americans were denied the right to vote. In some communities, African Americans were given different, harder tests than whites. In Texas, the use of the literacy test was rare. Texas favored other techniques to exclude African Americans.

Another legal barrier instituted to prevent African Americans from voting was the **poll tax,** an annual tax that had to be paid before one was allowed to vote. In 1902, an amendment to the Texas Constitution allowed poll taxes to be used by the state, county, and local governments of Texas.[10] The state imposed a rate of $1.50 per voter annually, while counties could impose a tax of up to $0.25 on each voter. Since most African Americans in Texas earned relatively lower incomes compared to whites, African Americans faced the choice between purchasing basic necessities versus participating in politics.

The poll tax prevented many poor whites from voting as well. Disenfranchising poor, rural white voters served a useful purpose: diluting the strength of the Populist Party. The Democratic Party feared the growing challenge of the Populist

Grandfather clause

the granting of voting rights only to those citizens whose grandfathers had the right to vote; used to bar African Americans from voting in the South after the end of Reconstruction.

Literacy test

a test of a prospective voter's ability to read and understand aspects of American government; used to bar African Americans from voting in many parts of the post-Reconstruction South, but not widely used in Texas.

Poll tax

an annual tax that had to be paid before one was allowed to vote; allowed by a 1902 amendment to the Texas Constitution and used to legally bar African Americans from voting.

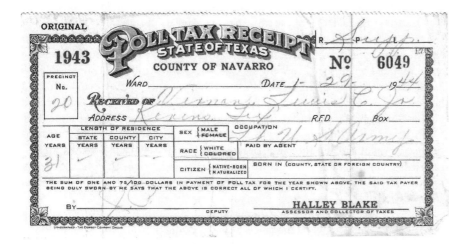

The poll tax was used to deny the right to vote to many African Americans in Texas. This actual poll tax receipt from Navarro County in 1943 shows that the poll tax had been paid in full, thereby allowing the individual to vote in upcoming elections.

Party, which was based in farmer and labor movements throughout the United States and directly challenged wealthy interests in Texas politics. Populists focused on the economic plight of poor, small- and medium-sized family farms and sought to shift the race-based politics of the Civil War, Reconstruction, and post-Reconstruction eras to a class-based politics in which the lower and middle classes could effectively vie with the upper classes for political power. As such, the poll tax served the Democratic Party well: African Americans were eliminated from voting, potential Populist voters were removed from the voting pool, and, consistent with Texas's traditional political culture, it was the "better" elements of society that were given the right to rule. The poll tax was instrumental in allowing the Democratic Party in the southern states to stave off any serious challenge to its supremacy and maintain its status as the majority party for decades. Racial appeals by traditional Democrats continued into the late 1940s and beyond. For example, Governor Allan Shivers in 1948 complained of "creeping socialism" by the national Democratic Party leadership and the need for "moral regeneration" or a "spiritual awakening" to prevent integration of the races.[11] He relied upon similar themes to confront integration of public schools in the 1950s as well.

A final technique for disenfranchising African American voters in southern states was the **white primary.** Essentially, participation in primary elections to nominate candidates for office was restricted to members of the party only, and membership in the party was limited to white voters. Because the primary election determined the Democratic Party nominee for the general election, and because the primary was restricted to white voters, the "white" primary guaranteed that parties and candidates responded only to issues of concern in the white population. Texas was unusual in that the use of the white primary occurred because of state law. All other states implementing the white primary did so as a matter of party rules or custom rather than law.[12]

Eliminating Barriers to Voting for African Americans

Ultimately, the removal of barriers to voting gave the national government significant control over state voter registration processes, and in so doing took power away from the states. However, because elected officials in states like Texas refused to ensure African Americans' equal rights, including the right to vote, assumption of control was a necessary step on the road to equality. The grandfather clause was eliminated when the U.S. Supreme Court issued its ruling in *Guinn v. United States* (1919). The Court in *Guinn* declared that the grandfather clause violated the Fifteenth Amendment of the U.S. Constitution. In doing so, the Court relied on the **Equal Protection Clause** of the Fourteenth Amendment to the U.S. Constitution. The Equal Protection Clause requires that state laws and state constitutions treat all citizens the same. Because the grandfather clause treated African Americans, whose grandfathers clearly did not have the right to vote, differently from whites, the grandfather clause violated the idea that the law must treat all citizens the same.[13]

Another barrier to voting was removed in 1965 with passage of the **Voting Rights Act of 1965 (VRA)** by the U.S. Congress. While the VRA did several things, most important here is that it eliminated the literacy test as a qualification to vote among those with at least a sixth-grade education. The removal of the literacy test greatly increased African Americans' access to the ballot box. This provision applied to all elections conducted by the states.

White primary

the attempt by the Democratic Party in Texas and other southern states to limit the voting in party primaries only to party members; in Texas, codified in state law.

Equal Protection Clause

clause of the Fourteenth Amendment to the U.S. Constitution requiring that state laws and state constitutions treat all citizens the same.

Voting Rights Act of 1965 (VRA)

a federal statute that eliminated literacy tests as a qualification to vote, greatly increasing African Americans' access to the ballot box.

Eliminating the poll tax proved to be more complicated. The poll tax in national elections was eliminated by the Twenty-fourth Amendment to the U.S. Constitution in 1964. However, states assumed that state and local elections, which clearly did not involve the national government, remained solely the domain of state law. Payment of the poll tax continued to be required for state and local elections for another year. In *Harper v. Virginia Board of Elections* (1966) the U.S. Supreme Court struck down the poll tax in Virginia state and local elections as a violation of the Equal Protection Clause of the Fourteenth Amendment to the U.S. Constitution.[14]

Challenging the white primary also proved difficult, especially in Texas. In the Texas-based case *Nixon v. Herndon* (1924),[15] the U.S. Supreme Court invalidated the white primary where required or sanctioned by state law. In response, the Texas Democratic Party, with the support of Texas's key political leaders, declared itself a "private organization." Twenty years later the Court threw out the white primary in *Smith v. Allwright* (1944).[16] The Court declared that the vital function of nominating candidates for office meant that political parties were public organizations. Not accepting of this decision, the Democratic Party in Fort Bend County attempted a "Jaybird" pre-primary in which only whites cast informal votes to consolidate support behind a single candidate who all whites would then back in the official primary. Seeing through this attempt at coordination and control, the U.S. Supreme Court outlawed the practice in *Terry v. Adams* (1953).[17] One estimate suggests that removing the barriers to voting had the immediate impact of allowing as many as 200,000 African Americans in Texas to vote.[18]

Hispanics and Voting Rights

The history of voting rights for Hispanics in Texas is a complex story. In the days of the Texas Republic and early statehood, some discrimination against Hispanics existed, but not to the extent faced by African Americans.[19] For example, the literacy test used widely throughout the South did not exist in Texas. Hispanics who sought to register did not have to interpret the state constitution or answer questions about the national government, and neither did African Americans or whites. Instead, Hispanics were often allowed to vote in the white primary and formed an important base of support for the Democratic Party in southern parts of Texas, although some scholars assert that the white primary did prohibit Hispanic voters.[20] Along the Mexican border, many local elected officials were Hispanic,[21] so at the local level at least the primary system did not prohibit Hispanic candidates from getting elected. In contrast, the poll tax did disenfranchise many Hispanics, just as it did poor whites and African Americans.[22] Therefore, the removal of the poll tax in national and state elections provided an opportunity for more Hispanics to register to vote.

Although the VRA originally applied only to attempts to disenfranchise African American voters, the renewal of the act in 1975 led to the extension of the VRA to Hispanic voters. After 1975, the VRA applied to states or counties with a history of low levels of voting, where elections were conducted only in English, and where more than 5 percent of the voting-age population was part of a language minority.[23] States like Texas and California are required to provide bilingual ballots that encourage Hispanic voters who are citizens to participate in elections. Provision for a bilingual ballot has also been applied to benefit Native Americans in Alaska, California, Oklahoma, New Mexico, and South Dakota. Asian Americans also are covered by this provision in selected counties across the United States.

The key source of disenfranchisement of Hispanics appears to have been economic harassment. Whites boycotted Hispanic businesses, linked bank loans to support for white candidates in the election, and fired Hispanics who engaged in political campaigns. In addressing discrimination against Hispanics voting in Bexar County, the U.S. Supreme Court identified the sources of discrimination to be primarily economic, educational, and linguistic in nature rather than legal.[24] Although significant in Bexar County, the use of economic and other tools to disenfranchise Hispanics varied by county.[25] Thus, rather than the formal and legal barriers that African Americans faced, the primary barriers to voting for Hispanics were intimidation tactics.

Voting Rights for Women, Members of the Armed Forces, and Younger Voters

Texas proved slightly more progressive in its extension of voting rights to women. The Wyoming Territory in 1869 was the first area of the United States to grant women the right to vote. Women's suffrage in Wyoming survived the transition to statehood in 1890, making Wyoming the first state in which women could vote. In 1893, Colorado became the first state in which a state legislature granted women the right to vote. The Texas legislature first considered the issue of women's suffrage in 1915, and by 1918 it had authorized women, or at least white women, to vote in primary elections. Two years later, in 1920, the Nineteenth Amendment to the U.S. Constitution gave women the right to vote in federal elections. Texas also proved somewhat forward-thinking by being the first state in the "Old South" to ratify the Nineteenth Amendment, and the ninth in the nation. Ultimately, the United States was one of the first countries to grant women the right to vote in national elections, following in the footsteps of Great Britain, which had granted women suffrage in 1919, and other former British colonies like New Zealand (1893) and Australia (1901).

Historically, members of the U.S. military and their families were denied the right to vote in some states if they were not residents of the state prior to joining the military. In Texas, a provision of the state constitution prohibited members of the U.S. military who moved to Texas during their tour of duty from establishing residency. Because residency is a requirement to vote, members of the military were effectively denied that right. Members of the military and their families were considered transients who should not influence or affect state and local politics, even though laws passed by the state legislature, county governments, and city councils applied to members of the military. In 1965, the U.S. Supreme Court struck down this provision of the Texas Constitution in *Carrington v. Rash* (1965).[26] Members of the military and their families were then allowed to establish residency like any other person moving to Texas and exercise the right to vote in state and local elections.

A further extension of voting rights concerned the voting rights of young adults. The right to vote was associated with being an adult, historically defined as having attained the age of twenty-one. However, in 1971 the Twenty-sixth Amendment to the U.S. Constitution lowered the minimum voting age to eighteen in federal elections. States quickly followed suit, lowering the minimum voting age to eighteen for state and local elections. This extension of voting rights to those between age eighteen and twenty-one stemmed in part from U.S. involvement in Vietnam. Young men of this era were fighting—and losing their lives—for their country in the Vietnam War but were unable to vote in national or state elections. The discrepancy between being able to die for one's country and not being able to participate in the selection of one's political leaders struck many as wrong, spurring passage of the Twenty-sixth Amendment. The voting rights of college students is another youth-focused issue. Today, Texas state law guarantees college students the right to choose where they will vote if the student spends weeks or months in different locations each year, including the community in which he or she attends college.[27] In the past, state and local governments attempted to prevent college students from registering to vote where they attended school if that location was different from their parent's residence. The argument against the participation of college students in local elections was similar to that against members of the military: they were viewed as "transient" rather than "permanent" members of the community. However, because college students use local government services like roads and pay local taxes like sales taxes they often do have an interest in the politics of the community in which they attend college. Once a student votes in an election he or she is more likely to vote in future elections. Thus, by allowing students to vote in the community where they attend college, a lifelong pattern of voting is encouraged. Since most votes in Texas occur on a weekday during the school year, students often find that voting in the community where they attend college is easier than returning home to vote.

The objection to college students' voting may evidence a deeper distrust. Some area residents view them as "outsiders" who might displace local political elites and change local ordinances in the community. In fact, attempts to prevent an early voting location on the campus of Stephen F. Austin State University (SFASU) in the 2008 general election were argued in these very terms by members of the community and by some members of the Nacogdoches County Commissioners Court. Despite the tremendous success of early voting in the 2008 presidential election, similar arguments led to a 4–1 vote against early voting at SFASU in the 2010 general election, including the governor's election. In any case, when students go off to college they have the right to choose whether to vote at their permanent home address or at their college address, but students must choose one or the other.

An interesting quirk regarding the rights of voters in Texas centers on the conduct of the voter on Election Day. With the exceptions of treason, felony, or disturbing the peace, voters in Texas are exempt from arrest while going to or returning from voting.[28]

The history of voting rights in Texas appears to be periodic attempts to restrict the right to vote to only the "right" kinds of voters: white and, at times, Hispanic males with better education and more money. The Democratic Party of the post-Reconstruction era sought to maintain its power base by writing the "rules of the game" to exclude African Americans and to prevent the state government from responding to the demands of all citizens. As a result, state politics and policy reflected primarily the wishes of those able to vote rather than those of all the citizens of Texas. Only after the civil rights era of the 1950s and 1960s took root did significant numbers of poorer whites and African Americans gain access to the ballot box. More recently, legal attempts to include Hispanics in Texas politics more completely—as voters, candidates, and elected officials—have proved increasingly effective. Efforts to include women, members of the military, and young voters in the election process proved less controversial.

The expansion of voting rights is a clear example of transition in Texas elections. The right to vote has broadened significantly over the course of Texas history. With few exceptions, citizens today age eighteen and older from all demographic groups are able to participate fully in the electoral process. However, the white establishment attempted to prevent both disenfranchised groups from voting to maintain the tradition of white dominance in Texas politics. It was largely through the actions of the national government that Texas was forced to change election rules and practices to be more inclusive. Texas has in turn significantly altered. As a result, the dynamics of state politics, forcing consideration of issues that matter to all of the state's citizens, changed as well.

If Texans object to the expansion of the national government's powers in the area of voting rights, we need only remember that the expansion occurred because elected officials in the state openly engaged in legal and social strategies to deny specific classes of individuals the right to participate in elections. Ultimately, the elected officials were reflecting the attitudes and beliefs of the majority white population at the time. Here the tyranny of the majority, as expressed in state government and its policies, demonstrates the need for a balance of power and checks on the powers of state governments by the national government. Of course, constitutional design also allows the state governments to check the powers of the national government.

Getting on the Ballot in Texas

As emphasized at the beginning of this chapter, who gets on the ballot is an important aspect of elections. Everyone running for office in the state of Texas must be a resident of Texas and of the relevant election district. A candidate must also be registered to vote. Beyond these requirements, getting on the ballot as a candidate results from one of two processes: nomination by a political party or qualifying as an independent candidate.

For candidates running with a party nomination, the candidate gets on the ballot either by competing in and winning a primary election or being selected from a party convention. Political parties that win 20 percent or more of the vote in the last governor's election must hold primary elections. To qualify for the primary election, a candidate must pay a filing fee. The filing fee varies from $5,000 for a candidate for U.S. senator to $300 for candidates for the state board of education. In lieu of paying the filing fee, candidates may qualify for a party primary by filing a petition with a set number of signatures from registered voters, varying from 5,000 signatures to the number of signatures equivalent to 2 percent of the vote in the governor's election in the state, county, or election district. If a political party receives 5 percent or more of the vote, but less than 20 percent, the party may use a primary election or nominating convention to place candidates on the general election ballot. However, the filing fee requirements remain in place. Parties with less than 5 percent of the vote in the most recent governor's election must first register with the Secretary of State's office by collecting the signatures of registered voters who support the party. A party must secure enough signatures to equal 1 percent of the total votes for all candidates for governor at the last election.

An **independent candidate,** a candidate running for office without a political party affiliation or nomination, must submit an application for a place on the general election ballot. In addition, the candidate must gather signatures of registered voters willing to sign a petition that the candidate's name should appear on the ballot. The number of signatures needed varies from 1 to 5 percent of the total votes for all candidates for governor at the last election. If the independent candidate is running for a countywide office, the candidate needs to collect 1 to 5 percent of the total votes for governor in that county. Because they lack a party affiliation,

Independent candidate

a candidate running for office without a political party affiliation.

Landslide Lyndon

Today, visitors to the Lyndon B. Johnson Presidential Museum in Austin can watch a mechanical figure of the former president lean on a split-rail fence and spin yarns about Texas. Johnson occupies a unique position in that he has both starred in and recounted many Texas legends.

The career of Lyndon Baines Johnson saw his rise from teacher in a poor school in Pearsall, Texas, to president of the United States. When "Pappy" O'Daniel, in what one newspaper called the "most constructive act" of his career, retired from the U.S. Senate, the battle to succeed O'Daniel pitted Johnson against former governor Coke Robert Stevenson. Stevenson was considered unbeatable by some but Johnson won the endorsement of many of the state's newspapers and "Ma" Ferguson, who remembered that Johnson attended the funeral of her husband while Stevenson skipped the service. Johnson concentrated on the large urban areas and zipped around the state by campaigning with a helicopter while Stevenson was content to drive around in an old Plymouth.

Stevenson finished first in the primary, easily besting Johnson by a vote of 477,077 to 405,617. However, lacking the majority needed to win the nomination, the two candidates faced off in a run-off election. Official returns from the run-off took three days to compile, before the Texas Election Board announced that Stevenson had won by 362 votes. However, "late returns" were still coming in, including what would become the legendary Box 13 from Alice, Texas, which belatedly revealed 203 uncounted ballots, 202 of them for Johnson. Upon further examination, the poll lists showed that Box 13's voters had signed in and voted in alphabetical order and

in identical handwriting. Amended returns gave Johnson an 87-vote margin statewide and the nickname of "Landslide Lyndon."

The State Democratic Executive Committee had the final word on the primary returns and voted 29 to 28 to certify the Johnson victory. While some of Johnson's critics have pointed to evidence of voter fraud in Alice, others point out that there was evidence of similar vote fraud on behalf of Stevenson in East Texas. As T. R. Fehrenbach concluded in his classic history of Texas, "Johnson's men had not defrauded Stevenson, but successfully outfrauded him."[i]

While Johnson's leadership of the nation as it tackled landmark civil rights legislation including the Civil Rights Act of 1964 and the Voting Rights Act of 1965 have given him a well-deserved place in history, it's worth remembering that Johnson, like many other leaders of his time, came to power under the wing of powerful party bosses and sometimes won high office by taking the low road.

i. T. R. Fehrenbach, *Lone Star: A History of Texas and the Texans,* updated ed., (Cambridge, Mass.: Da Capo Press, 2000), 659

independent candidates do not compete in primary elections in Texas. In fact, independent candidates cannot declare their intention to run for office until after primary elections are over and cannot have voters who participated in the primary elections sign the petition form that puts them on the ballot. Write-in candidates qualify by either paying a filing fee or, like independent candidates, completing a nomination petition. Once a candidate decides to run for a party nomination either by party primary or party convention, he or she cannot run as an independent candidate in the general election.

Even as Texas maintains its tradition of Texas ballot access for major-party candidates, independent candidates, and write-in candidates, another tradition endures in Texas, one whereby rules and procedures are used to make access to the ballot for minor-party candidates more challenging. The rule requiring minor parties to constantly reapply to have their party name and label on the ballot based upon statewide totals in the governor's election clearly favors the established Democratic and Republican parties. The hurdles put in place by Texas's ballot access rules and procedures reflect the traditional political culture that dominates much of Texas, that is, a desire to keep the "wrong" kinds of candidates and political parties off the ballot. Denying access to the ballot to these candidates and political parties minimizes challenges to existing political elites. Of course, periodically, a political party like the Libertarians does qualify automatically for access to the ballot.

Electronic Voting in Texas

In the wake of the 2000 presidential election, which saw a large number of irregularities in the state of Florida, Congress acted to create a single national standard for election procedures for presidential and congressional elections by passing the **Help America Vote Act (HAVA)** in 2002. Ultimately, many states and local governments began adapting procedures for non-federal elections to comply with HAVA simply because state and local elections are often held simultaneously with federal elections. Therefore, HAVA has had the effect of standardizing procedures for all elections to office—federal, state, and local—and in so doing has given the national government a degree of control in states' election affairs.

Help America Vote Act (HAVA)
federal statute enacted after the 2000 presidential election to effectively standardize election procedures.

HAVA mandates that every polling station utilize electronic voting equipment and have at least one voting booth that is accessible for those with a disability. HAVA also requires that state and local voting officials conduct educational activities and equipment demonstrations to allow voters to become familiar with the electronic voting equipment. While HAVA does not specify the exact equipment to be used, standards have nevertheless been set for the equipment. Congress, recognizing the expense of purchasing new equipment, provided limited funds to states and local governments to implement HAVA. In Texas, the Secretary of State's Elections Division certified several types of equipment, including optical scanners, touch-screen voting machines, and dial-controlled computer voting (E-slates). County governments may select from one of four companies to supply the equipment.

The shift to electronic voting is meant to overcome the perceived problems of other forms of balloting. Traditional paper ballots are subject to ballot-box stuffing, in which additional paper ballots are placed in the box to ensure a particular candidate wins. When questions arise about the final vote totals, paper ballots are recounted by hand, a process that is not particularly reliable. Lever-operated voting machines, if not maintained properly, can cause errors in tabulating vote results, and these machines do not have a paper record of the vote for comparison later if results are questioned. Punch card ballots, which were a primary cause of the difficulties in the 2000 presidential election in Florida, are among the least reliable, with high error rates both in counting the ballots and determining which candidate on the ballot was actually selected by the voter.[29] However, electronic voting methods, like touch screens and E-slates, are not without problems, including the possibility of software tampering, the lack of a paper ballot to verify results,[30] errors in saving votes to a database, and voter distrust of computer-based voting.[31]

At the time that Congress passed HAVA in 2002, about one-third of Texas's counties still used the paper ballot. Fourteen counties employed punch-card systems, and three counties used lever machines. All of these counties were required to replace all of their voting equipment with electronic systems. In 2000, the majority of counties employed optical scanners. With optical scanners, a voter marks a ballot, the ballot is scanned, and the results are added by the scanner's software to the database. Although optical scanners were allowed to continue under HAVA, counties using optical scanners were still mandated to have at least one E-slate or touchscreen system available at each polling place for those with disabilities. The passage of HAVA, then, meant that almost all of Texas's 254 counties needed to upgrade equipment, with a substantial proportion of them needing to replace their equipment entirely.[32]

The cost of these upgrades has been high. Estimates from the Texas Secretary of State's office suggest that more than $170 million was needed to comply with HAVA.[33] Funds were made available to counties from the state based upon a formula that included the number of voting precincts and voting-age-eligible population. Loving County, the smallest in population, with only fifty-four age-eligible voters, received $27,000 in 2003 and $40,000 in 2004. Implementation of HAVA in Harris County, with almost 2.5 million voters, cost over $6 million in 2003 and $12 million in 2004. In the trade-off between ensuring the accuracy of the vote and need to fund elections, Congress chose ensuring accuracy but passed most of the cost onto states and local governments. The limited funds provided by Congress were nowhere near the total cost to states and local governments to purchase the new voting equipment. Again, the role of the national government in promoting change in Texas elections becomes evident. The transition to electronic voting resulted from laws passed by the U.S. Congress.

Texas Pioneers: Early Voting

National elections are required by federal law to be held on the first Tuesday following the first Monday in November. State and local elections in Texas are also typically held on a Tuesday, and polls are open from 7:00 a.m. to 7:00 p.m. While these hours might seem extensive, in fact for many people who work from 8:00 a.m. until 5:00 p.m., with time needed for commuting to and from work, these hours may not be enough. To help Texans vote, Texas began in 1988 to experiment with **advanced or early voting,** which allows a voter to cast a ballot before an election without giving a specific reason. Historically, to cast a ballot before Election Day a voter had to qualify for an absentee ballot, documenting a specific reason for being absent on Election Day: for example, being on vacation, being on a business trip, or being away at college. In early voting, the local elections administrator opens polling to voters during specified times and days in the weeks leading up to the election. In Texas, early voting days include weekends. Voting is made "easier" and at the leisure of the voter, who can now avoid a hectic workday scramble to get to the voting booth before it closes on Election Day. Texas was an early adopter of early voting; its experiences and those of a handful of other states has led to the expansion of early voting nationwide. Many states now have some form of early voting. As shown in Figure 7.1, early voting has become quite popular in Texas, especially in presidential election years. In 2008, more than 5 million Texans took advantage of early voting, a record number for the state.

Advanced or early voting
a voting system that allows a voter to cast a ballot before an election without giving a specific reason, thus making voting more convenient for the voter.

Figure 7.1 Early Voting in Texas, 1996–2008

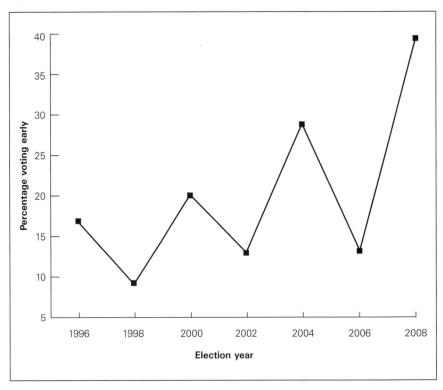

Source: Compiled by the authors based on data available from the Texas Secretary of State, Early Voting Information, www.sos.state.tx.us/elections/historical/earlyvotinginfo.shtml (accessed May 14, 2007 and August 4, 2010).

Primary election

intra-party election in which candidates compete to determine who will win the party's nomination in the general election.

Direct primary

a primary election in which the winning candidate directly receives the party nomination.

Indirect primary

a primary election in which voters elect delegates to a party convention; delegates are pledged to support a specific candidate seeking the party nomination.

Preference primary

a primary election in which voters indicate their choice to hold office, but the actual selection is left to the political party elites.

General election

an inter-party election in which candidates from two or more political parties and independent candidates compete for actual political office.

Types of Elections in Texas

Several types of elections exist. **Primary elections** are essentially intra-party elections. In these elections, candidates compete to represent a particular political party in a general election. Thus, the winner of a primary "wins" the party's nomination and a place on the ballot in the general election. A primary election may be a **direct primary,** in which the winning candidate automatically receives the party nomination, or it may be an **indirect primary** or **preference primary.** In an indirect primary, voters elect delegates to a party convention. Delegates are pledged to support a specific candidate seeking the party nomination. At the convention, the delegates vote among the various candidates. The winner receives the party nomination. In a preference primary, voters indicate their choice of candidate to hold office, but the actual selection is left to the political party elites.

Primary Elections versus General Elections

The winner of a political party's primary next moves on to compete in the **general election** as that party's candidate. General elections see candidates from two or more political parties vie for elected office. These elections are inter-party elections in which voters choose among several candidates representing different political parties and independent candidates. The winner of the general election wins office, for example, as governor, member of the state legislature, or judge.

Texas versus Oregon

While Texas serves as a pioneer in early voting, Oregon followed a different path in encouraging voter turnout by allowing "vote by mail." In the vote-by-mail system, the state of Oregon mails a ballot to every registered voter about two weeks before the election. At their leisure, voters mark the ballot and mail the ballot back in a special envelope. A voter may also hand-deliver the ballot to designated locations throughout the state.

Historically, states have allowed voters to receive a ballot early and mail it back only for absentee voting. Absentee voting required that the voter provide a legitimate reason for not being in the community on Election Day in order to cast an early ballot. In 1981, Oregon allowed limited experiments with mail-in ballots for all voters in local elections. In December 1995, Oregon extended the process to party primaries. By 1998, all elections in Oregon included the vote-by-mail system. One review of the research on the impact of voting by mail suggests that voter turnout increases between 5 to 10 percent over traditional in-person voting.[i]

The table to the right presents some statistics comparing turnout in Texas to turnout in Oregon since vote-by-mail became a statewide process in 1998.

Voter Turnout in Oregon and Texas

ELECTION	OREGON TURNOUT	TEXAS TURNOUT
2000 Presidential Election	65%	44%
2002 November General Election	51%	29%
2004 Presidential Election	71%	46%
2006 November General Election	52%	26%
2008 Presidential Election	66%	46%

Thinking Critically

- What is vote by mail?
- How is the vote-by-mail system similar to early voting in Texas?
- Do you think a vote-by-mail system would help boost voter turnout in Texas?
- Have you ever voted with early voting in Texas?
- Would you be more likely to vote if you could vote by mail?

i. Paul Gronke and Peter Miller, "Voting by Mail and Turnout: A Replication and Extension," paper presented at the Annual Meeting of the American Political Science Association, Chicago, Illinois, August 20, 2007.

In Texas, primary elections, in most instances, are direct primaries. Political parties use direct primaries to nominate candidates for all state offices, plus the U.S. House of Representatives and the U.S. Senate. In the presidential primaries, Texas and many other states use an indirect primary to nominate candidates for president. An alternative to the indirect primary is the caucus. In some states, parties are allowed to pick how their delegates are selected. In Texas, the two major parties must use a primary election. In 2008, however, the Texas Democratic Party adopted an unusual system, called the Texas Two-Step, to select delegates to the party's national convention, which is responsible for nominating the party's presidential candidate. The Texas Two-Step involved a traditional preference, or indirect, primary held in early March. The preference primary was used to choose 126 delegates for the national convention. However, an additional 67 delegates were selected through a caucus system that began at the precinct level on the evening of the primary. These caucuses essentially were precinct conventions. Over 3,000 delegates chosen at the precinct level moved on to county-level caucuses, which in turn chose delegates to district-level caucuses. Finally, results were aggregated at the state convention, where those final 67 delegates for the national convention were selected. This process took several months to complete. Whether or not it will be used by the Democratic Party in 2012 is uncertain. Republicans selected their delegates using a preference primary only. Details on the caucus system are found in the "Texas versus Iowa" box in Chapter 8.

Closed primary

an electoral contest restricted to party loyalists and excluding supporters of other political parties and independent voters.

Open primary

an electoral contest in which voters are not required to declare a party affiliation to participate, but must request a specific party's ballot at the primary; voters are subsequently barred from participating in the other party's primary.

Blanket or wide-open primary

a primary in which voters do not register party affiliations and receive ballot papers containing the names of all candidates from all political parties running for office; usually voters may choose only one candidate per office rather than one candidate per political party.

Three types of primaries exist: closed primaries, open primaries, and blanket or wide-open primaries. A **closed primary** restricts the voters who participate in the primary to party loyalists. Typically, prior to the primary, often when registering to vote, each individual voter must declare a party affiliation. At the primary, when a voter shows up to cast a ballot the voter's name is checked against a list of registered party supporters. Obviously, this approach limits the number of voters in the primary to those voters willing to specify a party affiliation. An advantage of the closed primary is the fact that candidates who win the party nomination more closely reflect the beliefs and ideas of the party faithful. On the flip side, candidates may not reflect the beliefs of the entire electorate because independent voters and supporters of other political parties are excluded from voting. A closed, enforced primary ensures that only the registered party supporters vote in the primary. However, some states and localities use a closed, unenforced primary. In this case, although voters register with a specific party affiliation, at the actual primary election a voter's name is not checked against a list of registered party supporters. A voter may therefore be registered with the Democratic Party but vote in the Republican Party primary, or vice versa. In states with closed primaries, political parties may hold their primaries on different days.

In an **open primary,** a voter is not required to declare a party affiliation. At the primary, the voter requests a specific party's ballot. The ballot contains only those candidates from the party that the voter requested. Once a voter participates in a specific party's primary, he or she is prohibited, usually by law, from participating in another party's primary. In some states, the parties may hold their primaries on different days. Independent voters often prefer the open primary because they are allowed to participate in at least one party's primary. Moreover, cross-party voting often occurs because Republicans may vote in the Democratic Party primary and vice versa. Of course, if a Republican chooses to vote in the Democratic primary, the voter is then barred from participating in the Republican primary. Also, open primaries are more subject to manipulation. For example, if a Democratic Party candidate is running unopposed in the Democratic primary, party officials may encourage Democratic voters to show up for the Republican primary and help the most extreme or easiest-to-defeat candidate win the Republican nomination. Republicans may likewise engage in the same behavior in a Democratic primary.

A few states use the **blanket or wide-open primary.** In this system, voters do not register a party affiliation. At the primary, voters receive ballot papers containing the names of all candidates from all political parties running for office. Voters still may choose only one candidate per office, not one candidate per political party. In the partisan blanket primary, the Democratic Party candidate with the most votes moves on to the general election as the Democratic nominee, and the Republican candidate with the most votes competes in the general election as the Republican nominee. The same results hold true for any and all other parties holding primary elections. The states of Alaska and California required use of the partisan blanket primary until the U.S. Supreme Court in *California Democratic Party v. Jones* (2000) upheld the right of political parties to choose their own primary system, holding that the First Amendment's right to association took precedence.[34] From 1935 until 2004, the state of Washington also used the partisan blanket primary.

Louisiana pioneered the use of the nonpartisan blanket primary. This system is a bit different from the partisan blanket primary systems. In Louisiana, the top two candidates regardless of party affiliation move on to the general election. In the 1970s and 1980s, a common outcome of the primary saw two Democrats competing in the general election, with no Republicans on the general election ballot.

Another unusual aspect of Louisiana's system is the fact that if a candidate wins a majority of the vote in the primary election, the candidate wins the office and no general election ensues. In effect, the primary becomes a general election. In 2004, voters in Washington adopted an amendment to the state constitution to change their partisan system to a nonpartisan blanket primary like Louisiana's. More recently, California voters moved in opposition to the U.S. Supreme Court ruling in *California Democratic Party v. Jones* (2000) when they approved Proposition 14 in June 2010. This ballot measure amends the California Constitution to require the use of the nonpartisan blanket primary in state and local elections.

Currently, Texas's primary system is technically a closed system, as required by state law. In practice, however, Texas's system is considered semi-open.[35] The designation semi-open is more appropriate because, as in an open primary, voters in Texas do not have to declare a party affiliation when registering to vote. However, the system becomes functionally closed at the primary election. Upon requesting a specific party's ballot at the primary, this information is recorded and in some counties even stamped on voter registration cards at the time. For the next year, the voters cannot change party affiliations. Since multiple primaries may be held in a given year, the voters become locked into voting in the same primary for twelve months. At the next primary, voters are automatically given the party ballot of their previously recorded party.

Another interesting requirement in Texas is that the winner of a political party's primary election must receive a majority of the vote, 50 percent plus one additional vote, in the primary election. If the leading candidate does not receive a majority in the initial primary election, a run-off election is held a few weeks later between the first- and second-place candidates in that party's initial primary election. Simply put, candidates must receive a majority of the political party's primary votes, not just the most votes.

The history of primaries in Texas is riddled with political manipulation to produce certain outcomes. In an effort to stave off defection to the Republican Party as national Democratic Party leaders began to emphasize civil rights legislation in the 1950s, election reforms in 1951–1952 allowed **cross filing.** In cross filing, a candidate may run simultaneously as a Democratic candidate and a Republican, essentially competing in both parties' primaries.[36] This tactic allowed Democrats to maintain control of the Republican Party as it held its first presidential primary election in Texas. Democratic voters were able to cross over to support Republican candidate Dwight Eisenhower for U.S. president all the while ensuring that state and local candidates who won the Republican primary were also loyal Democrats. Republicans labeled these Democratic voters "One-Day Republicans."[37] This practice seems unusual, but as recently as 1948 Texas Republicans had approached prominent Democrats, including candidates for governor, and requested that they run as Republicans.[38] Note that some states today allow a related practice called electoral fusion, in which more than one party nominates the same candidate in the general election, and the candidate carries both party labels on the election ballot.

Cross filing

a system that allows a candidate to run simultaneously as a Democratic and a Republican candidate, essentially competing in both parties' primaries.

Direct Democracy Elections

A final type of election is the direct democracy election, which emerged during the era of the Progressive reforms. At the state level, three of the Progressive Party's ideas associated with direct democracy and voter input into the decision-making process have been adopted: the referendum, the initiative, and the recall.

The nonpartisan blanket primary system used in Louisiana often seems attractive to voters from outside the state. The system differs from the closed primary by allowing independent and third-party voters to participate in the primary election because voters do not need to register a political party affiliation. In addition, the nonpartisan blanket primary differs from the traditional open primary in that voters do not have to choose a specific political party's primary in which to participate. Instead, a registered voter simply arrives at the polling place on Election Day and receives a ballot with all of the candidates from all of the political parties with all offices to be chosen listed. Here, voters can maximize cross-party voting by, for example, choosing a Republican for president, a Democrat for U.S. senator, a Libertarian for U.S. House of Representatives, and so forth. This ability to cross-party vote by office, which is impossible in other types of primaries because the ballot contains only candidates from a specific political party, is attractive to many voters. Since all registered voters may participate in the primary, proponents maintain that the system should produce more centrist or moderate candidates. This ability to produce centrist or moderate candidates was important in the California campaign to adopt the nonpartisan, blanket primary.[i] After all, by restricting the ballot to registered party supporters, the closed primary essentially limits participation to conservative or right-of-center voters for the Republican primary and liberal or left-of-center voters in the Democratic primary. Independent voters are forced to choose a side, or stay at home.

Does the nonpartisan blanket primary in Louisiana produce centrist, moderate candidates that reflect the views of the entire electorate rather than those of a

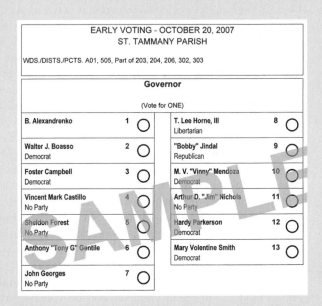

smaller number of partisan voters? Fortunately, evidence is readily available in the form of elections results from Louisiana. In fact, results from Louisiana governor's elections suggest that Louisiana's primary system does not necessarily produce centrist or moderate officeholders. For example, in 1991 the centrist incumbent governor Buddy Roemer, a one-time Democrat who became a Republican, received 27 percent of the vote to finish third place in a twelve-candidate field. Roemer's third-place finish meant he was eliminated. In second place, with 32 percent of the vote, was David Duke.[ii] Duke, a former member of the state legislature and once Grand Wizard of the Knights of the Ku Klux Klan, was clearly more extremist than Roemer. Edwin Edwards, a former

Normally, a law is passed by having the state legislature approve a bill; the bill is signed by the governor to become a law. In a referendum, the state legislature proposes a new law and places the proposed law on an election ballot. At the next election, citizens vote statewide to determine whether the new law is adopted or rejected. Twenty-two states use the referendum for approving new laws. Texas lacks this referendum process to enact laws. Another use of the referendum, as discussed in Chapter 2, is to approve formal changes and amendments to a state constitution. In this use, a state legislature submits the amendment to the voters of the state for approval. Forty-nine states, including Texas, require that amendments to the state's constitution be approved by voters through this second use.

state governor who had been indicted and tried several times for a variety of violations of federal racketeering laws, finished in first place with 34 percent of the vote. Edwards and Duke moved on to the general election in November. Edwards defeated Duke with 61 percent of the vote.

Another example is the 1987 gubernatorial election. In that race, Edwin Edwards received 28 percent of the primary vote and Buddy Roemer, then a Democrat, received 33 percent. While Roemer went on to become governor, third place in the primary went to Robert Livingston, the only Republican candidate, who received 18 percent of the vote.[iii] The fourth place finish of W. J. "Billy" Tauzin, at the time a conservative Democrat and now a moderate Republican, is interesting because Tauzin was arguably more centrist than either Edwards or Livingston. The evidence suggests that centrist candidates are often crowded out in Louisiana's primary system by more extreme candidates. Simply put, centrist and moderate candidates, if sufficient in number, can split the middle vote, which has the effect of allowing more extreme candidates to get just enough votes to move on to the general election.

Note in both of the above cases the top two candidates did not receive a majority of the votes within their political party. What mattered was finishing in one of the top two positions. Hypothetically, a six-candidate race in which the candidates evenly split the votes could produce a result in which the top two candidates move on to the general election having received no more than 16 or 17 percent of the vote. Compare this with Texas's semi-open system in which the Republican and Democratic candidates moving on to the general election must have received a majority of the votes in their respective political parties' primary.

The 2007 election of Louisiana's current governor, Bobby Jindal, illustrates another interesting feature of Louisiana's primary system. (A sample ballot from the 2007 blanket primary election for governor is pictured on the facing page.) Jindal received 54 percent of the vote in the primary election. Under Louisiana's system, by winning a majority of the vote Jindal automatically became governor. A general election for governor was not needed. Yet no other Republican candidates ran that year, while five Democratic candidates, one Libertarian, and four other candidates ran for office. Democratic fracturing in the wake of embattled incumbent Democrat Kathleen Blanco's decision not to run for reelection handed the Republicans control of the governorship at the primary. Of course, with 54 percent of the vote, Jindal legitimately represented the majority of Louisiana voters at the time.

Thinking Critically

- What are the advantages to Louisiana's non-partisan blanket primary?
- Why do you think people in California, or Texas, might be attracted to the system?
- What are the advantages to Texas's current semi-open system? (See text for details on Texas's system.)
- Which system do you prefer?

i.   John Howard, "Voters Approve Prop. 14, 'Open Primary,' " *Sacramento Capitol Weekly*, June 8, 2010, www.capitolweekly.net (accessed August 10, 2010).
ii. Louisiana Secretary of State, "Election Results," http://electionresults.sos .louisiana.gov/graphical# (accessed August 10, 2010).
iii. Ibid.

Another way to get citizens directly involved in law-making is the initiative. An initiative takes shape when citizens propose a new law by writing it out and then collecting the signatures of registered voters who support it on an initiative petition form. When a set number of registered voters, which varies by state, have signed the form, the form is submitted to the state's chief elections officer for certification. Once certified, the proposed new law is placed on an election ballot for voters state-wide to accept or reject. Sometimes the initiative petition is called simply a proposition. Like the referendum, states use the initiative petition to propose new laws or to amend the state constitution. Twenty-four states allow the initiative petition,[39] but not Texas.

The recall petition serves as a method for removing a sitting elected official before his or her term of office has finished. The recall operates in a manner similar to a petition: a specified number of signatures are collected on a petition calling for immediate removal of an elected official from office. Once enough signatures have been gathered, the petition is submitted to the state's chief elections officer for certification. Following the certification, voters at the next election determine whether the official remains in office. Eighteen states allow the recall petition for elected officials. Texas lacks the recall petition for state officials. However, local officials in Texas may be recalled in some cities and other local governments depending on the locality's plan of government and the Texas Local Government Code.

Too Much Democracy?

In Texas's general elections, voters are confronted with the long ballot, a Progressive era reform that made as many state and local offices as possible subject to direct election by the voters. The long ballot is so called because it is just that—long. A long ballot may contain choices for all of the following: the governor, the lieutenant governor, the comptroller of Public Accounts, the commissioner of the General Land Office, the commissioner of Agriculture, the attorney general, a state senator, a state representative, a member of the U.S. House of Representatives, a U.S. senator, members of the Texas Railroad Commission, members of the Texas Board of Education, a justice of the peace, county commissioners, county tax assessors, a mayor, members of the city council, city judges, county judges, and state court judges (including district court, appeals court, and the two high courts). All of this is quite an undertaking.

The sheer number of elected offices and candidates running for office means that voters are often overwhelmed at the polling place. One result is that voters tend to vote for the offices that appear higher on the ballot, while ignoring and leaving blank offices that are farther down. In so doing, voters are typically voting for the most "important" offices like the U.S. president, governor, or U.S. senator and leaving "lesser" offices at the county and local level blank. This phenomenon is called **roll off**.[40] For example, in 2010 the total number of votes cast for the statewide race for governor equaled almost 45,000 more than the total number of votes cast for lieutenant governor, a difference of 0.9 percent. More dramatic results occurred down ballot. There were over 1 million fewer votes, or approximately 20 percent fewer votes, for comptroller of Public Accounts compared with the vote for governor. Similar trends occur during presidential elections. In 2008, over 165,000 fewer votes were cast for U.S. senator compared with the number of votes cast for U.S. president, or approximately 2.1 percent fewer votes for U.S. senator. Farther down the ballot, nearly 370,000 fewer votes were cast for chief justice of the Texas Supreme Court compared with the votes for U.S. president, or 4.6 percent fewer votes. In that election, voters also filled positions on the Texas Court of Criminal Appeals, the state's highest criminal appeals court. Voters in 2008 elected three positions on the court, with the total number of votes varying by 1.8 million votes between the three positions. Almost 25 percent of voters rolled off the ballot between selecting a candidate for the chief justice position and the third position to be elected to the Texas Court of Criminal Appeals.

Another effect of the long ballot is **party-line voting** also known as straight ticket voting (see Chapter 5). Party-line voting occurs when a voter selects candidates on the basis of their party affiliation, that is, recording a vote for all Democratic candidates

Roll off

process in which voters mark off only the "more important" offices on a lengthy ballot—usually national or statewide offices—and leave the county or local office choices blank.

Party-line voting

process in which voters select candidates by their party affiliation.

or all Republican candidates. In this way, the voter avoids having to make tough decisions on an office-by-office or candidate-by-candidate basis.

The advantage of the long ballot is, of course, greater accountability of elected officials to the voters in the state, county, city, or other agency of state government. However, the long ballot, if used as intended by the Progressives, requires that voters ignore partisanship as a guide to selecting a candidate in the election. Instead, voters are expected to be well informed about all candidates and issues in the election, selecting wisely the most qualified candidate or the candidate with views closest to the voter's. Such expectations may be unrealistic given the sheer number of races to be decided on a lengthy ballot. Voters may tend to rely on heuristics, or "short cuts," to aid them in making their choices.[41] Short cuts include use of party labels,[42] name recognition, and ideology. Overall, the increase in the number of elected offices contributes to voter fatigue and raises the costs of voting. The unintended consequence is fewer voters turning out on Election Day.

Voter Registration and Turnout

The health of democracy is often measured, correctly or incorrectly, by using participation in elections as a benchmark. To some extent, this approach makes sense because efforts at civic education often stress voting as the "best" or "most important" form of having one's voice heard. In addition, the denial of the right to vote to African Americans has placed additional focus on exercising one's right to vote. Finally, elections are essential to concepts of modern representative democracy, thus turnout is important to ensuring representation.

Figure 7.2 tracks the rate of voter registration from 1970–2010 among the age-eligible population in the state of Texas. Beginning in 1974 and continuing into the 1990s, the rate of registration remains relatively stable, hovering in the low- to mid-60-percent range for most of the period. Registration peaks during presidential elections. From a high of 71.2 percent in the wake of the Watergate scandal in 1976, participation trends downward, reaching 70 percent in 1984. In 1994, the trend is toward higher rates of voter registration, leveling off in the low 80-percent range by the mid-2000s. Why did voter registration spike in the mid- to late-1990s? One important explanation is the impact of the 1993 Motor Voter Act. In addition, the implementation of online voter registration forms made access to registration easier for many potential new voters, leading to potentially higher registration rates. The advent of new technologies like computerized databases and better training of local election officials influenced the rates of voter registration as well. However, in recent years voter registration has declined, falling by 2010 to about 70 percent. This trend may only reflect the improved ability to update and purge voter registration records.

Another important consideration during elections is **voter turnout**. Voter turnout, or the number of people actually casting ballots in an election, in Texas resembles trends from across the United States. Voter turnout tends to be higher in presidential election years than in off-year, mid-term elections. Moreover, special elections and local elections tend to have very low levels of voter turnout.

Voter turnout is calculated one of two ways: as the percentage of ballots cast in the election based upon (1) the total number of registered voters or (2) the total population over age eighteen (or, voting age-eligible population). Often government officials like to report turnout based on the first method, in part because rates of turnout are inflated with the first measure. Obviously, the total number of

Voter turnout
the number of people casting ballots in a given election.

Figure 7.2 Rate of Voter Registration, 1970–2010

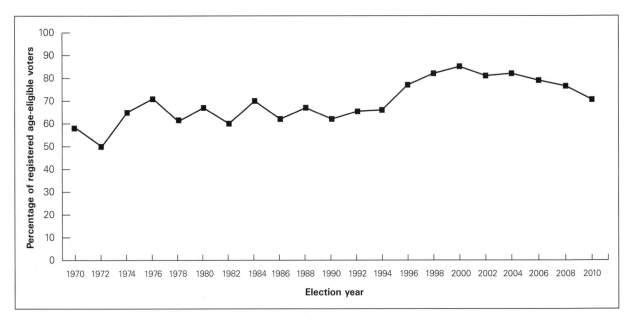

Source: Compiled by the authors based on data from the Texas Secretary of State, Turnout and Voter Registration Figures, www.sos.state.tx.us/elections/historical/70-92 .shtml (accessed May 14, 2007 and November 3, 2010).

registered voters is normally lower than the total number of people who are of eligible voting age.

This issue of using registered voters or age-eligible population is important when comparing voter turnout rates over time or across states. States sometimes change the eligibility requirements, for example southern states like Texas have clearly manipulated registration requirements to exclude African Americans, as discussed earlier. Also, registration processes and voter eligibility varies from state to state. North Dakota, as noted earlier, lacks any form of registration, so that anyone showing up on Election Day with a valid state driver's license or other proof of residency is allowed to vote. In neighboring Minnesota, voters are allowed to register to vote up to and on Election Day. These differences produce variations in the percentage of the age-eligible population that is registered to vote.

Thus, the more accurate figure, especially for comparison purposes, is to use the total population over age eighteen (or, voting age-eligible population). In general, voter turnout among the age-eligible population hovers in the 40 to 50 percent range for presidential elections but declines to the high 20 or low 30 percent range for mid-term, off-year elections. Recent elections are similar to these trends. In 2008, voter turnout was 59.9 percent of registered voters and 45.5 percent of age-eligible voters. Corresponding figures for 2010 were 37.5 percent of registered voters and 26.5 percent of age-eligible voters.[43] Interestingly, the gap between turnout among the age-eligible population and actual registered voters narrowed between 1992 and 2004. This narrowing of the gap between turnout and age-eligible population reflects the trend toward increased voter registration, whether as a result of the Motor Voter Act, ease of online registration, improvements in database management, or some other cause. Since 2004, the gap has grown wider again.

Figure 7.3 Turnout in Texas Special Elections, 1977–2009

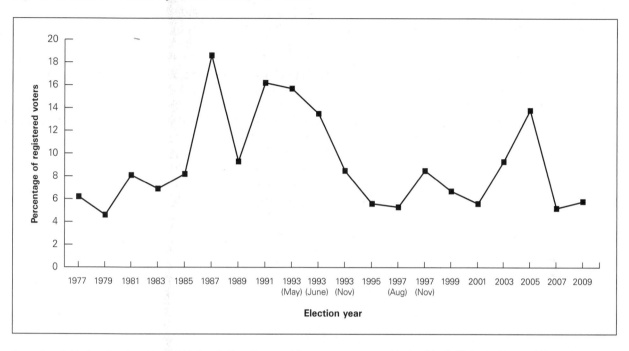

Source: Compiled by the authors from data available from the Texas Secretary of State, www.sos.state.tx.us/elections/historical/index.shtml (accessed May 14, 2007 and August 11, 2010).

What about voter turnout in special elections? Figure 7.3 shows the trends in voter turnout in special elections in Texas since 1977. With the exceptions of the May and June elections of 1993, all other special statewide elections since 1977 concerned amendments to the Texas Constitution. In general, voter turnout in special elections is quite low, never reaching higher than 35 percent of registered voters, or 20 percent of age-eligible voters. Two of the three most recent special elections, in 2003 and 2005, saw slight increases in the rate of turnout compared to earlier elections. In subsequent special elections, in 2007 and 2009, the rate of voter turnout fell to around 5 percent.

The 2005 special election involved a series of constitutional amendments, including a controversial proposal involving the definition of marriage. This amendment energized social conservatives who supported the language of the amendment, limiting marriage to a union between a man and a woman. However, many opponents, including gay and lesbian organizations, were also mobilized to vote to prevent passage of the amendment. Their efforts failed, however, when the amendment passed with 76.3 percent of the vote. The May 2007 amendment concerned a much less controversial topic: property tax rates paid by senior citizens. This relatively uncontroversial issue produced extremely low voter turnout (5.2 percent). Similarly, the special election of 2009 involved a series of amendments to the Texas Constitution concerning the powers of eminent domain and access to public beaches, among others issues.

So, why is voter turnout typically higher for presidential elections than for mid-term elections for governor, members of the U.S. House of Representatives, and the state legislature, and why do mid-term elections have higher voter turnouts than

Second order elections

elections for offices below the national executive level in countries with presidential systems like the United States or the national legislature level in parliamentary countries like Great Britain; generally viewed as less important in scope and impact on a country.

special elections? One answer lies in what scholars who compare elections across different countries refer to as **second order elections**.[44] Second order elections are elections for offices other than the national executive in presidential systems like the United States' or the national legislature in parliamentary systems like Great Britain's. The term "second order" refers to the fact that these elections are simply less important in scope and impact on the country as a whole, with less ability to shift the direction of the entire political system. Because the stakes are lower, voters see fewer benefits from voting and view the act of voting in these elections as less important. Another explanation is the issue of mobilization. Presidential elections in the United States are more likely to be discussed in the media and often more intensely advertised. What is more, the political parties and the candidates themselves through their campaign organizations are more aggressive in contacting potential voters to go out and to cast votes.

Voting behavior in Texas is in a state of transition. More and more Texans are now on the voter registration list, but this upward trend in registration is not reversing the general trend in low voter turnout. Voter turnout remains alarmingly low in special elections. Congressional and statewide elections not held in conjunction with presidential elections tend to have low voter turnout as well.

Who Votes?

In general, Texas is characterized by low rates of voter turnout compared to other states. Texas typically ranks near the bottom in voter turnout. Low voter turnout is a result of several factors. Certainly the long ballot, with its many races and candidates, is a deterrent for some voters. The focus on charismatic candidates and "personality" approaches to campaigns offers entertainment but little serious focus for some voters. While relatively easier than in the past, actually taking time to register to vote may be a deterrent, especially when a potential voter realizes that the list of registered voters is used by state and local courts to call people for jury duty. Lower turnout is also a result of Texas's traditionalistic political culture, which tends to cast a negative view on politics and political life in general; the state's strain of extreme individualism can make voting seem more of a chore than a right to be exercised. Finally, the relatively weak organizational nature of Texas's political parties limits their ability to mobilize voters. We will return to this theme in Chapter 8.

The rate of turnout in Texas is not stable across demographic groupings such as race/ethnicity, gender, and age. To illustrate these differences, the 2008 presidential elections provide an example of the patterns of turnout in an election in Texas. Table 7.1 provides comparisons between Texas, the U.S. average, Minnesota, and Hawaii. Minnesota had the highest turnout in 2008, while Hawaii had the lowest.

Note the differences in the rate of voter turnout between various demographic groups. For example, men are less likely to vote than women at the national level. That trend holds in each of the three states in the comparison. Non-Hispanic whites voted more than other ethnic groups. These trends are consistent with national trends on turnout by gender and ethnic group.

Throughout the United States and in Texas, voter turnout varies considerably by age group. The youngest voters, ages 18–24, consistently vote at levels much below the national or state average. While some improvement occurs in the 25–44 age bracket, the highest rates of voting occur among those over the age of 45, especially among those in the 65–74 age bracket. The trends in the 2008 election were consistent with prior presidential elections. However, these differences in turnout by age

Table 7.1 Voter Turnout Rates across Demographic Groups in the 2008 Presidential Election

CHARACTERISTIC	TEXAS	UNITED STATES	MINNESOTA	HAWAII
Sex				
Men	45.8%	55.7%	67.2%	46.6%
Women	51.6%	60.4%	74.2%	47.1%
Race/Ethnicity				
White, non-Hispanic	63.3%	64.8%	75.5%	60.6%
African American	61.8%	60.8%	45.5%	N/A
Asian	19.6%	32.1%	34.4%	49.2%
Hispanic	27.2%	31.6%	27.6%	N/A
Age				
18–24	32.7%	44.3%	58.6%	22.4%
25–44	39.9%	51.9%	65.6%	35.7%
45–64	58.2%	65.0%	76.1%	57.6%
65–74	72.0%	70.1%	80.0%	61.1%
75+	60.7%	65.8%	79.3%	64.7%

Source: U.S. Census Bureau, *Current Population Survey,* November 2008.

N/A = Not available.

level are important. Older Americans' propensity to vote leads candidates and parties to address disproportionately the concerns of older voters relative to those of younger voters.

Low voter turnout has consequences for Texas politics. Assuming there are differences in the policy preferences, party identifications, and other characteristics of voting behavior between the various ethnic groups, low voter turnout among African American and Hispanic voters in Texas means that fewer government decisions reflect these groups' beliefs. Similarly, government decision makers are less responsive to the concerns of younger voters because, as a group, they tend to vote less. In addition, lower turnout among various ethnic groups reduces the likelihood that minority candidates are elected to office. As a result, the system is less representative of the population as a whole.

Electoral Competition in Texas Elections

Merely holding an election to fill an office does not equate to democratic, representative government. Iraq under the rule of Saddam Hussein held regular elections for the presidency. In the Iraqi case, voters simply voted on whether Hussein should remain in office, not who among several choices should be president. Truly democratic elections require some degree of choice. A ballot with only one candidate hardly offers a choice. More importantly the choice must be between viable alternatives. In other words, elections imply not just a choice between A and B, but that both A and B have some possibility of actually winning the race.[45] This concept of two or more choices, each with some possibility of winning—or what is called electoral competition—is important for another reason. Electoral competition has been linked to higher rates of voter turnout.[46] Does Texas meet this standard of democratic elections? If not, what can be done to create a truly competitive Texas democracy?

In Texas, the dominance of the Democratic Party from the end of Reconstruction in 1876 until the civil rights era of the 1950s and 1960s challenged the democratic and representative nature of Texas politics. Disenfranchising African American and other voters certainly brings into question the representative nature of the system. However, the Democratic Party's attempts to limit the access of Republicans to the ballot process and to prevent competition from non-Democratic candidates also raises concerns about the nature of elections in Texas, and throughout the South. The era of so-called Yellow Dog Democrats began to end as the national Democratic Party in the 1950s and 1960s embraced civil rights, prompting Texans dissatisfied with this shift to look toward the Republican Party as an alternative.

The Republican Party started to become more competitive in Texas elections during the 1960s, when it began to see more votes in both state- and national-level elections. The number of Republicans elected to state and national office also began to increase. Perhaps the first cracks in Texas's stalwart association with the Democratic Party appeared in 1952 when Texas voters flocked to Republican presidential candidate and popular war hero Dwight Eisenhower. The real breakthrough occurred in 1961, when a little-known Republican professor of government at Midwestern State University in Wichita Falls, John Tower, won the U.S. Senate race and became the first Republican in Congress from the South since the late 1800s. In 1978, William Clements won the governorship and became the first Republican governor since Reconstruction. Since then, Texas Republicans have regularly won statewide elected offices and seats in the U.S. House of Representatives. Currently, both U.S. senators from Texas, Kay Bailey Hutchison and John Cornyn, are Republicans. The Texas delegation to the U.S. House of Representatives numbers twenty-three Republicans and nine Democrats. In 1996, Republicans won control of the Texas State Senate, and in 2002 they won control of both houses of the Texas Legislature for the first time since 1876. By 2006, Republicans controlled all six statewide elected offices, both houses of the Texas Legislature, and dominated other statewide elected offices such as the state supreme courts, the Railroad Commission, and the Board of Education. This domination continued through the 2010 election.

The trend toward Republican success in receiving more votes, holding more offices, and putting an end to the "Yellow Dog" Democratic dominance of Texas suggests that Texas politics has transitioned away from the traditional one-party system of the past. Similar transitions have occurred throughout the South, but the trend really began with Texas. Texas is often considered the least "southern" of the southern states,[47] and as such is something of a trend leader in southern development. The "Texafication" of American politics includes an emphasis on low taxes, high-tech industry-embracing policies, and limited spending on social welfare.[48] Republicans throughout the region and nation have capitalized in part on the success of Texas Republicans.

However, the rise of the Republican Party in Texas does not mean that Texas is now a two-party state. In fact, an alternative view argues that the Republican Party is simply replacing the Democratic Party in Texas. In this case, Republicans win elections in part because fewer Democratic candidates run for office. To examine this possibility, we looked at recent elections to statewide executive branch offices,

Campaigning in Texas

Election campaigns in Texas have regularly been the stuff of legends, starting in the era of the Republic of Texas. Running for his second term as president of Texas, Sam Houston was attacked by Vice President David Burnet, who described Houston as a drunken coward who failed to fight the Mexican Army before San Jacinto and possessed "beastly intemperance and other vices degrading to humanity." Houston responded by calling Burnet a hog thief. When Burnet became enraged and challenged Houston to a duel, Houston laughed off the challenge, in part, because he "never fought down hill."[i]

After statehood, this trend continued. In his 1857 run for the governorship, Houston gave speeches, sometimes with an antislavery message, that ranged from two to four hours. When pro-secession candidates attacked him, Houston responded by telling his audience that one candidate had left a political career in Arkansas because of a banking fraud scandal and that the other had killed two men in South Carolina before coming to Texas.

Race has been an issue in many Texas campaigns. However, the races under attack have not always been the same ones. Playing off the distrust of Germans resulting from World War I, opponents of James Ferguson claimed that the improper loans that had led to Ferguson's impeachment were from the Kaiser of Germany. Ferguson retorted that William P. Hobby, his opponent, had put "full-blooded Germans" in key government positions.

The U.S. Civil War as an issue still lingered as late as 1912. Governor Oscar B. Colquitt struggled in his reelection bid because he had criticized the state textbook board after they rejected a history book because it contained a photograph of Abraham Lincoln. Many Texans also flocked to see Colquitt's opponent, William Ramsay, who played upon southern sentiments in his speeches and had bands play "Dixie" during campaign events.

Radio and then television have played a role in Texas as they have in other states. Wilbert Lee "Pappy" O'Daniel used his radio show to launch his campaign for governor. The years since have seen the broadcast media of radio and television become the central tool of candidate's campaigns. While candidates still travel the state and personally interact with voters, the battles of advertising and of efforts to get covered by news organizations have become the primary concern of campaigns.

Today's campaigns are modern, with high-tech use of the Internet and other media. In the 2006 election, independent candidate Kinky Friedman (pictured) used the Internet to show Texans his "Kinkytoons" commercials that showed what the defenders of the Alamo would have done if led by today's parties. While not as colorful as Friedman, the other independent candidate, Carole Strayhorn, took to the television airwaves to paint herself as "one tough grandma." Trying to live up to the larger-than-life legacy of earlier Texas politicians, Democrat Chris Bell appeared in an ad as a giant figure looming over Texas landmarks like the Capitol Building and the Alamo. The larger-than-life Texas campaign is alive and well.

In general, campaigns in Texas are very much like those in the rest of the nation. The state's large size does require that candidates come up with a little more cash and produce a little more style. Texas voters also remain connected to their legends of Texas history, meaning that candidates will continue to use Texas icons like the Alamo and the cowboy heritage. Ironically, campaigns embrace the larger changes in the state by adopting new technologies like the Internet to transmit these time-tested messages of traditional Texas mythology.

i. Randolph B. Campbell, *Gone to Texas* (New York: Oxford University Press, 2004), 175.

to the U.S. Congress, and to both houses of the Texas Legislature. In general, the two major parties in Texas have run candidates for all six statewide elected offices in every election under consideration. Likewise, a Democratic and a Republican candidate normally appears on the ballot for elections to the U.S. Senate. In these types of elections, then, the two major parties appear to be competitive.

As illustrated in Table 7.2, most elections since 1992 for Texas's seats in the U.S. House of Representatives are contested by Democratic and Republican candidates alike. In fact, since 1992, both major parties have typically contested at least 70 percent of the seats. Although the low point occurred in 1998, with 60 percent of seats contested, the redistricting battles of 2002 and 2004 have generally led to a slight increase in the number of districts with both Democratic and Republican candidates. Thus, at the level of U.S. congressional elections, again the Republican and Democratic parties appear to be competitive.

In contrast to elections for national and major statewide offices, state legislative elections paint a somewhat different picture of electoral competition. Elections to the state legislature are much less likely to be contested by candidates from both major parties. In Texas Senate elections, rarely are more than half of the seats competitive. From 1992 until 2006, the general trend was declining competition between the two parties. Since 2006, more races for the Texas Senate have featured candidates from both political parties. In addition, the number of races contested only by a Democratic candidate has declined.

Texas House of Representatives elections tend to be one-party races. Since 1992, only between 26.7 percent and 49.3 percent of the 150 seats have been contested by both parties in an election. Again, while the general trend in the 1990s was toward less competitive elections, since 2000 both parties have contested around 40 percent or more of the seats. Yet the number of elections in which a Republican incumbent lacks a Democratic challenger has increased, while the number of elections in which a Democratic incumbent does not have a Republican challenger has declined. Overall, since the early 1990s two-party competition has ceased to be the norm.

Of course, third parties like the Libertarians or Greens field candidates in some elections. Getting on the ballot, however, is a huge hurdle, as illustrated at the beginning of this chapter, and these parties do not often present a real challenge to the major parties. For example, in 2008 the Libertarian Party fielded 80 candidates for the Texas House of Representatives. In 2006, 85 candidates for the Texas House of Representatives ran as Libertarians. Even when Libertarian candidates appear on the ballot, the party's candidates offer little real competition for the major parties. The 2008 election illustrates this situation. Libertarian candidates averaged about 7.5 percent of the vote in the districts they contested. The best performances by Libertarians in 2008 occurred in seats in which one of the two major parties failed to nominate a candidate. For example, in the 54th District, which includes Burnet, Lampasas, and parts of Bell Counties in Central Texas, the Libertarian candidate received 22 percent of the vote, providing the only opposition to the Republican incumbent, Jimmie Don Aycock.

Another method of assessing party competition in states is to develop a measure that takes into account the patterns of competition across gubernatorial elections, percentages of state legislature seats won by parties, the length of time the governorship and legislature are controlled by each party, and the proportion of time the parties divide control over state government. This method is called the Ranney Index. Calculated for 1999–2003, the Ranney Index places Texas in the range of two-party competition, but leaning toward one-party Republican control. In fact,

Table 7.2 Party Competition in Texas Elections

ELECTION/ YEAR	SEATS CONTESTED BY REPUBLICANS ONLY		SEATS CONTESTED BY DEMOCRATS ONLY		SEATS CONTESTED BY BOTH PARTIES	
	NUMBER	PERCENTAGE	NUMBER	PERCENTAGE	NUMBER	PERCENTAGE
U.S. House of Representatives (Texas)						
1992	2	6.7%	3	10.0%	25	83.3%
1994	5	16.7%	0	0.0%	25	83.3%
1996	2	6.7%	0	0.0%	28	93.3%
1998	5	16.7%	7	23.3%	18	60.0%
2000	3	10.0%	6	20.0%	21	70.0%
2002	4	12.5%	5	15.6%	23	71.9%
2004	4	12.5%	3	9.4%	25	78.0%
2006	1	3.1%	5	15.6%	26	81.3%
2008	6	18.8%	2	6.3%	24	75.0%
2010	6	18.8%	0	0.0%	26	81.3%
Texas Senate						
1992	4	12.9%	9	29.0%	18	58.1%
1994	6	19.4%	9	29.0%	16	51.6%
1996	5	33.3%	3	20.0%	7	46.7%
1998	5	31.3%	4	25.0%	7	43.8%
2000	6	40.0%	4	26.7%	5	33.3%
2002	10	32.3%	9	29.3%	12	38.7%
2004	6	40.0%	5	33.3%	4	26.7%
2006	7	43.8%	2	12.5%	7	43.8%
2008	5	33.3%	4	26.7%	6	40.0%
2010	8	50.0%	0	0.0%	8	50.0%
Texas House of Representatives						
1992	36	24.0%	61	40.7%	53	35.3%
1994	37	24.7%	62	41.3%	51	34.0%
1996	49	32.6%	43	28.7%	58	38.7%
1998	53	35.3%	44	29.3%	53	35.3%
2000	53	35.3%	57	38.0%	40	26.7%
2002	48	32.0%	35	23.3%	67	44.7%
2004	51	34.0%	39	26.0%	60	40.0%
2006	37	24.7%	43	28.6%	70	46.7%
2008	37	24.7%	39	26.0%	74	49.3%
2010	54	36.0%	38	25.3%	58	38.7%

Sources: Compiled by the authors from data available from the Texas Secretary of State, www.sos.state.tx.us/elections/historical/index.shtml (accessed May 14, 2007 and August 9, 2010); Texas Secretary of State, http://enr.sos.state.tx.us/enr/ (accessed November 3, 2010); and *Austin American-Statesman,* http://hosted.ap.org/dynamic/files/elections/2010/general/by_state/state_sen_house/TX_State_House.html?SITE=TXAUSELN&SECTION=POLITICS (accessed November 3, 2010).

Texas scores closer to traditional Republican states like Nebraska and North Dakota than "Solid South" Democratic-controlled states like Mississippi.[49] Moreover, Texas looks nothing like four of its neighboring states. Arkansas, Louisiana, New Mexico, and Oklahoma lean much more toward the Democratic Party (see Table 7.3).

While the Democratic and Republican parties contest elections throughout Texas, the patterns of party competition suggest that Republicans have emerged in recent years as a major competitor of the Democratic Party. The days of Democratic Party dominance are gone. Republicans now compete effectively to win statewide offices; in fact, Republicans now dominate these offices. At the federal level, Republican and Democratic candidates usually face each other for seats in the U.S. House of Representatives. At the level of state legislature, the Texas Senate is somewhat competitive. The Texas House of Representatives, however, features a high number of non-competitive races, with many districts dominated exclusively by one major party or the other. Thus, transition has come to electoral competition in Texas. Ultimately, Texas may be emerging as a Republican dominant state, in which

Table 7.3 Party Competition in U.S. States

STATE	RANNEY INDEX	RANK (MOST DEMOCRATIC TO MOST REPUBLICAN)
Top Five Democratic States		
Hawaii	0.735	1
Mississippi	0.716	2
Maryland	0.707	3
Rhode Island	0.700	4
Massachusetts	0.694	5
Texas	**0.378**	**36**
50-state average	0.483	n/a
States Bordering Texas		
Arkansas	0.657	9
New Mexico	0.617	12
Louisiana	0.577	15
Oklahoma	0.570	17
Top Five Republican States		
Wyoming	0.284	46
Kansas	0.284	46
Utah	0.249	48
South Dakota	0.247	49
Idaho	0.167	50

Source: Kendra A. Hovey and Harold A. Hovey, *CQ's State Fact Finder* (Washington, D.C.: CQ Press, 2007), 118.

Note: The Ranney Index runs from 0 to 1, with 0 indicating complete domination of the state governorship and legislature by Republicans and 1 indicating complete control by Democrats.

the Democratic Party has increasing difficulties even finding candidates to run for some offices.

In most elections in which an **incumbent,** or current officeholder, is running, the incumbent possesses a significant advantage over his or her challengers. The incumbent, by virtue of already holding office, is well known to voters. The advantage of having voters familiar with the identity of a candidate is called name recognition. Name recognition is also enhanced by media coverage of the incumbent's activities, speeches, and public appearances before and during the election campaign as he or she carries out the duties of office. Of course, challengers with previous office-holding experience in other elected positions will also have a degree of name recognition.

Incumbents are also advantaged by having an existing record of positions on issues, both from previous elections and in the context of decisions made while in office. This advantage is known as **position taking.** For executive branch offices, position taking taps into an incumbent's record of accomplishments, including programs created or abolished, new initiatives created, and so forth. In the legislature, incumbents are advantaged by having a record of votes on specific bills and resolutions. The legislator's position is therefore known based upon the voting record in the legislature. Presumably the incumbent has attractive positions to some of the voters, otherwise the incumbent would not likely have been elected in the first place.

Another positive aspect of incumbency is the ability to engage in **credit claiming.** Credit claiming occurs when an incumbent points out positive outcomes for which the incumbent is responsible. Credit claiming could include obtaining state funding for new buildings at a local community college or state university, sponsoring a bill that changed the penalties for underage consumption of alcoholic beverages, or taking a stand against perceived runaway spending by the legislature.

In elections to a legislature like the Texas Legislature or U.S. Congress, incumbents are also favored by **casework,** or solving problems for the people back home. However, the most important advantage of incumbency may be the advantage that an incumbent possesses in raising money for an election campaign. Incumbents typically raise much more money than non-incumbents during an election cycle. Organized interests, knowing the advantages that the incumbent has, contribute willingly to the incumbent's reelection campaign to remain in good standing with the incumbent or court new relationships with the incumbent.

Incumbent
the current officeholder.

Position taking
an incumbent's advantage in having an existing record of positions on issues, both from previous elections and in the context of decisions made while in office.

Credit claiming
the advantage derived from incumbents' ability to point to positive outcomes for which they are responsible.

Casework
the process of solving problems for constituents.

Campaign Finance in Texas

nevitably, the discussion of elections turns to the issue of money in elections. Campaign finance is important, because without money candidates and political parties have trouble getting out their message and voters have a difficult time gathering information and making decisions about which candidate they will vote for. Money also provides essentials for election campaigns like television and radio advertising and travel throughout the state or election district. It also pays for office space, telephones, websites, public-opinion polls, and campaign staff.

The issue of campaign finance is important to a discussion of the health of American democracy, voter participation, and outcomes of elections. In a large, diverse state like Texas, a well-funded campaign is often viewed as crucial. However, the sources of campaign financing raise concern: The questions of who is giving money to candidates and what candidates may be doing in return. When a group gives campaign contributions, it is typically doing so with the expectation that the candidate will at least listen to the group's concerns. The issue of campaign finance also raises the question of whether organized interests "buy" favorable legislation, court rulings, and executive decisions.

Because money matters, the issue of free speech comes to the forefront of the debate. On the one hand, campaign contributions are a form of political speech, because by contributing to a candidate's campaign, individual citizens or interest groups are indicating their political position. On the other hand, the cost of modern campaigns suggests that those with more money to contribute are "heard" more often, regardless of the opinions of the entire electorate or even a majority of voters. In 1976, the Supreme Court examined this issue, ruling that campaign contributions were a form of speech and that limits on contributions limited freedom of speech.[50] According to the Court, limits on what an individual contributes to his or her own campaign violate the First Amendment of the U.S. Constitution. Likewise, what an individual or organized interest spends on their own, independent of candidate campaign funds, cannot be limited. In 2003, the Court revisited this issue, allowing more limits to be placed upon independent spending by individuals and interest groups,[51] only to reverse itself again in 2007.[52] Additional provisions of campaign finance law that prohibited corporations and labor unions from spending money independent of candidates' and political parties' official campaign funds were eliminated by the U.S. Supreme Court in *Citizens United v. Federal Election Commission* (2010).[53]

Some countries, like Germany, have addressed this issue by providing **public financing** of elections. Essentially, the government covers the costs of an election by providing subsidies to parties and candidates or by providing a reimbursement for campaign costs. Thus, parties and candidates do not have to raise money for the campaign from private citizens or organized interests like labor unions, special interests, and corporations. A public finance system is in contrast to the reliance on **private financing.** Private financing occurs when individual citizens, interest groups, labor unions, and corporations make donations to candidates and political parties to cover the cost of an election.

The United States possesses a mixture of systems, with most elections privately financed. An exception is the U.S. presidential election, which features some public financing. In addition, the United States tends to emphasize reporting the sources of campaign finance, the size of donations, and the patterns of candidate spending rather than limiting campaign spending. Campaigns for federal offices, including U.S. president, U.S. Senate, and U.S. House of Representatives, are governed by federal laws like the Federal Election Campaign Act of 1974 and the Bipartisan Campaign Reform Act of 2002. The Supreme Court has also been active in this area, as evidenced above.

State and local elections are governed by state campaign finance laws and rulings by state courts. All state and local elections in Texas are privately financed. In Texas, there is an emphasis on **disclosure.** Disclosure is the idea that each candidate reports who has contributed money to the campaign and how much has been contributed by an individual or group. Texas does not place limits on how much an individual, interest group, labor union, or corporation may contribute. The logic here is that merely providing this information allows voters to become informed about who is supporting the candidates or constitutional referendums in an election. However, political organizations outside the state are limited to a contribution ceiling of $500.

Public financing

a system of campaign financing in which the government covers the cost of elections for political parties or candidates.

Private financing

a system of campaign financing in which citizens, interest groups, labor unions, and corporations donate funds to cover the cost of elections for political parties or candidates to cover the cost of an election.

Disclosure

the reporting of who contributes money to a campaign and how much is contributed by an individual or corporation.

Table 7.4 Campaign Spending for Candidates in the 2006 Texas Gubernatorial Election

CANDIDATE (PARTY AFFILIATION)	AMOUNT RAISED	AMOUNT SPENT	VOTES RECEIVED	MONEY SPENT PER VOTE
Rick Perry (Republican)	$20,199,539	$26,723,217	1,716,792	$15.57
Chris Bell (Democrat)	$7,359,018	$6,440,256	1,310,337	$ 4.91
Carole Strayhorn (Independent)	$9,084,635	$14,349,456	796,851	$18.01
Kinky Friedman (Independent)	$6,288,113	$5,246,550	547,674	$ 9.58

Source: Texas Ethics Commission and authors' calculations.

Texas campaign finance laws apply to both primary elections and general elections. The responsibility for collecting this information and providing it to the public rests with the Texas Ethics Commission. Candidates are required to file reports with the Texas Ethics Commission every month once a candidate begins to campaign. After an election, a final report must be filed within three months of the election. The Texas Ethics Commission maintains a searchable database for citizens on its website, www.ethics.state.tx.us.

Because state and local judges are elected in Texas, judicial elections are also covered by campaign finance laws. To alleviate fears that justice in Texas can be "bought" through campaign contributions, additional regulations limit the size of all contributions made to a candidate's campaign to get elected as a judge. The limits on individual donors depend on the size of the judicial district, ranging from $1,000 for judicial districts with a population of 250,000 or less to $5,000 for judicial districts with a population of one million or more; individual donors to candidates for statewide judicial offices are limited to $5,000 as well. Law firms may contribute up to six times the individual limits but individual members of the law firm are limited to $50 contributions. Similarly, statewide candidates may accept only $300,000 from political action committees (PACs). Judicial candidates may also opt to accept voluntary spending limits. Like contribution limits, the voluntary limit for a judicial office is based on the size of the judicial district. For example, the limit begins at $100,000 for districts that have less than 250,000 people and eventually rises to $500,000 for districts with more than one million people. The limit for statewide office is $2 million. Candidates accepting these limits enjoy an unusual reward—if their opponent exceeds the expenditure limits, the candidate is no longer subject to limits on contributions and expenditures.

The 2006 elections illustrate the role of money in Texas elections. Across all state government elections, $179.3 million was contributed to candidates running in executive, legislative, and judicial elections.[54] This figure includes races for the Texas Railroad Commission and State Board of Education. The race for governor accounted for over $49.2 million collected by the four major candidates in the primaries and general elections. The candidates spent over $52.7 million on the election.[55] Table 7.4 gives the amounts raised and spent for the four candidates seeking the governorship in the 2006 election. The table also calculates the spending per vote received.

The race for lieutenant governor proved more interesting. David Dewhurst, the Republican, raised $10.2 million for his reelection, while his Democratic opponent, Maria Alvarado, raised only $50,991. As might be expected, Dewhurst received 58 percent of the vote, compared with Alvarado's 37 percent. This situation suggests that a link exists between campaign finance and electoral competition. Running a well-financed campaign in a geographically large state like Texas is often a precondition to being a viable, competitive candidate in the election. Similar disparities in financing occurred in 2006, including for other statewide offices like Texas agriculture commissioner, comptroller of Public Accounts, and attorney general. Candidates for the Texas Senate pulled together over $28.5 million, averaging $433,885 per candidate. Comparable figures for all candidates running for the 150 seats in the Texas House of Representatives were $65.4 million, or $148,657 per candidate.

The sources of contributions provide interesting insight into Texas politics. As might be expected, the oil and gas industry contributed large sums of money. Across all races and candidates, oil and gas companies gave over $7.9 million. However, this level of giving placed the industry only third among top donors, trailing behind real estate ($8.9 million in contributions) and lawyers/lobbyists ($25.6 million in contributions). A list of the top individual or group contributors reveals that Bob J. Perry, the owner of a large home construction firm, contributed almost $3.8 million to various candidates for office, followed by Texans for Lawsuit Reform, a lawyer/lobbyist organization, which donated $3.4 million. David Dewhurst gave $2.7 million of his personal money to his own campaign for lieutenant governor, while Chris Bell's unsuccessful attempt to win the governorship included $1.7 million of his own personal fortune. Interestingly, the San Antonio-based H-E-B grocery store chain appeared in the list of top twenty contributors, only to announce a series of store closings not six months later in an effort to control costs and maintain profitability.

For the 2010 elections, campaign war chests for all candidates from all political parties for all races had exceeded $166 million by early November. Because candidates and organized interested have several months to complete their reporting of campaign contributions and campaign spending, this figure is estimated to cover 73 percent of the reports that must be filed. Most of the contributions were related to the governor's race, which accounted for over $83 million of the total. Among the candidates, Kay Bailey Hutchinson's unsuccessful attempt to take the Republican nomination for governor away from Rick Perry in the spring Republican primary saw her accumulate over $14 million in contributions, while Farouk Shami's unsuccessful bid to become the Democratic Party nominee topped $10.6 million in contributions. Rick Perry collected $28.3 million in his successful bid for the Republican nomination in the spring and his subsequent reelection in November. On the Democratic Party side, Bill White received just over $21.3 million in contributions for his run for the Democratic nomination and loss to Rick Perry in the general election.[56]

Among the top contributions to the campaigns for governor were the candidates themselves and candidate committees. This figure includes the $9.6 million that Farouk Shami contributed to his own unsuccessful campaign for the Democratic nomination for governor. Other important sources of campaign contributions to the governor's race in 2010 include the oil and gas industry (about $7.1 million), lawyers/lobbyists ($4.6 million), securities/investment industry ($3.8 million), and the real estate industry ($2.7 million). In some cases individual citizens who were not running for office gave substantial contributions, including businessman John McCall ($1 million) and home builder Bob Perry ($910,000).[57]

Winners and Losers

Politics involves decisions about who gets what, and thus it is not surprising that those groups that participate in politics are more likely to be the winners in a state's distribution of resources. In theory, the strength of democracies lies in the ability of average citizens to exert pressure on the political system. When democracies are working, policy represents compromise, but must take into account the needs of all groups in society. Historically differences in participation were created by institutional barriers to voting, ranging from outright denial of suffrage to certain groups to obstacles such as white primaries and poll taxes designed to stifle a particular group's participation. Removing these barriers to voting has occurred slowly and often as a result of federal imposition of election standards.

Unfortunately, in spite of the enfranchisement of minority groups in the state, minority participation in the electoral process remains significantly lower than white participation. Asian and Hispanic groups in particular exhibit extremely low levels of voting participation. Minorities will continue to struggle to make their voices heard as long as they keep their distance from the voting booth. Texas is one of the most diverse states in America, but this is not reflected in its voting patterns.

Voter turnout is also significantly lower among certain age groups. College-age voters are the least likely to show up at the polls and, therefore, the least likely to be represented by state policies. Because policies in Texas often ignore the needs of college-age voters, in times of budget crisis college students are often the first group that legislators target. The deregulation of tuition at state universities and Governor Perry's veto of appropriations for state community colleges are just two recent examples of such targeting. Groups in the state who remain apathetic will continue to be the first sacrificed in times of budget cuts.

Finally, the long ballot in Texas exerts a palpable cost, by increasing voter apathy throughout the state. Ironically, Texans resist changes to the election system, preferring to keep many of the most important public offices elected because Texans distrust government. Elected officials are theoretically more accountable to the people. Yet, in any given election, most Texans are not exercising that option. In some instances, voters face noncompetitive elections at the level of the state legislature. The result is that average Texans are becoming increasingly disconnected from the political process.

Conclusion

Texas elections, like all election systems, are designed to produce certain types of outcomes. Historically, election rules and voting rights were designed to disenfranchise African American voters and, to a lesser extent, poor rural white voters. The rules historically were also designed to allow the Democratic Party to maintain control over the election system. Thus until the 1960s white elites and the Democratic Party were clearly the winners of the electoral game. The transition of Texas politics toward inclusion of minorities and women occurred in large part through the actions of the national government in securing voting rights for disenfranchised groups, especially for African Americans and Hispanics. By increasing the national government's role a second transition was spurred: Congress and the U.S. Supreme Court moved into the area of elections by establishing over time a set of standards that all states must follow in the conduct of national, state, and local elections. The mandated use of electronic voting equipment is the latest example of this transition.

Beginning in the 1960s, the emergence of the Republican Party has altered Texas politics. An emerging Republican Party meant greater electoral competition in the state for the first time since the end of the Reconstruction era. However, while electoral competition has certainly increased at the level of seats for the U.S. House of Representatives and the U.S. Senate, the emergence of the Republican Party has not necessarily produced increased electoral competition at the level of the state legislature. Periods of alteration between Republicans and Democrats for statewide elected offices in the executive branch and various commissions have been recently replaced by Republican dominance. The absence of electoral competition in some elections, combined with voter apathy and disengagement by certain demographic groups, means that the true winners in Texas legislative politics may be those who contribute the money that finances the election campaigns. Candidates who are well financed do quite well. The organized interests who donate to campaigns expect some form of return for their efforts to fund the winner's campaign. We will explore the influence of these organized interests and the role of the political parties in this financing system more thoroughly in the next chapter.

Key Terms

advanced or early voting
blanket or wide-open primary
casework
closed primary
credit claiming
cross filing
direct primary
disclosure
Equal Protection Clause
general election
grandfather clause
Help America Vote Act (HAVA)
incumbent
independent candidate
indirect primary
literacy test
Motor Voter Act
open primary
party-line voting
poll tax
position taking
preference primary
primary election

private financing
public financing
roll off
second order elections
suffrage
voter turnout
Voting Rights Act of 1965 (VRA)
white primary

Explore this subject further at http://lonestar.cqpress.com, where you'll find chapter summaries, practice quizzes, key word flash cards, and additional suggested resources.

Rick Perry addresses delegates at the Texas Republican Party convention held in Dallas in June 2010.

CHAPTER 8

Parties and Organized Interests

The Texas Republican state convention that convened in June 2010 could easily have become a pep rally for a unified team heading to victory. Republicans held every statewide office as well as a majority in both houses of the state legislature. Pundits predicted that the Republican Party nationwide would have a good year as Democrats in Congress and the Obama administration struggled with a sputtering economy and oil gushing into the Gulf of Mexico. Meanwhile, polling in Texas showed Republicans leading in every statewide race as a slate of strong incumbents sought reelection.

While Texas Republicans were looking forward to good times ahead, that didn't mean that they did not have some old business to settle. With the luxury of front-runner status, many Republican delegates believed it was the right time to make their stand for the direction of the party. The convention brushed aside Rick Perry's reservations about including in the party's platform the kind of controversial immigration policy that had recently embroiled Arizona politics. The delegates also approved other tough stands in their new platform, including making English the official language, ending Social Security, replacing the income tax with a national sales tax, and repealing No Child Left Behind, President George W. Bush's signature education reform. Convention delegates took the unusual step of dislodging the current chair of the state party, Cathie Adams, in favor of Steve Munisteri because many Republicans were unhappy with the state party's finances and unsuccessful attempts to reach out to new voters. David Barton, a former vice chairman of the state party, rallied for language in the platform calling for the removal of fellow Republican Joe Straus from his position as Speaker of the Texas House of Representatives because many social conservatives considered him too liberal.

The consequences of these disagreements go beyond campaign stands and electoral politics. As we saw in Chapter 3, one of the reasons some Republicans had joined with Democrats before the 2009 legislative session to oust the previous Speaker, Tom Craddick, and replace him with Joe Straus was that Craddick had insisted legislators hold strictly to a conservative ideology even when doing so on some issues proved unpopular with constituents. Some of the criticism of Straus at the 2010 convention involved his efforts as Speaker to reach out to Democratic legislators. Ironically, some delegates in 2010 were ready to divide the convention because they were angry with legislators who had failed to remain unified behind Craddick when he was Speaker.

The debates at the 2010 Republican state convention reflect the tensions that can arise from the two basic functions of political parties. On the one hand, the party must try to represent the views of its members as faithfully as possible, and the Texas Republican Party is home to a large number of conservatives who hold strong views on important issues like immigration, same-sex marriage, and abortion. On the other hand, the party's candidates need to win office to advance those views and fear that strident language on immigration, for example, will alienate the growing Hispanic population in Texas or moderates and harm Republicans' chances of winning elections in 2010 and beyond. Thus, in summer 2010 Texas Republicans were grappling with holding to what they saw as traditional Texas values while thinking about the success of the party in Texas's future.

In this chapter we will look at the impact that political parties and organized interests have on the practice of democracy in Texas. Lurking in the shadows of the three branches of Texas government, political parties and organized interests remain unpopular but important partners in state politics. While organized interests and political parties can foster citizen participation, we will see that they often fail to represent the citizens of the state and have become hindrances to Texas's ability to keep pace with today's rapid changes.

As you read the chapter, think about the following questions:

★ How have political parties changed in Texas?

★ What are the main functions of political parties?

★ To what extent do parties and organized interests represent citizens of the state?

★ In what ways does Texas attempt to regulate interest group influence?

The Development of Political Parties in Texas

While the battle between political parties has often served as the premier forum for competition in U.S. politics, Texans have rarely enjoyed the benefits of a truly competitive party system. Early Texans were not strangers to political parties, but initially shunned them. Sam Houston had been a close political ally of Andrew Jackson, whose patronage system did much to build the early Democratic Party in the United States. Despite his Democratic roots, however, Houston generally avoided party labels in his Texas campaigns, and the state's earliest elections were dominated by personalities rather than parties.

Ironically, just as political parties were taking root in Texas, the national Whig Party collapsed in the mid-1850s. Its replacement, the Republican Party, held anti-slavery positions that ensured it would find little support in the state. The American or "Know-Nothing" Party, an anti-immigration party, aggressively cultivated Texans, forcing the Democratic Party to become fully organized in Texas for the first time in 1854.[1] Even as the Democratic Party was beginning to take hold in the state, the divisions that would culminate in the Civil War separated Texans into pro-union and secessionist factions and blotted out any chance of Republicans winning statewide office. The bitterness that followed Reconstruction was directed toward the Republican Party, allowing the Democratic Party to dominate the state for decades. The biggest challenges to the Democrats came from the Greenback Party in the 1870s and 1880s and the Populists or "People's Party" in the 1880s and 1890s.

The Populist Party, backed largely by small farmers looking to democratize the economic system, favored programs like a graduated income tax, an eight-hour workday, and government control of railroads. The Populists made the greatest gains in the American Midwest, but the party shared a common cause with the Farmer's Alliance (itself an outgrowth of the Grange Movement) that had organized in Lampasas, Texas, in the mid-1870s.[2] Texas's Populist Party built on the foundation of the fundamentalist churches, an especially important social network in early Texas, and one of the few that brought farm families together. Farmers thus often linked religious themes with their desire for relief from economic pressures.[3] Before fading from the Texas scene, the Populists won 44 percent of the vote for J. C. Kearby, their candidate in the 1896 election. Kearby ran with the support of the Republicans, who had not fielded their own candidate that year. Populists' call for government ownership of the railroads and limits on land ownership by corporations was decidedly at odds with the pro-business Republican Party. Eventually, the partnership with the Republicans and partnerships with other groups took their toll, undermining the consistency of the Populist ideological foundations. Meanwhile, some of their more popular ideas were appropriated by Democratic politicians like Governor Jim Hogg, who won the favor of many Texas farmers by taking on the railroads.

The next challenge to the Texas Democratic Party emerged from the Progressives, a formidable force for reform in much of the country. Because Texas's Progressives lacked the targets for reform that energized the party nationally, such as corrupt, big-city party machines and unfavorable economic policies, they turned instead to cultural issues like alcohol prohibition.[4]

Texas had a few local party machines through which local party officials dispensed patronage, offering government jobs, contracts, and other favors to party loyalists to perpetuate their power. George Parr's political machine ran Duvall County in South Texas for thirty years after Parr inherited it from his father, Archer. By working closely with poor Hispanics and getting to know them Parr earned their loyalty and their votes. He built a political and economic empire founded on money taken from businesses and government accounts. Parr's ability to deliver votes to friendly candidates made him a kingmaker in Texas; Parr was responsible for pushing local election officials to find the questionable votes that secured Lyndon Johnson's Democratic primary victory in the 1948 U.S. Senate campaign.

George Parr wasn't the first Texas official involved in creative ballot counting. In 1869, citizens in Navarro County were unable to cast their votes after the county's registrar absconded with the registration lists before the election. In the same year, Milam County ballots were never counted, and in Hill County an official took the ballots to another jurisdiction to count, with results that surprised many Hill County voters.[5] While Texas needed the reforms championed by the Progressive movement, changes were slow to come.

In general, the Progressives found themselves caught up in the prohibition movement because promoting political reform and banishing alcohol were seen as tools for building a better society. As with the Populists, churches played an important role and evangelicals and women's groups were drawn to the Progressive cause.[6] Also like the Populists, the Progressives saw much of their agenda absorbed by the Democrats.

The Republican Party in Texas slowly developed in the early twentieth century, only to suffer a major setback during the Great Depression, a disaster that many Texans blamed on President Herbert Hoover and the Republican Party. While the

In November of 2006, voters in Texas and in New York participated in elections for one of their U.S. senators. Texas voters selected from three candidates: a Republican, a Democrat, and a Libertarian. In New York, voters selected from among candidates from nine different political parties. One key difference between the two elections is the fact that in New York three political parties selected and listed the same candidate for U.S. senator–Hillary Clinton. She was the candidate for the Democratic Party, the Independence Party, and the Working Families Party. Her primary opponent, John Spencer, ran as the Republican Party candidate and as the Conservative Party candidate. In New York, the ballot is laid out so every party and candidate appears separately. As a result, Hillary Clinton's name appeared on the ballot three times and John Spencer's name appeared twice.

The practice of two or more parties legally running the same candidate for office is called electoral fusion. Electoral fusion is allowed in a handful of states, including New York. While electoral fusion was once practiced in Texas as a means of protecting Democratic dominance, it is now illegal.

The practice of electoral fusion allowed voters to support Hillary Clinton or John Spencer without voting for either of the two major parties. In addition, during the campaign both Clinton and Spencer had to address issues of concern not only for their respective party's base of voters but also for the additional parties that gave them a nomination.

U.S. Senate Election in New York, 2006

CANDIDATE	PERCENTAGE OF VOTES	PARTY
Hillary Rodham Clinton	60.1%	Democratic
John Spencer	27.0%	Republican
John Spencer	4.0%	Conservative
Hillary Rodham Clinton	3.6%	Independence
Hillary Rodham Clinton	3.3%	Working Families
Howie Hawkins	1.2%	Green
Jeffrey T. Russell	0.4%	Libertarian
Roger Calero	0.2%	Socialist Workers
William Van Auken	0.1%	Socialist Equity

Thinking Critically

- What is electoral fusion?
- How does electoral fusion allow third parties to participate in an election?
- How does electoral fusion legitimize voting for third parties?
- Why did Texas Democrats support electoral fusion in the past?
- Why did the practice become illegal in Texas?

depression and World War II hurt Republicans seeking statewide office, Texans were beginning to show more and more interest in Republican presidential candidates. In 1952, the Texas Democratic Party officially supported Republican candidate Dwight D. Eisenhower, and for the second time in Texas's history, a Republican presidential candidate carried the state. Texas Democrats avoided the Republican tide across the state in 1952 though, when every Democratic nominee for statewide office, except one, cross-filed for positions on the ballot as both Democrats and Republicans under the provisions of a 1951 law.

While the Democratic Party would eventually lead the nation in civil rights, from Reconstruction until the 1960s it often supported segregation and racism in Texas and elsewhere in the South. African Americans were barred from participating in Democratic primaries, and the party created special white primaries as a matter of law in Texas and as a matter of practice in other southern states. Since the Democratic Party enjoyed a virtual monopoly in statewide general elections,

African Americans were effectively shut out of any meaningful role in elections. Democratic governor James "Pa" Ferguson proclaimed, "A negro has no business whatever taking part in the political affairs of the Democratic Party, the white man's party."[7] Eventually, the civil rights issue split the Democratic Party of Texas, a breakup common throughout the southern states.

In the latter part of the twentieth century, Texas starred in the transition that saw southern states turn away from the Democratic Party and embrace the Republican Party. The Republicans finally broke the Democrats' dominance in 1961 and won statewide office for the first time since Reconstruction, when Republican John Tower won the U.S. Senate seat vacated by the election of Democrat Lyndon Johnson to the vice presidency. The Republicans did not win the governorship until 1978, when William Clements won a surprise victory. By 2000 Democrats were unable to effectively challenge Republicans for any statewide office. Thus, in less than forty years Texas went from being a state dominated by the Democratic Party to one dominated by the Republican Party. Exit polls from the 2010 election for governor revealed that 39 percent of Texas voters identified themselves as Republicans, 28 percent as Democrats, and 31 percent as independents.

Domination of a state by one party is not always the case in American politics. After the 2010 elections twenty states had divided government, with a governor faced with at least one house of the state legislature in the hands of the opposition party. Among the other states, ten had both the legislature and governor's mansions in the hands of Democrats while the other twenty were in the hands of Republicans.

The dominance of one party in Texas does not necessarily mean that there is no competition. It has often been said that Texas only has one party but has enough conflict for six. For much of the state's history its political battles were fought in the process of nominating Democratic candidates. With Republicans unable to mount a serious challenge, Texas politicians understood that the winner of the Democratic nominating primary was effectively the election winner. As such, it was the battles to win the primary that were most hotly contested.

While today the Republican Party dominates statewide elections—and appears well-positioned to continue to do so in the foreseeable future—citizen participation in politics in general and in party politics particularly has weakened; today, few voters take part in the primaries of either major party. For example, turnout for the primaries leading up to the 2010 election totaled only 7 percent of the state's voting-age population, with 3.6 percent of Texans voting in the Democratic primary and 7.9 percent voting in the Republican primary. In contrast, turnout for the Democratic primary during the 1970s when the Democratic Party dominated was generally between 15 percent and 19 percent. As Table 8.1 shows, in the 1970s less than 5 percent of Texans took part in the Republican primaries, a matter of little consequence since Republican gubernatorial candidates were seen as having little chance of winning office. However, since that time the stature

Table 8.1 Turnout as Percentage of Voting-Age Population in Primaries, 1970–2010

YEAR	DEMOCRATIC PRIMARY TURNOUT	REPUBLICAN PRIMARY TURNOUT
1970	14.1%	1.5%
1972	28.4%	1.5%
1974	18.4%	0.8%
1976	17.3%	4.0%
1978	19.3%	1.7%
1980	13.8%	5.3%
1982	12.3%	2.5%
1984	12.9%	3.0%
1986	9.3%	4.6%
1988	14.4%	8.3%
1990	11.9%	6.8%
1992	11.5%	6.2%
1994	7.9%	4.3%
1996	6.7%	7.4%
1998	4.7%	4.2%
2000	5.4%	7.8%
2002	6.5%	4.0%
2004	5.2%	4.3%
2006	3.1%	3.9%
2008	16.2%	7.7%
2010	3.6%	7.9%

Source: Texas Secretary of State's Office, www.sos.state.tx.us.

of the Republican Party has grown tremendously, even as participation rates in its primaries have not increased dramatically. It appears that the GOP hasn't grown into its new boots as far as voter electoral participation is concerned and, alongside the Democrats, is left to contend with the troubling trend of reduced voter participation. With just 7.9 percent of eligible citizens selecting the Republican nominees who were almost certain to win statewide offices in November 2010, it is fair to say that the parties have not succeeded in creating the broad participation and healthy competition that is necessary to respond to the juggernaut of change that is Texas.

Political Parties in Texas

Texas history has often strained traditional definitions of political parties. One classic definition of a political party comes from eighteenth-century British political philosopher Edmund Burke, who described a party as people "united for promoting by their joint endeavors the national interest, upon some particular principle in which they are all agreed."[8] As we've seen, Texas has experienced as much fighting within its parties as between them, straining the application of the traditional definition of parties to Texas politics. For example, while today's Republican Party can be labeled a conservative party, Republicans often clash on the meaning of conservatism as conflict over issues like immigration and abortion divide Texans who claim the conservative label. Further complicating matters, as we will see later, the Texas Republican Party disagrees with the national Republican Party, and even Texan and former U.S. president George W. Bush, on several issues.

Political party

any group, however loosely organized, seeking to elect governmental office-holders under a given label.

The realities of the **political party** in Texas are best captured by Leon Epstein's definition of a party as "any group, however loosely organized, seeking to elect governmental office-holders under a given label."[9] While this definition does not meet everyone's hopes for the function of party, it does match the realities of Texas's parties historically and distinguishes parties from interest groups, in that parties nominate candidates for office under their label while interest groups do not.

Texas provides an interesting case to examine the role that many political scientists want parties to play. Some scholars want politics to meet the standards of the **responsible party model** of politics, in which each party holds firmly to a consistent, coherent set of policies with a consistent ideology distinct from the other parties. The virtue of responsible parties is that they provide voters with clear choices and firm positions the parties are pledged to honor if elected. In contrast, political scientist Anthony Downs has described an **electoral competition model** in which parties move to the center of the political spectrum as they attempt to win votes, sacrificing the more purely ideological positions preferred by the proponents of the responsible party model. In this view, the political parties are more pragmatic than ideological and are ready to shift their issue stands from year to year in order to win office. Like American political parties in general, parties in Texas do not match either model perfectly. In fact, as we saw at the beginning of the chapter, Texans sometimes disagree about which model they prefer.

Responsible party model

the view that each party should hold firmly to a clear and consistent set of policies with a coherent ideology distinct from that of other parties to present voters with clear choices.

Electoral competition model

the view that parties make a pragmatic move to the center of the political spectrum as they attempt to win votes, sacrificing the more purely ideological positions.

Functions of Parties

State and local parties have a variety of important roles in a democracy. One of the most obvious is the nomination of party candidates. Since the distinguishing characteristic of a party is electing candidates under its label, selecting nominees is a central function of the state and local parties. Slating, or putting together a list of candidates for all positions, is often seen as an important role of state and local parties as they assemble teams of candidates ready to bring their party's ideas into a variety of offices.

Related to getting candidates on the ballot and elected is the need to seek out the right candidates. Thus, one of the most important functions of state and local parties is recruitment. As each party attempts to build a winning team it will seek out the most politically talented individuals for the next generation of politics. Precinct and county party leaders must be alert to the presence of individuals with the talent to take themselves and their party to victory in an election. Before he was president of the United States, George W. Bush was a Texas governor urged by state Republicans (and some Democrats) to run for president. Before that, he was a businessman urged into politics by local Republican leaders.

The next step for state and local parties is the function of supporting candidates. Both state parties provide logistical support and campaign staff training for party candidates. Some of the support is financial, with parties providing cash contributions as well as advertising and similar support. The parties also provide training for candidates and their campaign staffs.

One function that is rapidly expanding may define modern parties: fundraising. Headlines about presidential involvement in fundraising in the 1990s clouded the fact that much of the fundraising being done was actually for state parties. Fundraising and spending in campaigns has shifted to the states because federal laws restrict how much individuals can give to the national parties. State parties in general have faced few such restrictions and thus find themselves the recipients of the big checks their national parties cannot legally accept. While fundraising remains an area of controversy, the parties must raise funds to promote their agendas or help their candidates and thus remain locked in a money competition in which they try to raise more money than the other.

Another function that parties must spend money on is mobilizing voters. Through phone banks, door-to-door canvassing, mailings, and advertising the parties reach out to voters and encourage them to go to the polls. Of course, a party is most likely to reach out to those voters who will support the party's candidates. However, democracy in general can benefit from healthy competition if both parties reach out to voters and increase turnout in general.

Parties can also be an important tool for representation. Texas's one-party nature has often meant its general elections were not competitive, and the redistricting process described in Chapter 3 has divided the state even further by creating districts that are either heavily Republican or heavily Democratic. This means that many Texans live in districts in which it is unlikely that their party will be able to effectively compete. As a consequence, some citizens will see themselves as part of a **chronic minority,** a group destined to rarely win an election or achieve majority status. Such citizens will see few reasons to become actively engaged in politics and have little hope that their views will be reflected by their representatives in Austin. Parties can offer some hope that such views will be heard even if these views are transmitted by an elected official from another area of the state. For example, Democrats in areas that find themselves represented by Republicans in the Texas House and Senate may hope that Democrats from other parts of the state will give voice to their concerns and advance their cause.

The ultimate function of political parties is control of government, since the point of winning elections is getting party candidates into office. In some ways this

Chronic minority
a group that rarely wins elections or achieves majority status and thus sees few reasons to become actively engaged in politics.

Pappy O'Daniel

As we've noted, Texas's size has given an advantage to characters flamboyant enough to grab the voters' attention across the state. One of Texas's legendary governors, "Pass the Biscuits, Pappy" O'Daniel (pictured, left, with Harry Akin) is a fine example of the ability of a colorful outsider to push aside established party leaders and land on top of the state's power structure.

Wilbert Lee O'Daniel was born in Ohio but moved to Texas in 1925. As sales manager for a flour mill, O'Daniel would become well known as the host of a radio show featuring music from Bob Wills and Milton Brown's band, The Light Crust Doughboys. The show opened with someone saying, "Pass the Biscuits, Pappy," and mixed inspirational stories with music, including songs that O'Daniel penned with titles like "The Boy Who Never Got Too Big to Comb His Mother's Hair." In 1938, purportedly spurred by listener letters urging him to run for governor (although others suggest that wealthy business interests and a public relations expert had done the real urging), O'Daniel declared his candidacy, proclaiming the Ten Commandments as his platform and the Golden Rule as his motto. O'Daniel won the Democratic nomination without a run-off and, facing no real opposition, won the general election with 97 percent of the vote.

An estimated 100,000 people packed into Memorial Stadium in Austin to witness his inauguration, but O'Daniel quickly exhibited his lack of political skill by proposing a thinly disguised sales tax, making numerous questionable appointments, and forgetting his only specific campaign promise—a $30 a month pension for every Texan over 65. By the time of his reelection campaign, he was opposed by almost every newspaper in the state, with the *Dallas Morning News* proclaiming, "The highest office in the state has been the laughingstock of the United States for a year and a half."[i] Voters nevertheless returned O'Daniel to office, but he accomplished little in his second term beyond positioning himself for a move to the U.S. Senate by appointing Andrew Jackson Houston, Sam Houston's only surviving son, to fill a vacancy left after Sen. Morris Sheppard died in April 1941. Houston, the oldest man to serve in the U.S. Senate to that point, died the next year, leaving O'Daniel without an incumbent to worry about in the special election. O'Daniel's only serious primary challenger was a young ex-congressman named Lyndon Baines Johnson. Johnson led through much of the ballot counting, but late returns from rural districts gave O'Daniel a victory, leaving Johnson to await another day.

While O'Daniel's colorful character effectively swept Johnson aside in the Texas primary, it did nothing to endear him to the Washington establishment. And O'Daniel's down-home, colorful stylings won him few victories in the nation's capital. His public appeal made him a legend in Texas, but O'Daniel's leadership did little to leave any real legacy of accomplishment, either in Austin or Washington, D.C.

i. Randolph B. Campbell, *Gone to Texas* (New York: Oxford University Press, 2004), 394.

function of political parties goes against the constitutional order because our system of checks and balances and separation of powers is intended to keep any one faction from having too much influence. However, parties are elected so they will have influence and get things done, and their ability to coordinate the efforts of officials across the branches of government can be an important tool in creating the kind of leadership a state in transition needs.

The Consequences of Weak Parties

The scholar V. O. Key observed that Texas's geographic size makes it hard for well-formed political networks to function. Without closely knit political networks, it has been harder for parties to maintain enduring political organizations across the broad geographic expanse of the state. Those parties that were able to build personal followings did so through dramatic appeals to the public that were generally short-lived and created a political following based more on personality than policy goals. For example, it was his skills as a flour salesman rather than dependence on a well-ordered political machine that brought Wilbert Lee "Pappy" O'Daniel into the governorship. In contrast, other southern states saw the rise of personal political machines, such as the Longs in Louisiana, that spanned several generations.

With no well-organized party organization to provide resistance, political outsiders have often found their way into the Texas governor's mansion. In the absence of a well-established political order, working through the system has less value and a political newcomer's dramatic appeal can more easily win the election. While the early twentieth century saw some lively outsiders like James E. "Pa" Ferguson and Pappy O'Daniel, more recent elections have seen the rise of political newcomers like William Clements and George W. Bush leading the Republican revival in the state.

Party Organizations

Because of the role they play in the practice of democracy in the state, the organization and functioning of political parties is subject to some regulation by the state. The U.S. Supreme Court has ruled that state law can regulate the internal affairs of political parties only if it is "necessary to ensure that elections are orderly, fair, and honest."[10] Texas state law still places restrictions on the selection, composition, rules, and meeting dates of the state and local political party committees. In fact, Texas is rated a "heavy regulator," with some of the most extensive laws governing the state's parties.[11]

Political parties in the United States are composed of both temporary and permanent organizations. The **temporary party organizations** are gatherings of ordinary party members through primaries and in meetings known as caucuses and conventions. The **permanent party organizations** are the party officials selected by the temporary organizations to conduct the business of the party in between primaries, caucuses, and conventions.

While the temporary nature of party conventions may make them seem less important, like any democratic organization, America's political parties draw their legitimacy from the participation of citizens. As such, a political party is a **grassroots organization,** or a group in which power and decision making reside with average citizens. This relationship makes these gatherings of party members the foundation upon which the party claims legitimacy.

Citizens' participation in Texas's two major parties begins at the local level through primaries, elections in which ordinary citizens vote to choose the candidates that will represent a party on the ballot in the general election (see Figure 8.1). In Texas, the parties may also use primary elections to have party members vote on resolutions that voice demands for specific legislation or any other matter. Primaries have been part of Texas elections since the Terrell

Temporary party organizations
gatherings of ordinary party members such as primaries, caucuses, and conventions.

Permanent party organizations
the party officials selected by the temporary organizations to conduct party business between the primaries, caucuses, and conventions.

Grassroots organization
a group in which power and decision making reside with average citizens; the participation of average citizens is the foundation upon which these groups' legitimacy rests.

Figure 8.1 Texas Party Organization

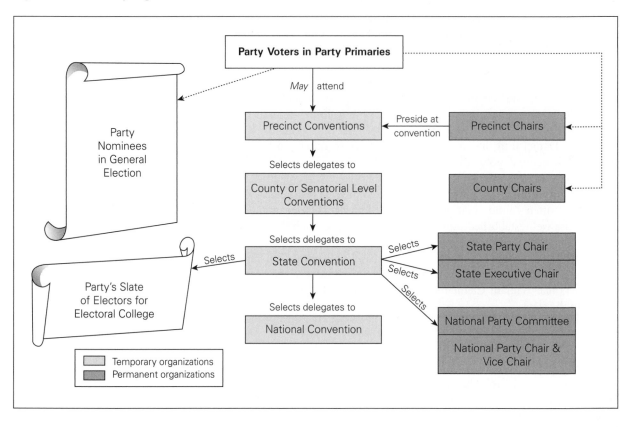

Election Law in 1905 mandated that major political parties use primaries to select their nominees. Prior to that, parties were free to make their nominations however they pleased, with nominees usually being chosen by nominating conventions composed of party leaders without input from average citizens. Progressives promoted primaries as a means to take the choice of candidates away from political bosses meeting behind the scenes and expand participation to ordinary citizens.

Current Texas law requires that the major parties (those that received 20 percent or more of the vote for governor in the last election) use primaries to choose their candidates for office. Parties whose candidate for governor received between 2 percent and 20 percent of the vote in the last election have a choice between nominating candidates by convention or by primary. Parties whose gubernatorial candidates received less than 2 percent of the vote must use conventions because of the costs involved in holding primaries. Primaries require separate voting booths for each party in every precinct in the state. To control costs, minor political parties like the Libertarian Party typically choose conventions when given the option of primaries.

For decades, the major political parties operated their primaries as they pleased, claiming along the way that their private status allowed them to set their own restrictions—including barring black voters. Until 1972, political parties paid for primaries, relying on hefty candidate filing fees to fund these elections.

As noted in Chapter 7, Texas party primaries are technically closed primaries with only party members allowed to vote. In practice Texas primaries are much more accessible and function as semi-open primaries in which any voter may participate without having previously registered a party affiliation. When Texans vote in a party's primary their voter registration cards are stamped with the name of that party. Under state law this "affiliates" citizens with a specific party for an entire year and thus makes them ineligible to participate in any other party's primary that year. While this affiliation does make them a member of the party for that year in some sense of the word, this affiliation does not obligate them to contribute to, vote for, or support in any way that party's candidates. By law, a party affiliation expires at the end of each voting year; before the primaries in the next set of elections two years later all voters receive new registration cards with no party affiliation, leaving them free to vote in whichever primary they choose. The impact of affiliating with a party by voting in its primary is that the citizen is excluded from participating in the nominating process of other parties or independent candidates. In addition, Texas's "sore loser law" prohibits someone from voting or running in the primary of one party and later running for office under the label of another party in the same year.

In states with more restrictive closed primaries citizens face a deadline before which they must declare their party affiliation; this can be as much as eleven months before the primary in which they wish to participate. One advantage of such strict rules is that they ensure that the people who vote in the primaries are "real" party members. A disadvantage is that voters who are excluded from the party's primary by such rules may feel less inclined to get behind the party's candidates.

The flexibility of Texas's primary voting system can create its own set of problems. For generations, many conservative Texans continued to vote in the Democratic primary since they could often nominate like-minded conservatives as Democrats and see them elected in November. Meanwhile, other conservatives sought to make the Republican Party more viable. Today, Democrats face a similar dilemma. Many vote in the Republican primary hoping to make that party's nominee as moderate as possible. Others will seek out the nominee who will most embarrass the Republican Party.

Under state law a political party's nominee must receive a majority of the total number of votes in the primary. Races that generate competition from three or more candidates raise the possibility that no nominee will get the required majority, necessitating a **run-off primary** in which the top two finishers from the first primary face off.

Local Parties

Party primaries also elect local party officers. In Texas, party members in each voting precinct elect by a majority vote a **precinct chair** and in a countywide vote select a **county chair.** These officers are responsible for managing the local affairs of their party for the next two years. To be eligible to be a county or precinct chair of a political party, a person must only be a qualified voter and not hold or be a candidate for any elective federal, state, or county office. To make participation as easy as possible, state law provides that a candidate for county chair or precinct chair not be required to pay a fee in order to get on the primary ballot.

At the county level each party has a county executive committee composed of a county chair and the precinct chair from each precinct in the county. This committee is the permanent committee that oversees the party's organization, fundraising,

Run-off primary
a primary that occurs if no nominee receives the required majority of the votes in the primary; the top two finishers face off in a second primary to determine the nominee for the general election.

Precinct chair; County chair
a precinct chair is selected by party members in each voting precinct by majority vote; a county chair is selected by countywide vote. These party officials are responsible for managing the local affairs of their party for the next two years.

and campaigning within the county. There is often little competition for these positions, and they sometimes go vacant because most Texans are content to leave the business of politics to others. However, in some areas conservative Christian groups have aggressively sought to win those positions in the Republican Party as a means of exerting more influence over party affairs, a strategy that has contributed to their success in gaining control of the Republican Party statewide. The success of conservative Christian political forces in Texas illustrates that big political victories are often built upon many small efforts.

While these local officials still have some influence, their role has diminished over the last century. The power of local party officials to select political candidates and select delegates to state and national conventions was lost as the parties became more democratic through the introduction of primaries. In addition, when campaigns relied on the labors of individuals communicating one-on-one, the local party was one of the few organizations positioned to mobilize the necessary human resources. Today, campaigns are increasingly in the hands of media-savvy campaign specialists and require less human effort and more cash to pay for advertising on television and radio and technical know-how to establish an effective presence on the Internet.

On the same day as the primary voting the parties hold precinct-level meetings, or **conventions** (in much of the nation these meetings are called **caucuses** when conducted at the local level), in which party members meet to conduct a range of party business. Primary conventions are temporary organizations in the party structure that convene on primary election day between 7:00 p.m. and 9:00 p.m., usually in the same location as the primary election. Sometimes, Republicans and Democrats hold their precinct conventions in different rooms in the same building, often the same school, church, fire station, or other building that hosted voting earlier that day. State law requires that a written notice at the polling place provide to primary voters the date, hour, and place for convening the precinct convention.

While these meetings are open only to party members, recall that party affiliation in Texas requires only showing up for the primary and requesting the party ballot. Minor parties that do not use primaries to nominate candidates obviously cannot require that citizens vote in their primary to participate in their party's convention. In these cases, a citizen wishing to participate in the convention of a party that has not held a primary may affiliate with that party simply by taking an oath prescribed by law: "I swear that I have not voted in a primary election or participated in a convention of another party during this voting year. I hereby affiliate myself with the _____ Party."

Precinct conventions are used to elect **delegates** (and alternates) who will attend the party's conventions held later at the county level or Texas senatorial district level. The number of delegates a precinct is allotted is based on how many members of the party voted in that precinct in that election. While selecting those party members to represent the precinct at future conventions is the primary function of the precinct conventions, attendees may also vote on resolutions related to political issues, especially those on which citizens want their party to take an official stand.

On the third Saturday after the primary election each of the major parties holds its **county or senatorial district convention.** A county convention is held in a county if the county is not situated in more than one state senatorial district. If a county is in more than one state senatorial district, a senatorial district convention is held in each part of the county that is in a different senatorial district. These conventions select delegates to the statewide convention and deal with other party business.

Conventions (caucuses)
meetings at which party members participate in a range of party business.

Delegates
party members elected to attend their party's conventions held later at the county level or the Texas senatorial district level.

County or senatorial district convention
held on the third Saturday after the primary election, a convention in which delegates to the statewide convention are selected.

State Parties

Texas's political parties hold their state conventions biennially in June. The convention includes delegates selected by the county or senatorial district conventions, although nominees for or holders of state or national government offices are entitled to attend a state convention of their party, but they may not vote in the convention unless they have been selected to serve as delegates by their county or senatorial district through the usual process.

While the state conventions are temporary party organizations, meeting on a few days every two years, they are important events because state parties really only take form when the parties' members gather in state conventions at this time. For example, state law requires that party rules must be approved by the party's state convention. While gathered, each state convention writes and approves their **party platform,** the document that officially spells out the issue stands of the party. Each issue position of the party platform is referred to as a **plank.** (See Table 8.2 for excerpts from the 2010 platforms for the Texas Republican and Democratic parties.)

Each party's state convention also selects a **state party chair** and **executive committee** to carry on the activities of the party between state conventions. By law, each party's state executive committee consists of one man and one woman from each state senatorial district. In addition, the state committees' chair and a vice chair must include a man and a woman. Texas's state party executive committee is typical of state party committees, if there is such a thing as a typical state party committee. As one text points out, "So great are the differences between these committees from state to state—in membership selection, size, and function—that it is difficult to generalize about them."[12] Texas's parties, like most of those in the South, are relatively weak. For example, Texas's party leaders do not make pre-primary endorsements, a practice more common in the Northeast and Midwest. The permanent officers of the parties do hold some authority, yet they are often rivaled by elected officials from their party. While the head of the Republican Party is selected by the state Republican Convention, Governor Rick Perry can rightfully claim that he reflects the wishes of the Republican voters statewide. Thus, the label of "party leader" is much more subjective than the official party organization charts would suggest.

Nominating Presidential Candidates

In addition to conducting the business of the state parties, the state party conventions in presidential election years must also select the party's delegates to the national party convention, representatives to the party's national committee, as well as the slate of electors who will be available to serve in the Electoral College.

Today, state law requires that major parties in Texas hold presidential "preference primaries" in presidential election years, in conjunction with their regular primaries. Texans may use this primary to express their preference for one of the candidates on the ballot or vote "uncommitted," if the rules of their party allow such a vote. While holding these primaries at the same time as the nominating primaries for other offices makes some sense by consolidating voting dates, it presents a dilemma in national politics as many states attempt to move their primaries earlier in the year to garner as much attention as possible from presidential candidates. Texas, which held its primaries in June for many years, moved its primary date up to early March in 1988 and joined the ranks of "Super Tuesday" primaries, so named because many of the large states held their party primaries on that Tuesday. In 2007, in response to moves by other states to hold their primaries even earlier,

Party platform
the document that officially spells out the issue stands of a party; written and approved at the party conventions.

Plank
an individual issue position of the party platform.

State party chair
individual selected at the state party convention to head the state executive committee; state law mandates that a man and a woman be chosen.

Executive committee
this group, selected at the state party convention, carries on the activities of the party between party conventions; by law, the committee consists of one man and one woman from each state senatorial district.

Table 8.2 Comparison of 2010 Texas Party Platforms

ISSUE	2010 TEXAS REPUBLICAN PARTY PLATFORM	2010 TEXAS DEMOCRATIC PARTY PLATFORM
Abortion	"We affirm our support for a human life amendment to the Constitution and we endorse making clear that the Fourteenth Amendment's protection applies to unborn children."	"Texas Democrats trust the women of Texas to make personal and responsible decisions about when and whether to bear children."
Homosexuality	"We believe that the practice of homosexuality tears at the fabric of society, contributes to the breakdown of the family unit, and leads to the spread of dangerous, communicable diseases."	"To protect our rights and freedoms, we support repeal of discriminatory laws and policies against members of the gay, lesbian, bisexual and transgender community."
Capital punishment	"Properly applied capital punishment is legitimate, is an effective deterrent, and should be swift and unencumbered."	"[T]he current system cannot ensure that innocent or undeserving defendants are not sentenced to death."
Immigration	"We oppose illegal immigration, amnesty in any form, or legal status for illegal immigrants." "We call on the Legislative, Executive and Judicial branches of these United States to clarify Section 1 of the 14th Amendment to limit citizenship by birth to those born to a citizen of the United States: with no exceptions."	"We support the creation of a policy that would establish a path to citizenship for the majority of those currently here . . . provided they qualify and seek to become part of our national community. We strongly oppose Republican proposals that they should be charged with a felony simply because they are undocumented."
Kindergarten	"We believe that parents are best suited to train their children in their early development and oppose mandatory pre-school and Kindergarten."	"Texas Democrats believe . . . Texas should maintain or extend the 22–1 class size limits and expand access to pre-kindergarten and kindergarten programs."
Bilingual education	"English is the language of commerce, therefore a successful tiered language instruction program with the following provisions is recommended: • Year 1: 70% English/30% Native language (Year 1 indicates first year of U.S. based education) • Year 2: 80% English/20% Native language • Year 3: 90% English/10% Native language • Year 4 and thereafter: 100% English (No bilingual education after year 3)"	"To make public education our highest priority, we believe the state should . . . reject efforts to destroy bilingual education."
Evolution versus intelligent design	"[We] support objective teaching and equal treatment of all sides of scientific theories, including evolution, Intelligent Design, global warming, political philosophies, and others. We believe theories of life origins and environmental theories should be taught as challengeable scientific theory subject to change as new data is produced, not scientific law. "	"In rewriting the curriculum for social studies, English language arts, and science, [members of the State Board of Education] repeatedly have dismissed the sound advice of professional educators. . . . Their skewed vision slights the contributions of racial and ethnic minorities."
Minimum wage	"We believe the Minimum Wage Law should be repealed."	"[W]e believe the minimum wage must be raised, enforced, and applied meaningfully across-the-board to restore lost purchasing power for all workers."

Sources: Excerpted from the 2010 Texas Democratic Party Platform, Texas Democratic Party, www.txdemocrats.org/issues/party_platform and from the 2010 Republican Party of Texas Platform, The Republican Party of Texas, http://www.texasgop.org.

the Texas Legislature considered moving its primary to February to avoid being left to vote on presidential nominations after a candidate had already won enough state and local votes to lock up the nomination. In 2008, Texas Republicans and Democrats cast their votes on March 4, by which date about two-thirds of the states had already voted. The problem for Texas is that many citizens prefer to nominate their candidates a little closer to Election Day. Moving up the nominating process would only extend an already long campaign season. Some states hold separate presidential primaries at different times from the primaries used to select other offices. Other states, like Kansas and Iowa, have opted not to hold a presidential primary in their state and rely on a caucus instead.

Texas's presidential primary has not always been binding. While voters filed through the voting booths during the day to vote in the primary, the number of delegates that their favorite candidate received was decided by party members who attended the precinct conventions that evening and at other conventions later in the spring. Today, while the party conventions select which individuals will be sent to the party's national convention as delegates, the allocation of these delegates between the competing candidates for president is determined by party rules, which use results from the presidential preference primary to allocate candidates on a districtwide or statewide basis. Currently, state law requires that at least 75 percent of delegates representing the state at the party's national convention be allocated based on the votes in the presidential primaries. However, the law does not dictate exactly how the parties use the results of primary voting in allocating delegates. For example, the Republicans have an elaborate system of allocating delegates using the vote counts at the congressional district and statewide level. A candidate who receives more than 50 percent of the votes within a congressional district is entitled to all of the delegates to the Republican convention from that district. When no candidate gets 50 percent, the delegates are divided between those candidates who received more than 20 percent of the vote.

In 2008, Texas came under scrutiny for its system of delegate allocation because candidate Hillary Clinton won the popular vote in the state's Democratic presidential primary but did not win the majority of the 228 delegates Texas sent to the Democratic National Convention.

The controversy resulted from Texas's complicated allocation process. **Allocation** refers to how many of the state's delegates will attend the national convention pledged to vote for a specific candidate or attend as undecided. Because the Texas Democratic Party wants to encourage participation in all stages of the nominating process, delegates are actually allocated in three ways: (1) allocation based on primary day votes, (2) allocation based on convention attendance, and (3) unpledged "super delegates."

Of Texas's 228 delegates only 126 (or 56 percent) were allocated based on the votes cast by Democrats in the primary on March 4. However, it's not as simple as counting up the votes statewide. Delegates are actually allocated to a candidate based on the proportion of votes they receive within each of the state's thirty-one Texas Senate districts (candidates who get less than 15 percent of the vote in the district get no delegates). So, on primary election night what looks like a statewide competition is actually thirty-one separate competitions.

Not all Senate districts are equal in the eyes of the Democratic Party because while all the districts have about the same number of Texans in them, they don't all have the same number of Democrats. Based on Democratic voter turnout in past elections, districts may select anywhere from 2 delegates (District 31 in West Texas) to 8 delegates (District 14 in Austin).

Allocation
the process by which party rules designate how many of the state's delegates to the national party convention will be pledged to vote for a specific candidate or attend as undecided.

While most states require parties to hold primaries to nominate candidates for the general election, Iowa uses a system of caucuses. The word "caucus" allegedly comes from a Native American word for a meeting between tribal leaders.[i] The Iowa caucus system developed in the late 1800s within political parties as a method of selecting delegates to political party conventions. The Iowa Caucuses operate similarly to a closed primary in that the participants must be registered with a political party. This process effectively limits the Republican caucuses only to Republicans and the Democratic caucuses only to Democrats.

On the night of the Iowa Caucuses, participants gather in over 2,000 local, precinct-level meetings. Historically, these meetings occurred in the homes of local party activists, creating a feeling of neighborliness among participants. In recent years, the meetings have occurred at a local school, library, church, or similar place. To some extent, the caucuses still take on the flavor of a giant precinct party.

The two major parties have slightly different rules concerning how the caucus proceeds. For the Republican Party, the caucus consists of participants dropping the name of a candidate in a hat. Results are then tabulated. At a separate meeting, participants choose delegates to attend a state convention, where the official nomination of party candidates for the general election takes place. At the Democratic caucus, participants break into groups based upon which candidate they support. If any group consists of less than 15 percent of the total number of participants, then the group members must realign with another group. Participants then lobby and persuade members of the group or groups with less than 15 percent to change their preference. When all remaining groups supporting a candidate are above 15 percent of the total participants at that location, delegates to the party county convention are allocated based upon the size of the groups. Note that "undecided" is an acceptable grouping. Here is a comparison of the results of the party caucuses since 1972, when the Iowa Caucuses gained their reputation as a presidential bellwether and grabbed the attention of candidates and the nation alike.

By tradition, the Iowa Caucuses are the first caucuses held in the United States. Because winning, or at least doing well, in the Iowa Caucuses creates momentum for a candidate's campaign and encourages financial support by donors, the Iowa Caucuses are very important to candidates running for U.S. president. As a result, critics suggest that Iowa carries too much weight in presidential elections, especially considering the relatively small and homogenous population.

While turnout for Texas primaries is quite low, and falling over the last two decades, the turnout rates for Iowa Caucuses appear to be increasing. However, turnout for the Iowa Caucuses is harder to determine simply because no official counts occur, and in contrast to closed primaries, lists of registered Democratic or Republican voters do not exist. Estimates of participation in the Democratic caucuses indicate that the percentage of the population that participates in the caucuses is increasing over time.[ii]

Another 67 of the state's 228 delegates (29 percent) are allocated to a candidate based on how many Democrats showed up at the party's precinct-level conventions and signed in for their favorite candidate. Thus, attending the precinct convention after voting in the primary is like casting a second vote for your candidate. The system has earned the nickname the "Texas Two-Step," which makes it sound more fun than voters find it actually to be.

While the Texas process has been criticized, Texas Democrats voted at the 2010 state convention to retain the two-step. Why would they do this? Remember, the parties do things other than nominate presidential candidates. If the parties give voters something kind of fun and interesting to do at the party convention (like support a favorite candidate), they stand a better chance of roping them into attending to the other, more mundane business of the party (for example, establishing rules and the party's platform). It's a kind of political bait-and-switch that

Results of the Iowa Caucuses since 1972

YEAR	DEMOCRATIC PARTY IOWA CAUCUS WINNER	NATIONAL PARTY NOMINEE	REPUBLICAN PARTY IOWA CAUCUS WINNER	NATIONAL PARTY NOMINEE
2008	Barack Obama	Barack Obama	Mike Huckabee	John McCain
2004	John Kerry	John Kerry	George W. Bush	George W. Bush
2000	Al Gore	Al Gore	George W. Bush	George W. Bush
1996	Bill Clinton	Bill Clinton	Bob Dole	Bob Dole
1992	Tom Harkin	Bill Clinton	George H.W. Bush	George H.W. Bush
1988	Richard Gephardt	Michael Dukakis	Bob Dole	George H.W. Bush
1984	Walter Mondale	Walter Mondale	Ronald Reagan	Ronald Reagan
1980	Jimmy Carter	Jimmy Carter	George H.W. Bush	Ronald Reagan
1976	Uncommitted	Jimmy Carter	Gerald Ford	Gerald Ford
1972	Edward Muskie	George McGovern	Richard Nixon	Richard Nixon

Thinking Critically

- Have you ever voted in a primary in Texas? Why or why not?
- Would you be more likely to participate in the Texas presidential primaries if they occurred earlier in the nomination process or if the candidates campaigned more actively in the state?
- What do you think the advantages or disadvantages of a system like the Iowa Caucuses would be if Texas changed to that system?

i. "Frequently Asked Caucus Questions," *Des Moines Register,* www.desmoines register.com (accessed November 5, 2007).

ii. Ibid.

makes sense because getting voters involved in the party makes them more likely to support their candidate.

The often-overlooked third leg of the Texas Two-Step rests on unpledged "super delegates." Super delegates are elected officials and party leaders who get invited to the national convention without going through the selection process required of ordinary Democrats. While this may be unfair in many regards, it is designed to connect the state's leading Democrats with the presidential nominating process.

The lack of strict national party rules for counting delegates reflects the independence of the state parties and the nature of American political parties. In 2007, for example, many states ignored the national party's threats to exert more control by reducing the number of delegates of those states that violated party rules and went ahead and moved their presidential primaries to dates earlier than those allowed by national party rules.

The State Parties and the National Parties

Although citizens generally consider parties to be consistent across all levels of government, there are actually significant differences between the expressed opinions of the parties. Because American parties are grassroots organizations in which power flows from the bottom up, the national parties are not able to impose their views on the state parties. Texas political parties vividly illustrate the inability of the national parties to control party members. For example, for years the national Democratic Party championed civil rights while the conservative Democrats who controlled the Texas Democratic Party often vigorously opposed civil rights legislation. More recently, the Texas Republican Party platform has consistently "demanded" the elimination of presidential authority to issue executive orders and the repeal of all previous executive orders, despite the fact that the executive order was used frequently by George W. Bush as well as by other Republican presidents.

The national party conventions have come to be dominated by the campaign organization of the presidential candidates rather than by the state parties. Because delegates to the national convention are selected based on attachment to national presidential candidates rather than service in the local party, the local party's role has been diminished. This undermines some of the representational role of parties as local concerns disappear into the shadow of national politics.

State and local parties in the United States are in a precarious position. While local party leaders remain important actors in recruiting party candidates and building the parties at the local level, the rise of mass media and candidate-centered campaigns have taken away some of the local parties' most important functions as vehicles for raising money and getting candidates' messages out. Some have called state and local parties "Mom-and-Pop Shops in the Information Age,"[13] and as citizens make more use of television and the Internet to learn about candidates, local parties may find less to do. This represents one way in which changes in the state may permanently transform the way the parties operate and who in the parties hold significant power.

Winners and Losers

Although the primaries and conventions may technically be open to any eligible voters willing to declare themselves members of the party, Texans generally seem increasingly uninterested in participating in the business of parties. In March 2010, only 7.9 percent of Texans went to the polls to choose between Texas Republicans Governor Rick Perry and U.S. Senator Kay Bailey Hutchison in a hotly contested gubernatorial primary; only 3.6 percent voted in the Democratic primary. With less than 12 percent of eligible Texans voting in the primaries that year, how representative are the nominees of the two parties? V. O. Key argued, "over the long run, the have-nots lose in a disorganized politics."[14] According to Key, when there are no strong parties, no one has the incentive and ability to mobilize disorganized interests. Without well-organized parties, some citizens will remain disorganized and their interests diffuse. Organization is especially important to anyone wishing to promote serious reform, since reform efforts require battling an entrenched status quo.

Domination by one party complicates matters. Without groups to mobilize the masses, there is no policy debate, leaving voters less informed and the meaning of election victories less clear. Without an ongoing agenda, party labels are much less meaningful and differences between parties are more difficult for voters to discern.

This means that new Texans looking to take their place in politics and old Texans interested in reforming the system will both need to be well organized as they promote change. This lesson applies most particularly to Hispanics as they increasingly attempt to exert influence in Texas politics and to Republicans as they seek to remove institutional barriers to their political rise.

Organized Interests in Texas Politics

Organized interests step into some of the vacuum left by the lack of party competition. With Republicans now winning statewide elections, as Democrats did a few decades earlier, some of the competition has moved from between the parties to between interest groups. Some organized interests have done well working with members of both parties while others have worked consistently with just one party.

In this text we use the term *organized interest* for what most textbooks, journalists, and citizens would label "special interests" or "interest groups." Many, if not most, of the forces tugging at the political system today are not the large membership organizations that we generally think of as interest *groups*.[15] Many important players in politics are individual citizens or businesses, rather than groups. Nowhere is this more evident than in Texas, where many individual businesses like AT&T and TXU Energy spend millions of dollars lobbying the Texas Legislature without benefit of joining a group, and where individuals like James Leininger pour millions of dollars into campaigns to advance issues like public school vouchers.

An **organized interest** is any organization that attempts to influence public policy decisions. "Organization" in this sense does not mean a collection of individuals.[16] Instead, organization reflects the direction of systematic efforts aimed at influencing the political process. Thus, organized interest sometimes refers to the systematic efforts of an individual. In addition, it should be clear that many of the organizations in politics are groups of corporations, not individuals. For example, the Chamber of Commerce, a very important group at the state and federal level, is a collection of businesses, not individual citizens.

Our definition is well suited for some of the key issues in this chapter. As we will see, many interests in the state may be special, but they are not organized and will not have a meaningful impact on the state's politics. In fact, one of our key arguments is that the failure of some interests to organize is fundamental to understanding who wins and who loses in Texas politics.

Organized interests in Texas benefit from the part-time nature of Texas government. Legislators meeting during the frantic 140-day legislative session find themselves moving through legislation quickly and needing help to sort out the issues. With little professional staff available, lawmakers are more reliant on the kind of information and assistance lobbyists dish out. The part-time commissioners who head bureaucratic agencies provide another entry point for interests' influence in the state. As governors look for citizens to occupy the boards that oversee so much of the Texas bureaucracy, they are likely to turn to wealthy donors—especially those with a connection to the policy area being regulated.

Interest Group Formation

A variety of factors play into Texans' decisions to join interest groups. Some of Texas's early organized interests were held together by the provision of **solidarity benefits,** social interactions that individuals enjoy from joining a group and from

Organized interest
an individual, group of people, or group of businesses that organizes its efforts to influence public policy.

Solidarity benefits
the social interactions that individuals enjoy from joining a group and from working together for a common cause.

working together for a common cause. Texas's size shaped its politics from its earliest days as the Patrons of Husbandry, more commonly known as "the Grange," formed in 1867 largely to escape rural isolation and address the educational and social needs of the farmers who found themselves widely dispersed on the Texas plains. Over time, the Grange became more engaged in economic matters and farmer protests. By 1875 the Grange had more than 1,000 lodges in Texas, claiming over 40,000 members in a state with about 250,000 voters.[17] When the Grange faded it was replaced by the Farmers' Alliance, which got its start in 1877 as an attempt by farmers to sell their goods without intermediaries. While modern Texans may not be as isolated as their ancestors, they still join a group to make new friends, find romance, or simply enjoy the sense of connection that is gained when working alongside others with similar interests.

The advantage of organizing political interests on preexisting social networks continues today. In modern Texas, churches, already homes to groups of people connected through religious communion, are particularly effective at mobilizing their members for political action. The impact of conservative Christians on the state is large; that impact is the result of the many groups, including the Texas Christian Coalition, the Texas Restoration Project, Texas Eagle Forum, and the American Family Association of Texas, that tap into the social networks already in place in churches.

Another motivation for group membership is the **expressive benefits** individuals gain from taking action to express their views. Many individuals and groups protest even in the face of widespread antipathy or hostility. While this behavior may seem irrational at some level, so is yelling at the television during sporting events—a behavior that is not limited to Texans.

According to **disturbance theory,** organized interests have become more numerous as society has changed. As society and the economy develop, becoming more complex and diverse, new interests emerge. These new interests begin to voice their concerns, which leads to the mobilization of established interests that seek to protect themselves from the challenges posed by emerging interests.[18] This theory helps to explain the rise in the number of organized interests active in politics in conjunction with the ongoing transformation of the state.

The **free-rider problem** occurs in the case of citizens who do not contribute to the efforts of a group even though they enjoy the results of the group's efforts. The problem arises because groups labor for **collective goods,** that is, benefits that once provided go to everyone and cannot be effectively denied to others, even those who did not contribute to the effort. Those who do not organize to advance their interest still enjoy as many benefits as those who do. The dilemma of the free-rider problem is that citizens will see little point in making an individual contribution to political efforts since their individual contribution is small and the work will go on without them. For example, all students may enjoy lower tuition, better facilities, and similar benefits from group action even if they do not belong to any student-oriented group or contribute to student organizations in any way.

The free-rider problem is common in politics, as well as in the rest of life. Government itself is a partial solution to the free-rider problem. It creates rules and compels citizens to share the burden of the advancement of a common good. Government partially solves the free-rider problem by jailing citizens who refuse to pay taxes or abide by common rules. College students are familiar with their own free-rider problem: roommates who eat groceries that another roommate paid for or who don't do their share of cleaning chores.

Expressive benefits

benefits that arise from taking action to express one's views; motivates group membership.

Disturbance theory

a theory of group formation that states that as societies become more complex and more diverse, new interests emerge to voice their concerns, prompting established interests to mobilize to protect the status quo.

Free-rider problem

occurs when citizens who do not contribute to the effort of a group nevertheless enjoy the results of the group's efforts.

Collective goods

benefits that, once provided, go to everyone and cannot be effectively denied to others, even those who did not contribute to the effort.

Two things can happen when Texans prefer to leave politics to others and fail to organize. First, nothing gets done. When only a few people who take an interest in an issue become active, their impact will be minimal. Second, when only a narrow slice of interested citizens becomes involved, the few who do take action may poorly reflect the views of others. In a process known as unraveling, a relatively small number of people take over an organization and define its goals in a way that drives away more moderate members. As moderate members fall away, the group becomes increasingly radical, driving away still more of those moderates until the organization no longer reflects the views of the majority of those interested in the issue.

Given these problems, what keeps like-minded Texans working together? One solution to the free-rider problem is the provision of **selective incentives,** or benefits that can be given to members but effectively excluded from non-members. For example, the Texas State Teachers Association proudly proclaims it is "Fighting for Public Schools." However, new members are drawn into the organization with the promise of savings on services ranging from shopping to snowboarding. Current members are encouraged to log in for updates by monthly drawings for "free stuff." Because these benefits go only to members, they can help organizations build membership. However, many observers may worry about the moral authority of groups built on free tote bags and discounted travel.

The fundamental dynamics of interest group organization often leave the citizens with the greatest needs facing the greatest barriers to getting organized. When they lack the resources to organize members or the money needed to finance campaign contributions or professional lobbying, some Texas citizens will remain at a disadvantage. For example, college students are impacted tremendously by decisions made by the Texas Legislature, Higher Education Coordinating Board, and other officials who control the costs of higher education in Texas. Administrators and regents of the schools are well represented. Students who wish to organize and be heard, however, are faced by apathy and a lack of resources on the part of their peers, which leaves them largely unorganized and in a weak position relative to other interests. As a result, it is easy for legislators to overlook students' views. Thus, in 2003, when Texas faced a budget crunch, the easiest solution for the Texas Legislature was to pass a law that allowed state schools to raise their tuition at will.

Selective incentives
benefits exclusively available to members of an organization.

Types of Interests in Texas

Probably the most visible organized interests in Texas are economic interests. These organizations attempt to produce economic benefits for group members. These might be corporations working individually or collectively to lower taxes, reduce regulation, or alter some other business policy to help their bottom line. As Table 8.3 indicates, many of Texas's businesses hire lobbyists to represent them in Austin. The large dollar amounts reflected in the table often conceal the full effort of these businesses, since some business leaders will lobby on behalf of their businesses without additional compensation.

Economic interests also include **labor unions,** which seek better pay or working conditions for their membership. For example, the Texas AFL-CIO spends much of its time lobbying for bread-and-butter issues such as raising the minimum wage and improving the quality of schools. There are about 500,000 labor union members in Texas. In a similar fashion, **professional associations** like the Texas State

Labor unions
organizations that represent the interests of working people seeking better pay and better working conditions.

Professional associations
organizations that represent the needs of professionals not represented by unions.

Table 8.3 Companies or Groups Spending More than $1 Million on Lobbying in Texas in 2009

LOBBYING CLIENT	INTEREST TYPE	CONTRACT VALUES
AT&T Corp.	Communications	$9,250,000
Energy Future Holdings Corp.	Energy	$3,240,000
Reliant Energy, Inc.	Energy	$2,540,000
McGinnis, Lochridge & Kilgore	Lawyers & Lobbyists	$2,175,000
Texas Trial Lawyers Association	Lawyers & Lobbyists	$1,850,000
American Electric Power	Energy	$1,800,000
Texas Association of Realtors	Real Estate	$1,770,000
Texas Medical Association	Health	$1,720,000
TXU Energy Retail Co.	Energy	$1,495,000
CenterPoint Energy	Energy	$1,485,000
Oncor Electric Delivery Co.	Energy	$1,470,000
Association of Electric Companies of Texas	Energy	$1,425,000
City of Houston	Ideological/Single Issue	$1,315,000
Wholesale Beer Distributors of Texas	Miscellaneous Business	$1,305,000
Baker Botts	Lawyers & Lobbyists	$1,285,000
ExxonMobil Corp.	Energy	$1,260,000
El Paso County	Ideological/Single Issue	$1,250,000
Texas Cable and Telecommunications Association	Communications	$1,245,000
Linebarger Heard Goggan Blair & Sampson	Lawyers & Lobbyists	$1,200,000
Verizon	Communications	$1,115,000
Luminant Holding Co.	Energy	$1,110,000
RRI Energy, Inc.	Energy	$1,050,000
City of Austin	Ideological/Single Issue	$1,045,000
Atmos Energy Corp.	Energy	$1,015,000
Henderson Global Investors, Inc.	Finance	$1,002,000
Locke Lord Bissell & Liddell	Lawyers & Lobbyists	$1,000,000
UnitedHealth Group	Health	$1,000,000

Source: Texans for Public Justice, "Austin's Oldest Profession: Texas' Top Lobby Clients and Those Who Service Them," May 2010, http://info.tpj.org/reports/austinsoldest 09/clients.html. Used by permission of Texans for Public Justice.

Teachers Association and the Texas Medical Association represent the needs of professionals who are not represented by unions. Some businesses work collectively through **trade associations,** organizations of similar businesses working together to advance shared goals. For example, the Texas Hospitality Association (THA) is a coalition of restaurants and bars that lobbies on state laws related to how the food and beverage service sector does business. THA's mission statement calls for the repeal of the state law that requires distilled spirits to be purchased only from a retail store.

In contrast, **public-interest groups** pursue noneconomic policies on behalf of the general public (even if not all members of the general public agree on the issues, policies, or solutions). For example, Texans for Public Justice attempts to promote better government by scrutinizing campaign finance and lobbying, while Texans for Lawsuit Reform seeks to reduce the abuse of the legal system. Some **single-interest groups** might also be considered public interest groups since the issue their members are grouped around is one that impacts the public in general. For example, the Texas Right to Life Committee and the Texas Abortion and Reproductive Rights Action League focus their efforts primarily on the issue of abortion, while the Texas State Rifle Association and Texans for Gun Safety square off over gun rights.

Another type of interest is other governments, often referred to as the **intergovernmental lobby**, in which different levels of government lobby each other. As a state, Texas sits in the middle of the intergovernmental lobby, lobbying the national government and being lobbied by cities, counties, and school districts. For example, the cities of Austin and Houston spent over $1 million each on lobbying in 2005, while the Metropolitan Transportation Authority of Harris County spent about $845,000 on its own lobbying effort. In addition, the state is lobbied on behalf of state institutions like universities. While some of this lobbying is done on a contract basis with professional lobbyists, many institutions like universities rely on their upper administration to represent them in Austin.

Texas state government works closely with members of the U.S. Congress to maximize federal grants coming into the state. For example, questions were raised about $1.2 million that Texas had paid for lobbying contracts spanning the period between 2003 and 2007. The Office of State-Federal Relations had hired outside lobbyists, including Washington, D.C., lobbyists with connections to the Jack Abramoff lobbying scandal in which Indian tribes were defrauded of millions of dollars on issues associated with Indian gaming. An article in the *Austin-American Statesman* indicated that the contract was awarded to the lobbying firm of Cassidy & Associates despite the fact that the company's bid was higher than that of some of the other bidders and the company itself was initially given lower scores based on the criteria of the contract.[19] The defense that the firm rose in the rating after its "references" were checked did little to reduce fears that favors were being traded. Some members of the Texas Legislature objected to paying professional lobbyists to work with Congress when members of Congress from Texas carried influence in Washington and there was a Texan in the White House.

While the idea of governments lobbying each other may sound odd, and the prospect of Texas paying millions of dollars for representation in Washington may seem wasteful, keep in mind that Texas receives over 37 percent of its budget—over $24 billion in 2009—from the national government. If paying lobbyists $1 million a year to represent the state's interests increased federal grants by only 1 percent, this outcome would equal a roughly twenty-fold return on lobbying dollars.

Trade associations
organizations of similar businesses, which work together to advance shared goals.

Public-interest groups
organizations that pursue noneconomic policies on behalf of the general public, even if all members of the general public do not agree on these issues or policies.

Single-interest groups
groups usually organized around one side of a single issue, such as pro-choice or anti-abortion groups.

Intergovernmental lobby
the lobbying that occurs between different levels of government, such as between the state and national government or between local governments and the state government.

Contributions of Organized Interests

Organized interests in Texas play the same kind of roles that they do in other states and countries. However, given the condition of Texas's parties, some of these functions are especially important in the state.

One of the primary functions of organized interests is to provide *representation* for groups to complement the geographic representation provided by elected officials. In an essentially one-party state like Texas, group representation may be especially important to many Texans who live in an area in which no one from their party/ideology holds office. Beyond that, Texans have interests that may be best represented based on something other than geography. For example, Texas's teachers come together through groups such as the Texas State Teachers Association to work on educational issues. Public school teachers, while a small part of any one community, comprise a huge bloc of voters across the state.

The *education* function is also very important since many of the issues that impact Texans' lives lie beyond their everyday experiences and knowledge. Organized interests in Texas help bring attention to issues and educate citizens about what their government is doing and how it impacts their lives. For example, environmental groups draw citizens' attention to environmental issues and help them understand the scientific and technical aspects of these issues as well as their potential impact on their physical or economic health.

Similarly, Texans may benefit from *program monitoring* as organized interest groups invest their effort in keeping an eye on the many large bureaucratic agencies and small boards that do much of the work of governing in the state. The average citizen has little time to do this and may lack the expertise to track levels of pollution or budget implementation issues. Organized interests serving as watchdogs may help uncover bureaucratic misbehavior in some cases and deter it in others.

Organized interests can also play an important role by providing program alternatives. In education, for example, teacher groups and other organized interests have put forward alternative reforms to public schools in Texas and helped give citizens alternatives that might never emerge from the education bureaucracy. Organized interests may not seem the best source of reform; however, they may prove more supportive of reform and innovation than bureaucrats and elected officials.

What Organized Interests Do

Organized interests utilize several strategies for influencing policy: electioneering, litigation, and lobbying. With **electioneering,** interests try to shape public policy by influencing who is elected to office. Seeking a statewide office like governor requires reaching into every corner of the state, which requires lots of advertising dollars. Most candidates find that they cannot raise enough money for such a campaign from individual donors contributing small amounts, therefore donors able to supply large amounts like organized interest groups become especially important in deciding which campaigns get off the ground.

Organized interests influence elections in a variety of ways. The most visible and perhaps the most important is through spending. Individuals like James Leininger have the resources to make large donations and through them can have a major impact. (See "Texas Legends" box on Leininger in Chapter 9.) However, most people do not have Leininger's resources. To make their voices heard, these people contribute to campaigns as part of a group in order to bring together enough money to also have an impact on the candidates. These contributions pass through

Electioneering

method used by organized interests to try to shape public policy by influencing who is elected to office, especially by serving as sources of campaign funding.

interest groups, usually a **political action committee (PAC)**. PACs are essentially the fundraising arms of organized interests set up in order to meet the requirements of state and federal campaign finance laws. During the 2007–2008 election cycle, 1,209 general-purpose PACs in Texas reported expenditures of over $119 million (a 21 percent increase over 2006). Over 52 percent of that amount was spent by business PACs. Ideological PACs, including single-issue PACs and PACs associated with political parties, totaled about 42 percent, while labor PACs accounted for just over 5 percent of PAC dollars.

Currently, the biggest spending PAC (independent of political parties) in Texas is Texans for Lawsuit Reform. In 2008, Texans for Lawsuit Reform spent about $4.3 million in an effort to elect legislators and judges who support its desire to reduce the cost of non-meritorious lawsuits. Stars over Texas spent almost $2 million in an unsuccessful effort to keep Tom Craddick as Speaker of the Texas House. The spending of the state's largest union PAC in 2008, the Fort Worth Firefighters, looks relatively small in comparison, at over $700,000. In fact, the $496,298 raised by the second-largest labor-related PAC, the Texas State Teacher's Association, is smaller than contributions made by some individual donors, for example, Tom Craddick, who donated $500,000 to Stars over Texas in October 2008.

Organized interests often supplement the money they give to candidates by spending money on their own advertising or providing materials that others may distribute. The Christian Coalition, for example, produces "voter guides," brochures that list the candidates' positions on issues important to the group that members can print and distribute at their own expense. Other organized interests have launched radio and television ad campaigns backing candidates or issues.

Organized interests may also provide other kinds of assistance to candidates. Labor unions and other groups with large memberships may provide volunteers to help staff phone banks, campaign door-to-door, stuff envelopes, or provide other kinds of help with campaigns. This is one area in which student groups hold an advantage. While they seldom have enough money to make large cash contributions, student groups can provide much-needed volunteers to campaigns. Students can help work phone banks, distribute campaign brochures, put up yard signs, and do other campaign work that is essential to campaigns.

Access can be promoted in a number of ways beyond traditional campaign contributions. Former House Speaker Tom Craddick was criticized for raising over a million dollars for renovation and upkeep on the Speaker's apartment in the Texas Capitol after AT&T and Dallas oilman T. Boone Pickens led the list of donors, each chipping in $250,000 for the apartment. While the money is controlled by the State Preservation Board, many people were concerned that gambling interests and other special interests were the source behind the money used for the Speaker's living quarters.

Sometimes organized interests turn to the courts for assistance and use litigation to advance their causes. While individuals who believe their rights have been violated may lack the resources to take their case to court, groups of people can band together to file lawsuits. For example, as mentioned in Chapter 3, the League of United Latin American Citizens (LULAC) filed a lawsuit challenging the Texas Legislature's redistricting plan on the grounds that it violated the voting rights of the Latino community in Texas according to the 1965 Voting Rights Act. The case resulted in a 2006 U.S. Supreme Court decision, *LULAC v. Perry*, that struck down the redistricting plan; the justices cited diluted representation in violation of the Voting Rights Act.[20]

In Texas law, **lobbying** is defined as contact by telephone, telegraph, or letter with members of the legislative or executive branch to influence legislation or

Political action committee (PAC)
the fundraising arm of an interest group that has been organized to meet the requirements of state and federal campaign finance laws.

Lobbying
direct contact with members of the legislative or executive branch to influence legislation or administrative action.

administrative action. Lobbying embraces a wide range of efforts. For example, during the legislative session Texans for Lawsuit Reform offers massages, manicures, and pedicures on top of the usual food and drink to the "ladies of the Legislature" at their annual "Girls Night Out" event at the Four Seasons Hotel in Austin. While the legislators and staffers in attendance were not offered money, sixteen of the roughly eighteen legislators who attended won $1,000 scholarships to be donated to the school of their choice.[21]

In fact, legislators benefit from a cozy relationship with organized interests in a variety of subtle ways during the legislative session. During the legislative sessions, carts of food zip around the capitol as legislative offices find themselves provided with meals and snacks. In the evening, legislators and their staffers can always find receptions and dinners funded by organized interests. While legislators are unlikely to sell their vote for a tray of bagels or a few cocktails, feeding a legislator is a step to building a relationship and helps create the access that lobbyists thrive on.

One technique is not entirely new, but has been facilitated by advances in mass communication. Via **grassroots lobbying** groups will attempt to influence legislators through public opinion. Grassroots lobbying is a legitimate extension of democratic principles in which groups of citizens spontaneously mobilize to build support for a cause. However, the misuse of public opinion has stirred concerns, as some groups have used negative or misleading information to advance their cause. One variation of grassroots lobbying is known as **astroturf lobbying.** As the name implies, astroturf lobbying simulates grassroots support in an attempt to influence legislators. Often done by specialized lobbying firms, astroturf lobbying involves political elites spending large amounts of money to create public opinion designed to advance a group's agenda. Sometimes this involves large donors using phone banks to urge citizens to contact legislators based on misleading or incomplete information.

One less democratic version of grassroots lobbying is **grasstop lobbying,** which is an attempt to influence legislators through key constituents or friends of legislators. Rather than calling upon thousands of citizens to contact their elected officials, grasstop lobbying efforts rely on the influence of a few key citizens to sway elected officials.

Lobby Regulation

For most of its history, Texas has had little meaningful regulation of lobbying activity, reflected in legends such as those about poultry magnate Lonnie "Bo" Pilgrim passing out $10,000 checks on the floor of the Texas Senate in 1989. In 1957, the Lobby Registration Act required that lobbyists disclose certain activities and began the process of reform. Today, Texas law prohibits contributions from thirty days before the start of a legislative session to twenty days after the session ends.

With millions of dollars at stake, it should come as no surprise that lobbying is a well-developed industry in Austin. In fact, as Table 8.4 reveals, almost two dozen Texans managed to earn $2 million or more as lobbyists in 2009. Texas law defines lobbying as communicating directly with a government official for the purpose of influencing legislation or administrative action. The law requires that persons seeking to influence policy this way register as a lobbyist if they expend more than $500 or receive more than $1,000 in compensation in a three-month period. Lobbyists in Texas must file reports that disclose the range of lobbyists' salaries and their clients.

Grassroots lobbying

attempts by organized interests to influence legislators through public opinion; extension of democratic principles in which groups of citizens spontaneously mobilize to build support for a cause.

Astroturf lobbying

a simulation of grassroots support, usually conducted by specialized lobbying firms; involves spending large sums of money to generate the appearance of public support to advance a group's agenda.

Grasstop lobbying

the attempt to influence legislators through key constituents or friends.

Overseeing lobbying in Texas is the Texas Ethics Commission (TEC), created by a constitutional amendment approved by Texas voters in 1991. The commission is composed of eight members, with no more than four members from the same party. Four of the commissioners are appointed by the governor, two by the lieutenant governor, and two by the Speaker of the Texas House.

The Texas Constitution provides the TEC with the authority to recommend the salary and per-diem payments of members of the legislature, the lieutenant governor, and the Speaker of the House of Representatives, subject to approval by the voters. The commission is also charged with administering laws related to political contributions to candidates, the election of the Speaker of the House, as well as regulation of lobbyists, personal financial disclosure of state officials, and other matters related to integrity in state government. The commissioners meet roughly every two months with an executive director selected by the commission to manage the commission staff and the daily work of the commission.

Today TEC rules prohibit officeholders from accepting certain gifts and track what government officials receive. Officeholders are prohibited from accepting anything in consideration of an official act and are not allowed to accept honoraria or other compensation for speaking if the invitation is related to their status as an officeholder. While travel expenses to a speech can be accepted, the officeholder may not accept any pleasure travel from a group. Lobbyists may pay for food for officeholders when they dine together.

The Center for Public Integrity, a national organization interested in government reform, estimated that in 2005 just over $173 million was spent on lobbying in the state, placing Texas second to California where $227 million was spent. While Texas's large size and population make the large amounts of money spent on lobbyists seem reasonable, in fact the dollar amounts are dramatic given that the Texas Legislature is in session for only 140 days every other year; the legislature in California, as in most other states, meets every year and spends more days each year in session.

The amounts spent by some companies and groups illustrate the level of interest in Texas policy. Communications giant AT&T spent just over $9.2 million lobbying in Texas in 2009, leading the pack of nineteen companies or groups spending over $1 million on lobbying that year.

While there is some debate about how much influence these large lobbying contracts actually have, there is no doubt that they have some impact. These companies did not become large by making investments that do not produce returns. Clearly, they have reaped some reward in keeping their views before the legislature.

Lobbying has long been a concern in Texas. However, there has often been disagreement about the proper relationship between lobbyists and legislators. For example, at one time it was considered acceptable for large companies to keep

Table 8.4 Texas Lobbyists with Contracts of $2 Million or More, 2009

LOBBYIST	MAX. VALUE OF CONTRACTS	NO. OF CONTRACTS
Carol McGarah	$3,415,000	52
Andrea McWilliams	$3,325,000	42
Russell T. Kelley	$3,210,000	51
Stan Schlueter	$2,975,000	27
Robert D. Miller	$2,925,000	30
Joe B. Allen	$2,900,000	102
Randall H. Erben	$2,800,000	31
Dean R. McWilliams	$2,440,000	31
Todd M. Smith	$2,435,000	24
Christopher Shields	$2,325,000	23
Michael Toomey	$2,295,000	31
Kristen Hogan	$2,250,000	90
Mignon McGarry	$2,185,000	24
Camm "Trey" Lary III	$2,165,000	108
Don A. Gilbert	$2,100,000	27
Ron E. Lewis	$2,085,000	27
David Sibley	$2,060,000	35
"Reggie" G. Bashur	$2,025,000	23
Virginia Martinez	$2,010,000	40
Arthur V. Perkins	$2,010,000	40
W. James Jonas III	$2,000,000	11
Natalie B. Scott	$2,000,000	39

Source: Texans for Public Justice, "Austin's Oldest Profession: Texas' Top Lobby Clients and Those Who Service Them," May 2010, http://info.tpj.org/reports/austinsoldest09/lobbyists.html. Used by permission of Texans for Public Justice.

The State of Washington tackles the issue of lobbying very differently than Texas. In 2007, one ranking of attempts to regulate lobbyists and their activities placed Washington as first in the nation, while Texas ranked twelfth.[i] Among the points of comparison was the fact that, in 2005, lobbyists spent over $173 million dollars lobbying in Texas and only $37 million in Washington. In Texas, there are nine registered lobbyists with the state government for every member of the state legislature. In Washington, the ratio is six lobbyists per member of the state legislature. More telling is the fact that seventy of the lobbyists in Texas were former members of the legislature now hired to lobby their former colleagues. In Washington, only fifteen former members of the state legislature work as lobbyists.

When it comes to defining and registering lobbyists and their activities, the two states differ in a number of areas. As the table comparing Texas with Washington shows, Washington's regulatory environment provides a more detailed accounting of the activities of lobbyists who attempt to influence the state government than does the Texas environment.

Thinking Critically

- Which provisions of Washington's lobbyist regulations not found in Texas do you find the most attractive?
- How do you think such provisions would change the dynamics of money in Texas politics?

i. The Center for Public Integrity, "In Your State—Washington" and "In Your State—Texas," www.publicintegrity.org/hiredguns/iys.aspx (accessed August 11, 2010).

Lobbying in Texas and Washington State

ACTIVITY REGULATED	TEXAS	WASHINGTON
Register if lobbying executive	Yes	Yes
Register if lobbying legislature	Yes	Yes
Minimum spent to qualify as a lobbyist	$500	$0
Must provide photo with registration form	No	Yes
Must report compensation	Yes	Yes
Must itemize all spending	No (only over $25)	Yes
Campaign contributions disclosed on registration form	No	Yes
Lobbyists' employers must file spending report	No	Yes
Online registration and reporting allowed	No	Yes
State conducts audits of lobbyist reports	No	Yes

Source: Compiled by the authors from data available at The Center for Public Integrity, "Lobby Disclosure Comparisons 2003," 2007, www.publicintegrity.org/hiredguns/comparisons.aspx (accessed August 11, 2010).

legislators who were also lawyers "on retainer." In this arrangement, members of the Texas Legislature would accept payments from companies even as they deliberated over legislation impacting that company.

The fluid movement of people between public service and lobbying enterprises concerns many Texans. This movement, known as the **revolving door,** sees legislators and members of the executive branch moving easily from government office to lobbying firm where, as former government officials, they are able to use the access they have developed through years in public service for private gain. According to the Center for Public Integrity, between the close of the 2005 legislative session and the start of the 2007 session, eight former legislators became lobbyists, helping Texas lead the nation in lawmakers turned lobbyists, with seventy having made the transition.[22] In 2007, renewed concern developed after Governor Perry issued an executive order

Revolving door
the phenomenon of legislators and members of the executive branch moving easily from government office to lucrative positions with lobbying firms.

calling for all sixth-grade girls to receive mandatory vaccines designed to protect them from cervical cancer. While many citizens applauded the governor's enthusiasm for combating cancer, others questioned the need for mandatory vaccines, particularly after it became public knowledge that Perry's former chief of staff was now a lobbyist for the vaccine's manufacturer. Stopping the revolving door, or even slowing it down, is politically difficult because it asks state legislators to support laws limiting their future careers. Also, limits on what officials do after their years of public service are limits on their First Amendment rights and may keep some from lobbying for causes they truly believe in or that their constituents would favor.

Some family members of legislative leaders have found jobs as well-paid lobbyists, suggesting that interest groups are buying influence through family members. One study found that at least six well-paid lobbyists had members of their family serving in high-level positions in Texas government.[23] One member of the legislature, Jim Pitts, had a twin brother, John, who worked as a lobbyist. While the two claim to have avoided discussing issues during the legislative session, the close connection illustrates the concern of many. Although an interest in politics is often shared in families, and it would not be unusual to find several members of a family ending up in different areas of politics, these close relationships and the size of the lobbying contracts raise concerns.

Winners and Losers

One important debate in the area of organized interests is always who wins and who loses. One perspective on this issue is the **pluralist perspective** that looks at politics as a collection of interests and argues that democracy is best practiced when citizens participate through groups. When many interests are represented, pluralists see wide participation and a healthy democracy. The leading voice of pluralism was the political scientist Robert Dahl who, in his classic *Who Governs?*, concluded that no single interest dominated and that politics was open to broad participation with organized interests representing the needs of real people.[24]

Critics of pluralism disagree with the idea that the presence of a large number of interest groups means that citizens are well served; some people, they argue, will be better represented by organized interests than others. C. Wright Mills maintained that the "power elite," the wealthy and powerful interests, were better represented than ordinary citizens.[25] As one scholar colorfully suggested, "the flaw in the pluralist heaven is that the heavenly chorus sings with a strong upper-class accent."[26] Most Texans don't have enough money to contribute to an interest group or hire the lobbyists and other staff needed to build support for their agenda. There are some groups that represent poor Texans but, ironically, these groups are generally funded and led by people who are not themselves poor. That is, poor Texans remain reliant on wealthy patrons to advocate for them.

One of the challenges to the pluralist view is that we have gone beyond simple pluralism and evolved into a system of **hyperpluralism,** in which many narrow groups are represented, often at the expense of the broader public interest. For example, the National Rifle Association may effectively represent many Texans on the issue of gun ownership, but that does not mean that its members are heard on issues unrelated to the NRA's narrow focus. As is evident from looking over the groups functioning in Texas, many businesses and groups labor in Austin on behalf of narrow interests while very few work on behalf of citizens in general.

Pluralist perspective
a view of politics that argues that democracy is best practiced when citizens participate through groups; a greater number of organized interests means wider participation and a healthier democracy.

Hyperpluralism
a view that the system today has evolved beyond simple pluralism and is now one in which many narrow interests are represented, often at the expense of the broader public interest.

Some of the arguments implicating organized interests have little to do with class or party. One view is that special interests have made it impossible to get rid of a government program that is no longer needed, whether it's a social program benefiting the poor or a subsidy benefiting businesses.[27] In this argument, organized interests have been successful at protecting their own spending, even if it is at the expense of everyone else's pocketbook. While all organized interests win in this state of affairs, they also all lose as taxpayers remain burdened with programs that are ineffective.

The ability of some groups to effectively organize while others remain unorganized produces clear winners and losers in the state. In Texas, businesses, and often individual businessmen and women, have effectively organized. Once organized, the relatively loose laws governing lobbying make it easy for them to exert considerable influence in Austin. Other groups, perhaps due to a lack of money or apathy, or both, fail to effectively organize and pay a high price. For instance, the vast majority of college and university students in Texas consistently show little interest in politics. In recent years, the Texas Legislature has approved increased tuitions, capped the number of hours students can attempt to carry or withdraw from, and, in one case, even seen the funding of Texas's community college health benefits vetoed by the governor. Governor Perry's veto, which would have forced community colleges across the state to raise tuition even more to cover funding, was so unpopular with community colleges and their supporters that the governor ultimately backed down.

Conclusion

Parties and organized interests can be both allies and enemies in the political process. While organized interests often support political parties, there are times when narrow interests will abandon the broader goals of the political parties and divide them instead. However, while the two political actors may at times clash, their impact on Texas politics is undeniable.

The importance of parties and organized interests in Texas is not in dispute; however, their place in Texans' hearts is less certain. V. O. Key, who defined much of our understanding of Texas and southern politics, noted, "As institutions, parties enjoy a general disrepute, but most of the democratic world finds them indispensable as instruments of self-government, as means for the organization and expression of competing viewpoints on public policy."[28] Organized interests similarly generate little fondness among the citizens of Texas, but Texans show little hesitation in supporting interests that serve their personal needs. Texans may dislike interest groups, but few states have systems in which lobbyists play a stronger role. They may express frustration and proclaim their political independence, but the citizens of Texas have proved unswervingly loyal to first the Democratic Party and now the Republican Party. Despite their disdain and doubts, Texans continually turn to these political institutions, ensuring them a place in the future of Texas politics.

Key Terms

allocation
astroturf lobbying
chronic minority

collective goods
conventions (caucuses)
county chair
county or senatorial district convention
delegates
disturbance theory
electioneering
electoral competition model
executive committee
expressive benefits
free-rider problem
grassroots lobbying
grassroots organization
grasstop lobbying
hyperpluralism
intergovernmental lobby
labor unions
lobbying
organized interest
party platform
permanent party organizations
plank
pluralist perspective
political action committee (PAC)
political party
precinct chair
professional associations
public-interest groups
responsible party model
revolving door
run-off primary
selective incentives
single-interest groups
solidarity benefits
state party chair
temporary party organizations
trade associations

Explore this subject further at http://lonestar.cqpress.com, where you'll find chapter summaries, practice quizzes, key word flash cards, and additional suggested resources.

Governor Rick Perry prepares to sign House Bill 1634 at an event at an Austin movie studio. The law provided $22 million to help bring jobs in the entertainment industry, including the production of movies, television programs, and video games, to Texas.

CHAPTER 9

Policy

In June 2007 the Texas Legislature passed HB 1634, creating the Texas Moving Image Industry Incentive Program to provide grants and tax breaks to films, television programs, commercials, and video games produced in the state. The idea was to bring the entertainment industry to Texas and create jobs. In signing the bill, Governor Rick Perry noted neighboring Louisiana's success with a similar program and told Texans that the entertainment industry "creates jobs, builds the economy and serves as an incubator for the development of the creative arts industry." The law provides that funds may be denied in cases where the Texas Film Commission, an agency attached to the governor's office, finds "inappropriate content or content that portrays Texas or Texans in a negative fashion."

In 2009, when Perry signed a revision of the law, he held the bill signing ceremony at Robert Rodriguez's Troublemaker Studios and boasted that the law was "strengthening our state's investment in a vital industry." The law, to some degree, had its desired effect and, according to Rodriguez himself, the revised legislation helped him keep the production of his new movie *Machete* in Texas.

Unfortunately, not everyone was looking forward to the movie or relishing the idea that their tax dollars had paid for its production when they read rumors that the hero of *Machete* was an illegal immigrant who was battling, in part, corrupt Texas officials. The possibility of funding a movie about people who illegally entered Texas and rose up against corrupt officials was more than many could stand. Some conservatives launched an offensive to make sure that tax dollars from the incentive program did not go to a "racist" movie.

Why would a Texas governor get tangled up in the politics of the movie industry? Surely such nonsense is best reserved for California and its governors, like Arnold Schwarzenegger. Actually, Perry is following a tradition of Texas governors going back to John Connolly, who realized that the future of the state economy had to be more than cowboys and oilmen and who wanted to find ways to diversify the state's economy. Perry was reaching out with his legislation to lasso new jobs for Texas, part of his strategy of economic development.

The clash over *Machete* dramatically reflects some of the challenges of economic development, especially in a state as dynamic as Texas. Giving tax breaks to bring in new business can create jobs, but it also brings tax dollars into businesses some citizens might want little to do with. While some Texans might feel that movies like *Machete* create an unflattering image of Texas, others focus more on the jobs created. As we noted in Chapter 1, Texas politics has often been about balancing the demands of new and old, and how best to bring in new businesses without alienating the old will be an ongoing challenge as the state continues to grow.

How effective will incentives for the entertainment industry be if studios know that they could be denied funding years after a shoot begins? And, how effective will Texas's incentives prove as more and more states offer more and larger incentives?

The state's funding of movies reflects the complexity and controversy of policy making. The debate over support for entertainment industry funding illustrates how Texas must continually adapt to the changing economy and strike a delicate balance in what jobs it funds.

Today, Texas government finds itself attempting to manage an interesting mix of tasks. Policy, the actions of government, can take a variety of forms. Some policies, like tax policy, are a constant reminder of government and its activities. Other policies, like education policy, are subtler in their costs and in their benefits.

In this chapter we will describe the policymaking process and examine types of policies generally as well as some of the specific policies that emerge from the process. Policy comes to Texans through a variety of actors in Texas government. Some policies result directly from the action of the Texas Legislature as it gathers every two years to write new laws. Many policies result from executive orders and other actions of the governor or other elected executives. Other policies emerge from the bureaucracy as it interprets the laws enacted by the legislature. Finally, local policies result from the actions of city or county governments. Government is seldom tasked with problems that have easy solutions. As we will see in the discussion of the issue of immigration at the end of the chapter, policy solutions are difficult because Texans often do not even agree on whether or not there is a problem. Texas government under different flags and constitutions has been struggling for generations to find solutions to the problems Texans face. However, a rapidly changing population continually redefines our old problems and generates new problems as immigration from other countries and other states continues to bring new people and new politics to Texas.

> ### As you read the chapter, think about the following questions:
>
> ★ What kinds of taxes do Texans pay?
> ★ Should Texas change its current tax system?
> ★ What does the government do to promote economic growth?
> ★ What are the challenges facing the education system in Texas?
> ★ How can Texans prepare for current and future transportation needs?

The Policymaking Process

Policy, or the actions and activities of government, is the bread and butter of governance. Scholars have identified five stages in the policymaking process, which are depicted in Figure 9.1. In the **agenda setting** stage, policymakers prioritize the various problems facing the state. These policymakers may discover the problem themselves through sources ranging from their own everyday experiences to formal legislative hearings, or a problem may be brought to their attention by individual citizens, interest groups, or media reports. In the

Policy
the actions and activities of government.

Agenda setting
the stage in which policymakers prioritize the problems facing the state.

Figure 9.1 The Policymaking Process

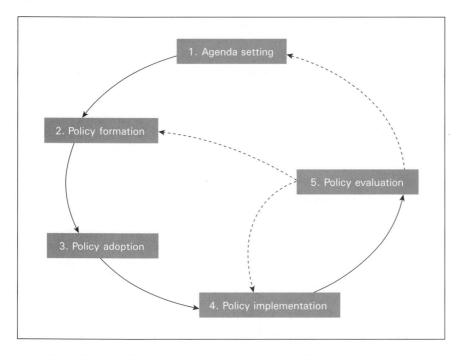

Source: Christine Barbour and Gerald C. Wright, *Keeping the Republic,* 4th Brief Ed. (Washington, D.C.: CQ Press, 2011), 475.

policy formation stage, possible solutions are developed and debated. Next, in the **policy adoption** stage, formal government action takes place with approval of the legislature or through administrative action by a member of the executive branch. After approval, policies move into the **policy implementation** stage, during which state agencies follow up on the actions of elected officials. In this stage bureaucratic agencies develop rules and regulations that detail the guidelines for how the policy will be carried out. Finally, in the **policy evaluation** stage, government agencies, the legislature, and interest groups assess the implementation of the policy to determine if its goals are being met.

Political scientists have categorized policies into three types: redistributive, distributive, and regulatory. **Redistributive policy** moves benefits (usually in the form of money) from one group to another in an attempt to equalize society by taxing people with higher incomes to provide benefits to people with fewer resources. **Distributive policy** is similar except that it attempts to meet the needs of citizens without targeting any one group as the source of money. As a result, distributive policies are easier to implement because their costs are widely dispersed and such policies face less opposition since no group is identified as the source of funds. **Regulatory policy** attempts to limit or control the actions of individuals or corporations. For example, businesses may face fines or other penalties as a disincentive for polluting or other socially undesirable outcomes. Thus, policy is at the heart of politics as the government resolves the question of who gets what from government.

Policy formation
the stage in which possible solutions are developed and debated.

Policy adoption
the stage in which formal government action takes place.

Policy implementation
the stage in which the policy is carried out in state agencies.

Policy evaluation
the stage in which the implementation of a policy is examined to see if policy goals are being met.

Redistributive policy
moves benefits, usually in the form of money, from one group to another in an attempt to equalize society.

Distributive policy
moves benefits to meet the needs of citizens but does so without targeting any one group as the source of money.

Regulatory policy
attempts to limit or control the actions of individuals or corporations.

Fiscal Policy: Taxes, Spending, and Budgets

 aybe the most obvious way of looking at who gets what from government is examining the money that Texas takes from its citizens (taxes) and puts into various programs (spending). While the intentions and effectiveness of spending merit specific discussion, we need to first look at **fiscal policy,** how government seeks to influence the economy through taxing and spending. This takes the form of policies to shape the health of the economy overall, as well as the taxing and spending policies the state uses to encourage some businesses and discourage others. The state may also provide a **subsidy,** an incentive designed to encourage the production or purchase of certain goods, to encourage some businesses or industries. For example, in 2009 the Texas Legislature appropriated $203 million for the state's Emerging Technology Fund to support startup companies in cutting-edge fields. Many cities offer grants and tax breaks to businesses thinking about relocating. While bringing jobs to an area might seem popular at first glance, these incentives creating subsidies for new businesses shift the tax burden to existing businesses that may not enjoy paying the tax bill for their new neighbors. In addition, tax dollars might be used to bring in businesses that are controversial (for example, nuclear power plants).

Taxes

Texans, not surprisingly, have never liked taxes. Settlers in Stephen F. Austin's colony complained about the 12.5 cents per-acre tax Austin charged to pay for survey fees and the militia needed for settlers' defense.[1] Today, Texans pay relatively little in state taxes. According to the Census Bureau in 2005, Texas taxes ranked forty-ninth out of fifty, with state taxes for each Texan in 2005 averaging $1,434, just slightly higher than South Dakota's $1,430 and well below the national average of $2,190 per person in state taxes.[2]

State Taxes

Today, Texas relies on a complicated mixture of over sixty separate taxes. Texas is one of seven states with no **income tax,** a tax calculated as a percentage of income earned in·a year. Two states (New Hampshire and Tennessee) have no general income tax but do tax dividend and interest income. While the idea of avoiding income tax is appealing, as Texas demonstrates, the lack of an income tax doesn't mean there will be no taxes since, as we're about to see, there are many, many other ways of raising revenue for the state. As Bob Bullock observed while he was serving as the state's comptroller, "There are only certain taxes known to civilized man, and Texas has nearly all of them, except the income tax."[3]

In 1961, Texas implemented its first **general sales tax,** an across-the-board tax imposed on goods and services sold within a jurisdiction, when it imposed a 2 percent sales tax on many goods sold. Over the next forty years that tax rate has increased to 6.25 percent and expanded to include more goods and services. In 1967, the Local Sales and Use Tax Act authorized cities to add a 1 percent local tax on all retail sales. Today, Texas cities, counties, transit authorities, and other special purpose districts have the option of imposing an additional local sales tax for a combined possible maximum for all state and local sales taxes of 8.25 percent. By 1967, the sales tax had become the largest source of tax revenue for Texas. In 2009, the state sales tax brought in $21 billion per year, accounting for about 55 percent

Fiscal policy

how government seeks to influence the economy through taxing and spending.

Subsidy

incentive designed to encourage the production or purchase of certain goods, to stimulate or support some businesses.

Income tax

a tax calculated as a percentage of income earned in a year.

General sales tax

an across-the-board tax imposed on goods and services sold within a jurisdiction.

of Texas taxes, by far the biggest source of tax revenue for the state. Texas's sales tax of 6.25 percent is the fourth highest state sales tax rate in the nation, a full point behind California's 7.25 percent sales tax.

Comparing state sales taxes is difficult because each state uses a different mixture of state and local sales taxes. For example, the state of New York imposes a sales tax rate of only 4 percent, but counties in New York have local sales tax rates that allow them to add an additional percentage, from 3 percent to 5.75 percent. Other states, like Connecticut, have a state-level sales tax with no local add-ons.

In addition to the general sales tax, Texas has a separate tax of 6.25 percent on the sale and rental or lease of motor vehicles. There is also a tax of 3.25 percent on the sale of manufactured housing. These taxes bring in another $3 billion per year, or 9 percent of the state's revenue.

Texas also taxes the sale of gasoline. The Gasoline and Diesel Fuel Tax charges consumers in Texas 20 cents on every gallon of gasoline they buy (on top of 18.4 cents a gallon in federal taxes). Texas's gas tax rate is one of the lowest in the nation (thirty-seventh out of the fifty states and the District of Columbia), coming in at half of New York's 44.5 cents a gallon but much more than Alaska's 8 cents a gallon. This generates almost $3 billion each year, or about 8 percent of the state's tax revenue. The Texas Legislature has not raised the gasoline tax since 1992, however, and these funds are not keeping up with the increasing costs of building and maintaining Texas roads. The state has increasingly turned to toll roads to keep pace with the needs of a growing state.

After oil erupted from the Spindletop well on January 10, 1901, ushering in an era of petroleum, taxes on Texas's oil production became a huge source of revenue that has kept many Texans from having to pay much in the way of taxes. By 1905, the state was raking in $101,403 a year from oil production alone. Texas still taxes the production of oil and gas with a **severance tax,** a tax on natural resources charged when they are produced or "severed" from the earth. These severance taxes, similar to a value added tax (VAT), that is common in Europe, take the form of Texas's "Oil Production" tax that takes 4.6 percent of the market value of oil produced, while the "Oil Regulation" tax takes three-sixteenths of a cent from each barrel of oil produced. The state also taxes the production of natural gas at 7.5 percent of market value. In addition, liquefied gas is taxed at a rate of 15 cents a gallon. While once a much larger portion of the state budget, the state's tax on oil and gas production today accounts for only about 6 percent of all state taxes.

Texas's **franchise tax** is its primary tax on business. That tax was significantly revised in the 2006 special session in order to help fund Texas public schools by expanding the types of businesses taxed. At the same time, the method of calculation of the tax was changed. Today, the franchise tax is based on the "taxable margin" (a variety of measures approximating profit) of the company (70 percent of total revenue, total revenue minus the costs of goods sold, or total revenue minus compensation, whichever is less). In 2009, the franchise tax generated $4.2 billion, or about 11 percent of all state taxes.

Like other states, Texas uses the so-called **sin tax,** or a tax on products or activities that some legislators want to discourage, to generate additional income. The objects of sin taxes make inviting targets, as elected officials look for places to impose taxes on the least sympathetic products possible. While the federal government has its own **excise tax,** a tax paid at the time of purchase with the cost of the tax usually included in the price of the product, on alcoholic beverages, Texas has separate tax rates on liquor, beer, wine, malt liquor, and mixed drinks. While some

Severance tax

a tax on natural resources charged when the resources are produced or "severed" from the earth.

Franchise tax

the primary tax on businesses in Texas, which is based on the "taxable margin" of each company.

Sin tax

tax on products or activities, such as cigarettes or gambling, that some legislators would like to discourage.

Excise tax

a tax paid at the time of purchase, with the cost of the tax included in the price of the product.

Every year, the Tax Foundation, a nonpartisan tax research group based in Washington, D.C., calculates "Tax Freedom Day" to illustrate what portion of the year citizens must work to pay their federal, state, and local taxes. In 2010, it estimated that the average American works about 99 days out of the year to pay his or her taxes, making "Tax Freedom Day" April 9.

By the Tax Foundation's estimate, Tax Freedom Day comes a few days earlier (April 5) to Texans, placing Texas thirty-second among the fifty states in terms of total state taxes paid per capita. The most heavily taxed state, according to the Tax Foundation, is Connecticut, although some of Connecticut citizens' heavy tax burden results from their prosperity, as a high average income in the state results in high federal income taxes.[i] Connecticut state taxes average $3,674 per person, compared to an average of $1,646 per person in Texas.[ii] Citizens of Connecticut face taxes of 5 percent on income over $10,000, as well as a 6 percent state sales tax (local governments are not allowed to add to that rate). One of the reasons for Connecticut's high taxes is that its citizens are relatively prosperous, with a median household income in 2006–2008 of $68,411, compared to Texas's median household income of $49,078 and the national average median of $52,175.[iii] Because households in Connecticut have higher incomes, they naturally pay higher federal income taxes.

Overall, the highest rates of taxation could be found in the Northeast, with Connecticut, New Jersey, New York, and Maryland having the four highest rates in the nation. In contrast, taxes were generally lower in the South, with Oklahoma, Alabama, Mississippi, Tennessee, and Louisiana among the least taxed states.

Thinking Critically

- Can you think of some advantages of living in a high-income-tax state like Connecticut? What might these be?
- Can you identify problems in Texas that might be better addressed if the state had more revenue? Can you offer some examples?
- Can you think of other ways the state might raise revenue without imposing income taxes?

i. Tax Foundation, Special Report: Americans Celebrate Tax Freedom Day, April 2010, www.taxfoundation.org/taxfreedomday.
ii. U.S. Census Bureau, States Ranked by Total State Taxes: 2009, www.census.gov/govs/statetax/09staxrank.html.
iii. U.S. Census Bureau, State Fact Sheets, www.census.gov.

alcohol is taxed by volume, mixed drinks are taxed at 14 percent of sales. In 2009, Texas's taxes on alcohol totaled almost $800 million. This is a small portion (2 percent) of the total state taxes, as a contribution of a single product, but Texans might be surprised to realize that they drink enough to average over $40 in alcohol tax for every Texan of drinking age.

The rise in the state's tax on cigarettes, passed in May 2005 to help pay for schools, illustrates the complexities of the sin tax. On January 1, 2007, the state's tax on a pack of cigarettes leapt a full dollar for a total tax of $1.41 a pack, driving the cost of most packs of cigarettes to over $4 and making the state's tax one of the highest in the region. Some Texans contemplated quitting smoking, an effect intended by groups like the American Cancer Society that lobbied for the increase. Others saw the tax increase as a way of offsetting the healthcare costs to a state that sees over 20,000 people a year die from smoking-related illnesses. With about half of the revenue from the tobacco tax designated for funding of public schools, imposition of the tax may seem an easy way to raise revenue at the expense of unpopular products. However, these taxes can be problematic. Because Louisiana's 36-cent tax per pack is one of the lowest in the nation, some Texans simply cross state lines to buy their cigarettes, just as New Mexico's smokers streamed into Texas when New Mexico increased its tax by 70 cents per pack in 2003. With convenience stores

Map 9.1 Tax Freedom Days, 2010

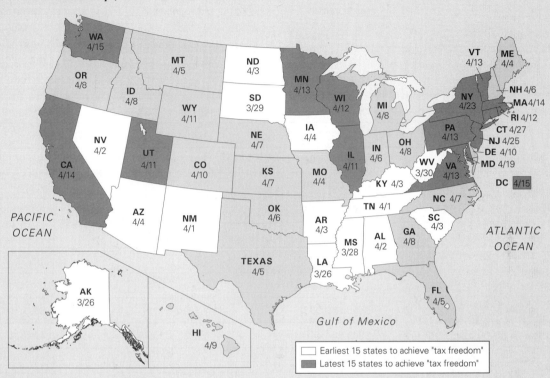

Earliest 15 states to achieve "tax freedom"

Latest 15 states to achieve "tax freedom"

Source: Adapted from Tax Foundation, "America Celebrates Tax Freedom Day: Tax Freedom Day by State and Rank, Calendar Year 2010," http://www.taxfoundation.org/taxfreedomday. Used by permission of Tax Foundation.

claiming that cigarettes account for over one-quarter of their sales, the outflow of Texas customers results in a significant loss of revenue, depriving Texas merchants of customers and the state of Texas of taxable sales.

The general mixture of taxes is spelled out in Table 9.1. As the table demonstrates, while Texas's tax rates may be low, the system is far from simple as the state looks to a wide variety of sources for its tax dollars.

Property Taxes

While Texas's state taxes are lower than most other states, local governments impose a significant local **property tax,** a tax on the value of real estate that is paid by the property owner. And while the Texas Constitution forbids a statewide property tax, cities, counties, and local school districts charge property taxes that they rely heavily on for their revenue. In Texas, the balance of responsibility for funding public schools has been a source of major conflict, requiring special legislative sessions to resolve. In 2006, the Texas Legislature reduced school property taxes by one-third. The plan traded lower school property taxes for higher taxes on businesses, smokers, and used-car purchasers. While the legislature's reform promised significantly lower taxes, about two-thirds of local school boards in the state opted to increase

Property tax

a tax on the value of real estate that is paid by the property owner; used by county and local governments to fund such programs as public schools.

Table 9.1 Texas State Taxes by Source, Fiscal Year 2009

	2009 REVENUE	PERCENTAGE OF TOTAL TAX REVENUE	PERCENTAGE OF ALL SOURCES OF REVENUE
Tax Collections			
Sales tax	$21,014,065,089	55.6%	24.9%
Motor vehicle sales/rentals	$2,600,939,347	6.9%	3.1%
Motor fuels taxes	$3,032,770,482	8.0%	3.6%
Franchise tax	$4,250,332,029	11.2%	5.0%
Insurance taxes	$1,257,314,168	3.3%	1.5%
Natural gas production tax	$1,407,739,109	3.7%	1.7%
Cigarette and tobacco taxes	$1,556,793,276	4.1%	1.8%
Alcoholic beverage taxes	$796,948,327	2.1%	0.9%
Oil production tax	$884,510,773	2.3%	1.0%
Inheritance tax	$2,004,064	0.0%	0.0%
Utility taxes	$518,883,903	1.4%	0.6%
Hotel tax	$343,544,448	0.9%	0.4%
Other taxes	$156,607,998	0.4%	0.2%
Total taxes	$37,822,453,013	100%	44.9%

Source: Texas Comptroller, "Revenue by Source for Fiscal Year 2009," www.window.state.tx.us/taxbud/revenue.html.

Note: May not sum due to rounding.

Ad-valorem tax

a tax based on property value, which is subject to periodic appraisals.

Appraisal

the official estimate of a property's value.

the rates after the legislature had reduced them.[4] While the increases were relatively small and within the limits created by the law, they served to reduce the size of tax cuts the legislature sought.

These complications result from a mixed funding system that leaves local school boards dependent on the state for much of their money at the same time the boards remain subject to state rules on how they raise remaining revenues. Many local school boards are faced with rising utility bills and staff costs even as the legislature has capped available funding. Locally elected school boards are left with few alternatives, having little choice but to raise property taxes.

Setting property tax rates may seem like a simple process. However, the property tax is an *ad-valorem* tax, a tax based on the value of property. Even if the property tax rates remain the same, governments may raise the tax on citizens by increasing the amount of the **appraisal,** the official estimate of a property's value. This problem is especially serious in growing areas like Dallas, which saw a 60 percent rise in property values from 2000 to 2005.[5] This creates what critics call a "stealth tax increase," even though the state government had no hand in increasing property values. Currently the state caps the annual increase in a home's taxable value to 10 percent. Senior citizens and others living on fixed incomes may have trouble keeping up with the taxes on their property as values rise. Rising property values create a significant problem for seniors today, who, after paying off a $250-a-month thirty-year mortgage, for example, now find themselves paying that much in property taxes every month. To protect seniors, Texas offers a cap on school taxes and the Texas Constitution was amended in 2003 to allow (but not require) cities and counties to cap seniors' taxes. While this may give retired Texans some protection against rising rates, it shifts the burden for taxes to others and may present a serious problem for areas with high numbers of retirees.

Winners and Losers

The type of taxes Texas uses creates obvious winners and losers. A **progressive tax,** such as the federal income tax, places higher rates on people with higher incomes. A **regressive tax,** in contrast, takes a higher proportion of income from people with lower incomes than from people with higher incomes. Sales taxes are often cited as examples of regressive taxes, even though everyone pays the same tax rate on purchases. Critics of sales taxes point out that people with lower incomes tend to spend a larger share of their income on the kind of items taxed at sale.

Progressive tax
a graduated tax, such as an income tax, which taxes people with higher incomes at higher rates.

Regressive tax
a tax, such as a sales tax, that taxes everyone at the same rate, regardless of income; has a greater impact on those with lower incomes.

Some Texans have advocated an income tax like those used by other states to shift more of the state's tax burden to people with higher incomes. While critics complain about the complexity of an income tax system with exemptions and schedules of deductions, the vast array of current state taxes is evidence that Texas has already created a complicated system without an income tax. Even some conservative legislators privately concede that replacing Texas's long list of taxes with a single income tax based on calculations already done for federal income taxes would actually simplify taxation in the state. These legislators worry that if the state does away with small taxes in favor of an income tax, nothing would prevent the state from gradually reinstating these small taxes whenever the government needed more money.

So choosing who to tax and how to structure taxes is a clearly visible statement by the government of who wins and who loses. Thus, it is not surprising that the Texas Legislature, currently faced simultaneously with increased costs and statewide tax fatigue, has largely avoided the problem altogether. In some cases, creative but surreptitious alternatives (such as the growing number of toll roads or significant increases in university tuition and fees) are filling the gap. In other cases, citizens are left with an education system, healthcare system, and even basic infrastructure that are inadequate to their needs. As Texans grapple with the difficult issue of who pays, it appears everyone loses.

Other Sources of Revenue

While the taxes outlined so far generated almost $38 billion dollars in 2009, they accounted for less than half (45 percent) of state revenue. This raises the question of where the state gets the rest of its revenue. As Table 9.2 indicates, tax revenues are only part of the funding picture.

Federal Grants

The large share of the state budget that comes from the federal treasury might surprise many Texans. In 2009, Texas received about $30.8 billion from the federal

Table 9.2 Texas State Revenue by Source

Revenue by Source	2009 REVENUE	PERCENTAGE OF ALL SOURCES OF REVENUE
Tax collections	$37,822,453,013	44.9%
Federal income	$30,859,931,204	36.6%
Licenses, fees, fines, and penalties	$7,198,061,506	8.5%
Interest and investment income	$1,346,545,322	1. 6%
Lottery proceeds	$1,581,961,572	1.9 %
Sales of goods and services	$427,644,257	0.5%
Settlements of claims	$564,752,988	0.7%
Land income	$788,045,918	0.9%
Contributions to employee benefits	$270,553	0.0%
Other revenue	$3,695,796,980	4.4%
Total revenue	$84,285,463,312	100.0%

Source: Texas Comptroller, "Revenue by Source for Fiscal Year 2009," www.window
.state.tx.us/taxbud/revenue.html.

Note: May not sum due to rounding.

Permanent School Fund

a fund set aside to finance education
in Texas; the state's largest source of
investment income.

government, accounting for about one-third of the state's finances. As the federalism discussion in Chapter 2 illustrates, some of these federal monies generally come with strings attached while others pay for programs in which the state and federal government partner. These large dollar amounts account for much of state leaders' willingness to accept federal rules.

Relative to other states, Texas has not fared that well with federal dollars. A study by the Tax Foundation found that in 2004 Texas ranked thirty-sixth out of fifty states on federal funds received relative to federal taxes paid by residents of the state. Overall, Texas received $0.94 for every $1.00 Texans paid in federal taxes.[6]

Licensing and Lottery Funds

Rounding out the revenue picture for Texas are various funding sources that together account for about one-fifth of all state revenues. Some of this money comes from the licensing of various professions and businesses. While these fees resemble taxes on certain professions, the argument that they simply offset some of the specific expenses associated with licensing justifies counting these fees as something different from taxes. In addition, the state receives money from fines paid by those found guilty of traffic and other offenses.

In 2009, the state received over $1.3 billion in income from returns on its bank balances and other investments. The largest source of investment income came from the state's **Permanent School Fund,** a fund set aside to finance education in Texas.

Texas also makes money from a state lottery. Half of the proceeds of lottery ticket sales go into the prizes, with the state and retailers dividing the rest. In 2009, the state brought in $1.6 billion based on $3.7 billion in lottery ticket sales. Of that $1.6 billion, just under $1 billion was used to help fund public education in Texas. While criticized by a variety of groups, the lottery remains a part of Texas state finances for the same reason as the other taxes, fees, and revenue sources noted here: no one has found a more popular way to replace the money it generates. For example, many conservative members of the Texas Legislature find the state's profits from gambling distasteful. However, eliminating the Texas lottery would require increasing taxes or cutting popular programs to offset the revenue lost. Thus, taking this revenue source off the books would be politically difficult.

Spending and Budgeting

 exas government has not always been frugal. During the three years of Mirabeau Lamar's presidency, the government of Texas spent about $4.85 million while taking in only about $1.08 million.[7] Lamar had reversed Sam Houston's policy of cooperating with the Native American tribes, and the hostilities spawned by Lamar's desire to wipe Native Americans off the face of the state cost Texas dearly. By contrast, Houston's administration spent only about half a million dollars in the three years after Lamar's presidency.

As the Texas economy changes and Texans' expectations for government change, spending in Texas shifts. One of the fundamental causes of a growing state budget is a growing state population. For example, 2006 saw spending on public safety and corrections surge by 27.8 percent, in part because more Texans means more crime. As Table 9.3 details, Texas spends its money on a wide array of functions. While some details of the policies in these areas will be discussed later in this chapter, our concern here is how overall spending is managed.

Texas has a **"pay-as-you-go" system** that requires a balanced budget and permits borrowing only under a very few circumstances. The Texas Constitution provides that state borrowing cannot exceed $200,000 unless such borrowing is needed to "repel invasion, suppress insurrection, or defend the State in war" or unless such borrowing is approved by voters. The Texas Legislature may declare an emergency, but doing so requires getting a four-fifths vote of each house before the spending limit can be exceeded.[8]

While many Texans might assume that balancing the state budget is relatively simple, the system created to ensure that the budget stays balanced has spawned some unique features in Texas government, especially in the role of the Comptroller of Public Accounts. At the beginning of each legislative session, the Texas Constitution requires that the comptroller certify how much money will be in the state's accounts in the two years ahead that the legislature is budgeting for. For example, when the Texas Legislature convened in January 2009, Comptroller Susan Combs reported to the legislature that revenue "from all sources and for all purposes should total $167.7 billion."[9] This estimate from the comptroller effectively became the ceiling for state spending that the legislature had to operate under. The constitution also provides that a bill cannot be considered passed by the legislature unless the comptroller has authorized that the amount to be spent by the bill is available. If the comptroller finds that legislation would exceed the state's budget, the comptroller must notify the legislature so that additional revenue can be found or the appropriation in the bill reduced. These provisions put the Texas comptroller in a unique—and powerful—position. As former comptroller Carole Strayhorn pointed out, "The comptroller's office is a constitutional office; there's nothing like it in any other state. I tell the legislature what they can spend, and I certify that the budget is balanced. Unless and until I certify that budget, there is no appropriations bill, and there is nothing for the governor to line-item veto."[10]

The constitution does allow the state to sell revenue bonds to finance activities specified in Article 3. These bonds are sold to investors and then paid back with the

Table 9.3 State Spending by Function, Fiscal Year 2009

GOVERNMENT FUNCTION	AMOUNT	PERCENTAGE OF TOTAL
General government—executive departments	$2,475,761,834	2.80%
General government—legislative	$141,750,457	0.20%
General government—judicial	$254,971,650	0.30%
Education	$33,120,732,460	37.40%
Employee benefits	$2,928,101,148	3.30%
Health and human services	$33,492,032,588	37.80%
Public safety and corrections	$5,043,393,457	5.70%
Transportation	$6,722,847,158	7.60%
Natural resources/recreational services	$2,069,187,656	2.30%
Regulatory agencies	$356,325,497	0.40%
Lottery winnings paid	$491,322,426	0.60%
Debt service	$1,005,304,449	1.10%
Capital outlay	$473,903,973	0.50%
Total net expenditures	$88,575,634,753	

Source: Texas Comptroller, "Texas Annual Cash Report, Fiscal Year 2009," http://www.window.state.tx.us/taxbud/expend.html.

"Pay-as-you-go" system
a fiscal discipline, adopted by Texas and many other states, that requires a balanced budget and permits borrowing only under a very few circumstances.

Table 9.4 Trends in Spending, 1978–2009

FISCAL YEAR	TOTAL EXPENDITURES
1978	$7,864,096,032
1979	$8,600,168,100
1980	$10,210,907,514
1981	$11,367,553,831
1982	$12,074,204,469
1983	$13,539,476,462
1984	$14,348,917,194
1985	$16,526,569,692
1986	$17,692,682,714
1987	$17,918,188,233
1988	$19,432,790,686
1989	$20,695,147,589
1990	$22,680,257,166
1991	$25,602,753,536
1992	$29,290,095,003
1993	$33,388,708,598
1994	$35,638,096,003
1995	$39,337,381,101
1996	$39,669,455,477
1997	$41,460,006,691
1998	$43,223,731,907
1999	$45,687,044,389
2000	$49,707,754,236
2001	$52,669,367,487
2002	$55,739,143,025
2003	$60,270,447,962
2004	$60,718,645,275
2005	$64,693,009,292
2006	$68,833,163,941
2007	$74,500,815,546
2008	$81,935,831,778
2009	$88,575,634,753

Source: Texas Comptroller, "Texas Expenditure History by Function," www.cpa.state.tx.us/taxbud/expend_hist.html.

revenue from the services they provide. For example, Texas often issues tuition revenue bonds that may pay for new buildings on college campuses with student fees set aside to pay back the debt. Overall, Texas has a very low state debt burden; in 2007 it ranked last among the ten most-populous states in state debt per capita. At the end of the 2009 budget year, Texas had about $34 billion in outstanding state bonds.[11]

The Legislative Budget Board (LBB) was created in 1949 to help coordinate the budgeting process in Texas, a process that had previously been a haphazard collection of individual appropriations bills. As outlined in Chapter 3, the LBB is co-chaired by the Speaker of the Texas House and the lieutenant governor. The presence of the presiding officers of both houses, as well as the chairs of key committees, ensures that the LBB wields tremendous political clout.

The LBB is responsible for budgeting, looking at the balance of taxing and spending as well as the performance of state agencies. While the LBB enjoys tremendous influence because it prepares the initial budget estimate that will be considered during the legislative session, its work continues beyond the initial proposal. During the legislative session the LBB staff provides analysis for the legislative committees involved in budgeting. Texas law requires each bill in the legislature to have a "fiscal note" prepared by the LBB staff that estimates the cost of the bill. Because elected officials tend to want to spend more than they have, many critics feel that the fiscal notes have become politicized and that they often ignore the true costs of bills favored by the leadership. At the end of the 2007 legislative session, Governor Perry complained that fiscal notes were no longer providing accurate pictures of the costs of legislation and warned that he would no longer sign bills with inaccurate fiscal notes.[12]

Between sessions, the LBB or the governor may recommend prohibiting a state agency from spending money appropriated to it by the legislature. The LBB or the governor may also transfer money from one state agency to another or change the purpose for which an appropriation was made. Such recommendations by the LBB must be approved by the governor in order to go into effect while recommendations by the governor require approval by the LBB.

While the state's constitution establishes numerous barriers to state debt, these provisions have not always proved enough to stop increased state spending. Despite the fact that Texas has been a conservative state, spending continues to rise. As Table 9.4 demonstrates, spending in the state has been increasing steadily for the past thirty years. Some of this increase can be explained by inflation and the fact that the state's population has roughly doubled in the same time frame. However, Texas's government has grown dramatically, under both Republicans and Democrats, and this growth reflects the increased demands of a growing and changing state.

Education Policy

During 2009 over 6 million Texans were in the state's educational system at some level. About 573,000 were in nursery school, preschool, or kindergarten; 1.8 million were in elementary school (grades 1–5); another 1 million were in middle school (grades 6–8); and 1.3 million were in high school (grades 9–12).[13] In addition, 1.36 million people were enrolled in institutions of higher education and almost 90,000 were enrolled in community and state colleges or state technical colleges (Table 9.5).

Education is important even to those Texans not in school because the state's education system strengthens the economy of the state by providing the state's businesses with the qualified workforce needed to be competitive today, while the research conducted at the state's universities leads to the innovations needed for the future. The importance of schools to the state's businesses was reflected in 2007 when a new group calling itself "Raise Your Hand, Texas" sought educational reforms. Although the organization is chaired by the former lieutenant governor, Bill Ratliff, most of the board members are current or former heads of major corporations like Texas Instruments, Continental Airlines, and AT&T, reflecting the ongoing interest of business in public education.

Table 9.5 School Enrollment, 2009

SCHOOL TYPE	ENROLLMENT
Kindergarten and earlier	573,656
Elementary (1–5)	1,826,286
Middle (6–8)	1,031,877
High (9–12)	1,296,385
Total K–12	*4,728,204*
State-funded workforce continuing education	89,908
Two- and four-year colleges and universities	1,225,071
Medical, dental, and health-related institutions	18,646
Total higher education	*1,333,625*
Total enrollment	6,061,829

Sources: Texas Education Agency, *Pocket Edition, 2008–2009 Texas Public School Statistics*, http://ritter.tea.state.tx.us/perfreport/pocked/2009/pocked0809.pdf; Texas Higher Education Data, http://www.txhighereddata.org/.

Public Schools: Education in Grades K–12

Education policy in the state's public schools is especially complicated because it brings together the efforts, money, and rules of federal, state, and local governments. In the 2007–2008 school year, Texas public schools received 45.7 percent of their revenues from local taxes, 44.8 percent from the state, and 9.5 percent from the federal government. As the sources of money indicate, while federal laws like No Child Left Behind have continued to increase federal involvement in Texas public schools, the financial responsibility for schools remains mostly with state and local officials.

Combined, state and local government spent over $51 billion on Texas public schools, averaging $11,024 per pupil.[14] Given the large investment of tax dollars and with the future of the state's children at stake, the education issue is primed for conflict. At the same time, various political groups seeking to bring their concerns into the schools up the ante, triggering debates about emotional issues like prayer and contraceptives as well as other societal concerns.

Political battles over education are nothing new, predating the state and even the Republic. The authors of the Texas Declaration of Independence included in their list of grievances that Mexico had "failed to establish any public system of education, although possessed of almost boundless resources (the public domain) and, although, it is an axiom, in political science, that unless a people are educated and enlightened it is idle to expect the continuance of civil liberty, or the capacity for self-government." During his presidency Mirabeau Lamar earned the title of "Father of Texas Education"[15] by championing education in the new republic and setting aside three leagues of land for each county to support elementary schools. Despite Lamar's vision, the limited value of this land combined with Texans' reluctance to finance schools and the preference of many for private schools delayed realization of a public school system until the Constitution of 1868 centralized the public schools.

James Leininger

Dr. James Leininger is a man on a mission to transform education in Texas. Leininger began his journey to become the state's leading advocate of school vouchers twenty years ago when he discovered that some of the employees of his very successful hospital bed company were functionally illiterate despite having high school diplomas. Initially, he tried to help by personally sponsoring a mentoring program. When his mentoring program failed to produce change, Leininger became interested in vouchers, certificates given to parents that could be used to pay for education for their children at the school of their choice, as a means of allowing students to find their way into better schools. He began by offering scholarships to help poor students pay the $3,000 needed to attend public schools in other districts or private schools. Over the years, students in his privately funded scholarship program have enjoyed a 100-percent graduation rate and 95 percent have gone on to college.

In 1993 Leininger began working with the Texas Legislature to create a state-funded voucher system. In the years since, he has backed voucher-friendly candidates and worked directly with the legislature. In the 2006 election he pumped over $5 million into campaigns, backing Republican candidates who favored vouchers. In five races, Leininger backed Republican challengers to the Republican incumbents in that party's primary, in one race accounting for 96 percent of a candidate's campaign funds. While the flood of money was alarming to some, Leininger's massive spending generally failed to be decisive. Despite spending about $2.5 million in five Republican primary races, three of the five candidates that Leininger backed failed to unseat the incumbent.

In 2007 Leininger announced that he would be ending his privately financed voucher program for 2,000 students and urged the legislature to approve a state-funded system. While he has ended his own program Leininger plans on continuing to support pro-voucher candidates and a statewide voucher program in Texas.

While Leininger has not won approval for vouchers, he has been attacked for his efforts to reform education. Leininger attributes the bad press coverage he has received to misunderstanding and misrepresentation of the voucher issue. However, some of the concerns emerge from the fact of one person playing such a large role in an election.

The foundation of the modern public school system in Texas was laid in 1949 when the legislature passed the Gilmer-Aikin Act (named for Rep. Claud Gilmer and Sen. A. M. Aikin) that guaranteed Texas children twelve years of school with a minimum of 175 days of instruction per year. The legislation also redesigned the state's governance of public education by replacing the nine-person appointed State Board of Education with commissioners elected by voters in districts.

Texas education was further transformed by the civil rights era, although change proved slow. In 1954, the U.S. Supreme Court issued the landmark *Brown v. Board of Education*[16] decision that declared segregated public schools to be a violation of the Equal Protection Clause of the U.S. Constitution. Despite the Court's unanimous agreement in the original decision and in a follow-up decision known as *Brown II*[17] handed down in 1955 and calling for desegregation "with all deliberate speed," little progress was seen in Texas in the decade after the *Brown* decisions, and students in many areas remained separated by race. Eventually, the U.S. Department of Justice filed a lawsuit against the State of Texas resulting in a 1970 decision by Judge William Wayne Justice, the chief judge of the U.S. District Court for the Eastern District in Tyler, to desegregate the state's public schools and give the court authority to oversee the state's implementation of desegregation.[18]

Since that time Texas has labored to improve the quality of public schools through various reform movements, while still addressing the need for equality. In the 1980s the Perot committee, led by wealthy businessman H. Ross Perot, pushed for reforms and saw the Texas Legislature adopt many of its recommendations in a special session in the summer of 1984. The **Education Reform Act** required that teachers and administrators take the "Texas Examination of Current Administrators and Teachers" (TECAT) to assure basic competency before being recertified. Students were also tested periodically, beginning Texas's long experimentation with standardized testing that would ultimately spread across the nation during the presidency of George W. Bush. The act also included the "no-pass, no-play" rule that kept students with an average below 70 in any subject from taking part in extracurricular activities. The new law also called for more funding for poor school districts that lacked resources because of the reliance on local property taxes to fund schools. Some of these reforms proved unpopular as "no pass" sometimes meant "no play" for high school football players. Additionally, poor school districts felt they did not receive enough money; others resented the increased taxes needed to equalize school districts. While these reforms eventually cost then governor Mark White his reelection bid, most of the reforms he signed into law have endured.

Despite the end of legal segregation, the inequality between school districts remains one of the most vexing problems in Texas politics. Texas traditionally used a system of local control and local financing for its public schools. While the Texas Legislature mandated a statewide curriculum in 1981 and continues to dictate most of what local schools must teach, much of the financial responsibility for these mandates remains with the local school district. This reliance on local funding left the public schools largely dependent on property taxes, meaning that school districts located in areas with high property values were able to provide more resources for their students, while other school districts have had to get by with much less.

In 1989, the Texas Supreme Court's unanimous decision in *Edgewood Independent School District v. Kirby*[19] forced the funding issue, when the court ruled that Texas's system violated the Texas Constitution's requirement of free and efficient schools. The court noted that two schools in Bexar County illustrated the inequity as the Edgewood Independent School District had $38,854 in property taxes per student while Alamo Heights had $570,109 in property taxes per student. After three failed special sessions of the legislature, the fourth session produced a bill to raise sales taxes one-quarter of a cent and increase taxes on cigarettes. While this financing scheme did not satisfy the court, it did hold off further reform (thanks to court appeals by the state) until the early 1990s. In 1993, the Texas Legislature passed a law that established an equalized wealth level for schools and created a process for redistributing money between districts. In subsequent years, this law became known as the "Robin Hood" plan because it took money from "rich" school districts and gave it to "poor" districts. During a 2006 special session of the Texas Legislature called to try to resolve the inequality, the legislature expanded the business tax in

Education Reform Act
a 1984 statute that requires teachers and school administrators to take a test to assure basic competency before being recertified; students are also tested periodically to monitor progress and are required to pass an exam before being allowed to graduate.

an effort to provide sufficient funding for the state's schools. However, this did not offset the accompanying cut in property taxes mandated by the legislature, and as a result 60 percent of schools are expected to have to make use of their reserve funds to meet operating expenses in the 2010–2011 school year.[20] Advocates of under-funded school districts are planning another lawsuit that will likely drag the legislature back into the school funding battle again.

In the 2008–2009 school year, Texas had 8,322 schools in 1,235 school districts and charter schools. These schools educate about 4.7 million people, using about 327,000 teachers and another 319,000 administrators and support staff.[21] Today, the system is run by the Texas Education Agency, which is overseen by a commissioner of education appointed by the governor, and a State Board of Education (SBOE) composed of fifteen members elected from districts, with the chair appointed by the governor. The SBOE meets every few months and decides broad education issues like curriculum and standards for passing state-mandated exams.

States, and increasingly the national government, have been demanding more accountability from local school districts, and Texas has become a focal point of the debate on accountability because of the state's early embrace of standardized testing and George W. Bush's rise to the presidency based partly on his promise to do for the nation's schools what he had done for the Texas public schools. Actually, the assessment craze did not begin with Bush. As mentioned earlier, the Education Reform Act signed into law by Governor Mark White in 1984 required students in odd-numbered grades to take tests in language arts and math. It also required students to pass an exam before they could receive their diploma. In 1990, the **Texas Assessment of Academic Skills (TAAS)** was implemented and used to create higher standards for state assessment. In 2003, TAAS was replaced by **Texas Assessment of Knowledge and Skills (TAKS).** The TAKS exams test students annually on reading in grades 3 through 9 and mathematics in grades 3 through 11. Students also are tested on writing in grades 4 and 7; on English Language Arts in grades 10 and 11; on science in grades 5, 10, and 11; and on social studies in grades 8, 10, and 11. These tests are designed to create a standard by which student progress can be tracked and schools evaluated based on that progress. In 2006, 81 percent of Texas schools met the standards of the federal government's **"No Child Left Behind" Act (NCLB).** However, 291 Texas schools faced penalties under NCLB for failure to demonstrate progress on test scores annually for two years in a row. After two years of failing to show progress, schools that receive federal money to help low-income students are required to allow students to transfer to another campus (and provide transportation). After three years without progress, schools are required to provide extra tutoring or other help for students.

These exams have spawned some unintended consequences. Studies funded by the *Dallas Morning News* found evidence of massive amounts of cheating on the 2005 and 2006 exams. According to the newspaper's analysis, more than 50,000 students' exams showed evidence of cheating. Evidence of cheating was three times as frequent in schools that had been underperforming—where the pressure to cheat would have been greatest. For example, in one previously underperforming school district, science scores went from 23 percent below the state average to 14 percent above; evidence of cheating was found in half of the district's eleventh grade science exams.[22] Such results were eight times more common in the eleventh grade exams that determine graduation than at other grade levels. Confronted with these figures, Texas officials generally were content to call these results "anomalies" rather than proof of cheating.[23] Because schools see their ratings and teachers see their raises tied to test scores, concerns go beyond student cheating and extend to "educator-led"

Texas Assessment of Academic Skills (TAAS)

a standardized test implemented in 1990 to create higher standards for state educational assessment.

Texas Assessment of Knowledge and Skills (TAKS)

replaced TAAS in 2003; a standardized test given to students starting in grade 3 to assess reading and math skills; also mandates periodic tests in writing, language arts, science, and social sciences.

"No Child Left Behind" Act (NCLB)

the federal education act, based on the Texas standardized testing statutes, that requires schools to institute mandatory testing to track student progress and evaluates schools based on that progress.

cheating, in which teachers or school administrators aid students or change answers after the exam to produce higher passing rates. Further, state officials have little incentive to follow up on the evidence of cheating, since it would undermine their claims to progress.

In 2007, the Texas Legislature removed the requirement that seniors pass the TAKS test before they could graduate after 16 percent of Texas seniors failed to pass the test by graduation, meaning that 40,182 students did not graduate with their classmates in the spring of that year. While some school districts allowed students who had met other requirements to participate in graduation ceremonies, many school districts rejected students' pleas to be allowed to walk across the stage with their classmates. Under the revised law, Texas high school students will no longer be taking the annual TAKS exams; instead, they will be required to take separate end-of-course exams at the end of each year in high school in the four core subject areas: English, math, science, and social studies. Students will have to score an average of 70 on the tests in each subject in order to graduate; the tests must count for 15 percent of a student's final grade in the class.

While the roots of the federal government's No Child Left Behind law may be in Texas, the state, like every other state, has battled parts of this federal law. States have challenged federal standards and asserted their desire to use their own standards. NCLB was designed to provide accountability in public schools, but very few parents have taken advantage of rules that allow students to transfer out of low-performing schools. Texans in general have some doubts about the consequences of NCLB, with a 2006 poll finding 56 percent of Texans worried that there is too much emphasis on testing, 27 percent saying there is the right amount of testing, and a mere 13 percent preferring more emphasis on testing.[24]

Recently, the debate over school performance has been clouded by the Texas Education Agency's introduction of the "Texas Projection Measure," which uses a complicated formula to predict whether a student will pass TAKS assessments at a future grade. Accountability ratings released in July 2010 saw 31 percent of Texas schools rated "exemplary" and another 37 percent rated "recognized." In 2009, only 8 percent of campuses were rated "exemplary" and 41 percent were rated "recognized."[25] Contrasted with a recent poll that shows that 61 percent of Texans believe academic standards are too low, the TEA's assessment of schools may not provide a credible measure of schools' performance.[26] While the state's system of testing was intended to help citizens evaluate local schools, in fact these credibility concerns leave Texans in doubt about the validity and value of these high-stakes tests in public schools, seriously undermining the entire process.

As if fighting over funding and accountability were not enough, the Texas State Board of Education also attempts to control what is taught in the state's classrooms through a set of increasingly detailed standards known as the Texas Essential Knowledge and Skills (TEKS), which shapes the 48 million textbooks the state purchases for students. These standards often prove controversial because they include issues ranging from the treatment of evolution in science classes to discussions of race in social studies. Social conservatives have been behind the most recent efforts to transform these standards to meet their worldview, but other groups have politicized the standards before. In 2010, the conservative members of the SBOE won changes to curriculum standards that emphasize the virtues of a free market system and deemphasize the concept of separation of church and state. The SBOE's deliberations proved controversial, with several days of tense hearings that attracted national attention and demonstrated how politicized issues like education have become.

Overall, Texas's record on public schools has been mixed. While scores on standardized tests have indicated some progress, Texas's graduation rate (65.1 percent) lags slightly behind the national average (68.8 percent), with pockets of lower rates in some areas, including Houston (42.2 percent), Dallas (42.8 percent) and Fort Worth (50.0). This means that the class of 2010 in Texas saw over 135,000 Texans fail to graduate.[27]

In many ways, the struggles of Texas public schools dramatically reflect the basic dilemmas of public policy. Citizens want as much efficiency as possible, and in response legislators create systems of accountability. However, accountability proves costly and generates unintended consequences, like cheating, which then leads to more oversight, more bureaucracy, and more expense.

Higher Education

The relationship between the state's politicians and the University of Texas has been a stormy one. Located in Austin, right under the nose of the Texas government, the University of Texas has proved an appealing target for political hotheads who have sought to reach across town and squash testy academics. Governor James Ferguson battled with the University of Texas faculty, a battle that helped lead to his impeachment. In the 1940s the regents of the University fired four economics professors who had supported federal labor laws, eliminated funding for social science research, and banned John Dos Passos's *U.S.A.* trilogy shortly before it won a Pulitzer Prize.

Permanent University Fund (PUF)
an endowment funded by mineral rights and other revenue generated by 2.1 million acres of land set aside by the state; investment returns support schools in the University of Texas and Texas A&M systems.

Higher education in Texas has been aided by the **Permanent University Fund (PUF).** The PUF was created by the Constitution of 1876, which added one million acres to the one million acres previously granted to the University of Texas. Initially, the land, spread over nineteen counties in West Texas, generated little money. Most of the value of that land was in grazing leases that netted about $40,000 in 1900. In 1923, the PUF changed dramatically when the Santa Rita well struck oil on university lands, and by 1925 the PUF fund was growing at about $2,000 every day. Today, the PUF totals over ten billion dollars and provides support for schools in the University of Texas and Texas A&M systems. The PUF is an endowment, meaning that the principal from this account cannot be spent and that only investment returns can be used. In recent years these returns have averaged about $350 million dollars a year, which is made available to the eighteen universities and colleges in those systems. PUF funds may be used only for construction and renovation projects or certain "academic excellence" programs.

Today, higher education in Texas brings together a wide variety of institutions seeking to serve students beyond K–12. Texas has 145 institutions of higher education, including 35 public universities, 41 private colleges and universities, 50 public community college districts, 2 independent junior colleges, 7 public technical and state colleges, 9 public health-related institutions, and 1 independent health-related institution.[28] While large institutions like the University of Texas and Texas A&M enjoy the most visibility, the system involves a variety of institutions that may have widely different goals. As the Texas economy continues to diversify, higher education must meet the demands of the global market by providing the state's citizens with the increasingly diverse set of skills required to maintain competitiveness.

Higher Education Coordinating Board
a group of thirteen appointed by the governor for six-year terms to oversee higher education policy in Texas.

Much of higher education policy in Texas is overseen by the **Higher Education Coordinating Board,** which is made up of thirteen citizens appointed by the governor for six-year terms. The governor also appoints the chair and vice chair.

No board member may be employed in education or serve on a community college board of trustees. The board selects a full-time commissioner of higher education to run the organization. The board meets quarterly and is responsible for setting the broad direction of education policy—within the boundaries established by Texas law. For example, in October 2000 the Higher Education Coordinating Board approved "Closing the Gaps," a long-term plan intended to guide higher education in Texas for the next fifteen years. It proposed adding 500,000 students to the rolls of higher education institutions, increasing the number of degrees awarded, and improving the quality of programs and research, all by 2015.

The state's universities find themselves caught between conflicting demands. In 2010, the state's colleges and universities had to return 5 percent of their current budget and then start mapping out 10 percent in budget cuts for the coming years. These cuts came at an especially difficult time as many people were returning to college campuses in response to the economic downturn. At the same time, the Higher Education Coordinating Board proposed a new funding formula that shifted the basis of calculation from the number of students enrolled at the beginning of the semester to the number of students who actually finished the semester. While state leaders want more students brought into higher education this new formulation, which places an emphasis on funding students likely to succeed, may encourage schools to turn away some at-risk students.

Access

If a college degree is a ticket to a better future, a key question is who has access to higher education in Texas. The coordinating board reported in 2006 that African Americans and Hispanics made up about 55 percent of Texas's college-aged population, but only 36 percent of the students in higher education in the state.[29] The Texas appellate courts specifically addressed the issue of minorities in higher education in 1996 in *Hopwood v. Texas*;[30] the courts ruled that race-based admission violated the U.S. Constitution. That standard has been loosened by a subsequent U.S. Supreme Court case which ruled that although race couldn't be the sole deciding factor, it could be used as a factor in university admissions decisions. The use of race in university admissions remains a complicated matter. In 1997, the Texas Legislature approved a law that guaranteed students in the top 10 percent of their high school class admission to any university in the state. While this allows every community in the state a chance to place their students in the most exclusive universities, critics complain that it overlooks some students from highly competitive school districts and demanding private schools. In 2009, the University of Texas and its allies won their battle to modify the law and restrict the students automatically admitted to the University of Texas to those in the top 8 percent. In fall 2006, 71 percent of students entering the University of Texas came in through the top-ten-percent rule, limiting the school's ability to bring in students from out of state or those who have distinguished themselves through special abilities, like music, that are not fully reflected in a student's general academic performance.

The battle over college admissions reflects issues of representation found in many policy areas. The coalition that stood behind the ten-percent rule included not just representatives of minority and border districts whose populations were the initial focus of the legislation, but legislators from rural districts as well who saw it as a means of ensuring that their students had a chance to attend the University of Texas and Texas A&M too.

Beyond admissions, tuition is a major access issue because tuition and fees pose a barrier to college for many students as costs rise. In 2003, the state legislature deregulated tuition, allowing each school to raise its tuition as it saw fit. Since then, colleges have responded to declining state funds for schools by turning to their students to make ends meet. By 2008, the average cost of tuition in state schools had risen 63 percent since deregulation.[31]

As Table 9.6 illustrates, the state's success in the classroom has been mixed compared to that of other states. Texas must continue to invest wisely in education as its students prepare to compete for jobs globally. Today, the newest wave of immigrants competing for jobs may arrive digitally, citizens of far-away countries like India and China, who, thanks to the Internet, may be in a position to compete for work as effectively as if they were living next door. These "digital immigrants" are already providing services for Texas firms, ranging from technical assistance in call centers for some of the state's high-tech firms to accounting services outsourced from some of the state's largest corporations.

Table 9.6 State Education Performance Measures

MEASURE	TEXAS	NATIONAL AVERAGE	TEXAS RANKING
Average graduation rates for public high school students, 2006	72.5%	73.4%	35
Percentage of public high schools offering advanced placement in the four core subject areas, 2009	38.0%	33.9%	24
Estimated rate of high school graduates going to college by state rank, 2006	55.4%	62.0%	41
In-state tuition prices at public two-year institutions by state rank, 2010	$1,736	$2,982	4
In-state tuition prices at public four-year institutions by state rank, 2010	$7,724	$6,784	34
Full-time freshman-to-sophomore retention rates at public two-year institutions by state rank, 2007	57.8%	59.0%	18
Full-time freshman-to-sophomore retention rates at public four-year institutions by state rank, 2007	72.8%	78.0%	40
Three-year graduation rates of associate degree-seeking students by state rank, 2007	18.0%	27.8%	40
Six-year graduation rates of bachelor's degree-seeking students by state rank, 2007	50.2%	56.1%	32
Adults ages 25–64 with less than a high school diploma by state rank, 2008	13.2%	11.3%	50
High school graduates going to college by state rank, 2006	55.4%	62.0%	41
Percentage of 25- to 34-year-olds with an associate degree or higher	27.4%	41.6%	41

Source: The College Board, The College Completion Agenda 2010 Progress Report.

Health and Human Services

American federalism has increasingly entwined state government with national policy related to health and human services through federal-state partnerships. Generally, Americans think of such policies as coming from Washington, D.C. In fact, the states play an important role in delivering many of the benefits, in partnership with the federal government. Moreover, each state faces a unique set of challenges. In 2009, for example, Texas had one of the highest rates of poverty (17.2 percent) in the nation, well above the national average of 14.3 percent and over twice the rate in New Hampshire (7.8 percent).[32] Texas is home to three of the nation's five counties of 250,000 or more people with the highest rates of poverty: Cameron (33.5 percent), Hidalgo (34.8 percent), and El Paso (25.2 percent). All told, Texas spends over $25 billion a year on 200 different programs, with 48,000 state workers engaged in the broad category of health and human services. While there is not space here to describe (or even list) all these programs, a few of the state's programs merit some discussion here.

Texas provides assistance to some families through **Temporary Assistance for Needy Families (TANF),** which replaced Aid to Families with Dependent Children (AFDC). Under this program eligible households receive monthly cash payments and Medicaid benefits. Today, recipients must accept the terms of a Personal Responsibility Agreement that requires them to stay free of alcohol or drug abuse, seek and maintain employment, and take part in parenting and other programs if asked. In May 2010 about 48,000 Texas families were receiving TANF, including about 97,000 children and 18,000 adults, with the average recipient receiving about $70 a month.[33]

Families may also qualify for the **State Nutritional Action Plans (SNAP)** (Texas's version of the Food Stamps program) that helps low-income seniors, people with disabilities, low-income single people, and families in need buy food from local retailers. While the benefits are available to adults with no children, they must work at least twenty hours a week or meet other work requirements in order to qualify. Adults without dependent children that do not meet work requirements are limited to three months of benefits in a thirty-six-month period. These benefits cannot be used for hot ready-to-eat foods, cigarettes, alcoholic beverages, cosmetics, or paper goods. In July 2010 almost 3.5 million Texans were receiving an average of $124 a month in benefits. The majority of recipients (1.95 million) were children under eighteen.

Health care is quickly becoming a major issue in American politics, and Texas faces an especially daunting task. In 2009, Texas had the highest percentage of people without health insurance (26.1 percent), well over the national average of 16.7 percent uninsured, and dramatically higher than Massachusetts, the state with the lowest rate (4.4 percent).[34] Texas also led the nation in the highest percentage of uninsured children (21 percent).

A variety of programs address the healthcare needs of Texans. **Medicare** is a federal health insurance program that serves about 2.85 million Texans who average about $8,000 in benefits each year. Medicare is available to senior citizens who have worked and paid into the Medicaid system for ten or more years. This means that today about 82 percent of the state's Medicare recipients are age 65 or over; the remainder qualify for Medicare because of disability. There are actually several components to Medicare. Part A covers in-patient hospital care, while Part B covers doctors' fees and other "out-patient" costs. In 2003, President George W. Bush signed legislation adding "Part D," which extended Medicare coverage to provide prescription drugs.

Temporary Assistance for Needy Families (TANF)
federal program that provides eligible households with monthly cash payments and Medicaid benefits.

State Nutritional Action Plans (SNAP)
Texas's version of food stamps that helps low-income seniors, people with disabilities, and single people and families in need buy food from local retailers.

Medicare
a federal health insurance program available to senior citizens who have worked and paid into the Medicare system for ten or more years.

Medicaid

a federal program providing medical coverage for low-income people and some elderly and disabled people.

State Children's Health Insurance Program (SCHIP)

a federal-state program that offers health insurance and medical care to the children of families that make too much to qualify for Medicaid but not enough to afford private health insurance.

The **Medicaid** program provides medical coverage for people with low incomes and some elderly or disabled people. Currently, there are almost 3 million people covered by Medicaid, with most (65 percent) under 19 years of age. Medicare has a fixed standard that is consistent across all states, while Medicaid allows each state some discretion in how funds are used. Texas shares the cost of coverage of its citizens with the federal government. For every dollar Texas spends on Medicaid, the federal government matches with about $1.50.

For those families making too much to qualify for Medicaid but not enough to afford private health insurance, the **State Children's Health Insurance Program (SCHIP),** a federal-state program, offers the children in these families health care, including regular checkups, immunizations, prescription drugs, hospital visits, and many other health care services.[35]

The 8,500 employees of the Texas Health and Human Services Commission (HHSC) are responsible for overseeing these policies in the state. Like many Texas agencies, the HHSC is overseen by a council of nine citizens appointed by the governor. The day-to-day operations of the commission are conducted by the executive commissioner, a professional administrator appointed by the governor, who works with the council to develop rules and policies for the commission.

One experiment in privatization in Texas has been in the area of social welfare. Texas has been experimenting with using private contractors to manage call centers and other tasks previously handled by state employees in HHSC. So far, the results have been less than clear. Critics say that service has suffered while the savings have been smaller than expected. Advocates of privatization argue that service in general has been good and that the long-term savings will be significant.

Environmental Policy

Regulation

government rulemaking and enforcement intended to protect citizens from being harmed by private firms.

Given its wide open spaces and the individualistic nature of its citizens, it is perhaps not surprising that concern about the environment has been slow to develop in Texas. Even in a conservative state like Texas, however, there is some need for regulation. **Regulation** can be defined as government rulemaking and enforcement intended to protect citizens from harm by private firms. While federal regulations generally attract the most attention, much of the regulatory task is left to the states.

Texas's first environmental policies were passed after hundreds of Texas oil wells drilled in the late 1890s dumped unusable crude oil onto the ground. Air pollution made its first major appearance in Texas in 1901 when oil from an uncapped well was set on fire by a passing train, sending clouds of black smoke over Beaumont and generating a rain that damaged the paint of the houses in the town.[36] Still, environmental regulation has remained relatively low on Texas's priority list. Until recently, most of the state's environmental policy was focused on protecting the quality of water. Texas did not begin to address air quality until 1965 when the Texas Legislature created the Air Control Board. The board, appointed by the governor, was empowered to monitor air quality in the state, but the law required that the board consider any adverse impact that its rulings might have on existing industries and economic development. In 1990, the Air Control Board was combined with the Texas Water Commission, effectively putting environmental policy in the hands of a single agency, the Texas Natural Resource Conservation Commission (TNRCC). In 2002, the TNRCC's name was changed to **Texas Commission on Environmental Quality (TCEQ).** In 2010, the TCEQ had 2,980 employees working

Texas Commission on Environmental Quality (TCEQ)

the agency that oversees state environmental policy, including air and water quality.

Texas versus California

Anyone who has watched a television game show like The Price Is Right with luxury car models being given away as prizes is familiar with the idea of "California emissions standards." While the U.S. government has enacted a series of minimum standards regarding auto emissions, California has long been at the forefront of this activity, regularly creating standards that exceed those required by the U.S. government. Since the 1970s, California has enacted the most restrictive standards regarding the gases coming out of the exhaust pipes on cars, trucks, and other automobiles. Eleven other states have also enacted auto emission standards beyond the minimum standards set by the U.S. government.

Several agencies in California are involved in the regulation of auto emissions including the California Environmental Protection Agency, the Department of Public Health, and the Department of Consumer Affairs—Bureau of Automotive Repair. Key pollutants subject to regulation include carbon dioxide, hydrocarbons, and ozone. These agencies in the past led the United States in developing additional equipment on vehicles to limit emissions, in requiring the use of unleaded gas, and in mandating routine inspections of vehicles. For example, California required the use of fuel injectors and catalytic converters long before they became standard across the United States. Current efforts by California include those to increase sales of zero-emission vehicles, to encourage the use of alternative fuels, and to boost the fuel efficiency of cars.

Opponents of California's efforts at regulation note that the result of such differing regulations is differences in automobile standards across states. This variation creates additional costs to makers of cars, which is then passed onto the people who buy cars and trucks. In the end, they argue, the United States government should be the appropriate level of government to regulate auto emissions.

Texas, in contrast, maintains little state legislation above and beyond the minimum standards established by the U.S. government. One of the few requirements in Texas is the imposition of annual auto emission standards in metropolitan areas like Houston with consistently high levels of air pollution linked to automobiles. Texas also requires all state, city, and county governments that own fifteen or more vehicles to purchase some low-emission vehicles

Thinking Critically

- How is California a leader in the regulation of auto emissions?
- How does California's attempt to regulate auto emissions affect the size and scope of government?
- Do you think that Texas and other states should set standards that are stricter than those set by the U.S. government?
- What do you think the advantage of Texas adopting stricter emissions standards might be?

out of sixteen offices throughout the state. About 85 percent of the commission's $539 million operating budget for the 2010 fiscal year came from fees it charged clients, with about 9 percent of the budget coming from the federal government and only 3 percent from the state. The surging Texas economy and the growth of Texas's major cities gave the state its share of environmental headaches. Houston and the Dallas–Fort Worth Metroplex have some of the highest ozone levels in the nation, and smog warnings are not unusual in the summer. In 2000, Houston held the distinction of having the worst air quality in the nation, leading to new EPA emission standards for automobiles in those areas.

In the language of economics, government regulation protects citizens from negative externalities. An *externality* occurs when costs are imposed on someone who is not participating in a transaction. For example, a citizen who does not make, own, drive, or ride in an automobile still must live with the pollution created by cars. This is a problem in a free-enterprise system, which assumes that costs and benefits involve just those people buying and selling a product. Those people involved in a transaction express their desire for cleaner or safer products as they shop by favoring products with those qualities and avoiding those without them. An individual not taking part in a transaction has no influence on shaping the characteristics of a product through market participation, thus creating the need for government involvement. In short, if you're not buying or selling a product you have no way of dealing with its impact on your own life without regulation.

While environmental policy has most often been the concern of the federal government, many states have taken their own paths, even with regard to problems that go beyond state lines such as global warming. California, for example, has been a pioneer in aggressively pursuing environmental policies that go well beyond federal standards. In contrast, the TCEQ has found itself battling federal authority in an effort for less strident rules. The federal government's Environmental Protection Agency had rejected the TCEQ's "flexible" permits system that allowed industrial plants to comply with emissions limits for the entire facility rather than the limits for individual emission points within the facility created by federal rules. Texas's approach would have effectively allowed polluters to avoid some federal emission requirements. Texas officials have focused more on protecting the jobs of Texas businesses while federal officials have emphasized public health and safety.

At the same time, Texans worry about the possibility of electricity shortages, resulting in the kind of rolling blackouts that struck California in the early 2000s. In response to the rising demand for power, in 2005 Governor Perry expedited the approval of new coal power plants. TXU, the state's largest energy producer, planned eleven new plants, citing the growing demand for electricity and Texans' fondness for large homes and air conditioning. Despite the power industry's claim that these new coal plants would be cleaner than their predecessors, many Texans resisted the locating of these plants near their homes. This triggered several **NIMBY** ("not-in-my-backyard") battles as communities lobbied to keep the plants away from them, even if the electricity flowed into their homes. Even "green" power has generated some NIMBY debates, as the wind mills and power lines required to transmit the energy they generate blight the landscape and intrude onto citizens' lands.

The Public Utility Commission (PUC) of Texas is charged with protecting consumers. In 1975, the Texas Legislature passed the Public Utility Regulatory Act that created the PUC to regulate the rates and services of telephone companies everywhere in the state, as well as electric, water, and sewer utilities in unincorporated areas of the state. The PUC is headed by three commissioners appointed by the governor to six-year terms. While utility regulation is not an especially exciting topic to most Texans, the rising costs of electricity have awakened citizen interest and drawn the notice of Texas politicians.

Transportation

ransportation has always been a concern in Texas, given the need to connect the broad expanses of a large state and provide farmers a way of transporting their produce to markets. Texas's transitions have been borne on a transportation system that continues to evolve with the state.

In the latter half of the nineteenth century, Texas farmers, usually suspicious of railroads and other big companies, quickly realized that without railroads the state's economic growth would stall because Texas's rivers were not large enough to carry goods. While the Constitution of 1876 had defined railroads in a way that allowed

NIMBY

acronym for "not in my backyard"; local efforts to prevent the situating of potentially harmful activities, such as industrial waste disposal, in nearby areas.

rate regulation, the state began looking for ways to bring the railroads into the state. The Texas Legislature passed a Land Grant Law that offered over 10,000 acres of land for each mile of track the railroads put down. In addition, numerous Texas cities began offering deals to the railroads in hopes of bringing them—and the prosperity and jobs that came with them—to town. Cities competed against each other and money was often passed under the table. As we saw in Chapter 6, some towns, like Abilene, thrived when the railroad arrived while others, like Buffalo Gap, withered when they didn't.

In 1890, Attorney General James Stephen Hogg decided that his office was not able to keep up with the enforcement of regulations on the state's railroads. Hogg advocated for the creation of a Railroad Commission, making the call for a commission a centerpiece of his campaign for governor. While the railroads labeled Hogg "communistic," his reforms were appealing to voters and Hogg became Texas's first native-born governor in 1891.

Texas roads have played a vital role in the economic health of the state for generations. The state's "farm-to-market" roads helped Texas farmers and ranchers bring goods to towns and cities. Since the 1950s, highways have played a vital role in bringing products to store shelves. While Texas today already has over 305,000 miles of public roads, the state's growth demands even more to get people to and from work and to convey goods coming and going north into other states and south into Mexico. Today, most Texans think about transportation policy in terms of rush-hour traffic and urban traffic jams. About 8.5 million Texans ride alone to work every day, while another 1.3 million carpool. On average, Texans have to travel about 25 minutes to work.

Recognizing that past investments in transportation had benefitted the state, Governor Perry in 2004 proposed the next generation of transportation policy: the Trans Texas Corridor. This system would have included over 4,000 miles of roads, railways, and pipelines to move goods from Mexico to Oklahoma. The corridor was to include ten highway lanes and six lines for rail travel, at a cost of about $183 billion over fifty years.[37] To meet this ambitious goal, Perry embraced privatization, allowing companies to build and maintain roads in return for the right to charge citizens tolls to drive on them. Reaction to Perry's plans was mixed. On the one hand, allowing private firms control of some Texas roadways offered the potential of efficiency and savings as the profit incentive motivated these companies to find the least expensive way to provide roads. In addition, privatization would free up money that the state could then invest in other areas. On the other hand, some Texans—both Democrats and Republicans—harbored doubts. Critics worried that Texans could see their land taken by the government through **eminent domain** and then handed to private firms. Resistance was heightened when it became apparent that the Trans Texas Corridor's largest investor would be a Spanish company, Cintra. Because of the concerns about eminent domain and foreign investors, the conservatives most likely to back privatization of government services like roads were also those most likely to oppose the government's taking of private land to build this toll road. This dilemma helped create the discord in the Republican Party this led to challenges within the party to Perry's 2006 reelection campaign and fed the ultimately successful rebellion against his plan in the legislature.

The demise of the Trans Texas Corridor plan did not end the debate over transportation. While Texas has increased its use of toll roads, the Texas Department of Transportation is still struggling to find enough money to build and maintain the roads and railways that Texans rely on every day.

Eminent domain
the power of government to take private property for public use, generally for public functions such as roads.

Private Property and Takings

One of the most pervasive legends in Texas is that of private property. Most Texans view their property as coming exclusively under their own control. However, this is increasingly false.

The idea of "takings" emerges from the Fifth Amendment to the U.S. Constitution that prohibits the taking of private property "for public use, without just compensation." Traditionally, this clause has been examined in the light of eminent domain, the power of government to take property for public use. Generally, eminent domain has been used to take private property for government use for public functions such as roads. Recently, the limits of eminent domain have been tested as the government has taken private property for public uses like the Dallas Cowboys' new stadium in Arlington or toll roads operated by private firms. In this more expansive use of power, the taking of private property is justified for general economic development, even though privately owned, that will create jobs and other advantages for the entire community. Thus "public use," doesn't exclude private profit.

Another use of the takings label deals with the impact of regulation on the value of private property. One example of regulatory takings would be environmental regulations that place restrictions on the uses of private property designated as "wetlands." These rules restricting how individuals use their property may diminish the value of property. In this case, the government is restricting use of property to promote the general welfare, which is certainly a public concern. However, for many years the courts did not support compensating citizens for regulatory takings. Restrictions on land use are not unique to environmental regulation. Property owners in cities face restrictions on how they use their land. Zoning rules prohibit building businesses in residential areas. However, environmental regulations reach outside cities to the rural areas, where many people have retreated in their attempt to avoid rules imposed by government and their neighbors.

The problem of takings reflects a cost of government that frequently does not show up on the balance sheet of costs and benefits. Sometimes, government regulation requires costly action, like altering coal plants to produce less pollution, with the cost being passed along as higher utility bills. At other times, government policies restrict citizens' uses and enjoyment of their own property.

However, without some ability to extend its authority onto private property the government would lack the ability to create and enforce meaningful rules related to the environment or public safety, since pollution and other problems don't honor property lines. Without such rules, individuals could block the flow of creeks and cut off water supplies to, or cause flooding for, other citizens. Neighborhoods could find adult businesses placed next to family homes or schools. Thus, the matter of who wins and who loses involves a balancing act in which the government must weigh the public safety against the rights of individual property owners.

The divisions among both Republicans and Democrats on the Trans Texas Corridor illustrates that state policy often fails to break down neatly as liberal versus conservative or Republican versus Democrat. While some conservatives embraced the potential efficiencies of privatization, others resented the taking of privately owned land for private toll roads. And while some liberal constituencies favored the expansion of roadways and the opening of the door to increased trade with Mexico, others doubted the benefits of free trade, worrying about a flood of cheap goods and labor from Mexico. Transportation policy is an example of how Texas's economic growth and rapid change continuously redefine politics and create new challenges.

Immigration

Perhaps the most dynamic and challenging policy issue facing Texas today is immigration. It shouldn't be surprising that a president from Texas remained conflicted in the nation's debate over immigration. Coming from one of the largest destinations for illegal immigrants, some expected President George W. Bush to be an avid advocate of tight border security and "getting tough" on illegal immigration. Because Texas provides education and other social programs for immigrants, you might expect an ex-governor of Texas to have wanted to aggressively turn away immigrants at the border. However, the Texas economy's heavy reliance on immigrant labor convinced Bush that immigrant workers were an important part of the Texas and American economies. The fact that Bush has had more experience with the issue of illegal immigration than most people, but holds a less ideological view than most Americans, is instructive. As is often the case, the immigration issue is more complicated than it would first appear, and President Bush's approach reflected the complicated relationship between Texas and immigrants. Today, Governor Perry, another staunch conservative, has rejected some of the most dramatic elements of the Arizona immigration law at the center of current debate, despite the law's popularity with some conservatives. Clearly, there's more to the immigration issue.

In some ways, the debate over illegal immigrants tells us more about Texas politics than about immigration. Immigration is a federal issue, and it is the U.S. Department of Homeland Security's Citizenship and Immigration Services that takes the lead in sealing the U.S. border and managing the flow of legal immigrants into the country. Despite this, many state and local officials make public proclamations and pass new rules aimed at immigration.

Some of this conflict results from differences among Texans over who bears the costs and reaps the benefits of immigrants. In fact, the costs and benefits are spread unevenly, benefitting some and costing others. It is estimated that while illegal immigrants cost the state of Texas $1.16 billion, they pay $1.58 billion in state taxes and fees. In contrast, local governments in Texas pay about $1.44 billion in costs like indigent care, law enforcement, and other services that stem from the immigrants while generating only $513 million in taxes. In addition, it costs local school districts about $957 billion to educate the estimated 151,000 children of illegal workers. While an increase in government taxing and spending results from the presence of an estimated 1.4 million undocumented immigrants in Texas, in fact the Texas Comptroller's Office has estimated that their *absence* would cost the state's economy $17.7 billion dollars.[38] The distribution of costs and benefits to the government and the private sector reflects the origins of some divisions. Clearly many Texas cities and school districts bear a disproportionate burden from illegal immigration. At the same time, the profit generated by their labors clearly benefits the state. The forces of the free market will continue to draw immigrants into the U.S. economy, if not into citizenship.

The experience of Cactus, Texas, illustrates the degree to which some businesses and local economies rely on immigrant labor. On December 12, 2006, Immigration and Customs Enforcement (ICE) officers raided the Swift meat-packing plants in Cactus, a small town of 2,639 in the Texas Panhandle, arresting 292 workers. Some of those arrested had lived and worked in Cactus for over fifteen years. The arrest and deportation of these workers left families torn apart and large numbers of job openings that Swift scrambled to fill. As these families and the community tried to

patch themselves together, the plant, now woefully shorthanded, found itself offering employees who referred good job candidates a bonus of $650 for unskilled
candidates and $1,500 for experienced ones.[39]

While the influx of people into the United States remains a federal issue, border states like Texas bear the burden of following up on the promises of the U.S.
Constitution. One of the most important legal cases in the dispute over illegal
immigration occurred in Tyler, Texas. In the 1982 case *Plyler v. Doe*,[40] the U.S.
Supreme Court ruled that School Superintendent Jim Plyler could not charge
illegal immigrants residing in Tyler $1,000 in tuition to attend public schools in
Tyler. In the majority opinion written by Justice William Brennan, himself the
son of Irish immigrants, the Court pointed out that the Fourteenth Amendment
required that states provide equal protection of the law to "any person within its
jurisdiction" and that the language of that amendment had been intentionally
designed to protect the rights of aliens living in the United States. Reflecting on
the decision more than twenty years later, in 2007, Plyler remarked, "It would
have been one of the worst things to happen in education—they'd cost more not
being educated."[41]

The issue of immigration captures Texas's ongoing struggle with change and
highlights the two political parties' attempts to balance new and old. The political
dynamic behind one aspect of the immigration debate was illustrated by former
Republican congressman Dick Armey, for years one of the state's leading conservatives, who complained that after years of Republicans courting Hispanic voters
in Texas his party was throwing away its future on the immigration issue: "Who
is the genius that said, 'Now that we've identified that [the Hispanic commu-
nity] is the fastest growing demographic in American, let's do everything we can
to make sure we offend them?' Who is the genius that came up with that bright
idea?"[42]

Conclusion

While some Texans worry that immigration from Mexico will transform the politics of Texas, a broader view of Texas history reveals that change is the Texas way of life. Native American populations were challenged by the Spanish and later the Mexican governments; those governments would, in turn, see themselves pushed out by the Anglo settlers who first moved Texas to independence and then to statehood. Texas's union with the United States was quickly undone by secession and the decision to join the Confederate States. The end of the Civil War saw Texas's return to the United States, but under terms imposed by the Radical Republicans, whose Reconstruction government was rooted in the North. Eventually, Reconstruction ended, leaving Texas to find its way through a century that saw more demographic than political change. During the last century and a quarter Texas has seen its population explode as immigrants from all over the United States and the world converged on the state, once again seeking the opportunity promised by Texas.

Texas has never stayed the same, and today it remains in the enviable position of being a place where people see opportunity. The promise of opportunities that draws one set of people to Texas today will inevitably draw others in the future, and the immigrants from Central and South America are only the latest chapter in the changes that define the state.

Occasionally, Texans become so engrossed in recounting our colorful and larger-than-life traditions that we don't notice that dramatic events like the Alamo are the markers of great change, but change has always been with us. This is not surprising. As each regime departs, it leaves behind a little of its legacy, its traditions, and its own legends. While not always entirely compatible, these myths form a kind of patchwork quilt that makes up the Texas of today.

Texas's myths and legends are often stories of change. Stephen F. Austin became the Father of Texas by bringing new settlers to Texas before he played a key role in the revolutionary movement that the new settlers brought about. The battle of the Alamo is a pivotal point in the transition from Mexican to American rule and immediately served as a powerful symbol that motivated the Texas army to defeat Santa Anna's army at San Jacinto.

What is especially appealing about many of Texas's legends is the degree to which we all share them. Standing in line to visit the Alamo, you will encounter people of every race. These people are not drawn to the Alamo because the battle there was between the Anglo and Mexican forces but because the battle defines a dynamic state that draws people of every race and nationality. The defenders of the Alamo took their stand for change rather than against it, and future generations of Texans will—each in their own way—do the same.

Key Terms

ad-valorem tax
agenda setting
appraisal
distributive policy
Education Reform Act (1984)
eminent domain

excise tax
fiscal policy
franchise tax
general sales tax
Higher Education Coordinating Board
income tax
Medicaid
Medicare
NIMBY
"No Child Left Behind" Act (NCLB)
"pay-as-you-go" system
Permanent School Fund
Permanent University Fund (PUF)
policy
policy adoption
policy evaluation
policy formation
policy implementation
progressive tax
property tax
redistributive policy
regressive tax
regulation
regulatory policy
severance tax
sin tax
State Children's Health Insurance Program (SCHIP)
State Nutritional Action Plans (SNAP)
subsidy
Temporary Assistance for Needy Families (TANF)
Texas Assessment of Academic Skills (TAAS)
Texas Assessment of Knowledge and Skills (TAKS)
Texas Commission on Environmental Quality (TCEQ)

Explore this subject further at http://lonestar.cqpress.com, where you'll find chapter summaries, practice quizzes, key word flash cards, and additional suggested resources.

Declaration of Independence of the Republic of Texas

UNANIMOUS
DECLARATION OF INDEPENDENCE,
BY THE
DELEGATES OF THE PEOPLE OF TEXAS,
IN GENERAL CONVENTION,
AT THE TOWN OF WASHINGTON,
ON THE SECOND DAY OF MARCH, 1836

When a government has ceased to protect the lives, liberty and property of the people from whom its legitimate powers are derived, and for the advancement of whose happiness it was instituted; and so far from being a guarantee for the enjoyment of those inestimable and inalienable rights, becomes an instrument in the hands of evil rulers for their oppression; when the Federal Republican Constitution of their country, which they have sworn to support, no longer has a substantial existence, and the whole nature of their government has been forcibly changed without their consent, from a restricted federative republic, composed of sovereign states, to a consolidated central military despotism, in which every interest is disregarded but that of the army and the priesthood—both the eternal enemies of civil liberty, and the ever-ready minions of power, and the usual instruments of tyrants; When long after the spirit of the Constitution has departed, moderation is at length, so far lost, by those in power that even the semblance of freedom is removed, and the forms, themselves, of the constitution discontinued; and so far from their petitions and remonstrances being regarded, the agents who bear them are thrown into dungeons; and mercenary armies sent forth to force a new government upon them at the point of the bayonet. When in consequence of such acts of malfeasance and abdication, on the part of the government, anarchy prevails, and civil society is dissolved into its original elements: In such a crisis, the first law of nature, the right of self-preservation—the inherent and inalienable right of the people to appeal to first principles and take their political affairs into their own hands in extreme cases—enjoins it as a right towards themselves and a sacred obligation to their posterity, to abolish such government and create another in its stead, calculated to rescue them from impending dangers, and to secure their future welfare and happiness. Nations, as well as individuals, are amenable for their acts to the public opinion of mankind. A statement of a part of our grievances is, therefore, submitted to an impartial world, in justification of the hazardous but unavoidable step now taken of severing our political connection with the Mexican people, and assuming an independent attitude among the nations of the earth.

The Mexican government, by its colonization laws, invited and induced the Anglo-American population of Texas to colonize its wilderness under the pledged faith of a written constitution, that they should continue to enjoy that constitutional liberty and republican government to which they had been habituated in the land of their birth, the United States of America. In this expectation they have been cruelly disappointed, inasmuch as the Mexican nation has acquiesced in the late changes made in the government by General Antonio Lopez de Santa Anna, who, having overturned the constitution of his country, now offers us the cruel alternative either to abandon our homes, acquired by so many privations, or submit to the most intolerable of all tyranny, the combined despotism of the sword and the priesthood.

It has sacrificed our welfare to the state of Coahuila, by which our interests have been continually depressed, through a jealous and partial course of legislation carried on at a far distant seat of government, by a hostile majority, in an unknown tongue; and this too, notwithstanding we have petitioned in the humblest terms, for the establishment of a separate state government, and have, in accordance with the provisions of the national constitution, presented the general Congress, a republican constitution which was without just cause contemptuously rejected.

It incarcerated in a dungeon, for a long time, one of our citizens, for no other cause but a zealous endeavor to procure the acceptance of our constitution and the establishment of a state government.

It has failed and refused to secure on a firm basis, the right of trial by jury; that palladium of civil liberty, and only safe guarantee for the life, liberty, and property of the citizen.

It has failed to establish any public system of education, although possessed of almost boundless resources (the public domain) and, although, it is an axiom, in political science, that unless a people are educated and enlightened it is idle to expect the continuance of civil liberty, or the capacity for self-government.

It has suffered the military commandants stationed among us to exercise arbitrary acts of oppression and tyranny; thus trampling upon the most sacred rights of the citizen and rendering the military superior to the civil power.

It has dissolved by force of arms, the state Congress of Coahuila and Texas, and obliged our representatives to fly for their lives from the seat of government; thus depriving us of the fundamental political right of representation.

It has demanded the surrender of a number of our citizens, and ordered military detachments to seize and carry them into the Interior for trial; in contempt of the civil authorities, and in defiance of the laws and constitution.

It has made piratical attacks upon our commerce; by commissioning foreign desperadoes, and authorizing them to seize our vessels, and convey the property of our citizens to far distant ports of confiscation.

It denies us the right of worshipping the Almighty according to the dictates of our own consciences, by the support of a national religion calculated to promote the temporal interests of its human functionaries rather than the glory of the true and living God.

It has demanded us to deliver up our arms; which are essential to our defense, the rightful property of freemen, and formidable only to tyrannical governments.

It has invaded our country, both by sea and by land, with intent to lay waste our territory and drive us from our homes; and has now a large mercenary army advancing to carry on against us a war of extermination.

It has, through its emissaries, incited the merciless savage, with the tomahawk and scalping knife, to massacre the inhabitants of our defenseless frontiers.

It hath been, during the whole time of our connection with it, the contemptible sport and victim of successive military revolutions and hath continually exhibited every characteristic of a weak, corrupt and tyrannical government.

These, and other grievances, were patiently borne by the people of Texas until they reached that point at which forbearance ceases to be a virtue. We then took up arms in defense of the national constitution. We appealed to our Mexican brethren for assistance. Our appeal has been made in vain. Though months have elapsed, no sympathetic response has yet been heard from the Interior. We are, therefore, forced to the melancholy conclusion that the Mexican people have acquiesced in the destruction of their liberty, and the substitution therefor of a military government—that they are unfit to be free and incapable of self-government.

The necessity of self-preservation, therefore, now decrees our eternal political separation.

We, therefore, the delegates, with plenary powers, of the people of Texas, in solemn convention assembled, appealing to a candid world for the necessities of our condition, do hereby resolve and DECLARE that our political connection with the Mexican nation has forever ended; and that the people of Texas do now constitute a FREE, SOVEREIGN and INDEPENDENT REPUBLIC, and are fully invested with all the rights and attributes which properly belong to the independent nations; and, conscious of the rectitude of our intentions, we fearlessly and confidently commit the issue to the decision of the Supreme Arbiter of the destinies of nations.

RICHARD ELLIS, president of the convention and Delegate from Red River.

Charles B. Stewart

Thos Barnett

John S. D. Byrom

Franco Ruiz

J. Antonio Navarro

Jesse B. Badgett

Wm D. Lacey

William Menefee

Jno Fisher

Mathew Caldwell

William Mottley

Lorenzo de Zavala

Stephen H. Everitt

Geo W. Smyth

Elijah Stapp

Claiborne West

Wm B. Scates

M.B. Menard

A.B. Hardin

J.W. Bunton

Thos J. Gasley

R.M. Coleman

Sterling C. Robertson

Benj. Briggs Goodrich

G.W. Barnett

James G. Swisher

Jesse Grimes

S. Rhoads Fisher

John W. Moore

John W. Bower

Saml A. Maverick from Bejar

Sam P. Carson

A. Briscoe

J. B. Woods

Jas Collinsworth

Edwin Waller

Asa Brigham

Geo. C. Childress

Bailey Hardeman

Rob. Potter

Thomas Jefferson Rusk

Chas. S. Taylor

John S. Roberts

Robert Hamilton

Collin McKinney

Albert H. Latimer

James Power

Sam Houston

David Thomas

Edwd Conrad

Martin Parmer

Edwin O. LeGrand

Stephen W. Blount

Jas Gaines

Wm Clark, Jr.

Sydney O. Penington

Wm Carrol Crawford

Jno Turner

Test. H. S. Kimble, Secretary

Notes

Chapter 1 Introduction

1. V. O. Key, *Southern Politics in State and Nation* (Knoxville: University of Tennessee Press, 1984), 267.
2. John Steinbeck, *Travels with Charley: In Search of America* (New York: Bantam Books, 1961), 231.
3. Randolph B. Campbell, *Gone to Texas* (New York: Oxford University Press, 2004), 15.
4. James L. Haley, *Passionate Nation: The Epic History of Texas* (New York: Free Press, 2006), 6.
5. Campbell, *Gone to Texas,* 41.
6. Ibid., 85.
7. Ibid., 88.
8. Ibid., 80.
9. Ibid., 186.
10. Haley, *Passionate Nation,* 272.
11. Campbell, *Gone to Texas,* 207.
12. Ibid., 299.
13. Ibid., 350–351.
14. Ibid., 366.
15. Christine Barbour and Gerald C. Wright, *Keeping the Republic,* 4th brief ed. (Washington, D.C.: CQ Press, 2011), 23.
16. Daniel J. Elazar, *American Federalism: A View from the State* (New York: Thomas Y. Crowell, 1966), 86.
17. "In Texas, 31% Say State Has Right to Secede from U.S., but 75% Opt to Stay," Rasmussen Reports, April 17, 2009, www.rasmussenreports.com/public_content/politics/general_state_surveys/texas/in_texas_31_say_state_has_right_to_secede_from_u_s_but_75_opt_to_stay.
18. Campbell, *Gone to Texas,* 15.
19. T. R. Fehrenbach, *Lone Star: A History of Texas and the Texans* (Cambridge, Mass.: Da Capo Press, 2000), 24.
20. U.S. Census Bureau, "Selected Social Characteristics in the United States: 2006–2008, American Community Survey: Texas," www.factfinder.census.gov.
21. Ibid.
22. Elizabeth Cruce Alvares, ed., *Texas Almanac, 2006–2007* (Dallas: Dallas Morning News, 2006), 519.
23. Jared Bernstein, Elizabeth McNichol, and Karen Lyons, "Pulling Apart: A State-by-State Analysis of Income Trends," Center on Budget and Policy Priorities and Economic Policy Institute, January 2006.
24. U.S. Census Bureau, "Census Brief: Warmer, Older, More Diverse: State-by-State Population Changes to 2025," CENBR/96-1, December 1996.

25. James E. Crisp, *Sleuthing the Alamo: Davy Crockett's Last Stand and Other Mysteries of the Texas Revolution* (New York: Oxford University Press, 2004), 59.
26. Anna J. Hardwicke Pennybacker, *A New History of Texas for Schools* (Tyler, Texas, 1888), 49.
27. Terrence Stutz, "Texas Won't Cover Tejanos at Alamo," *Dallas Morning News*, March 12, 2010.

Chapter 2 Texas Constitution

1. David Schmudde, "Constitutional Limitations on State Taxation of Nonresident Citizens," *Law Review of Michigan State University–Detroit College of Law* (spring 1999): 95–169.
2. Ibid., 125.
3. *South Dakota v. Dole,* 483 U.S. 203 (1987).
4. Thomas Dye, *American Federalism: Competition Among Governments* (Lexington, Mass.: Lexington Books, 1989).
5. Rick Perry, press release, March 21, 2010, at http://governor.state.tx.us/news/press-release/14396/.
6. Newt Gingrich and Rick Perry, "Let the States Lead the Way," *The Washington Post*, November 6, 2009.
7. "Attorney General Abbott: Texas and Other States Will Challenge Federal Health Care Legislation," March 21, 2010, www.oag.state.tx.us/oagNews/release.php?id=3269.
8. Randolph B. Campbell, *Gone to Texas* (New York: Oxford University Press, 2004).
9. Robert Calvert, Arnoldo De León, and Gregg Cantrell, *The History of Texas* (Wheeling, Ill.: Harlan Davidson Press, 2002).
10. Stephen F. Austin, quoted in John Cornyn, "The Roots of the Texas Constitution: Settlement to Statehood," *Texas Tech Law Review* 26 (1995): 1089–1184.
11. Campbell, *Gone to Texas*.
12. Texas Constitution (1836), General Provisions, sec. 10.
13. Texas Constitution (1836), General Provisions, sec. 6.
14. Texas Constitution (1876), art. 6, sec. 2.
15. Cornyn, "The Roots of the Texas Constitution."
16. Roy R. Barkley and Mark F. Odintz, eds., *The Portable Handbook of Texas* (Austin: Texas State Historical Association, 2000).
17. Campbell, *Gone to Texas*.
18. Cornyn, "The Roots of the Texas Constitution."
19. Texas Constitution (1845), art. 3, sec. 1.
20. Joe Ericson, "An Inquiry into the Sources of the Texas Constitution," Ph.D. Dissertation, Texas Tech University (1957). See also Janice C. May, *The Texas State Constitution: A Reference Guide* (Westport, Conn.: Greenwood Press, 1996).
21. Campbell, *Gone to Texas*.
22. Texas Constitution (1866), art. 8, sec. 1.
23. Ericson, "An Inquiry into the Sources of the Texas Constitution."
24. May, *The Texas State Constitution*.
25. Ibid.
26. Texas Constitution (1876), art. I, sec. 1.
27. Originally a state treasurer was also included in the plural executive, but this office was eventually dissolved.
28. Oklahoma is the only other state to have two high courts.
29. Calvert, De León, and Cantrell, *History of Texas*.
30. Only the constitutions of South Carolina, Arkansas, and Alabama have been amended more times.
31. Texas Secretary of State, www.sos.state.tx.us/elections/historical/70-92.shtml.
32. May, *The Texas State Constitution*.
33. Campbell, *Gone to Texas*, 371.
34. Bill Ratliff, quoted in Juan B. Elizondo, Jr., "Time to Rewrite Constitution," *Austin American-Statesman,* October 28, 1999.
35. Bill Stouffer, chair of Common Cause Texas, quoted in Elizondo, "Time to Rewrite Constitution."

Chapter 3 Texas Legislature

1. House Journal, 80th Legislature, Regular Session, Proceedings, 17–22.
2. April Castro and Liz Austin Peterson, "Texas House Speaker Refuses to Step Down Amid Uproar," *Arkansas Democrat-Gazette,* May 27, 2007, 7A.
3. "Speaker Fight: Legal Arguments," *Daily Sentinel* (Nacogdoches), May 27, 2007.
4. Castro and Peterson, "Texas House Speaker Refuses to Step Down Amid Uproar."
5. Laylan Copeland, "How the House Speaker's Race Was Won," *Austin American-Statesman,* January 6, 2009, www.statesman.com/search/content/region/legislature/stories/01/06/0106 speaker.html.
6. House Journal, 81st Legislature, Regular Session, Proceedings, 8–15.
7. Ross Ramsey, "Two Factions in the State's Majority Party," *The Texas Tribune,* November 15, 2010, www.texastribune.org/texas-politics/republican-party-of-texas/two-factions-split-texas-republicans/.
8. James Madison, *Federalist* No. 51, in *The Federalist Papers,* ed. Clinton Rossiter (New York: Penguin Putnam, 1999), 288–293.
9. 369 U.S. 186 (1962).
10. 377 U.S. 533 (1964).
11. Keon S. Chi, *The Book of the States: 2006 Edition,* vol. 38 (Lexington, Ky.: Council of State Governments, 2006), Table 3.2, 68–70.
12. Ibid.
13. R. G. Ratcliffe and Janet Elliot, "Along Trail of Stalled Bills, Budget Goes to Perry," *Houston Chronicle,* March 20, 2009, www.chron.com/disp/story.mpl/special/legislature/6447856 .html.
14. R. G. Ratcliffe and Peggy Fikac, "Five State Agencies Left Wondering by Lawmakers," *Houston Chronicle,* June 2, 2009, www.chron.com/disp/story.mpl/metropolitian/6455230 .html.
15. Ben Wear, "Borrowing, Stimulus Boost TxDOT Road Plans," *Austin American-Statesman,* July 30, 2009, www.stateman.com/news/content/news/stories/local/2009/07/30/0730txdot .html.
16. Mike Ward, "In Just 30 Hours, Legislature Sends 2 of 3 Bills to Perry, Then Adjourns: Governor Says He's Happy with Special Session Results," *Austin American-Statesman,* November 13, 2009, www.statesman.com/news/texas-politics/in-just-30-hours-legisla ture-sends-2-of-56639.html.
17. Texas Constitution (1876), art. 3, sec. 8.
18. Texas Constitution (1876), art. 3, sec. 21.
19. National Council of State Legislatures, "NCSL Backgrounder: Full and Part-Time Legislatures," http://www.ncsl.org/?tabid=16701 (accessed August 10, 2010).
20. Ibid.
21. Chi, *The Book of the States,* vol. 38, Table 3.13, 94–99.
22. Peverill Squire, "Measuring State Legislative Professionalism: The Squire Index Revisited," *State Politics and Policy Quarterly* 7, no. 2 (2007): 211–227.
23. Texas State Constitution (1876), art. 3, sec. 6; art. 3, sec. 7.
24. Thomas M. Spencer, *The Legislative Process, Texas Style* (Pasadena, Texas: San Jacinto College Press, 1981), 20–21.
25. Texas Constitution (1876), art. 3, sec. 8.
26. Chi, *The Book of the States,* vol. 38, Table 3.2, 72–73.
27. Adapted from Kendra A. Hovey and Harold A. Hovey, *CQ's State Fact Finder* (Washington, D.C.: CQ Press, 2007), Table D-8, 109; Keon S. Chi, *The Book of the States,* vol. 36 (Lexington, Ky.: Council of State Governments, 2004), Table 3.4, 85.
28. Legislative Reference Library of Texas, "81st Legislature (2009)—Statistical Profile," www.lrl.state.tx.us/legis/profile81.html, and "78th Legislature (2003)—Statistical Profile," www.lrl.state.tx.us/legis/profile78.html.
29. Peter Slevin, "After Adopting Term Limits, States Lose Female Legislators," *Washington Post,* April 22, 2007, A04.
30. Steven Smith, Jason M. Roberts, and Ryan J. Vander Wielen, *The American Congress*, 4th ed. (New York: Cambridge University Press, 2006), 26.

31. Ibid.
32. Quoted in Iain McLean, "Forms of Representation and Systems of Voting," in *Political Theory Today,* ed. David Held (Cambridge, UK: Polity Press, 1991), 173.
33. David M. Farrell, *Electoral Systems: A Comparative Introduction* (New York: Palgrave, 2001), 11.
34. Texas Constitution (1876), art. 3, sec. 2; art. 3, sec. 25.
35. "State and Federal Law Governing Redistricting in Texas," 2001, Texas Legislative Council, Austin, www.tlc.state.tx.us/pubspol/redlaw01/redlaw01.pdf (accessed August 1, 2007).
36. *White v. Register,* 412 U.S. 755 (1973).
37. U.S. Department of the Interior, Census Office, *Report of the Population of the United States at the Eleventh Census: 1890* (Washington, D.C.: Government Printing Office, 1895), 41–42.
38. U.S. Census Bureau, "State and County Quick Facts: Nacogdoches County, Texas," 2007, http://quickfacts.census.gov/qfd/states/48/48347.html (accessed August 1, 2007).
39. U.S. Census Bureau, "State and County Quick Facts: Dallas County, Texas," 2007, http://quickfacts.census.gov/qdf/states/48/48113.html (accessed August 1, 2007).
40. 526 U.S. 541 (1999).
41. Texas Constitution (1976), art. 3, sec. 2.
42. Sam Attlesey, "Panel OKs Map Favoring GOP," *Dallas Morning News,* November 29, 2001.
43. 548 U.S. 204 (2006).
44. Spencer, *The Legislative Process,* 22–23.
45. Chi, *The Book of the States,* vol. 38, Tables 3.11 and 3.12, 90–93.
46. Keith Hamm and Robert Harmel, "Legislative Party Development and the Speaker System: The Case of the Texas House," *Journal of Politics* 55, no. 4 (1993): 1140–1151.
47. Ibid., 62.
48. Rep. Wayne Christian (R-9th District), email correspondence with the author, August 11, 2007.
49. Charles W. Wiggins, Keith E. Hamm, and Charles G. Bell, "Interest Group and Party Influence Agents in the Legislative Process: A Comparative State Analysis," *Journal of Politics* 54 (1992): 82–100.
50. Michelle G. Briscoe, "Cohesiveness and Diversity among Black Members of the Texas State Legislature," in *Politics in the New South: Representation of African Americans in Southern State Legislatures,* ed. Charles E. Menifield and Stephen D. Shaffer (Albany: State University of New York, 2005).
51. Rep. Jim McReynolds (D-12th District), interview with the author, Nacogdoches, Texas, August 8, 2007.
52. Hamm and Harmel, "Legislative Party Development," 1140–1151.
53. Kathryn Birdwill, "Bill Requires Universities to Limit Credit Hours Needed to Earn Degree," *Daily Sentinel* (Nacogdoches), January 6, 2006.
54. Chi, *The Book of the States,* vol. 38, Tables 3.25 and 3.26, 125–130.
55. Chi, *The Book of the States,* vol. 38, Table 3.18, 109–110.
56. Spencer, *The Legislative Process*, 31–32.
57. W. Gardner Selby, "It's Not Every Day a Legislator Travels Oversees while Voting in the Texas House," *Austin American-Statesman,* April 27, 2007.
58. Chi, *The Book of the States,* vol. 38, Table 3.14, 100–101.
59. Anthony Champaign et al., *The Austin Boston Connection: Five Decades of House Democratic Leadership, 1937–1989* (College Station: Texas A&M University Press, 2009).

Chapter 4 Governors and Bureaucracy in Texas

1. Paul Burka, "Teflon," *Texas Monthly,* January 28, 2010, www.texasmonthly.com/blogs/burkablog/?p=60.
2. "U.S. House Dems Add Caveat to Texas School Funds," *Huntsville Item,* July 3, 2010, http://itemonline.com/local/x1703948231/House-Dems-add-caveat-to-Texas-schools-funds.

3. National Conference of State Legislatures, *State Budget Update: July 2009* (Lexington, Ky.: Council of State Governments, 2009).

4. Daniel Murph, *Texas Giant: The Life of Price Daniel* (Austin, Texas: Eakin Press, 2002).

5. Texas Constitution (1876), art. 4, sec. 4.

6. Texas Constitution (1876), art. 4, sec. 6.

7. Kenneth E. Hendrickson, *The Chief Executives of Texas* (College Station: Texas A&M University Press, 1995).

8. Ibid.

9. Jim Yardley, "The 2002 Elections: Races for Governor: In Texas, Republican Who Inherited Top Job Is the Winner Outright," *New York Times,* November 6, 2002.

10. Jim Yardley, "In First, Texas Hispanic Seeks to Be Governor," *New York Times,* September 5, 2001.

11. Keon S. Chi, *The Book of the States: 2009 Edition,* vol. 41 (Lexington, Ky.: Council of State Governments, 2009).

12. "College Football Coaches See Salaries Rise in Down Economy," *USA Today,* November 10, 2009.

13. Chi, *The Book of the States,* vol. 41.

14. Jay Root, "Governor Perry's Temporary Digs Costs Texas Big Bucks," CBS News, May 17, 2010, www.cbsnews.com/stories/2010/05/17/national/main6491367.shtml.

15. Frederic A. Ogg, "Impeachment of Governor Ferguson," *American Political Science Review* 12, no. 1 (February 1918): 111–115.

16. Cortez A. M. Ewing, "The Impeachment of James E. Ferguson," *Political Science Quarterly* 48, no. 2 (June 1933): 184–210.

17. Texas Constitution (1876), art. 4, sec. 10.

18. Texans for Public Justice, "Governor Perry's Patronage," April 2006, http://info.tpj.org/reports/pdf/Perry%20Patronage2010.pdf.

19. Texans for Public Justice, "No Donor Left Behind: Gov. Perry Reaps $6 Million from Regents Appointees," April 7, 2010, http://info.tpj.org/press_releases/pdf/RegentstoPerry.april2010.pr.pdf.

20. Brittany Pieper, "Another Former Tech Regent Says the Governor Pressured Their Resignation," KCBD News Channel 11, September 12, 2009, www.kcbd.com/Global/story.asp?S=11120348.

21. Brian McCall, *The Power of the Texas Governor: Connally to Bush* (Austin: University of Texas Press, 2009).

22. Polly Ross Hughes, "Senators: Perry Evading Law with Expired Appointments," August 29, 2007, www.corridorwatch.org.

23. Randy Lee Loftis, "State of Neglect: Revolving Door Lets Lawmakers Profit from Capital Floor Time," *Dallas News,* January 7, 2009.

24. R. G. Ratcliffe, "Court Limits Perry's Power over Agencies," *Houston Chronicle*, February 21, 2007.

25. R. G. Ratcliffe, "Perry Muscle Flexing Falls Flat," *Houston Chronicle,* February 25, 2007.

26. Margaret R. Ferguson, "Roles, Functions, and Powers of the Governors," in *The Executive Branch of State Government,* ed. by Margaret R. Ferguson (Santa Barbara, Calif.: ABC-CLIO, 2006).

27. Chi, *The Book of the States,* vol. 41.

28. Texas Constitution (1876), art. 4, sec. 11.

29. Thad Beyle and Margaret Ferguson, "Governors and the Executive Branch," in *Politics in the American States: A Comparative Analysis,* 9th ed., ed. Virginia Gray and Russell L. Hanson (Washington, D.C.: CQ Press, 2008).

30. "Poll: Texas Governor Perry Job Approval Up Post Hurricanes," December 6, 2005, www.foxnews.com.

31. Kavan Peterson, "Governors Lose in Power Struggle over National Guard," January 12, 2007, www.stateline.org.

32. Ibid.

33. Beyle and Ferguson, "Governors and the Executive Branch," Table 7-5.

34. Paul Burka, quoted in McCall, *The Power of the Texas Governor.*

35. Beyle and Ferguson, "Governors and the Executive Branch," 203–204.

36. Ibid.
37. Ibid.
38. Ibid.
39. Texas Constitution (1876), art. 4, sec. 1.
40. Keon S. Chi, *The Book of the States: 2006 Edition,* vol. 38 (Lexington, Ky.: Council of State Governments, 2006).
41. Texas Constitution (1876), art. 4, sec. 22.
42. Jonathan W. Singer, *Broken Trusts: The Texas Attorney General versus the Oil Industry, 1889–1909* (College Station: Texas A&M Press, 2002).
43. HB 7 transferred the Texas Performance Review and the Texas School Performance Review to the Legislative Budget Board.
44. Steven Quinn, "Texas Tops in Wind Energy Production," *USA Today,* July 25, 2006.
45. "Texas Leases Offshore Wind Tracts," October 3, 2007, http://www.msnbc.msn.com/id/21113169/.
46. Sunset Advisory Commission, "Guide to the Texas Sunset Process," 2009, www.sunset.state.tx.us/htm.

Chapter 5 Texas Judicial System

1. Christy Hoppe, "Governor Perry Replaces Head of Agency Investigating Texas Arson Findings," *Dallas Morning News,* Thursday October 1, 2009.
2. Steve Mills, "Cameron Todd Willingham: Former Head of Texas Forensics Panel Probing 1991 Fire Says He Felt Pressured by Gov. Perry Aides," *Chicago Tribune,* October 12, 2009.
3. Texas Constitution (1876), art. 5, sec. 1.
4. Office of Court Administration, *Annual Report for the Texas Judiciary, Fiscal Year 2009* (Austin: Office of Court Administration, 2009).
5. Ibid.
6. Texas Constitution (1876), art. 4, sec. 19.
7. *Annual Report for the Texas Judiciary*, Fiscal Year 2009.
8. *Annual Report for the Texas Judiciary*, Fiscal Year 2009.
9. Texas Constitution (1876), art. 5, sec. 15.
10. *Annual Report for the Texas Judiciary*, Fiscal Year 2009.
11. Ibid.
12. Texas Constitution (1876), art. 5, sec. 8.
13. Texas Watch Foundation, "The Texas Supreme Court by the Numbers: A Statistical Analysis of the Texas Supreme Court, 2005–2006," Court Watch press release, www.txwfoundation.org.
14. Ibid.
15. Anthony Champagne and Greg Thieleman, "Awareness of Trial Court Judges," *Judicature* 76 (1991): 271–277.
16. Honorable Thomas Phillips, quoted in "The Texas Judiciary: Is Justice for Sale?" League of Women Voters panel discussion, Tyler, Texas, broadcast as part of a PBS *Frontline* special, September 25, 2007.
17. Texas Constitution (1876), art. 5, sec. 1A.
18. State Commission on Judicial Conduct, Fiscal Year 2009 Annual Report, State of Texas, www.scjc.state.tx.us/pdf/rpts/AR-FY09.pdf.
19. Texas Research League, "The Texas Judiciary: A Proposal for Structural-Functional Reform," in *Texas Courts: Report 2* (Texas Research League, 1991), 25.
20. 1993 Citizens' Commission on the Texas Judicial System, www.courts.state.tx.us/tjc/publications/cc_tjs.pdf.
21. Texans for Public Justice, "Billable Ours: Texas Endures Another Attorney-Financed Supreme Court Race," October, 25, 2006.
22. Ibid.
23. Texas Watch Foundation, "Hecht Votes with Mega-Donors to His Personal Legal Fund 89% of the Time: Judge's Actions Raise Serious Questions about His Impartiality," July 17, 2007, www.txwfoundation.org.

24. Ibid.

25. Kings College in London, International Center for Prison Studies, "Prison Brief—Highest to Lowest Rates," www.kcl.ac.uk/depsta/law/research/icps/worldbrief/wpb_stats.php?area=all&category=wb_poptotal.

26. Ibid.

27. State Profile of Texas, www.pewpublicsafety.org.

28. Karen Brooks, "Jail Bill Targets Dallas: Legislature: House Wants Staffing Rules, Monitors for Poor Performers," *Dallas Morning News,* May 11, 2007, www.dallasnews.com/ shared content/dws/news/texassouthwest/stories/051107dntexjai1.380a0e5.html.

29. Mike Ward, "Privately Run Prisons Come Under Fire at Capitol," *Austin American-Statesman,* October 13, 2007.

30. Gregory Hooks, Clayton Mosher, Thomas Rotolo, and Linda Lobao, "The Prison Industry: Carceral Expansion and Employment in U.S. Counties, 1969–1994," *Social Science Quarterly* 85 (March 2004): 1.

31. Ward, "Privately Run Prisons."

32. Holly Becka and Jennifer LaFleur, "Texas' Youth Jail Operators Have Troubled Histories," *Dallas Morning News,* July 30, 2007, www.dallasnews.com/sharedcontent/dws/dn/latest news/stories/072907dnmettyccontracts.37bfd89.html.

33. 536 U.S. 304 (2002).

34. 543 U.S. 551 (2005).

35. David Dobbs, quoted in "The Texas Judiciary: Is Justice for Sale?"

36. Max B. Baker, "Poll: Death Penalty Losing Support," *Fort Worth Star Telegram,* June 10, 2007; R. A. Dyer, "Poll Indicates Iraq War Is Texans' Top Concern," *Fort Worth Star Telegram,* June 14, 2007.

37. "Hello? Hello?! Criminal Justice," *Fort Worth Star Telegram,* October 31, 2007; ABC News, "Judge, We Close at 5," October 12, 2007.

38. Ford Fessenden, "Deadly Statistics: A Survey of Crime and Punishment," *New York Times,* September 22, 2000.

39. Christy Hoppe, "Executions Cost Texas Millions: Study Finds It's Cheaper to Jail Killers for Life," *Dallas Morning News,* March 8, 1992.

Chapter 6 Local Government in Texas

1. "There Will Be Water," *Bloomberg Businessweek,* June 12, 2008.

2. Julian Aguilar, "Fort Stockton Challenges Williams Over Water Use," *The Texas Tribune,* April 21, 2010, www.texastribune.org (accessed July 2, 2010).

3. Julian Aguilar, "Clayton Williams' Company, Fort Stockton Keep Battling," *The Texas Tribune,* April 30, 2010, www.texastribune.org (accessed July 14, 2010).

4. *Clinton v. Cedar Rapids and Missouri River Railroad Co.,* 24 Iowa 455 (1868).

5. *Hunter v. Pittsburg,* 207 U.S. 161 (1907).

6. Texas Constitution (1876), art. 9, sec. 1.

7. Paul Ciotti, "Money and School Performance: Lessons Learned from the Kansas City Desegregation Experiment," *Policy Analysis,* no. 298 (Washington, D.C.: CATO Institute, 1998).

8. Texas State Historical Association, "The Handbook of Texas Online: Loving County," www.tsha.utexas.edu/handbook/onlinearticles/LL/hc113.html (accessed October 2, 2007).

9. Texas Constitution (1876), art. 9, sec. 1(1).

10. Texas Association of Counties, "Some Facts about Texas Counties," www.county.org/counties/fact.asp (accessed August 18, 2007).

11. National Association of Counties, "About Counties: Data and Demographics—Texas," www.naco.org (accessed August 18, 2007).

12. Texas Constitution (1876), art. 9, sec. 14.

13. Texas Local Government Code, chap. 158, sec. 158.001.

14. Stan Reid and Tim Brown, *Texas Counties with Civil Service Systems: Research Report* (Austin: Texas Association of Counties, 2004), 2.

15. Texas Local Government Code, chap. 118.

16. "New Recycling Program Biz," *Kennedale News,* January 14, 2010, www.kennedalenews .com (accessed July 9, 2010).

17. Greene County, Missouri, "Personal Property Tax: Frequently Asked Questions," http:// www.greenecountymo.org/spane/personalproperty.htm (accessed October 4, 2007).

18. Texas Local Government Code, chap. 6, sec. 6.001 and chap. 22, secs. 22.031–22.042.

19. Texas Local Government Code, chap. 7.

20. Texas Local Government Code, chap. 24, sec. 24.021.

21. Texas Local Government Code, chap. 6, sec. 6.002; chap. 7, sec. 7.002; and chap. 8, sec. 8.002.

22. Texas Municipal Association, *Annual Survey of Members* (Denton: Texas Municipal Association, Inc.: 2007).

23. Robert Brischetto, "Cumulative Voting at Work in Texas" in *Voting and Democracy Report: 1995* (Takoma Park, Md.: FairVote–Center for Voting and Democracy, 1995).

24. Emily Ramshaw, "State Law Would Usurp City Control of Zoning, Neighborhood Control," *Dallas Morning News,* March 2, 2007.

25. Texas Local Government Code, chap. 43, sec. 43.055.

26. Texas Constitution (1876), Art. 7.

27. Texas Education Code, chap. 11, secs. 11.301 and 11.303.

28. Texas Education Code, chap. 11, secs. 11.051–11.058.

29. Texas Education Code, chap. 11, secs. 11.151–11.170.

30. Texas Education Agency, "SBOE History and Duties," www.tea.state.tx.us/sboe/ sboe_ history_duties.html (accessed September 5, 2007).

31. Texas Constitution (1876), art. 7, sec. 8.

Chapter 7 Elections: Texas Style

1. Dave Montgomery, "Libertarians Believe America's Political Mood Is Swinging Their Direction," Fort Worth *Star Telegram,* June 9, 2010, www.star-telegram.com/2010/ 06/08/2249822/libertarians-believe-americas.html (accessed July 22, 2010).

2. Naureen Khan, "Libertarians, Convening in Austin, Pick Candidates for November," *Austin American-Stateman,* June 12, 2010, www.statesman.com/news/texas-politics/ libertarians-convening-in-austin-pick-candidates.html (accessed July 22, 2010).

3. Jason Embry, "Democrats Head to Court in Effort to Stop Greens," *Austin American-Stateman,* June 23, 2010, www.statesman.com/news/texas-politics/democrats-head-to-court-in-effort-to-stop-7.html (accessed July 22, 2010).

4. Ibid.

5. Jim Vertuno, "Texas Green Party Files Appeals for Candidates," *Austin American-Stateman,* June 28, 2010, www.statesmen.com/news/texas/texas-green-party-files-appeal-for-candi dates-77439.html (accessed July 22, 2010).

6. Texas Election Code, chap. 11, sec. 002.

7. Texas Election Code, chap. 16, secs. 002–003.

8. Texas Secretary of State, "County Voter Registration Officials," 2010, www.sos.state .tx.us/elections/voter/county.shtml (accessed August 6, 2010).

9. Texas Secretary of State, "Election Duties," 2010, www.sos.state.tx.us/elecctions/voter/ votregduties.shtml (accessed August 6, 2010).

10. Texas Constitution (1876), art. 7, sec. 3.

11. Ricky F. Dobbs, *Yellow Dogs and Republicans: Allan Shivers and Texas Two-Party Politics* (College Station: Texas A&M University Press, 2005), 80.

12. Michael J. Klarman, "The Supreme Court and Black Disenfranchisement," in *The Voting Rights Act: Securing the Ballot,* ed. Richard M. Valelly, (Washington, D.C.: CQ Press, 2006).

13. The courts do allow for some limitations, primarily where the health and safety of citizens are concerned. Laws may discriminate on the basis of age; for example, statutes prohibit- ing children from driving are perfectly legal. Imagine if ten-year-olds were allowed to drive!

14. 383 U.S. 663 (1966).

15. 273 U.S. 534 (1924).

16. 321 U.S. 649 (1944).

17. 345 U.S. 461 (1953).
18. Klarman, "The Supreme Court and Black Disenfranchisement," 154.
19. Abigail M. Thernstrom, *Whose Votes Count?* (Cambridge, Mass.: Harvard University Press, 1987), 55.
20. Chandler Davidson, "The Voting Rights Act: A Brief History," in *Controversies in Minority Voting,* ed. Bernard Grofman and Chandler Davidson (Washington, D.C.: The Brookings Institution, 1992).
21. Thernstrom, *Whose Votes Count?* 56.
22. Texas State Historical Association, "Civil Rights Movement," in *The Handbook of Texas Online,* www.tsha.utexas.edu/handbook/online (accessed August 7, 2007).
23. Thernstrom, *Whose Votes Count?* 52.
24. Ruth P. Morgan, *Governance by Decree: The Impact of the Voting Rights Act in Dallas* (Lawrence: University of Kansas Press, 2004), 50–51.
25. Thernstrom, *Whose Votes Count?* 56–57.
26. 380 U.S. 775 (1965).
27. Texas Secretary of State, "Student Voters," 2010, www.sos.state.tx.us/voter/student-voters.shtml (accessed August 4, 2010).
28. Texas Constitution (1876), art. 6, sec. 5.
29. Donald P. Moynihan, "Building Secure Elections: E-Voting, Security, and Systems Theory," *Public Administration Review* 64 (2007): 515–528.
30. Ibid., 518.
31. Paul S. Herrnson et al., "Early Appraisals of Electronic Voting," *Social Science Computer Review* 23 (2005): 274–292.
32. Jeffrey S. Connor, *Amended Texas State Plan Pursuant to the Help America Vote Act of 2002* (Austin: Elections Division, Office of the Secretary of State, 2005), 3.
33. Ibid., 15.
34. 530 U.S. 567 (2000).
35. John F. Bibby and Thomas M. Holbrook, "Parties and Elections," in *Politics in the American States: A Comparative Analysis,* 8th ed., ed. Virginia Gray and Russell Hanson (Washington, D.C.: CQ Press, 2004), 63.
36. Dobbs, *Yellow Dogs and Republicans,* 70.
37. Ibid., 88.
38. Alexander Heard, *A Two-Party South?* (Chapel Hill: University of North Carolina Press, 1952), 104–105.
39. John G. Matsusaka, "2005 Initiatives and Referendums," in *The Book of the States: 2006 Edition,* vol. 38, ed. Keon S. Chi (Lexington, Ky.: The Council on State Governments, 2006), 307.
40. In some rare cases, voters do mark local and state races and leave "higher" offices, such as U.S. Senate or U.S. House of Representative races, unmarked. However, this pattern is much, much rarer than "roll off." As a result, political scientists do not really have a term to describe this phenomenon—"roll on" seems a bit silly.
41. Samuel L. Popkin, "Information Shortcuts and the Reasoning Voter," in *Information, Participation, and Choice,* ed. Bernard Grofman (Ann Arbor: University of Michigan Press, 1993), 19.
42. Ibid., 22–27; Anthony Downs, *An Economic Theory of Democracy* (New York: Harper and Row, 1957), 85.
43. Texas Secretary of State, "Election Night Returns," 2010, http://enr.sos.state.tx.us/enr/ (accessed November 5, 2010); Texas Secretary of State, "Turnout and Voter Registration Figures (1970–current)," 2010, www.sos.state.tx.us/elections/historical/70-92.shtml (accessed November 5, 2010).
44. Karlheinz Reif and Hermann Schmitt, "Nine Second-Order Elections: A Conceptual Framework for the Analysis of European Election Results," *European Journal of Political Research* 8 (1980): 3–44.
45. William H. Riker, *Liberalism against Populism* (Prospect Heights, Ill.: Waveland Press, 1982), 5; Robert A. Dahl, *A Preface to Democratic Theory* (Chicago: University of Chicago Press, 1956), 132.
46. James Endersby, Steven Galatas, and Chapman Rackaway, "Closeness Counts in Canada," *The Journal of Politics* 64, no. 2 (2002): 610–631. Specific cases finding a link in the United

States at the state level include Harvey J. Tucker, "Contextual Models of Participation in U.S. State Legislative Elections," *Western Political Quarterly* 39, no. 1 (1986): 67–78; Gregory A. Caldeira and Samuel C. Patterson, "Contextual Influences on Participation in U.S. State Legislative Election," *Legislative Studies Quarterly* 7, no. 3 (1989): 359–381; and Samuel C. Patterson and Gregory A. Caldeira, "Getting Out the Vote: Participation in Gubernatorial Elections," *American Political Science Review* 77, no. 3 (1983): 675–689.

47. Earl Black and Merle Black, *The Rise of the Southern Republicans* (Cambridge, Mass.: Belknap Press, 2002), 88.
48. Ibid., 23–24.
49. Bibby and Holbrook, "Parties and Elections," 87–88.
50. *Buckley v. Valeo,* 424 U.S. 1 (1976).
51. *McConnell v. Federal Election Commission*, 540 U.S. 93 (2003).
52. *Federal Election Commission v. Wisconsin Right to Life*, 551 U.S. 449 (2007).
53. 558 U.S. 50 (2010).
54. National Institute of Money in State Politics, "State at a Glance: Texas 2006 Candidates," www.followthemoney.org (accessed June 16, 2007).
55. Because Carole Strayhorn competed first in the Republican primary and then as an independent candidate in the general election, the figures include her spending in both the primary and general elections.
56. National Institute of Money in State Politics, "State at a Glance: Texas 2010 Candidates," www.followthemoney.org (accessed November 5, 2010).
57. Ibid.

Chapter 8 Parties and Organized Interests

1. Alwyn Barr, *Reconstruction to Reform: Texas Politics, 1876–1906* (Dallas: Southern Methodist University Press, 2000), 5.
2. T. R. Fehrenbach, *Lone Star: A History of Texas and the Texans* (Cambridge, Mass.: Da Capo Press, 2000), 618.
3. Ibid., 624.
4. Lewis L. Gould, *Progressives and Prohibitionists* (Austin: University of Texas Press, 1973), 39.
5. Fehrenbach, *Lone Star,* 415.
6. Gould, *Progressives and Prohibitionists*, 39.
7. Randolph B. Campbell, *Gone to Texas* (New York: Oxford University Press, 2004), 350.
8. Edmund Burke, *Works,* vol. I (London: G. Bell and Sons, 1897), 375.
9. Leon Epstein, *Political Parties in Western Democracies* (New York: Praeger, 1967), 9.
10. *Eu v. San Francisco County Democratic Central Comm.*, 489 U.S. 214 (1989).
11. Paul Allen Beck, *Political Parties in America*, 8th ed. (New York: Longman, 1997), 67–68.
12. Marc J. Hetherington and William J. Keefe, *Parties, Politics, and Public Policy in America*, 10th ed. (Washington, D.C.: CQ Press, 2007), 21.
13. John Kenneth White and Daniel M. Shea, *New Party Politics: From Jefferson and Hamilton to the Information Age* (Boston: St. Martin's Press, 2000), 174.
14. V. O. Key, *Southern Politics in State and Nation* (New York: Knopf, 1949), 307.
15. Anthony J. Nownes, *Pressure and Power: Organized Interests in American Politics* (Boston: Houghton Mifflin Company, 2001).
16. Ibid., 8.
17. Campbell, *Gone to Texas,* 313.
18. David Truman, *The Governmental Process: Political Interests and Public Opinion*, 2nd ed. (New York: Knopf, 1971).
19. Tara Copp, "State Lobbyist Bid Fell Short," *Austin American-Statesman,* January 25, 2006, 1A.
20. 548 U.S. 204 (2006).
21. Laylan Copelin, "Wined, Dined and Rubbed the Right Way," *Austin American-Statesman,* January 30, 2007.
22. Center for Public Integrity, "Statehouse Revolvers: Study Finds more than 1,300 Ex-legislators among 2005 State Lobbying Ranks," October 12, 2006, www.publicintegrity.org/hiredguns/report.aspx?aid=747.

23. Pete Slover and Robert T. Garrett, " 'Kinfolk' Lobbyists Prospering," *Dallas Morning News,* May 5, 2005, 1A.
24. Robert A. Dahl, *Who Governs?* (New Haven, Conn.: Yale University Press, 1961).
25. C. Wright Mills, *The Power Elite* (New York: Oxford University Press, 1956).
26. E. E. Schattschneider, *The Semisovereign People* (New York: Holt, Rinehart and Winston, 1960), 34–35.
27. Jonathan Rauch, *Government's End: Why Washington Stopped Working* (New York: Public Affairs, 1999).
28. Key, *Southern Politics*, 11.

Chapter 9 Policy

1. James L. Haley, *Passionate Nation: The Epic History of Texas* (New York: Free Press, 2006), 81.
2. U.S. Census Bureau, "States Ranked by Total State Taxes and Per Capita Amount: 2005," www.census.gov/govs/statetax/05staxrank.html.
3. Quoted in Dave McNeely and Jim Henderson, *Bob Bullock: God Bless Texas* (Austin: University of Texas Press, 2008), 174.
4. Laurie Fox, "School Districts Opt for Extra Tax," *Dallas Morning News,* September 22, 2006.
5. Kevin Krause, "Senior Property-tax Freeze Considered," *Dallas Morning News,* July 31, 2007.
6. Tax Foundation, "Federal Tax Burdens and Spending by State," Special Report no. 139, October 19, 2007.
7. Haley, *Passionate Nation*, 231.
8. Texas Constitution (1876), art. 3, sec. 49.
9. Texas Comptroller, "Biennial Revenue Estimate, 2008–2009," January 2007, 3, www.window.state.tx.us/taxbud/bre2008/BRE_2008-09.pdf.
10. Evan Smith, "One Ticked-Off Grandma," *Texas Monthly,* December 2003, 163.
11. Legislative Budget Board, "Fiscal Size-Up, 2010–2011 Biennium," 17.
12. Rick Perry, "Message," May 26, 2007, www.governor.state.tx.us/divisions/press/bills/letters/letter3-052607.
13. Texas Education Agency, *Pocket Edition, 2008–2009 Texas Public School Statistics,* http://ritter.tea.state.tx.us/perfreport/pocked/2009/pocked0809.pdf.
14. Ibid.
15. Haley, *Passionate Nation,* 232.
16. 347 U.S. 483 (1954).
17. 349 U.S. 294 (1955).
18. Judge Justice's order in the *United States v. Texas* case is generally referred to as "Civil Order 5821."
19. 777 S.W. 2d 391 (Tex. 1989).
20. Jenny Lacoste-Caputo and Gary Scharrer, "Expect Another School-funding Lawsuit," *Houston Chronicle*, August 1, 2010.
21. Texas Education Agency, "2006–2007 Texas Public School Statistics."
22. Joshua Benton and Holly Hacker, "Analysis Shows TAKS Cheating Rampant," *Dallas Morning News,* June 3, 2007.
23. Joshua Benton, "TAKS Analysis Suggests Many Graduates Cheated," *Dallas Morning News,* June 11, 2006, 1A.
24. Terrence Stutz, "Most Say School Testing Overemphasized," *Dallas Morning News,* February 22, 2006, 3A.
25. Texas Education Agency, "2010 Accountability System," July 2010, http://ritter.tea.state.tx.us/perfreport/account/2010/statesummary.html.
26. University of Texas/*Texas Tribune*, "Texas Statewide Survey, May 14, 2010 through May 20, 2010," http://static.texastribune.org/media/documents/UTTT_May_2010_Poll-Education.pdf.
27. "Diplomas Count 2010," *Education Week*, June 10, 2010, 24–25.
28. Texas Comptroller, "Texas in Focus: A Statewide View of Opportunities," 2008, 55.

29. Texas Higher Education Coordinating Board, "Closing the Gap by 2015: 2006 Annual Progress Report," July 2006, 3, www.thecb.state.tx.us/reports.

30. 78 F.3d 932 (5th Cir. 1996).

31. Brian Thevenot, "Tuition Rising Fast While State Support Drops," *Texas Tribune,* January 18, 2010, http://www.texastribune.org/texas-education/higher-education/tuition-rising-fast-while-state-support-drops/.

32. U.S. Census Bureau, "Poverty: 2008 and 2009 American Community Surveys," http://www.census.gov/prod/2010pubs/acsbr09-1.pdf.

33. Texas Health and Human Services Commission, "TANF Cases and Recipients by County, May 2010," www.hhsc.state.tx.us.

34. U.S. Census Bureau, "Current Population Survey," Table HI06, "Health Insurance Coverage Status by State for All People: 2009," http://www.census.gov/hhes/www/cpstables/032010/health/h06_000.htm.

35. "Heal Program Enrolling Fewer Kids," *Dallas Morning News,* March 1, 2006, 4A.

36. Randolph B. Campbell, *Gone to Texas* (New York: Oxford University Press, 2004), 326.

37. Pamela M. Prah, "Wanna Buy the Brooklyn Bridge? Some States Aren't Joking," *State of the State Report: A Stateline.org Report,* 2007, 16, http://archive.stateline.org/flash-data/Stateline's_State_of_the_States_2007.pdf.

38. Texas Comptroller, "Undocumented Immigrants in Texas: A Financial Analysis of the Impact to the State Budget and Economy," December 2006.

39. Isabel C. Morales and Al Dia, "Swift Plant Raid Devastated Cactus," *Dallas Morning News,* February 11, 2007, 1A.

40. 457 U.S. 202 (1982).

41. Katherine Leal Unmuth, "Tyler Case Opened Schools to Illegal Migrants," *Dallas Morning News,* June 11, 2007.

42. "Texas Monday Talks: Dick Armey," *Texas Monthly,* January 2007, 66.

Glossary

Administrative federalism the process whereby the national government sets policy guidelines, then expects state governments to pay for the programs they engender without the aid of federal monies. (Ch. 6)

***Ad-valorem* tax** a tax based on property value, which is subject to periodic appraisals. (Ch. 9)

Advanced or early voting a voting system that allows a voter to cast a ballot before an election without giving a specific reason, thus making voting more convenient for the voter. (Ch. 7)

Agenda setting the stage in which policymakers prioritize the problems facing the state. (Ch. 9)

Allocation the process by which party rules designate how many of the state's delegates to the national party convention will be pledged to vote for a specific candidate or attend as undecided. (Ch. 8)

Amendment a formal change to a bill made during the committee process. (Ch. 3)

Annexation a process whereby areas adjacent to a city are added to the city, thereby extending the city limits. (Ch. 6)

Appellate jurisdiction the authority to hear an appeal from a lower court that has already rendered a decision; an appellate court reviews the court record from the original trial and does not hear new evidence. (Ch. 5)

Appointment power the ability to determine who will occupy key positions within the bureaucracy. (Ch. 4)

Appraisal the official estimate of a property's value. (Ch. 9)

Astroturf lobbying a simulation of grassroots support, usually conducted by specialized lobbying firms; involves spending large sums of money to generate the appearance of public support to advance a group's agenda. (Ch. 8)

At-large election an election in which a city or county is treated as a single district and candidates are elected from the entire district as a whole. (Ch. 5)

Auditor a county officer appointed by the district judge to oversee county finances. (Ch. 6)

Beyond a reasonable doubt the standard burden of proof necessary to find a defendant guilty in a criminal trial; the defendant is presumed innocent. (Ch. 5)

Bicameral a legislature that consists of two separate chambers or houses. (Ch. 3)

Bill a proposed new law or change to existing law brought before a legislative chamber by a legislative member. (Ch. 3)

Blanket or wide-open primary a primary in which voters do not register party affiliations and receive ballot papers containing the names of all candidates from all political parties running for office; usually voters may choose only one candidate per office rather than one candidate per political party. (Ch. 7)

Block grant national funds given to state and local governments for a broad purpose; comes with fewer restrictions on how the money is to be spent. (Ch. 2)

Blocking bill a bill regularly introduced in the Texas Senate to serve as a placeholder at the top of the Senate calendar; sometimes called a "stopper." (Ch. 3)

Budget power the executive's ability to exert influence on the state's budget process. (Ch. 4)

Casework the process of solving problems for constituents. (Ch. 7)

Categorical grant national money given to states and local governments that must be spent for specific activities. (Ch. 2)

Ceremonial duty an appearance made by the governor as the most visible state officeholder that can function as a source of power; includes appearances at events and performance of ceremonial functions. (Ch. 4)

Chronic minority a group that rarely wins elections or achieves majority status and thus sees few reasons to become actively engaged in politics. (Ch. 8)

Chubbing the act of delaying action on the current bill before the Texas House of Representatives to prevent action on an upcoming bill. (Ch. 3)

Citizen initiative a citizen-initiated petition that forces consideration or votes on certain legislation and amendments, rather than having these actions come from the legislature. (Ch. 3)

Citizen legislature a legislature that attempts to keep the role of a state legislator to a part-time function so that many or most citizens can perform it; normally, a citizen legislator is provided minimal compensation, offered few staffing resources, and has short or infrequent legislative sessions. (Ch. 3)

City charter in home rule cities, a plan of government that details the structure and function of the city government; similar to a constitution. (Ch. 6)

Civil case a case in which an aggrieved party sues for damages claiming that he or she has been wronged by another individual. (Ch. 5)

Civil defendant the party alleged to have committed the wrong at issue in the suit. (Ch. 5)

Closed primary an electoral contest restricted to party loyalists and excluding supporters of other political parties and independent voters. (Ch. 7)

Closed rider a rider that is not made public until after the legislature has voted on the bill, either when the bill goes to a conference committee for reconciliation or when the governor prepares to sign the bill into law. (Ch. 3)

Cohesion unity within a group; in politics, when members of a political party or special caucus vote together on a bill or resolution. (Ch. 3)

Collective goods benefits that, once provided, go to everyone and cannot be effectively denied to others, even those who did not contribute to the effort. (Ch. 8)

Commissioners court the governing body for Texas counties, consisting of four elected commissioners and the judge from the county constitutional court. (Ch. 6)

Committee a formally organized group of legislators that assists the legislature in accomplishing its work, allowing a division of labor and an in-depth review of an issue or a bill before review by the entire chamber. (Ch. 3)

Compensatory damages monetary damages designed to compensate the injured party. (Ch. 5)

Concurrent jurisdiction a system where different levels of courts have overlapping jurisdiction, resulting in a confusing and ill-defined system. (Ch. 5)

Concurrent powers powers such as taxing and spending and the ability to establish courts and charter banks that are shared by the national and state governments. (Ch. 2)

Concurrent resolution a legislative act that expresses an opinion of the legislature; must pass in both houses. (Ch. 3)

Confederal system a type of government where the lower units of government retain decision-making authority. (Ch. 2)

Conference committee an official legislative work group that meets on a limited basis to reconcile the different versions of a bill that has passed in the Texas House and Senate. (Ch. 3)

Constable an elected county officer who acts as a judicial officer for minor criminal and civil cases. (Ch. 6)

Constitution a written document that outlines the powers of government and the limitations on those powers. (Ch. 2)

Contract outsourcing a process whereby a government entity contracts with a private company to perform a service that governments traditionally provide, such as a contract to collect trash and garbage. (Ch. 6)

Conventions (caucuses) meetings at which party members participate in a range of party business. (Ch. 8)

County attorney the county official who represents the county in legal activities and offers legal advice to the county government. (Ch. 6)

County chair (*see* Precinct chair)

County civil service commission the agency administering the county's civil service system; develops job definitions, qualification processes, employee classifications, and other aspects of the system. (Ch. 6)

County clerk the elected county official who maintains county records and in some counties oversees elections. (Ch. 6)

County or senatorial district convention held on the third Saturday after the primary election, a convention in which delegates to the statewide convention are selected. (Ch. 8)

Credit claiming the advantage derived from incumbents' ability to point to positive outcomes for which they are responsible. (Ch. 7)

Criminal case a case in which an individual is charged by the state with violating the laws and the state brings the suit. (Ch. 5)

Criminal defendant a person charged with committing a crime. (Ch. 5)

Crisis manager the responsibility to act as a policymaker, coordinator of resources, and point person in the wake of natural and man-made disasters. (Ch. 4)

Cross filing a system that allows a candidate to run simultaneously as a Democratic and a Republican candidate, essentially competing in both parties' primaries. (Ch. 7)

Cumulative voting a system that allows voters to take the total number of positions to be selected in a district and concentrate their votes among one or a few candidates. (Ch. 5)

Delegate an elected official who acts as an agent of the majority that elected her or him to office and carries out, to the extent possible, the wishes of that majority. (Ch. 3)

Delegated powers the powers listed in Article I, Section 8 of the U.S. Constitution that are expressly granted to the national government. (Ch. 2)

Delegates party members elected to attend their party's conventions held later at the county level or the Texas senatorial district level. (Ch. 8)

De novo to hear an appeal with a new trial, most commonly taken in the absence of an official case record. (Ch. 5)

Dillon's Rule the principle that regardless of the type of local government, all local governments are creatures of the state government and have only those powers specifically granted to them by the state. (Ch. 6)

Direct primary a primary election in which the winning candidate directly receives the party nomination. (Ch. 7)

Disclosure the reporting of who contributes money to a campaign and how much is contributed by an individual or corporation. (Ch. 7)

Distributive policy moves benefits to meet the needs of citizens but does so without targeting any one group as the source of money. (Ch. 9)

Disturbance theory a theory of group formation that states that as societies become more complex and more diverse, new interests emerge to voice their concerns, prompting established interests to mobilize to protect the status quo. (Ch. 8)

Education Reform Act a 1984 statute that requires teachers and school administrators to take a test to assure basic competency before being recertified; students are also tested periodically to monitor progress and are required to pass an exam before being allowed to graduate. (Ch. 9)

Electioneering method used by organized interests to try to shape public policy by influencing who is elected to office, especially by serving as sources of campaign funding. (Ch. 8)

Electoral competition model the view that parties make a pragmatic move to the center of the political spectrum as they attempt to win votes, sacrificing the more purely ideological positions. (Ch. 8)

Emergency clause language that makes a bill effective immediately upon being signed into law rather than subject to the customary ninety-day waiting period. (Ch. 3)

Eminent domain the power of government to take private property for public use, generally for public functions such as roads. (Ch. 9)

Empresario an entrepreneur who made money colonizing areas of the Mexican territories. (Ch. 1)

En banc an appeal that is heard by the entire court of appeals, rather than by a select panel of judges. (Ch. 5)

Equal Protection Clause clause of the Fourteenth Amendment to the U.S. Constitution requiring that state laws and state constitutions treat all citizens the same. (Ch. 7)

Excise tax a tax paid at the time of purchase, with the cost of the tax included in the price of the product. (Ch. 9)

Exclusive jurisdiction a particular level of court with the sole right to hear a specific type of case. (Ch. 5)

Executive committee this group, selected at the state party convention, carries on the activities of the party between party conventions; by law, the committee consists of one man and one woman from each state senatorial district. (Ch. 8)

Expressive benefits benefits that arise from taking action to express one's views; motivates group membership. (Ch. 8)

Extradition the constitutional requirement that states deliver someone suspected or convicted of a crime in another state back to that state so they can face trial or sentencing. (Ch. 2)

Federalism a form of government based on the sharing of powers between the national and state governments. (Ch. 2)

Filibuster an effort to kill a bill by engaging in unlimited debate and refusing to yield the floor to another member, ultimately preventing a vote on the bill. (Ch. 3)

Fiscal federalism use of national financial incentives to encourage policies at the state level. (Ch. 2)

Fiscal policy how government seeks to influence the economy through taxing and spending. (Ch. 9)

Floor debate period during which a bill is brought up before the entire chamber for debate. (Ch. 3)

Floor whip a party member who reminds legislators of the party's position on a bill and encourages members to vote with the rest of the party caucus. (Ch. 3)

Franchise tax the primary tax on businesses in Texas, which is based on the "taxable margin" of each company. (Ch. 9)

Free-rider problem occurs when citizens who do not contribute to the effort of a group nevertheless enjoy the results of the group's efforts. (Ch. 8)

Full faith and credit clause the constitutional requirement that court judgments or legal contracts entered into in one state will be honored by other states. (Ch. 2)

General election an inter-party election in which candidates from two or more political parties and independent candidates compete for actual political office. (Ch. 7)

General law city the default organization for Texas cities, with the exact forms of government, ordinance powers, and other aspects of city government specified in the Texas Local Government Code. (Ch. 6)

General sales tax an across-the-board tax imposed on goods and services sold within a jurisdiction. (Ch. 9)

Gerrymandering the practice of incumbents creating very oddly shaped electoral districts to maximize their political advantage in an upcoming election. (Ch. 3)

Grandfather clause the granting of voting rights only to those citizens whose grandfathers had the right to vote; used to bar African Americans from voting in the South after the end of Reconstruction. (Ch. 7)

Grand jury a panel of twelve jurors that reviews evidence, determines whether there is sufficient evidence to bring a trial, and issues an indictment. (Ch. 5)

Grassroots lobbying attempts by organized interests to influence legislators through public opinion; extension of democratic principles in which groups of citizens spontaneously mobilize to build support for a cause. (Ch. 8)

Grassroots organization a group in which power and decision making reside with average citizens; the participation of average citizens is the foundation upon which these groups' legitimacy rests. (Ch. 8)

Grasstop lobbying the attempt to influence legislators through key constituents or friends. (Ch. 8)

Help America Vote Act (HAVA) federal statute enacted after the 2000 presidential election to effectively standardize election procedures. (Ch. 7)

Higher Education Coordinating Board a group of thirteen appointed by the governor for six-year terms to oversee higher education policy in Texas. (Ch. 9)

Home rule city a city that has been granted greater freedom in the organization and functioning of city government; can make structural and administrative changes without seeking permission from the state. (Ch. 6)

Horizontal federalism refers to the relationship between the states. (Ch. 2)

Hyperpluralism a view that the system today has evolved beyond simple pluralism and is now one in which many narrow interests are represented, often at the expense of the broader public interest. (Ch. 8)

Ideological caucus a special caucus in the state legislature that promotes an ideological agenda. (Ch. 3)

Impeachment formal procedure to remove an elected official from office for misdeeds; passage of the articles of impeachment by the House merely suggests that there is sufficient evidence for a trial, which is then conducted by the Senate. (Ch. 4)

Income tax a tax calculated as a percentage of income earned in a year. (Ch. 9)

Incumbency advantage the advantage enjoyed by the incumbent candidate, or current officeholder, in elections; the advantage is based on greater visibility, proven record of public service, and often better access to resources. (Ch. 5)

Incumbent the current officeholder. (Ch. 7)

Independent candidate a candidate running for office without a political party affiliation. (Ch. 7)

Indictment a document that formally charges a defendant with committing a crime. (Ch. 5)

Indirect primary a primary election in which voters elect delegates to a party convention; delegates are pledged to support a specific candidate seeking the party nomination. (Ch. 7)

Individualistic political culture the idea that individuals are best left largely free of the intervention of community forces like government and that government should attempt only those things demanded by the people it is created to serve. (Ch. 1)

Informal power an attribute of personal power based on factors such as electoral mandate, political ambition ladder, personal future as governor, and performance ratings rather than on constitutionally enumerated powers. (Ch. 4)

Initiative a mechanism that allows voters to gather signatures on a petition in order to place statutes or constitutional amendments on a ballot. (Ch. 2)

Instant run-off a type of election in which second-place votes are considered in instances where no candidate has received a majority of the vote; a winner is determined by adding together the first and second place votes. (Ch. 3)

Intergovernmental lobby the lobbying that occurs between different levels of government, such as between the state and national government or between local governments and the state government. (Ch. 8)

Interim committee a legislative work group that is created during periods when the legislature is not in session to provide oversight of the executive branch and monitor public policy. (Ch. 3)

Introduce [a bill] to officially bring a bill before a legislative chamber for the first time. Introducing a bill is the first step in the formal legislative process. (Ch. 3)

Issue caucus a special caucus in the state legislature that promotes bipartisan and cross-chamber support for policies and bills advocating positions inside a relatively narrow range of policy areas or political issues. (Ch. 3)

Joint resolution a legislative act whose approval by both chambers results in amendment to the Texas Constitution; a resolution must be approved by voters at the next election. (Ch. 3)

Judicial federalism a system in which judicial authority is shared between levels of government. (Ch. 5)

Jurisdiction the court's sphere of authority. (Ch. 5)

Justice of the peace an elected county officer who acts as a judicial officer for minor criminal and civil cases. (Ch. 6)

Killer amendment language added to a bill on an unrelated or controversial topic in order to make the bill unacceptable to the majority of the legislature who will then vote against the bill. (Ch. 3)

Labor unions organizations that represent the interests of working people seeking better pay and better working conditions. (Ch. 8)

Legislative Budget Board (LBB) the group that develops a proposed state budget for legislative consideration. (Ch. 3)

Legislative Redistricting Board (LRB) created by a 1948 amendment to the Texas Constitution, this group steps in if the state legislature is unable to pass a redistricting plan or when a state or federal court invalidates a plan submitted by the legislature; the LRB is active only with respect to redistricting of the state legislature. (Ch. 3)

Legislative role the executive's role in influencing the state's legislative agenda. (Ch. 4)

Lieutenant governor the presiding officer of the Texas Senate, elected directly by the voters. (Ch. 3)

Line-item veto the ability of the executive to selectively veto only some parts of an appropriations bill. (Ch. 3)

Literacy test a test of a prospective voter's ability to read and understand aspects of American government; used to bar African Americans from voting in many parts of the post-Reconstruction South, but not widely used in Texas. (Ch. 7)

Lobbying direct contact with members of the legislative or executive branch to influence legislation or administrative action. (Ch. 8)

Long ballot a system in which almost all of the positions in a state are elected rather than appointed. (Ch. 2)

Machine politics a system of patronage whereby political organizations, led by a local party boss, disperse city jobs, government contracts, and other benefits to maintain control of city governance; power once acquired is typically used for personal gain. (Ch. 6)

Magistrate functions the authority to conduct the preliminary procedures in criminal cases, issuing search and arrest warrants, conducting preliminary hearings, and setting bail for more serious crimes. (Ch. 5)

Majority election a type of election in which a candidate must receive 50 percent of the vote plus one additional vote to be declared the winner; simply winning the most votes is not sufficient. (Ch. 3)

Majority-minority district an election district in which the majority of the population comes from a racial or ethnic minority. (Ch. 3)

Manifest Destiny the belief that U.S. expansion across the North American continent was inevitable. (Ch. 2)

Mark-up process whereby a committee goes line-by-line through a bill to make changes without formal amendments. (Ch. 3)

Medicaid a federal program providing medical coverage for low-income people and some elderly and disabled people. (Ch. 9)

Medicare a federal health insurance program available to senior citizens who have worked and paid into the Medicare system for ten or more years. (Ch. 9)

Merit-based civil service system a system in which people receive government jobs based upon a set of qualifications and formal training; job promotion and pay raises are based upon job performance. (Ch. 6)

Minority and women's caucuses special caucuses in the state legislature that represent the unique concerns and beliefs of women and ethnic groups across a broad range of policy issues. (Ch. 3)

Moralistic political culture rare in Texas, the view that the exercise of community pressure is sometimes necessary to advance the public good; it also holds that government can be a positive force and citizens have a duty to participate. (Ch. 1)

Motor Voter Act the National Voter Registration Act that allows citizens to register to vote when applying for or renewing their driver's license. (Ch. 7)

Multi-member district (MMD) an election system in which the state is divided into many election districts, but each district elects more than one person to the state legislature. (Ch. 3)

Municipal bond a certificate of indebtedness issued by a city that serves as a pledge by the city to pay back the loan over time with interest; used to raise money for services and infrastructure; may also be issued by other forms of local government such as counties, school districts, and special districts. (Ch. 6)

Municipal utility district (MUD) a special district that provides water, sewer, or similar services to individuals and businesses outside city limits. (Ch. 6)

Name recognition making a voting choice based on familiarity with or previous recognition of a candidate's name. (Ch. 5)

NIMBY acronym for "not in my backyard"; local efforts to prevent the situating of potentially harmful activities, such as industrial waste disposal, in nearby areas. (Ch. 9)

"No Child Left Behind" Act (NCLB) the federal education act, based on the Texas standardized testing statutes, that requires schools to institute mandatory testing to track student progress and evaluates schools based on that progress. (Ch. 9)

Nonpartisan or bipartisan independent commission a system of drawing electoral district lines that attempts to remove politics from the process of redistricting. (Ch. 3)

One person, one vote shorthand term for the requirement of the U.S. Supreme Court that election districts should be roughly equal in population. (Ch. 3)

Open primary an electoral contest in which voters are not required to declare a party affiliation to participate, but must request a specific party's ballot at the primary; voters are subsequently barred from participating in the other party's primary. (Ch. 7)

Ordinance a law enacted by a city government. (Ch. 6)

Organized interest an individual, group of people, or group of businesses that organizes its efforts to influence public policy. (Ch. 8)

Original jurisdiction the authority to hear the initial case; the evidence and the case record are established in this court. (Ch. 5)

Oversight the process whereby the legislature reviews policies and decisions of the executive branch to make sure that the executive branch is following the intentions of the legislature. (Ch. 3)

Pardon an executive grant of release from a sentence or punishment in a criminal case. (Ch. 4)

Partisan election a type of election in which candidates' names and party affiliations appear on the ballot. (Ch. 6)

Party affiliation a candidate's identifiable membership in a political party, often listed on an election ballot. (Ch. 3)

Party caucus the organization of the members of a specific legislative chamber who belong to a political party. (Ch. 3)

Party caucus chair a party leader whose main job is to organize party members to vote for legislation on the floor. (Ch. 3)

Party-line voting process in which voters select candidates by their party affiliation. (Ch. 7)

Party platform the document that officially spells out the issue stands of a party; written and approved at the party conventions. (Ch. 8)

Party primary an electoral contest to win a political party's nomination for the right to appear as its candidate on the ballot in the general election. (Ch. 3)

Patronage when individuals who supported a candidate for public office are rewarded with public jobs and appointments. (Ch. 4)

"Pay-as-you-go" system a fiscal discipline, adopted by Texas and many other states, that requires a balanced budget and permits borrowing only under a very few circumstances. (Ch. 9)

Permanent party organizations the party officials selected by the temporary organizations to conduct party business between the primaries, caucuses, and conventions. (Ch. 8)

Permanent School Fund a fund set aside to finance education in Texas; the state's largest source of investment income. (Ch. 9)

Permanent University Fund (PUF) an endowment funded by mineral rights and other revenue generated by 2.1 million acres of land set aside by the state; investment returns support schools in the University of Texas and Texas A&M systems. (Ch. 9)

Petit jury a trial jury; jurors attend a trial, listen to evidence, and determine whether a defendant is innocent or guilty. (Ch. 5)

Plaintiff the party claiming to have been wronged and bringing the suit. (Ch. 5)

Plank an individual issue position of the party platform. (Ch. 8)

Plural executive an executive branch in which the functions have been divided among several, mostly elected, officeholders rather than residing in a single person, the governor. (Ch. 4)

Pluralist perspective a view of politics that argues that democracy is best practiced when citizens participate through groups; a greater number of organized interests means wider participation and a healthier democracy. (Ch. 8)

Plurality election a type of election in which the candidate with the most votes wins the election. (Ch. 3)

Policy the actions and activities of government. (Ch. 9)

Policy adoption the stage in which formal government action takes place. (Ch. 9)

Policy evaluation the stage in which the implementation of a policy is examined to see if policy goals are being met. (Ch. 9)

Policy formation the stage in which possible solutions are developed and debated. (Ch. 9)

Policy implementation the stage in which the policy is carried out in state agencies. (Ch. 9)

Political action committee (PAC) the fundraising arm of an interest group that has been organized to meet the requirements of state and federal campaign finance laws. (Ch. 8)

Political ambition ladder the manner in which a political figure has come up through the ranks, working through various levels of state governmental offices and positions on the way to the top position; climbing several levels on the ladder can increase a politician's contacts, allies, and political savvy. (Ch. 4)

Political culture the shared values and beliefs of citizens about the nature of the political world that give the public a common language as a foundation to discuss and debate ideas. (Ch. 1)

Political party any group, however loosely organized, seeking to elect governmental officeholders under a given label. (Ch. 8)

Politico an elected official who is expected to follow the wishes of the electorate on some issues but on others is permitted more decision-making leeway; a hybrid of the trustee and delegate. (Ch. 3)

Poll tax an annual tax that had to be paid before one was allowed to vote; allowed by a 1902 amendment to the Texas Constitution and used to legally bar African Americans from voting. (Ch. 7)

Popular mandate the claim that a newly elected official's legislative agenda is the will of the people based on a high margin of victory in a general election. (Ch. 4)

Popular sovereignty a government where the power to govern is derived from the will of the people. (Ch. 2)

Position taking an incumbent's advantage in having an existing record of positions on issues, both from previous elections and in the context of decisions made while in office. (Ch. 7)

Post-adjournment veto a veto that occurs after the legislature has adjourned, leaving the legislature unable to overturn it. (Ch. 4)

Precinct chair; County chair a precinct chair is selected by party members in each voting precinct by majority vote; a county chair is selected by countywide vote. These party officials are responsible for managing the local affairs of their party for the next two years. (Ch. 8)

Preference primary a primary election in which voters indicate their choice to hold office, but the actual selection is left to the political party elites. (Ch. 7)

Preponderance of evidence the burden of proof in a civil case, which is lower than that in a criminal case; the plaintiff must show merely that the defendant is likely to have committed the wrong. (Ch. 5)

Presidential republicanism the practice in the South of voting for Republicans in presidential elections but voting for conservative Democrats in other races, a practice that continued until animosity over Reconstruction faded and the Republicans demonstrated their electability in the South. (Ch. 1)

President pro tempore a presiding officer elected by the members of the Texas Senate; takes over when the lieutenant governor is unavailable. (Ch. 3)

Primary election intra-party election in which candidates compete to determine who will win the party's nomination in the general election. (Ch. 7)

Private financing a system of campaign financing in which citizens, interest groups, labor unions, and corporations donate funds to cover the cost of elections for political parties or candidates to cover the cost of an election. (Ch. 7)

Private prison a private, for-profit prison corporation that staffs and runs prison facilities in a state. (Ch. 5)

Privatization a process whereby a government entity sells off assets or services to a private company which is then responsible for providing a service; for example, a school district sells its buses to a private company and then allows the company to provide transportation to schools. (Ch. 6)

Privileges and immunities the constitutional requirement that states may not fundamentally treat citizens of other states differently than their own citizens. (Ch. 2)

Professional associations organizations that represent the needs of professionals not represented by unions. (Ch. 8)

Professional legislature a legislature that meets annually, often for nine months of the year or more; a professional legislator is provided a professional-level salary and generous allowances to hire and keep support and research staffs. (Ch. 3)

Progressive tax a graduated tax, such as an income tax, which taxes people with higher incomes at higher rates. (Ch. 9)

Property tax a tax on the value of real estate that is paid by the property owner; used by county and local governments to fund such programs as public schools. (Ch. 9)

Prosecutor a lawyer who represents the government and brings a case in criminal trials. (Ch. 5)

Public financing a system of campaign financing in which the government covers the cost of elections for political parties or candidates. (Ch. 7)

Public-interest groups organizations that pursue noneconomic policies on behalf of the general public, even if all members of the general public do not agree on these issues or policies. (Ch. 8)

Punitive damages larger monetary awards designed to punish the defendant and, perhaps, send a message to the larger society. (Ch. 5)

Quorum the minimum number of members in a legislative body who need to be present for it to conduct business; in the Texas Senate, a quorum is eleven members. In the Texas House of Representatives a quorum is one hundred members. (Ch. 3)

Recess appointment a gubernatorial appointment made while the Senate is not in session; requires Senate approval within ten days of the next legislative session. (Ch. 4)

Recidivism a former inmate's resumption of criminal activity after his or her release from prison. (Ch. 5)

Redistributive policy moves benefits, usually in the form of money, from one group to another in an attempt to equalize society. (Ch. 9)

Redistricting the periodic adjustment of the lines of electoral district boundaries. (Ch. 3)

Referendum a mechanism that allows voters to cast a popular vote on statutes passed by the state legislature; the legislature can place measures on the ballot for voter consideration. (Ch. 2)

Regressive tax a tax, such as a sales tax, that taxes everyone at the same rate, regardless of income; has a greater impact on those with lower incomes. (Ch. 9)

Regulation government rulemaking and enforcement intended to protect citizens from being harmed by private firms. (Ch. 9)

Regulatory policy attempts to limit or control the actions of individuals or corporations. (Ch. 9)

Removal power the power of the governor to remove an appointee; in Texas, the governor may remove his or her own appointees with the consent of two-thirds of the Texas Senate. (Ch. 4)

Representation the relationship between an elected official and the electorate. (Ch. 3)

Reserved powers the specification in the Tenth Amendment that all powers not delegated to the national government belong to the states. (Ch. 2)

Resolution a legislative act that expresses the opinion of the legislature on an issue or changes the organizational structure of the legislature. (Ch. 3)

Responsible party model the view that each party should hold firmly to a clear and consistent set of policies with a coherent ideology distinct from that of other parties to present voters with clear choices. (Ch. 8)

Revolving door the phenomenon of legislators and members of the executive branch moving easily from government office to lucrative positions with lobbying firms. (Ch. 8)

Rider an addition to a bill that deals with an unrelated subject such as changing some aspect of law or public policy or spending money or creating programs in a specific member's district. (Ch. 3)

Roll call vote a form of voting for which a permanent record of each member's vote is created; used with more important votes. (Ch. 3)

Roll off process in which voters mark off only the "more important" offices on a lengthy ballot—usually national or statewide offices—and leave the county or local office choices blank. (Ch. 7)

Run-off election a type of election in SMDM that is held when an election fails to yield a clear majority winner in the initial balloting; the run-off is limited to the top two vote-getters from the initial election, ensuring a majority win. (Ch. 3)

Run-off primary a primary that occurs if no nominee receives the required majority of the votes in the primary; the top two finishers face off in a second primary to determine the nominee for the general election. (Ch. 8)

Second order elections elections for offices below the national executive level in countries with presidential systems like the United States or the national legislature level in parliamentary countries like Great Britain; generally viewed as less important in scope and impact on a country. (Ch. 7)

Select committee a temporary legislative work group created by the lieutenant governor or Speaker of the Texas House of Representatives for a special purpose; called a joint committee when the lieutenant governor and Speaker of the Texas House of Representatives create a select committee with members from both chambers. (Ch. 3)

Selective incentives benefits exclusively available to members of an organization. (Ch. 8)

Senatorial courtesy the informal requirement that a gubernatorial appointee have approval of her or his own state senator in order to obtain support within the Senate. (Ch. 4)

Severance tax a tax on natural resources charged when the resources are produced or "severed" from the earth. (Ch. 9)

Sheriff the elected county official who oversees county law enforcement. (Ch. 6)

Simple resolution a legislative act that addresses organizational issues; may be limited to a single house. (Ch. 3)

Sin tax tax on products or activities, such as cigarettes or gambling, that some legislators would like to discourage. (Ch. 9)

Single-interest groups groups usually organized around one side of a single issue, such as pro-choice or anti-abortion groups. (Ch. 8)

Single-member district (SMD) an election system in which the state is divided into many election districts, and each district elects just one person to the state legislature. (Ch. 3)

Solidarity benefits the social interactions that individuals enjoy from joining a group and from working together for a common cause. (Ch. 8)

Speaker of the House the presiding officer of the Texas House of Representatives. (Ch. 3)

Speaker pro tempore officer that presides over the House of Representatives when the Speaker is unavailable; akin to the president pro tempore in the Texas Senate. (Ch. 3)

Special caucus an organization of members of the state legislature who share a common interest or have constituencies with a common interest. (Ch. 3)

Special session the ability to require the legislature to meet outside its regular session; in Texas the governor can invoke this power "on extraordinary occasions" for a thirty-day period to consider an agenda the governor has predetermined. (Ch. 4)

Standing committee a permanent, chamber-specific formal work group that typically exists across sessions and across elections. (Ch. 3)

State Children's Health Insurance Program (SCHIP) a federal-state program that offers health insurance and medical care to the children of families that make too much to qualify for Medicaid but not enough to afford private health insurance. (Ch. 9)

State Nutritional Action Plans (SNAP) Texas's version of food stamps that helps low-income seniors, people with disabilities, and single people and families in need buy food from local retailers. (Ch. 9)

State of the state address the constitutional requirement that the governor address the state legislature about the condition of the state; the state of the state address occurs at the beginning of each legislative session as well as at the end of the governor's term. (Ch. 4)

State party chair individual selected at the state party convention to head the state executive committee; state law mandates that a man and a woman be chosen. (Ch. 8)

Straight ticket voting the practice of selecting all the candidates for office who are running under a party label simply by checking off a single box marked with the party label. (Ch. 5)

Structuring the vote the way in which political parties align support or opposition to bills. (Ch. 3)

Subsidy incentive designed to encourage the production or purchase of certain goods, to stimulate or support some businesses. (Ch. 9)

Succession a set order, usually spelled out in the constitution, denoting which officeholder takes over when the sitting governor resigns, dies, or is impeached. (Ch. 4)

Suffrage the legal right to vote. (Ch. 7)

Sunset review process a formal assessment of the effectiveness of all statutory boards, commissions, and state agencies. (Ch. 4)

Sunshine laws laws designed to make government transparent and accessible. (Ch. 4)

Supremacy clause the section in the U.S. Constitution that guarantees that the national government is the supreme law of the land, and national laws and the national constitution supersede state laws and state constitutions. (Ch. 2)

Tax assessor the elected county officer who collects county taxes and user fees. (Ch. 6)

Temporary Assistance for Needy Families (TANF) federal program that provides eligible households with monthly cash payments and Medicaid benefits. (Ch. 9)

Temporary party organizations gatherings of ordinary party members such as primaries, caucuses, and conventions. (Ch. 8)

Term limit a legal limitation on the number of terms an elected official may serve in office. (Ch. 3)

Texas Assessment of Academic Skills (TAAS) a standardized test implemented in 1990 to create higher standards for state educational assessment. (Ch. 9)

Texas Assessment of Knowledge and Skills (TAKS) replaced TAAS in 2003; a standardized test given to students starting in grade 3 to assess reading and math skills; also mandates periodic tests in writing, language arts, science, and social sciences. (Ch. 9)

Texas Commission on Environmental Quality (TCEQ) the agency that oversees state environmental policy, including air and water quality. (Ch. 9)

Trade associations organizations of similar businesses, which work together to advance shared goals. (Ch. 8)

Traditionalistic political culture the idea, most prevalent in the parts of Texas most like the Old South, that government has a limited role concerned with the preservation of the existing social order. (Ch. 1)

Treaty of Guadalupe Hidalgo signed on February 2, 1848, this agreement between the United States and Mexico ended the Mexican-American War and recognized the Rio Grande as the boundary between Texas, now part of the United States, and Mexico. (Ch. 1)

Trustee an elected official who is entrusted to act in the best interests of the electorate based on his or her knowledge; he or she is understood to be generally better informed than the broader electorate. (Ch. 3)

Turnover when current officeholders step down from office and are replaced by new office-holders; turnover may result from retirement, defeat in an election, or term limits. (Ch. 3)

Unfunded mandate legislation passed by the national government imposing requirements on state and local governments, which bear the costs of meeting those requirements. (Ch. 2)

Unitary system a type of government where power is vested in a central governmental authority. (Ch. 2)

Vertical federalism the distribution of power between the national and state governments. (Ch. 2)

Veto power the formal power of the executive to reject bills that have been passed by the legislature; in Texas, a veto can be overridden only by a two-thirds vote in both houses. (Ch. 4)

Voter turnout the number of people casting ballots in a given election. (Ch. 7)

Voting Rights Act of 1965 (VRA) a federal statute that eliminated literacy tests as a qualification to vote, greatly increasing African Americans' access to the ballot box. (Ch. 7)

White primary the attempt by the Democratic Party in Texas and other southern states to limit the voting in party primaries only to party members; in Texas, codified in state law. (Ch. 7)

Zoning policy policy whereby the city restricts what individuals and entities may do with their property, usually by designating certain areas of the city for industrial, commercial, or residential uses. (Ch. 6)

Image Credits

Chapter 1 Introduction

Page xxii: © Clarke Conde/Alamy
Page 5 (map): The Granger Collection, New York
Page 6: © Vince Streano/Corbis
Page 7: The Granger Collection, New York
Page 10: The Library of Congress
Page 15: © Stephen Saks Photography/Alamy
Page 18: Wyatt McSpadden, all rights reserved

Chapter 2 Texas Constitution

Page 30: © Bob Daemmrich/Corbis
Page 39 (map): The Granger Collection, New York
Page 47: http://en.wikipedia.org/wiki/Image:Edmund_Davis.jpg

Chapter 3 Texas Legislature

Page 60: © Bob Daemmrich/Bob Daemmrich Photography, Inc./Corbis
Page 72: Courtesy of Ken Collier
Page 77: AP Photo

Chapter 4 Governors and Bureaucracy in Texas

Page 100: © Bob E. Daemmrich/Sygma/Corbis
Page 107: AP Photo/David Breslauer
Page 112: © Bob E. Daemmrich/Sygma/Corbis
Page 125: AP Photo

Chapter 5 Texas Judicial System

Page 130: © Benjamin Cawthra/Alamy
Page 137: http://en.wikipedia.org/wiki/File:Roybean2.jpg
Page 147: © Bettmann/Corbis
Page 151: Per-Anders Pettersson/Getty Images

Chapter 6 Local Government in Texas

Page 156: © Ocean/Corbis
Page 165: © Stock Connection Distribution/Alamy
Page 170: © Stephen Saks Photography/Alamy
Page 178: AP Photo

Chapter 7 Elections: Texas Style

Page 188: © Nick Anderson of the *Houston Chronicle*, dist. by The Washington Post Writers Group. Reprinted with Permission.
Page 193: From the collection of Edward Lynn Williams, Farmers Branch, Texas
Page 199: Lyndon Baines Johnson Library and Museum
Page 206: Ballot image provided by the Louisiana Secretary of State's Office
Page 215: AP Photo/Harry Cabluck

Chapter 8 Parties and Organized Interests

Page 226: AP Photo/LM Otero
Page 234: *ND-41-A004-01*, Austin History Center, Austin Public Library

Chapter 9 Policy

Page 258: AP Photo/Harry Cabluck
Page 272: AP Photo/Jack Plunkett
Page 284: AP Photo/Tony Gutierrez
Page 286: "Candorville" © 2004 Darrin Bell, www.Candorville.com

Inside back cover (map): International Mapping Associates

Index

Tables, figures, boxes, maps, and notes are indicated by t, f, b, m, and n, respectively, after page numbers. Alphabetization is letter-by-letter (e.g., "Educational attainment" precedes "Education Code").

At-large elections, 141, 169, 175–177
Attorney general
    constitutional parameters of office of, 50
    on Legislative Redistricting Board, 81
    role of, 121–122
Auditors, county, 166
Austin, Stephen F., 6–7, 40, 43, 124, 147*b*

B
Bache, Richard, 11
Baker v. Carr (1962), 64, 81
Ballots. *See also* Long ballot
    appearing on, 198–200
    bilingual, 195
Barbour, Christine, 261*n*
Barr, Alwyn, 302*n*
Barton, David, 227
Bassett, Samuel, 131
Battle, William J., 16
Bean, Roy, 137*b*
Beck, Paul Allen, 302*n*
Bell, Charles G., 296*n*
Bell, Christopher, 215*b*, 222
Bernstein, Jared, 293*n*
Beyle, Thad, 117–118, 120, 297*n*
Beyond a reasonable doubt standard, 146
Bibby, John F., 301*n*
Bicameral legislature, 63
Bill of Rights, Texas, 43, 48, 50
Bill of Rights, U.S., 33
Bills, legislative
    amendment of, 89–90, 95
    blocking, 94
    calendar committee, 93–94, 94*t*
    chubbing, 95
    defined, 73
    filibuster, 95
    floor debate, 95
    introduction of, 91–92
    killer amendment, 95
    process, 91–97, 93*f*
Bipartisan Campaign Reform Act of 2002, 220
Bipartisan independent commissions, 81
Black, Earl, 302*n*
Black, Merle, 302*n*
Blackshear, Edward, 16
Blanco, Kathleen, 117, 207*b*
Blanket primaries, 204
Block grants, 37
Blocking bill, 94
Board of Education, State (SBOE), 126, 182, 274, 275
Board of Pardons and Paroles, 116, 151
Boards and commissions, 124–126. *See also specific boards and commissions*
Boards of education, local, 181–182
Bonds
    municipal bonds, 180
    revenue bonds, 269–270
Bonnie and Clyde, 147*b*
Brewster County, 162

Brischetto, Robert, 300*n*
Briscoe, Dolph, 104, 108
Briscoe, Michelle G., 296*n*
Brown, Tim, 299*n*
Brown v. Board of Education (1954), 19, 272–273
Brown v. Board of Education (*Brown II,* 1955), 273
Budgets. *See also* Legislative Budget Board (LBB)
    city, 180
    comptroller and, 122–123
    federal funding for, 249, 267–268
    governor's budget power, 114
    "pay-as-you-go" system, 269
    policy, 268–270, 269–270*t*
    state shortfall, 67
Buffalo Gap, 170*b*, 283
Bullock, Bob, 18*b*
Bureaucracy, 111–112*t*, 120–124. *See also specific boards and commissions*
    accountability of, 126–128
    sunset review process, 126–128, 127*f*
    sunshine laws, 126
Burke, Edmund, 232
Burnet, David G., 9, 215*b*
Bush, George W.
    Florida vote for president (2000), 124
    governor succession and, 108
    Hurricane Katrina and, 117
    immigration policy and, 285
    political experience of, 104
    popular mandate of, 117
    vetoes as governor, 115

C
Caldeira, Gregory A., 302*n*
Calendar committee, 93–94, 94*t*
California
    death penalty, compared to Texas, 152–153*b*
    environmental regulation compared to Texas, 281*b*, 282
    legislature in, 64, 69
    lobbying in, 253
    primary elections in, 204–205
    sales tax in, 263
    state constitution, 54
    term limits in, 71
    voting rights in, 195
California Democratic Party v. Jones (2000), 204–205
Calvert, Robert, 294*n*
Campaign finance, 219–223, 221*t*
Campbell, Randolph, 294*n*, 302*n*, 304*n*
Campbell, Thomas, 15–16
Cantrell, Gregg, 294*n*
Capital punishment. *See* Death penalty
Casework, 219
Categorical grants, 36–37
Catholicism, 22, 40, 42
Caucuses
    partisanship and, 97
    party caucus, 85–86
    party caucus chair, 83

Permanent School Fund, 123, 126, 268
Permanent University Fund (PUF), 276
Perot, H. Ross, 273
Perry, Bob J., 222
Perry, Rick
    as agriculture commissioner, 123
    appointment powers and, 112–113
    approval ratings for, 120
    budgeting and spending policy and, 270
    campaign spending by, 221*t*
    compensation of, 109
    as crisis manager, 116
    death penalty cases and, 131
    elections of, 101
    entertainment industry bill, 259–260
    environmental policy and, 282
    executive orders by, 122, 254–255
    executive powers and, 128
    on healthcare reform, 38
    influence of, 101
    legislative special sessions called by, 115
    as lieutenant governor, 83
    patronage by, 112
    reauthorization of TxDOT, 67–68
    redistricting and, 82
    second-term election, 119
    state convention (2010), 227–228
    stimulus package and, 67, 101–102
    succeeding Bush as governor, 108
    tea party movement and, 31–32, 38–39
    terms of, 108
    Trans-Texas Corridor and, 101, 283
    vetoes by, 115–116
Peterson, Kavan, 297*n*
Petit juries, 146
Phillips, Thomas, 142
Picard, Theresa, 167
Pickens, T. Boone, 157, 251
Pilgrim, Lonnie "Bo," 252
Pitts, Jim & John, 255
Plaintiffs, 146
Platforms and planks, 239, 240*t*
Plural executive, 50, 110, 111–112*t,* 120–121
Pluralist perspective, 255
Plurality elections, 78
Plyler v. Doe (1982), 286
Policy, 259–288
    adoption, 260
    agenda setting, 260
    budgeting and spending, 268–270, 269*t,* 270*t*
    defined, 260
    distributive, 261
    education, 271–278
    environmental, 280–282
    evaluation, 261
    fiscal, 262–267
    formation, 261
    health and human services, 279–280
    immigration, 285–286
    implementation, 261

process, 260–261, 261*f*
    redistributive, 261
    regulatory, 261
    transportation, 282–284
Political action committees (PACs), 144–145, 221, 250–251
Political ambition ladder, 120
Political history and culture, 1–29
    confederacy period, 12–13
    current status of, 20–21
    definition of political culture, 20
    Democratic Party dominance, 14–15
    geography and, 3–4
    Great Depression and New Deal, 17, 19
    Mexican independence, 7
    Reconstruction era, 13–14
    reform era, 15–17
    Republic of Texas, 9–11
    statehood, 11–12
    Texas revolution, 7–9
    tradition of change, 21–25
Political parties, 227–257. *See also specific parties*
    affiliation of legislative members, 70
    development of in Texas, 228–232
    electoral competition by, 214–218, 217–218*t*
    functions of, 232–235
    interest groups and, 245–255
    legislative organization of, 85–86
    local, 237–238
    national, 244
    organization of, 235–244, 236*f*
    platforms and planks, 239, 240*t*
    presidential candidate nomination and, 239–243
    primaries, 70. *See also* Primary elections
    state, 239
    third parties, 189
Politico approach to representation, 73
Polk, James K., 11, 12, 42
Poll taxes, 51, 192–195
Popkin, Samuel L., 301*n*
Popular mandate, 117
Popular sovereignty, 33
Population growth, 21–22, 21*t,* 24–25, 52
Populist Party, 15, 193–194, 228–229
Port of Houston Authority, 184
Position taking, 219
Post-adjournment vetoes, 115
Poverty, 279–280
Powers
    constitutional distribution of, 34–36, 35*f*
    of governor, 102–103, 110–120
    state constitutions and, 34, 51
Precinct chairs, 237
Preference primaries, 202
Preponderance of evidence standard, 148
Presidential republicanism, 19
President pro tempore, 84, 108
Presiding officers, legislative, 84
Primary elections, 202–205
    "Jaybird" pre-primaries, 195
    legislative qualifications and, 70

two-step system, 203, 242–243
  voter turnout for, 231, 231*t*
  white primaries, 194
Prisons, privatization of, 148–150, 154
Private financing of campaigns, 220
Privatization
  of government services, 167, 283–284
  of prisons, 148–150, 154
  of welfare services, 280
Privileges and immunities, 36, 68
Probate courts, 137–138
Proctor, Bernadette D., 304*n*
Professional associations, 247, 249
Professional legislatures, 68–69
Progressive Party, 229
Progressive taxes, 267
Project V.O.T.E. (Voters of Tomorrow through
    Education), 124
Property rights, 39, 43, 283–284, 284*b*
Property taxes, 167–168, 184, 185–186, 265–267
Prosecutors, 146
Public financing of campaigns, 220
Public health officer, 166
Public Information Act of 1973 (Texas), 126
Public-interest groups, 249
Public schools. *See* Education
Public Utility Commission (PUC), 126, 282
PUF (Permanent University Fund), 276
Punitive damages, 148

Q
Quorum, 95

R
Race and ethnicity. *See also specific racial and ethnic*
    groups
  city government elections and, 176
  Constitution of 1836 and, 41
  districting and, 81
  of judges, 140, 140–141*f*, 146
  legislative caucuses and, 87
  of legislature members, 76, 76*t*, 78
  representation of, 52
  of state population, 21–22, 22*t*
  Vermont compared to Texas, 25*b*
  voter turnout and, 223
  voting rights and, 51, 196–198
Rackaway, Chapman, 302*n*
Radical Republicans, 45
Railroad Commission, 15, 124–125, 125*b*, 283
Railroads, 282–283
"Raise Your Hand, Texas," 271
Ramsay, William, 16, 215*b*
Rangers, 147*b*
Ranney Index, 216, 218, 218*t*
Ratliff, Bill, 57, 108, 271
Rauch, Jonathan, 303*n*
Recalls, 208
Recess appointments, 113
Recession, effect on legislature, 67

Recidivism, 149–150
Reconstruction era, 13–14, 44–47
Records, state, 124
Redistributive policies, 261
Redistricting, 28, 70–71, 79, 81–83, 82*b*
Referendum. *See* Initiative and referendum
Regressive taxes, 267
Regulation, 261, 280
Reid, Stan, 299*n*
Reif, Karlheinz, 301*n*
Religion, 22, 23*t*, 40, 49*b*
Removal powers, 113, 143
Representation
  defined, 73
  judicial, 139–143, 140–141*f*
  theories of legislative representation, 73–76
Republican Party
  Anything But Craddick (ABC), 62
  caucus, 86–87
  development of, 228–232
  electoral competition and, 214, 216–218
  governor's office and, 106, 108
  judicial representation and, 142
  legislative leadership and, 83–85
  platform, 240*t*
  Reconstruction era and, 45
  redistricting and, 28, 81
  state convention (2010) and, 227–228
Republic of Texas, 9–11, 161
  Constitution of 1836, 41–42
  Declaration of Independence, 271, 289–292
Reserved powers, 34, 35*f*
Resolutions, 92
Responsible party model, 232
Revenue bonds, 269–270
Revenues, state, 122–123, 267, 268*t. See also* Taxes
  federal funds as, 249, 267–268
  licensing and lottery revenues, 268
Revisions to constitution, 55, 57–58
Revolving door phenomenon, 254–255
Reynolds v. Sims (1964), 64
Rhode Island
  governors of, 109
  legislature in, 68
  local governments in, 159–160
Rice, William Marsh, 13
Richards, Ann, 103, 106, 107*b*, 108, 115
Riders, 96
Riker, William H., 301*n*
Roberts, Jason M., 295*n*
"Robin Hood" plan of school district funding, 273
Rockwall County, 162
Rodriguez, Robert, 259
Roemer, Buddy, 206–207*b*
Roll call votes, 96
Roll off voting pattern, 208
Roper v. Simmons (2005), 150
Ross, Nellie T., 106
Rotolo, Thomas, 299*n*
Runnels, Hardin R., 12–13